THE HISTORY OF POLIT
NATIONAL CONTEXT

In this volume a distinguished international team of contributors characterises the nature of, and recent developments in, the history of political thought in their respective countries. The essays scrutinise not only the different academic histories and methodological traditions on which the study of the history of political thought has drawn, but also its relationship to cultural and political debates within nations. This collection represents a major contribution to the history of ideas, in which political thought has always been central, whilst reflecting the disciplinary tensions – and national differences – of what remains a 'borderline' subject, located at the intersection of history, politics and philosophy. The different national characteristics taken on by political discourse, and the complex relationship these characteristics have to the aspirations of the discipline itself, are considered in these wide-ranging essays, which cover the history of political thought in the UK, the USA, France, Germany, Italy, Central and Eastern Europe.

DARIO CASTIGLIONE is Senior Lecturer in Political Theory at the University of Exeter. His main research interests are in the history of political philosophy and constitutional theory. His recent publications as editor include *Shifting the Boundaries: Transformation of the Languages of Public and Private in the Eighteenth Century* (1995, with Lesley Sharpe) and *The Constitution in Transformation: European and Theoretical Perspectives* (1996, with Richard Bellamy).

IAIN HAMPSHER-MONK is Professor of Political Theory at the University of Exeter. He is co-founder and editor of the journal *History of Political Thought*. His publications include *A History of Modern Political Though* (1992), and more recently he has edited *History of Concepts – Comparative Perspectives* (1998, with Karin Tilmans and Frank van Vree), *The Demands of Citizenship* (2000, with Catriona McKinnon) and *Evidence and Inference* (forthcoming 2001, with William Twining).

IDEAS IN CONTEXT

Edited by Quentin Skinner (*General Editor*), Lorraine Daston, Dorothy Ross and James Tully

The books in this series will discuss the emergence of intellectual traditions and of related new disciplines. The procedures, aims and vocabularies that were generated will be set in the context of the alternatives available within the contemporary frameworks of ideas and institutions. Though detailed studies of the evolution of such traditions, and their modification by different audiences, it is hoped that a new picture will form of the development of ideas in their concrete contexts. By this means, artificial distinctions between the history of philosophy, of the various sciences, of society and politics, and of literature may be seen to dissolve.

The series is published with the support of the Exxon Foundation.

A list of books in the series will be found at the end of the volume.

THE HISTORY OF
POLITICAL THOUGHT
IN NATIONAL CONTEXT

Edited by
Dario Castiglione
and
Iain Hampsher-Monk

CAMBRIDGE
UNIVERSITY PRESS

CAMBRIDGE UNIVERSITY PRESS
Cambridge, New York, Melbourne, Madrid, Cape Town, Singapore,
São Paulo, Delhi, Dubai, Tokyo, Mexico City

Cambridge University Press
The Edinburgh Building, Cambridge CB2 8RU, UK

Published in the United States of America by Cambridge University Press, New York

www.cambridge.org
Information on this title: www.cambridge.org/9780521174930

First published 2001
First paperback edition 2011

A catalogue record for this publication is available from the British Library

ISBN 978-0-521-78234-0 Hardback
ISBN 978-0-521-17493-0 Paperback

To our friends in the Political Thought Conference

Contents

Contributors

TERENCE BALL is Professor of Political Science at the Arizona State University. He is the author of *Rousseau's Ghost: a novel* (1998), *Reappraising Political Theory* (1995), and co-editor (with Joyce Appleby) of *Jefferson: Political Writings* (1999) and (with Richard Bellamy) of the forthcoming *Cambridge History of Twentieth-Century Political Thought*.

DARIO CASTIGLIONE is Senior Lecturer in Political Theory at the University of Exeter. His main research interests are in the history of political philosophy and constitutional theory. His recent publications as editor include *Shifting the Boundaries: Transformation of the Languages of Public and Private in the Eighteenth Century* (1995, with Lesley Sharpe) and *The Constitution in Transformation: European and Theoretical Perspectives* (1996, with Richard Bellamy).

JANET COLEMAN is Professor of Ancient and Medieval Political Thought at the London School of Economics. She is the co-founder and editor of the journal *History of Political Thought*. Her recent publications include *A History of Political Thought from the Ancient Greeks to Early Christianity* (2000) and *A History of Political Thought from the Middle Ages to the Renaissance* (2000). She edited and contributed to *The Individual in Political Theory and Practice* (1996), directing this research group which formed part of a European Science Foundation Project on the 'Origins of the Modern State in Europe'.

STEFAN COLLINI is Reader in Intellectual History and English Literature at the University of Cambridge. He is the author of several publications in intellectual history, including *That Noble Science of Politics* (1983, with Donald Winch and John Burrow), *Matthew Arnold* (1994) and *English Pasts* (1999), and editor of *British Intellectual History 1750-1950* (2000, 2 vols.).

ANGELO D'ORSI is Professor of History of Political Thought at the University of Turin. His main research interests are in the history of culture and intellectuals in the twentieth century and the history of historiography. His recent publications include *Guida alla storia del pensiero politico* (1995), *Alla ricerca della storia* (1996, rev. edn 1999) and *La cultura a Torino tra le due guerre* (2000).

MALACHI HACOHEN is Associate Professor of History at Duke University, where he teaches Modern European intellectual history. His current research interests focus on the Congress for Cultural Freedom and post-war transatlantic liberalism. He is the author of *Karl Popper in esilio* (1999) and *Karl Popper – the Formative Years, 1902–1945: Politics and Philosophy in Interwar Vienna* (2000).

IAIN HAMPSHER-MONK is Professor Political Theory at the University of Exeter. He is co-founder and editor of the journal *History of Political Thought*. His publications include *A History of Modern Political Thought* (1992), and more recently he has edited *History of Concepts – Comparative Perspectives* (1998, with Karin Tilmans and Frank van Vree), *The Demands of Citizenship* (2000, with Catriona McKinnon) and *Evidence and Inference* (forthcoming 2001, with William Twining).

JEREMY JENNINGS is Professor of Political Theory at the University of Birmingham. He is the author or editor of numerous books and articles, including *Georges Sorel: the Character and Development of his Thought* (1985), *Syndicalism in France* (1990), *Intellectuals in Politics* (1996) and the Cambridge Texts edition of Georges Sorel, *Reflections on Violence* (1999).

WOLFGANG J. MOMMSEN is Professor Emeritus of Modern History at the University of Düsseldorf. He was Director of the German Historical Institute in London from 1977 to 1985 and President of the International Commission for Historiography from 1990 to 1995. He is co-editor of the *Max Weber – Gesamtausgabe* and of several historical journals. He has published extensively on Max Weber, German and British history in the nineteenth and twentieth centuries, and the history of historiography. His most recent publication is *Politik und Kultur in der neueren deutschen Geschichte* (2000).

VICTOR NEUMANN is Professor of Modern and Contemporary History of Central and South Eastern Europe at the University of the West of Timisoara. His main research interests are in Romanian and East-Central European intellectual history. His publications include *The*

Temptation of Homo Europaeus (1993) and *Identités multiples dans l'Europe des Régions* (1997).

MELVIN RICHTER is Professor Emeritus of Political Science at the Hunter College, City University of New York. A founder of the 'Conference for the Study of Political Thought', he is the author of *The Politics of Conscience. T.H. Green and his Age (1966)*, *The Political Writings of Montesquieu* (1977) and *The History of Concepts: a Critical Introduction* (1995).

PIERRE ROSANVALLON is Professor of History and Political Philosophy and Director of the Centre de Recherches Politiques Raymond Aron at the École des Hautes Etudes en Sciences Sociales in Paris. Chairman of the Fondation Saint-Simon, his many publications include *Le sacre du citoyen* (1992), *Le peuple introuvable* (1998) and *The New Social Question: Rethinking the Welfare State* (2000).

QUENTIN SKINNER is Regius Professor of Modern History at the University of Cambridge, and a Fellow of Christ's College, Cambridge, and of the British Academy. His many publications include *The Foundations of Modern Political Thought* (2 vols., 1978), *Machiavelli* (1981), *Reason and Rhetoric in the Philosophy of Hobbes* (1996) and *Liberty before Liberalism* (1998).

ROBERT WOKLER is Senior Research Fellow at the University of Exeter. His main research interests are in the history of political thought and particularly Rousseau and the Enlightenment, on which he has published extensively. A joint editor of *Diderot's Political Writings*, his recent publications as author or editor include *Rousseau* (1995), *Rousseau and Liberty* (1995) and the forthcoming *Cambridge History of Eighteenth-Century Political Though* (with Mark Goldie).

Preface

The idea for this book derives from conversations between the two editors – two different nationals with different national upbringings in the history of political thought. Whilst one of them was learning about yet a third and fourth national context (Iain Hampsher-Monk was at the Netherlands Institute for Advanced Study as the guest of the Dutch *Begriffsgeschichte* project), the other – Dario Castiglione – organised a conference in Exeter, at which exponents of a range of different national histories of political thought were invited to speak on the topic. Whilst the participants judged the conference a great success, we were aware that the original invitation was likely to produce a disparate set of responses, not only in terms of content but in terms of how the history of political thought was construed. And so indeed it proved.

Although the conference *provoked* the book, there remained much to be done before a coherent volume could result. New papers were commissioned in order to fill gaps, a great deal of rewriting, editing and translation was undertaken and time – and length – limits imposed on the authors. Given all this, and a range of other circumstances (not least the current external forces shaping university life – which often seem devised specifically to prevent academics from doing the kinds of things they thought they were there to do – namely teach and conduct research), it has taken a long time to bring the volume to its present shape, and we are aware that we have tried the patience and good will of some of our earlier contributors. We hope they will think the result worth it – for we do.

That result does not claim any closure or ultimate coherence, but rather, as we explain in the introduction, reveals – as we originally hoped it would – the way national context shapes not only different histories, but even different conceptions of 'histories'.

A book so long in the making incurs many debts. We are, as we have already said, grateful to our original contributors for their patience and to those others who attended the conference for their comments; to

Richard Fisher and many others at Cambridge University Press for their help and guidance; to the two referees for comments and suggestions; and to Steven Davidson and Jamie Gaskarth for assistance with preparing the typescript for publication.

1 Introduction
The history of political thought and the national discourses of politics

Dario Castiglione and Iain Hampsher-Monk

A number of studies over the past two decades have explored the national context of movements and ideas with a predominantly universalist character or aspiration.[1] Although this has often meant a revision in our understanding of how such ideas and movements developed and of the impact they made, the approach chosen did not entirely go beyond the now widely accepted scholarly othodoxy of presenting ideas 'in context' – even if the identity of the appropriate context often remains a point of contestation.

The idea of this volume – of nationally contextualising the history of political thought – presents, however, a number of difficulties that were not germane to these other studies. This is so on account of the peculiar nature of the subject of our investigation, which can be understood both as an academic discipline, 'the history of political thought', but also in more substantive terms as a form of discourse, the history of 'political thought'. Such an ambivalence is exemplified to the point of ambiguity in the chapters comprising the volume. As we collected, reflected and commented on the essays provided by our illustrious contributors, we realised in just how many directions this particular field can be ploughed. Hence rather than offering a state-of-the-art picture, the present volume opens up an array of problems for the location and study of the history of political thought. From such a perspective, the 'national context' approach functions to place in sharp relief the intricate web of issues in which our subject matter is implicated. Indeed, as Stefan Collini rightly notices in his postscript, the use of the anglophone expression 'history of political thought' can only heuristically designate the subject of this volume, since equivalent expressions of which use is made in other national traditions to designate the 'discipline' – though not necessarily the 'discourse' – diverge from each other in important

[1] Cf., for instance, Roy Porter and Mikulas Teich (eds.), *The Enlightenment in National Context* (Cambridge, 1981).

respects. In this introduction, we point to some facets of chapters within this book that comprise the kaleidoscopic picture that a 'national tradition' perspective gives of the history of political thought.

We begin with what is perhaps the less obvious of the two meanings already identified, but which, in a sense, is partly to blame for the complications besetting the other. It has been suggested that a 'political culture' is a 'set of discourses and practices' through which members of a political community make claims upon each other and interact politically.[2] One of the operations which comprise a political culture is to 'define the meanings of the terms in which the claims are framed'. Reconstructing the history of political thought – not necessarily as a self-standing activity, but as part of the exercise of political reflection in which some form of memory is involved – is one of the ways in which such an operation is carried out. This would seem fairly uncontroversial. But addressing the history of political thought in the way in which the chapters of this book do – from within, and sometimes across, different national contexts – is mildly, and in diverse ways, subversive of a well-established account of the history of political thought. It is subversive because it suggests a particularist reading of what is often understood, if not in its genesis at least in its consolidation and development, as a cosmopolitan or even universalist (at least, if one might be permitted the phrase, 'Western universalist') enterprise. So paradoxically, it would appear that modern nation-states give rise to particularist political cultures where people who reflect on the character of these cultures nevertheless see them as the bearers of a common historically articulated body of works and practices derived from classical Greece via important way-stations such as Rome, medieval Christianity and feudalism, the Renaissance, Reformation and Enlightenment – a complex process well described in Janet Coleman's chapter. One prominent and persistent idea within national histories of political thought is therefore a pre- or trans-national narrative linking philosophers who self-consciously ad-dressed one another across spatial and cultural divides from which – at least in aspiration – they felt themselves emancipated. Such a view inspired the early modern essays in the genre, which emerged from the attempts of thinkers in the natural law tradition to identify their own provenance.[3] The persistence of this universalist and cosmopolitan ideal

---

[2] Keith Baker, *Inventing the French Revolution: Essays on French Political Culture in the Eighteenth Century* (Cambridge, 1990), pp. 4–7.

[3] Cf. R. Tuck, 'The "Modern" Theory of Natural Law', in A. Pagden (ed.), *The Languages of Political Theory in Early-Modern Europe* (Cambridge, 1987), pp. 99–119; I. Hont, 'The Language of Sociability and Commerce: Samuel Pufendorf and the Theoretical Foundations of the "Four Stages Theory"', in Pagden (ed.), *The Languages of Political Theory*, pp. 253–76; and K. Haakonssen, *Natural Law and Moral Philosophy*

is central to the argument developed by Malachi Hacohen on the intellectual self-image of the assimilated Jews in *Mitteleuropa* at a dramatic historical juncture of the twentieth century, and it plays an important part – if mainly through its absence – in Victor Neumann's reconstruction of the troubled past of that region.

To the extent that such a narrative is truly nationally conditioned, this old universalist ideal is subverted. Yet it is only mildly so, not least because we have already come to suspect that such an ideal is unattainable, and moreover that it may distract attention from the very circumstances which enable us to make sense of political-theoretical productions. Indeed there might be said to be another account of the history of political thought which is essentially political, particularist and related to, if indeed it is not the condition of, a free society. John Pocock has written of 'a certain kind of history . . . which is the creation of a political society that is autonomous, in the sense that it takes decisions and performs actions with the intention and effect of determining its character and the conditions under which it exists'.[4] This would ensure that the political society is both making its history and narrating it – two activities that, in Pocock's own account, are often hard to separate. The intuition that a history of political thought is in some way related to the nurturing and sustenance of politics in a society, and is, in turn, determined by it, is one on which we shall have more to say below. More generally, the fact that, in the modern world, political society has coincided with communities acting within the boundaries of nation-states gives a particular significance to the way in which the national context may determine both the role and the understanding of political thought and of its history. The issue at stake here is not therefore what separate national traditions may have contributed *to* the history of political thought, but whether there could be a shared narrative account *of* it which can be considered, in any meaningful sense, 'the same' discourse of politics. On this account, the universalist ideal may turn out to be unfeasible because it represents an unhistoricized version of that which can only be understood as historical.

Whilst recognising that the influence of the national character of political cultures might be subversive of one kind of ideal of the history of political thought, the perceived absence, or political inadequacy, of a

(Cambridge, 1996). A similar, universalist and cosmopolitan inspiration can be found in the origins of the history of philosophy as a genre, cf. Eugenio Garin's account in 'La storia "critica" della filosofia del settecento', in *Dal rinascimento all'illuminismo: studi e ricerche* (Pisa, 1970), pp. 241–84.

4 J.G.A. Pocock, 'The Politics of History: the Subaltern and the Subversive', *Journal of Political Philosophy* 6, 3 (1998), pp. 219–34.

national culture can dominate it. Such a consideration is at the centre of the contributions of Wolfgang Mommsen and Victor Neumann. The reason, in both cases, is to be found in the strongly *discoursive* nature of political theory as an activity that can only be sustained in societies where a minimum amount of liberty and freedom of expression is guaranteed. In so far as the history of 'political thought' contributes both to maintaining a certain stability of meanings in a political culture and to ensuring a 'conversation' between generations, self-reflexive political thinking is indeed as Pocock suggests a necessary, though not sufficient, condition for a free society. It is this deeply communicative nature of political thought that emerges in Coleman's analysis of the role of the classical canon in the history of political thought. In a different sense, this is also true of the way in which issues of interpretation and understanding have exercised historians of political thought in the past two or three decades, bringing back to the forefront of the discipline issues of meaning, intentionality and empathetic understanding. The essays by Quentin Skinner, Melvin Richter, Pierre Rosanvallon, Terence Ball, Jeremy Jennings and Iain Hampsher-Monk bear witness to this in diverse ways and with various agendas in mind, but they seem to agree that the restoration of agency and language as central concerns has contributed to revitalise an interest in the history of political thought, and that this has come about as part of wider cultural processes affecting each national culture in peculiar ways.

This cultural quality of political thought and of its history is no less evident when one considers the converse example: cosmopolitanism. This is illustrated by Hacohen's discussion of Popper and of how his construction of the history of the 'Open Society' and its enemies is deeply rooted in the experiences of his generation of Jewish cosmopolitan intellectuals. This, in itself, does not make his ideas less compelling, but it puts them in a different perspective, questioning some of the claims of a cosmopolitan culture successfully to displace the nation state as the focus and bearer of a history of political thought. Yet, the possibility of a 'rooted' cosmopolitanism suggests that the 'national' dimension is neither the only nor necessarily the main dimension through which to define the context of the history of political thought. It is intriguing, for instance, to notice how a number of authors (for example, Arendt) appear in different national contexts both bringing in new meanings and at the same time being re-interpreted within the new context.

None of the chapters in this collection seems to assume the 'national' dimension of political thought should be taken as a cipher for the 'national character' of a political culture, but they do see it as something more directly cultural and/or political. Indeed, some of the chapters suggest that deep-down the relevant histories often *reflect* current political debates and preoccupations. In France, as Jennings and Rosanvallon notice, the question of structure/agency with its ideological overtones has taken centre stage; in Germany, as indicated by Mommsen, the 'ever present' past of the Nazi experience has cast a long shadow on the post-war generations; in the United States, according to Ball, the positivist culture of the 1950s, the Vietnam crisis in the 1960s and the issues of identity recognition more recently have all contributed to the changing focuses of the discipline; while in Britain, finally, and as differently argued by Robert Wokler and Iain Hampsher-Monk, public concern has remained, perhaps more silently and even against the grain of scholarly intellectual postures, a reflex in the profession.

In so far as this book, as a whole, shows that substantive and methodological developments in the history of political thought reflect a 'national' and more directly 'political' dimension of the historical enterprise – though in the qualified forms just discussed – it is fair to assume that its study cannot be completely separated from its being a constitutive part of the national political culture. In this respect this collection achieves the twofold objective of putting national traditions within the context of their own political culture and discussing the more general relationship between history of political thought and political discourse at large.

But as already noted, and as Collini aptly reminds us in his postscript, there is a whole cluster of issues that pertain to the history of political thought as an academic discipline and in which the 'national' dimension plays as important a role as the one we have briefly suggested in relation to political discourse. Collini himself explores most of these issues by taking a sharply and rightly sceptical view of discipline-history. He may also be right in suggesting that the 'internalist' approach often adopted by the 'historians' of political thought to their own subject misses the culturally embedded nature of the discipline, and that one may have therefore to turn to intellectual historians and historians of higher education for an adequate historical account.[5] But, as the great majority of the chapters of this collection also show, there is a stubborn resistance about the self-conscious representation that the historians of political thought have of their own discipline, which makes it difficult to keep it within the strict walls of the citadel of higher education – if not in fact, at least in aspiration. This is surely for the reason indicated above: the intricate, partly parasitic, relationship that the subject has with political

[5] S. Collini, 'General Introduction', in S. Collini, R. Whatmore and B. Young (eds.), *British Intellectual History 1750–1950* [published in both companion volumes: *Economy, Polity, and Society* and *History, Religion, and Culture*] (Cambridge, 2000), pp. 14–15.

culture and political discourse at large; but also because of the ambiguity
– as for other histories – of being in between the reality and the
representation, the fact and the account, the linguistic utterance and its
interpretation. The process of identifying, collecting and converting the
sequence of political ideas, or articulations, of a culture into a written
sequence and endowing them with significant (or even canonical) status
must – as a number of our contributors emphasise – be recognised as
just that: a process, contingent, diverse and invariably culturally particu-
larised. But this particularisation is done at different levels, none of
which is entirely insulated, so that the internalisation of the political
culture may well pass through academic and institutional channels, but
not without escaping the peculiar filter offered to the historians of
political thought by the possibility of reflecting on the more directly
political material which they handle professionally.

Arguably, it is this residual *political* dimension that complicates
matters for the historian of the discipline. This is true in relation to both
its identity, its corpus and its approach. Many of the chapters of this
volume, and in particular those by D'Orsi, Wokler and Collini, which
offer a longer view of the formation of the discipline itself, stress the
borderline nature of the history of political thought - an academic
subject that occupies a, perhaps imaginary, terrain in between history,
politics, law and (moral) philosophy. As illustrated by those same
chapters, the reasons for this – and the location of the terrain – are
contingent and mainly dependent on developments in national systems
of higher education. Its borderline character has, however, created a
series of elective affinities that – at a time of increasing specialisation,
and in spite of much talk about the virtues of interdisciplinarity – make
its academic and intellectual location an intractable problem. None the
less, with politics' progressive gain of academic respectability, the
history of political thought seems to have found its more natural place
within it.[6] As remarked by Collini, this has been no easy cohabitation,
but it has partly, and perhaps paradoxically, secured the more theoretical
and philosophical character of the discipline. This is firstly because,
within the more general discipline of politics and government, the
history of political thought has appropriated to itself (or, depending on
the point of view, it has been relegated to) the role of 'political theory' –
a place, however, never fully assured. Secondly, this arises because this
cohabitation creates, from the body of texts selected as the proper object
for the study of the history of political thought, an elected form of

---

[6] Such a process is not solely circumscribed to the anglophone world, although there are
differences in the motivating reasons and the ways in which it has been taking shape.

discourse through which a society asks itself philosophical questions about politics.

Moreover, it is the inextricably 'political' character of the subject that keeps alive the tension between 'history' and 'theory' within the discipline. This was the main theme of the conference that we organised at Exeter in 1994 and from which the project of the present volume started and, in some ways, departed. As illustrated by the contributions of Richter, D'Orsi, Skinner, Rosanvallon and Hampsher-Monk, that persistent tension, and the methodological and interpretative issues that come with it, are not immune to the national dimension. The predominance within a national culture of a particular academic approach may, for instance, direct the historical research to the identification of a particular theoretical construction as its proper object, this being variously conceived as either an author, an ideology, a politico-philosophical text, a language, ordinary usage, *mentalités*, or *Begriffen*.

The very tension between theory and history plays no less important a part in supporting the 'canonical' structure of the discipline, in spite of the contextualist strictures that can be directed against this. It is perhaps part of the practice of most disciplines whose subject matter consists of rather abstract and theoretically inclined modes of thinking for its practitioners to be fixed in answering questions set by their predecessors, while they are more immediately addressing a contextualised and contextualisable set of intellectual problems. This 'vertical' dimension of the history of political thought, as opposed to the more 'horizontal' preoccupations of cultural and intellectual history, is the cardinal sin of the discipline – as it is perhaps of other discipline-histories – but it is also part of its genetic code. Some of the chapters of this volume illustrate how this vertical dimension is often conditioned by strong 'national' preoccupations, which partly determine who, in different contexts, are the authors that make it to the canon. More in-depth and comparative studies on the university curricula and on temporal variation of both it and the interpretations given to the 'canonical' authors would be needed to further illuminate this fascinating story. Here, as in other respects, the volume points in a direction rather than offering a complete treatment of the subject.

But there is something else that should be noted about the vertical dimension of the history of political thought, tempered as it is by the contextualist revolution. The continuous temptation of constructing its canon on the basis of the supposed influence of certain authors on political society is partly to be explained by the implicit, and slightly idealistic, faith in the strongly discursive nature of politics as a human activity – in the face of and often in reaction to the occasional denial that comes from history. By tracking political history, however, the history of political thought offers a particular reading of it. The political experience or problems in national contexts may establish a distinctive agenda for political theory. This may then bequeath a particular history of political thought as a result of a series of thinkers meditating on the identity or significance of a particular national event – the French Revolution, for example, in relation to which even thinkers preceding the event (famously, Rousseau) need to be situated. The experiences of Nazism and Fascism before the war, and of Communism in Eastern Europe, have also dominated the way in which the history of political thought contributes to a more general self-reflection going on in political society.

Yet, for all that we have said on the 'political' dimension of the history of political thought as a discipline, one of the effects of the subject entering the academy is, paradoxically, that of being deprived of its political character. This is part of a process – visible in modern liberal democracies with institutionalised higher education – of at least seeming to detach such histories from the politics of the society which gave rise to them, a process which is intensified by the professionalisation of the academic world which produces such histories. Such processes can be contested and resisted, as some of the chapters in this collection intimate, and the process of doing so is one of reasserting the political character of the history of political thought and perhaps even its intimate link to the development of modern society which supports it.[7] Or it can be seen as part and parcel of the development of modern society. The resistance to it would only serve to satisfy the slightly nostalgic need to reassert the supposedly 'universal' role of the intellectual, as historian of political thought, in a world perceived as growing progressively indifferent, while it may only be more differentiated and segmented, and where, as Collini suggests, we are no longer dealing, if we ever were, with 'the public', but more prosaically with overlapping publics.

As suggested earlier, the introduction to the interplay of national – or in some cases cosmopolitan – and academic traditions, of universalist aspirations and particularist preoccupations, of highly or lightly politicised histories, presented in this book is intended as a beginning and not in any sense as a final product. The process of recreating mutual awareness of various national academic traditions is one that has begun in earnest only in the authors' academic lifetimes. The results are often intriguing. A recent European Science Foundation network on the

---

[7] For a fairly recent statement of this position, cf. Bernard Crick, 'The Decline of political Thinking in British Public Life', *Critical Review of International Social and Political Philosophy*, 1, 1 (1998), pp. 102–20.

'Origins of the Modern State in Europe' revealed there were distinct national connotations of every term in that title! The creation of a common academic forum within which the history of political thought is pursued and debated seems to promise not a simple return to the universalist Enlightenment ideal, but the creation of a more differentiated – though perhaps fractal – field of investigation. Although the *paroles* may be different and bear each their own distinct patois, the *langue*, with all its resources, is a recognisably shared one.

2   The voice of the 'Greeks' in the conversation of mankind

Janet Coleman

Canonical difficulties

Having recently completed two volumes treating those political theorists who are most frequently discussed in university courses dealing with the history of Western political thought from the ancient Greeks to the sixteenth-century Renaissance, I have been aware, from the beginning, of being faced with a number of problems that required resolution.[1] During the past thirty years we have witnessed methodological debates concerning the proper way to study the history of political thought. Questions have been raised as to the very nature of a discipline that seeks to study political theorising as an activity that depends on its being engaged at discrete and contingent historical moments. In effect, this raises a very old question: is political theorising a cognitive activity of agents who, as a consequence of their socio-historical contexts, must engage a prudential form of reasoning in what are always taken to be changing circumstances? Or is political theorising some timeless activity of minds engaged in clarifying a necessary and unchanging truth about politics that is judged to be somehow independent of the particularities of agents' lived lives and the conventional languages they use to reveal their thoughts about it? In what follows, I propose some of my own conclusions in response to questions concerning what we should take the history of political thought to be for us today, why political theorising is thought to have a history, and of what it is a history. In consequence, I propose what appear to me to be the most satisfactory methods of studying old texts that are held to be important, not least because they reveal a variety of paths taken on the winding road to 'state' formation in the Western European tradition.

Perhaps the most prominent issue has had to do with those thinkers who have been included, unproblematically, as constitutive of the canon

---

[1] J. Coleman, *A History of Political Thought*: vol. I, *From Ancient Greece to Early Christianity*; vol. II, *From the Middle Ages to the Renaissance* (Oxford, 2000). What follows is based on the introduction to vol. I, here modified and expanded.

itself. Those writers (such as Plato, Aristotle, Cicero, Augustine, Aquinas, Machiavelli) who are *traditionally* considered to have contributed most influentially to political debate on the principles and practices of good government across the centuries are taken to be the key figures in the history of European political thought. But this is not an uncontentious statement. Just how we evaluate who contributed most and how we determine which authors and which of their works ought to be included on the list of 'great political theorists and theories' are hotly debated questions, not least by those who teach courses called 'the history of political thought' in European and North American universities.

The debate over the 'canon' consists in asking: how has the tradition become what we have taken it to be, and why have certain thinkers been traditionally included while others have not? Why, for instance, have there been no women?[2] Why, until very recently, are most of the 'great names' in this constructed tradition of an intellectual elite mainly dead, 'white' and male?

There has been considerable irritation expressed over the fact that even in recently published histories of Western political thought, the history of feminism has been relegated to footnotes. But a good deal of writing on the political tradition of dead, white males has precisely made the point that whatever else the history of much of Western political theorising is, it is, and was meant to be, a male and white enterprise. Women's voices, black voices, colonial and immigrant voices, non-Christian voices other than those of the pagan ancient Greeks and Romans are, for the most part, absent. We should not thereby assume that dead, white males were the only distinguished theorists who existed in the past and who exerted their influence. But it was the seminal male-authored political theories that led first to a focus on sexual difference, to the extent that the early 'state' became an exclusive preserve of men, and more recently, to the contemporary modern liberal state with its persistent denial of difference and, implicitly its favouring of men as universal models of citizen rationality and behaviour. A history of 'our'

---

[2] See the various responses to this question in, for instance, M.L. Shanley and C. Pateman (eds.), *Feminist Interpretations and Political Theory* (Oxford, 1991); C. Pateman, *The Sexual Contract* (Cambridge, 1988); D. Coole, *Women in Political Theory: From Ancient Misogyny to Contemporary Feminism* (Hemel Hempstead, 1988); E. Kennedy and S. Mendus (eds.), *Women in Western Political Philosophy* (Brighton, 1987); A. Saxonhouse, *Women in the History of Political Thought: Ancient Greece to Machiavelli* (New York, 1985); J.B. Elshtain, *Public Man Private Woman: Women in Social and Political Thought* (Princeton, N.J., 1981); G. Lloyd, *The Man of Reason: 'Male' and 'Female' in Western Philosophy*, 2nd edn (London, 1993); S.M. Okin, *Women in Western Political Thought* (Princeton, N.J., 1978); S. Rowbotham, *Women, Resistance and Revolution* (Harmondsworth, 1972).

political thought, that is, the varieties of political theorising that have dominated and structured the West's 'state', is a history of narratives that have either edited out alternative discourses or subsumed other voices within the dominant (male, white and Christian) discourses. No matter how eloquent the women or any other marginalised group of the past, they were not taken explicitly to have helped to construct the modern state and it is precisely for this reason that contemporary feminisms have challenged dominant male-stream political theories of all kinds. The reconstruction of a history, say, of feminisms in order to liberate women's voices from the past is, therefore, a different enterprise from the one that seeks to uncover and reconstruct what has been called the European, patriarchal state and its political theories. I shall try to explain, below, why I believe this to be the case.

Nor is the canon of 'great political theorists' as stable as some may think. It does not always include the same thinkers, nor give the same thinkers similar weight. This becomes clear when we go beyond the Anglo-American university and consider what different continental European traditions take to be the 'great thinkers' on the principles and practices of good government. But in general, it remains true that when we select those names that appear on all lists, we confront what have only quite recently been shown to have been cultural prejudices concerning race, gender and religion. And it is these prejudices which have, through complex processes of exclusion and selection, determined which voices were, in fact, taken seriously in the past. One could say that the canon of great texts is an extraordinary expression of Europeans' prejudices about themselves and others. This is precisely why it is important.

There is no doubt that for specialists in any period, certain authors who are relatively or virtually unknown today appear at the time to have been much read and influential. Specialist historians wonder why their names and texts gradually disappeared from the references of subsequent generations and they try to provide some answers. Indeed, there are periods when the sources for past conceptual usages are difficult for us to obtain not least because those texts which do survive for us to read are those that were allowed to survive by later rememberers of past usages deemed useful to them in a later present. Such texts are retrospective nominations. Furthermore, when we study the political theory produced from the period of the ancient Greeks to the sixteenth-century Renaissance, we can see an exclusion and selection process operating in the testimonies of those who wished to make explicit to contemporary and future readers of their works which authors *they* believed to have influenced them. As a consequence, and retrospectively, the *traditional* canon of thinkers *is* surprisingly small and relatively stable and it goes back a long way. Furthermore, it is a canon of thinkers whose works show them to have been engaged in discussing issues that are not considered by us, today, to be focused uniquely on politics. What they had to say about politics was often a consequence of what they had to say about language, about the nature of being and existence, about cosmology and nature, about what they took to be a peculiarly human access to what was thought to be beyond the human. In other words, what we take to be the subject of their theorising, 'politics', is today a much narrower domain of human thought and action than they often believed it to be.

Most of us would, however, agree *where* the history of Western political theorising begins for us: in ancient Greece followed by ancient Rome. Today, however, we need to explain why this is so, because students come to read translations of Greek and Latin political and philosophical texts without any background in the culture or language of classical antiquity. This is a relatively new phenomenon. As recently as the first quarter of the twentieth century it was thought that a training in Greek and Latin was the prerequisite for being considered an educated person, even if we are under no illusions about the degree of fluency in either 'dead' language that was acquired by a nineteenth- and early twentieth-century elite of students. Furthermore, today's students often learn about the history of political thought in university departments which focus more directly on modern political and social sciences where the historical and cultural contexts in which these theories were first generated are not necessarily discussed or even thought to be relevant to an understanding of these texts. Today, as never before, we need to ask and answer the question: why should we think the ancient Greeks followed by the ancient Romans, and thereafter, Christian medieval and Renaissance thinkers who selectively absorbed 'Greek' and 'Roman' lessons and adapted these to a Judaeo-Christian biblical world view, to be worthy of study, either in their own right or as relevant to our current concerns?

It seems to me that there are at least three interrelated reasons for beginning a study of the history of political thought with the ancient Greeks. The first two are so generally accepted as to be thought (wrongly, I believe) to require little further discussion. They concern firstly, what we take to be 'the language of politics' itself and the range of its application. ('Language' is used here in its generic sense to include the many distinct discourses that developed over time.) Related to this is, secondly, the belief that philosophy has a history within which political theorising has played a determining role. Most people who are somewhat familiar with what is often referred to as 'the classical heritage' would agree that in some sense we owe to the Greeks our very willingness to accept that there is a distinctive 'language of politics' as well as the belief that what we think of as the discipline of philosophy began with them. But I would suggest that the reason we accept that there *is* a language of politics *and* a history of philosophy owes rather a lot to the third reason we begin with the ancient Greeks, and this is not often discussed by historians of political thought. I want to argue here that we begin with the Greeks because of the way in which a European (Euro-American, in fact) identity has come to be constructed over the centuries.[3] It is this constructed identity which has determined the significance to us of, firstly, the language of politics and, secondly, the history of philosophy in the first place. And it is also this process of constructing an identity, a conceptual enterprise that pre-dates the emergence of nationalisms and their respective discourses, which has ensured the exclusion of other voices from the traditional canon. Let us begin, then, with the third reason for starting with the ancient Greeks.

The construction of a European identity

European cultural identity came to be intimately tied to its purported foundations in ancient Greek culture and values not only during the Middle Ages but even more so during the sixteenth and seventeenth centuries. During this period the ancient world was intensely re-investigated as the inspirational source of a number of key contemporary issues. Perhaps the most prominent of these concerned how emergent national states understood the possible range of *legitimate* constitutions and their respective relations to citizens and subjects. Scholars declared Greece to have initiated something peculiarly European – a tradition of 'legitimate' government. Consequently, they separated ancient Greece from its actual cultural ties to its geographical neighbours in the semitic Middle East and Asia Minor. But they were not the first to insist that Greece stood out as different from those supposed 'non-European' traditions of autocratic, indeed often tyrannous government, despite their awareness that there had been Greek tyrants too.[4] Learned men during the medieval and Renaissance periods of Western European

[3] See for instance C.J. Richard, *The Founders and the Classics: Greece, Rome and the American Enlightenment* (Cambridge, Mass., 1994); W. Haase and M. Reinhold (eds.), *The Classical Tradition and the Americas* (Berlin and New York, 1994).
[4] J. F. McGlew, *Tyranny and Political Culture in Ancient Greece* (Ithaca, N.Y., 1993); G. Giorgini, *La città e il tiranno, il concetto di tirannide nella Grecia del vii–iv secolo a.c.* (Milan, 1993).

history also acknowledged the Greeks, and their heirs, the Romans, as superior to other civilisations. They lamented the loss of the traditions of Greco-Roman culture in their own times and nostalgically sought to revive and pass on the traditions of their illustrious forebears, however inadequately.

Important recent, but controversial, studies have emphasised, however, that ancient Greek cities displayed more affinities with the contractual trading republics of the Oriental societies of the Levant and Mesopotamia and with the cities of the medieval and modern Oriental (Arab) world which are their heirs than with anything that developed in Western Europe.[5] It is beyond doubt that European political institutions were, in fact, derived far *less* from ancient Greek *practices* than from Roman law and Canon (Church) law supplemented by an extensive knowledge of the Old and New Testaments, and from an indigenously developed feudalism and a common law that was based on local practices and immunities from monarchical powers during the European Middle Ages. Ancient Greece contributed little to these practices. Indeed, certain ancient Greek practices, such as direct democracy, for which they are honoured today, were subject to severe criticism (by the Greek philosophers Plato and Aristotle), if not to 'editing' early on (for instance, by the historian Polybius in the second century BC, by the Roman Cicero in the first century BC and by Plutarch in the first and second centuries AD), as the legacy of ancient Greece was reconstructed by later self-proclaimed heirs who wished to favour a society based on differential rank rather than one based on the ancient Athenian acknowledgement of the equal potential of all free men to take turns in ruling and being ruled. During the Middle Ages and the Renaissance, emergent European nation-states and city-states did not see themselves as the legitimate heirs of the *historical* ancient Greek *polis*/city-state of which they knew little, but of that ancient *polis* reinterpreted by moral and political philosophers such as Plato and Aristotle and, thereafter, the Roman Cicero and other Roman historians, by the fifth-century Christian theologian St Augustine, the thirteenth-century scholastic theologian St Thomas Aquinas, and a variety of Renaissance civic humanists who drew selectively on all of these philosophical, theological and historical moralisers.

Furthermore, even if some of the most distinctive features of Plato's and Aristotle's preferences for monarchical or aristocratic constitutions

[5] M. Bernal, *Black Athena, the Afroasiatic Roots of Classical Civilization, vol.* I (London, 1987); P. Springborg, *Royal Persons, Patriarchal Monarchy and the Feminine Principle* (London, 1990) and Springborg, 'The Contractual State: Reflections on Orientalism and Despotism', *History of Political Thought* 8 (1987) pp. 395–434.

can be shown to reveal 'Eastern' influences,[6] the Eastern sources, none
the less, came to be ignored early on, indeed much earlier than during
the early modern period and for important reasons. The point is that
although some have argued for examples of democracy prior to the
Greeks, for instance, the tribal democracies of early Mesopotamia, their
impact as well as the impact of actual Athenian direct democracy on
later European society was to be virtually nil.[7] If ancient Athenian
democracy was itself to play virtually no role in the forging of Roman,
medieval, Renaissance and early modern political institutions, a history
of political thought must try to explain not only why this was so, but also
why the Greeks are still thought to be 'our' beginnings. What was the
reason for the most distinctive of ancient Athenian *practices*, a practice of
direct democracy or rule by the *demos* or mass, not surviving into later
periods while ancient political *theories*, composed by more or less anti-
democratic thinkers, did survive?

There is no doubt that the 'idea of ancient Greece' was exploited – in
what today we may regard as historically inaccurate ways – to serve
medieval, Renaissance and early modern Europeans' prejudices about
themselves and others. None the less, ancient Greek culture *was* at the
heart of a constructed European identity and this identity was in the
process of being formulated well before the sixteenth and seventeenth
centuries. Through the descriptions, often critical, of the workings of its
political institutions, and even more so through the doctrines of its
various schools of philosophy, through its sciences including medicine,
its drama, architecture and sculpture, and its tradition of historical
writing concerned with narrating events in Greek history and explaining
why they happened as they did, ancient Greece played a foundational
role in the development of the Roman and Christian civilisations which
chronologically succeeded it. Even when the writings of the Greeks were
later misread, awkwardly translated into other languages or deliberately
misconstrued in order to serve prejudices and beliefs the Greeks could
not or would not have shared (and they had plenty of their own which it
is the purpose of a history of political thought to reveal), educated men
took them to have set the agenda for the on-going debates in almost all
fields of intellectual endeavour, not least concerning the principles and
practices of good government and government's service to men of
principled behaviour. Ancient Greece educated ancient Rome in a
selective way, or rather, the Romans took the lessons they 'chose' and
with the development of Christianity, both theologically and institution-

---

[6] Springborg, *Royal Persons*, p. 405.
[7] M. Finley, *Democracy, Ancient and Modern* (London, 1973).

ally, the Greek legacy, as it came to be construed by various Church Fathers with the Bible dominating their thoughts, was not forgotten.

Instead of calling the ancient Greeks the first Europeans we could say that educated Europeans have thought of themselves as having inherited a range of values and certain institutions from ancient Greece. But it is more accurate to say that educated Europeans have thought of themselves as having inherited *ways of thinking about and discussing values and institutions* from that extraordinary culture that flourished in several centres in the Aegean, on the western shores of modern-day Turkey and in southern Italy, most notably during the sixth to fourth centuries BC. The Romans and then various 'schools' of Christian thinkers interpreted Greek values and institutions in a variety of ways and then applied these interpretations to their own historical experiences during subsequent centuries. In retrospect, it undoubtedly came to be the case that what they took to be shared values and similar institutions were nothing of the kind. But that Europeans of a later date believed in a shared discursive inheritance across the centuries indicates that they worked within a tradition of understanding that insisted on a fusion of different horizons, a largely unproblematic dialogue across the centuries, where they absorbed what they took to be intelligible to them in their own contexts and omitted what was judged to be of no apparent use or relevance.

Plato and Aristotle, who more than any other ancient Greeks set the norms for the subsequent tradition of *political philosophy*, often tell their audience that they mean to criticise and to provide a hostile commentary on some of the most revered values and practices of the city in which they lived – Athens. But when we read these philosophers and recognise that at times they are hostile witnesses, we cannot be certain that they are telling us how institutions actually operated or what *ordinary* people thought of the values and systems of rules by which they lived their daily lives. Indeed, the history of political thought comprises the voices of a selection of men who, in their own times, were anything but ordinary themselves, and (more importantly) neither were they considered such by future readers of their works. They were taken to be 'simply' the *best* of their age. Therefore, we can examine to what extent Plato and Aristotle appear to have shared or rejected their contemporaries' values by reading what they tell us are the opposing positions to their own. From these accounts we *try* to build up a picture of what it must have been like to be an ancient Greek and participate in their discussions. But we must be careful not to assume that we arrive at certainty in these matters for the following reasons. The voices from the page are today presumed to give accounts that, on the one hand, are taken to be *normative* for their societies and, on the other, stand out as *atypical* in being perhaps more reflective, synthetic or critical than would be those of many of their ordinary contemporaries, were the latter's views preserved for us to examine. Only through a comparative examination of all surviving voices could we come to some view on the degree to which Plato or Aristotle, for instance, were representative of ancient Greek attitudes on a range of issues. But in the construction of a European intellectual tradition, representativeness of the 'ordinary' lived life of the culture from which these philosophers came was not seen to be an issue because it was *assumed* that their voices were exemplary of the *best* of their tradition and, therefore, the ones worthy of being heard.

It is also important for us to realise that what we can uncover to have been ancient Greek attitudes, *in general*, to slaves, to women, to non-Greeks, to honour, birth, leisure, to politics and society, even to democracy, freedom and equality (whether they were attitudes that were rejected or modified by contemporary political philosophers or were apparently accepted by them and even justified philosophically and logically), were attitudes with which we now may have no sympathy. Furthermore, the *meaning* of Athenian values in their ancient contexts did not survive unchanged in later periods of history and in different cultures that, none the less, *can* trace their intellectual roots to ancient Greece. For instance, in translating from Greek to Latin, Romans often referred to what they took to be the same virtues in Greek society as in their own, but it can be established that they often meant rather different things by 'the virtues' than the Greeks appear to have meant. Nor did the philosophies of Plato and Aristotle, massively influential though they were on later European culture, survive unscathed in subsequent inter-pretations. Later thinkers believed themselves to be followers of Plato or Aristotle but, in the process of writing commentaries on their works and making these philosophers' theories their own, they changed them. The fate of great persons who have put their mark on the ages is that commentary very soon comes between their work and posterity. The commentary qualitatively goes beyond the works upon which it is commentary. 'More seriously yet: it becomes autonomous and generates a superimposed tradition which, driven by its own logic, obliterates the work from which it has issued, masks it, distorts it, and makes it disappear.'[8] A study of the history of political thought can show us that the *historical contexts* in which certain ideas became dominant, the dominant ideas themselves changing through commentaries and re-

---

[8] J.-F. Durvernoy, *La Pensée de Machiavel* (Paris, 1974), p. 3.

interpretations undertaken in different contexts, can answer some of the questions that philosophy cannot.

In general, then, we need to come to some decision concerning the degree to which the Greek legacy – *ways of thinking about and discussing values and institutions* – has been affected by specific historical and cultural milieux: ours, theirs, and those intervening cultures between them and us.

Interpretative difficulties

There is, however, another related problem to which we must find a solution: we must try to assess whether we can apply any of the values argued for in earlier political theory to our own situations, or to the world as we think it is. This can be decided only after we have come to some decision about whether we believe that there is a possibility of our understanding what earlier political theorists meant at all, given that they lived in conditions that are not those of Western, post-industrial, modern society and we, of course, do not live in societies that are like theirs. To what extent do we have, as it were, other things on our minds of which the Greeks, indeed any earlier political theorists, had not the slightest conception? And to what extent did they similarly have things on their minds with which we may have no sympathy and, worse, no comprehension at all? To say that Europeans have constructed their histories and their identities, taking the Greeks as their beginnings, does not at first help us to understand how we can be certain that when *we* read their texts, we grasp what *they* meant. Is there a method by which we can read the political theory of past authors without imposing our current agenda on them, without confusing our interests with theirs?

To raise this as a problem of understanding is to raise an issue that was *not* one during earlier centuries in which Europeans were in the process of forging their identity with the Greeks at the beginning. For centuries it had been thought that one *could* read the writings of, say, Greeks and Romans, and see there portrayed behaviour that was thought to be admirable in any age. The past was read about for no other reason than that it was thought to be exemplary and capable of being imitated.[9] It was reckoned to be a useful past. Hence, a four-teenth-century thinker such as Petrarch, the Italian poet who was enamoured of what he took to be the personality and values of the first century BC pagan Roman Cicero, could imagine having an unproble-matic conversation with Cicero in Latin. Petrarchan 'speaking' with

---

[9] See J. Coleman, *Ancient and Medieval Memories: Studies in the Reconstruction of the Past* (Cambridge, 1992).

someone from the ancient Roman world did not involve considering that the ancient might not understand him for the reason that each came from such different worlds of experience and value that their words might refer to different things, Cicero's words conveying resonances that had been lost over the centuries to a Christian, late medieval, Italian user of Latin. Petrarch and other medieval and Renaissance users of Latin were aware that language *use* had changed over the centuries; indeed they increasingly damned the deviation of medieval Church Latin from ancient Roman styles and tried to revive the latter. But while they acknowledged that Latin had changed over the centuries, indeed, according to them, had declined as a means of eloquent expression, they did not believe that *values* had changed or that different social experiences might have led good men in different cultural milieux not only to exalt different virtues but to build political systems that reflected these different values. Therefore, it was relatively unproblematic for earlier Europeans to converse with those whom they admired in the past and thus to build up a picture of their chosen ancestors as being very much like themselves. For them there was an undoubted continuity between good and virtuous men throughout history. It was the construction of this continuity, the construction of a continuous European cultural identity with the Greeks at the beginning, that enabled medieval and Renaissance thinkers to raise to prominence the first two reasons I proposed for our beginning the history of political thought with the Greeks: the language of politics and the history of philosophy, that is, the language of 'our' politics and the history of 'our' philosophy.

The language of politics

If we turn to the language of politics as a reason for beginning the history of political thought with the ancient Greeks, we see that it is not only that certain contemporary words for specific types of constitution such as democracy and monarchy derive from the Greek; indeed, our current political vocabulary (even the word 'politics' itself) derives from the Greek. It is also that the Greeks came to speak about 'the political' in a systematic way within a detailed and unified world view and this is what makes them the beginning of a tradition of political discourse where 'the political' is somehow privileged and in which we share. By believing it possible to give a human account of the social world and then asking what role, if any, the gods, or good and bad luck might play in this account, the ancient Greeks fashioned a range of explanations which are still recognisable ways of speaking, for instance, about the motivation behind men's actions within social structures, and whether or not these structures should be viewed as having developed naturally or by convention. By enquiring into the nature of social reality they discussed the roles played in that reality by human consciousness and agency. Through observation, description and commentary on their own activities of reaching decisions in public and then obeying collective judgement, they came to formulate political theories that argued for the *principles* on which well-run societies must be based. In this way, they defined reasonable principles to guide human behaviour, on the one hand, and to justify a variety of social and political structures according to which they operated, on the other. Today, when we speak about a systematic and rational understanding of nature, of human psychology, of principles of human conduct and the relation, for example, between self-interest and morality, that is, one's own good and its relation to the good of others with whom one lives in community, we may not all come to the same conclusions on these matters any more than did the Greeks, but we are giving an account of 'the political' in a language that was developed to a high degree in ancient Greece.

In privileging 'the political' as an exclusive realm in which certain values such as freedom, equality and justice can be realised through rational debate followed by consistent behaviour (even if what we mean by these values in liberal democratic societies is not quite what the Greeks meant when they spoke of freedom, equality and justice), Greek discourse ensured that later generations would associate notions of participation, rights and freedoms with a distinct sphere of 'civilised' human living, the political realm that was, in the Greek world, confined to male soldier-citizens of the *polis*. Rationalising activity carried on within a distinct and exclusive sphere of collective life has thereafter been taken, for good or ill, to be characteristic of a peculiarly Western understanding of the purpose of social institutions and their relation to free individuals who make choices about the ways they live their lives.[10]

The privileging of 'the political' was related to and perhaps dependent on another characteristic of Greek thought. It has often been noted, not least by the Greeks themselves, that there emerged a tendency in the Greek world to develop different methods for investigating distinct but interconnected subjects of study. The natural world, morality and ethics, logic and language, human psychology and theories of knowledge, human history and explanations of why things had happened in the ways they had, although related to one another, were also distinguished as discrete areas in which expertise and understanding could be

[10] See the feminist debates on the gendered political realm alluded to in n. 2 above.

acquired. In this way, those Greeks who specialised in one or more of these varied subjects of enquiry with distinct methods of proceeding helped to set the agenda for what would become the education curriculum in the West, most notably the liberal arts as they were taught in medieval European universities and which survived well into the seventeenth and eighteenth centuries, and in some cases beyond. The specification of what subjects constituted the arts and sciences in the early modern period and debates concerning what methods of investigation were appropriate to each go back to the Greek division, and especially to Aristotle's systematic version of the division of subjects, each with its own methodology and vocabulary, each with its own 'mode of knowing' or 'science' peculiar to it.

The history of philosophy: from the pre-Socratic naturalists to moral philosophy

This division of subject matter to be investigated follows the development of Greek speculation itself. The history of philosophy is thought to begin with what are known as the pre-Socratic naturalists (seventh to fifth century BC) who were concerned with enquiring into the nature and origins of the universe (*kosmos*).[11] It gradually shifts to those engaged in a more critical philosophy (fifth to fourth century BC), concerned with the foundations of morality and knowledge. Because we still take these kinds of concerns to be central to many contemporary major philosophical concepts, the beginnings of Greek philosophical discussions are considered to be inextricably involved in the historical origins of philosophy as it is still practised. Most notably, the vocabulary of reflective and critical thought in ancient Greek has contributed key terms to our own philosophical vocabulary (*physis* – nature, *aletheia* – truth, *logos* – discourse, account, reason). How, when and from what origins Greek philosophy arose are questions which have been controversially answered from the time of Aristotle onwards. In general, however, Greek philosophy is said to have begun from a view of the world or *kosmos* as a well-ordered totality of concrete and relatively discrete things governed by uniform periodicity, a balance of cosmic opposites that are proportionately and symmetrically structured. The cosmic structure was taken to conform to an intelligible formula and this is the tradition from which the philosophical rationalism of Plato

---

[11] See M. Gagarin and P. Woodruff (eds.) *Early Greek Political Thought from Homer to the Sophists* (Cambridge, 1995), introduction pp. ix–xxxi and texts in translation; G.S. Kirk and J.E. Raven, *The Presocratic Philosophers* (Cambridge, 1957) and revised editions with M. Schofield; A.P.D. Mourelatos (ed.), *The Pre-Socratics* (New York, 1974).

and Aristotle would emerge.[12] Indeed, Aristotle took the naturalists to be the first philosophers, concerned as they were with law and regularity, change and stability in the universe. Not only was nature viewed by some of them as an all-inclusive system, ordered by immanent law. The natural world was somehow the result of reason which, for some thinkers, was not itself part of nature but sovereign over it. A normative, necessary, rationalistic explanation of all that is, and which assumes a well-ordered universe, sometimes conflicted with an assumption that men can argue *from* reason and appearance *to* justified conclusions about objective reality. But in all cases, the pre-Socratic naturalists did not defend their arguments by appealing to the evidence of observation alone.[13] Rather, they relied on *principles* which were not derived from observation. They framed their scientific theories so that the use of observation relied on and, indeed, confirmed the theoretical principles of the sort they discovered. Hence, prior to observation for them was the assumption that natural processes conform to general laws and such laws are not known from authority or tradition but by *logos*, that is, by reason, by giving an account or an argument.

The shift from the focus on how the 'world' came into existence and to be as it is, to the question 'what do I have to know and then do in order to live a worthwhile human life which is what I desire above all else?' is the shift in focus that marks off the beginning of our subject, moral and political philosophy, from other philosophies in the ancient world. So the history of political thought in one sense, as a part of a history of philosophy, is thought to have begun in ancient Greece with the kind of distinct philosophical investigation which, as systematic reasoning, was consciously brought into the communal life. There it asked ordinary men to consider questions of virtue and vice, good and evil, justice and injustice, and the respective roles played by *nature* and *convention* in the constitution of a good society and the understanding of man's role within it and its institutions. Once this occurred, we confront discussions of human awareness and activity in a universe whose reality is governed by laws which somehow circumscribe human freedom, enabling men to distinguish between their capacities to cause 'events' or actions and to be caused or determined by them. But aspects of these

---

[12] D. Furley, *The Greek Cosmologists* (Cambridge, 1987); D. Furley and R.E. Allen (eds.), *Studies in Presocratic Philosophy*, 2 vols. (London, 1970–5); Mourelatos (ed.), *The Presocratics*; W.K.C. Guthrie, *A History of Greek Philosophy*: vol. I, *The Earlier Presocratics and the Pythagoreans* (Cambridge, 1962); vol. II, *The Presocratic Tradition from Parmenides to Democritus* (Cambridge, 1965).

[13] G.E.R. Lloyd, *Magic, Reason and Experience: Studies in the Origins and Development of Greek Science* (Cambridge, 1979).

discussions have a peculiar, even discordant, ring to contemporary liberal democratic ears.

To ask questions about the limits of human autonomy, about the extent to which humans can be the architects of their lives, individually and collectively, given their place in the natural and customary schemes of things, *however* one understands these to be arranged, is to ask not only about humans in general, but about the nature of the reality in which they are situated and within which and because of which they behave in what are taken to be peculiarly human ways. To ask these kinds of questions and also to try to find some answers is to engage in a kind of thinking that is meant to transcend time and one's own culture. It is meant to 'raise' the discussion to levels of abstraction that would allow people from a variety of different cultures to move beyond opinions prominent in their own society in order to discover the truth about such issues. On this view, the logic of certain kinds of arguments should be able to transcend people's opinions that tie their views to the historical times and conditions in which the argument may have first been made.

Certain Greeks thought it possible to enquire comprehensively, systematically and according to general laws and principles in order to disclose what they took to be evident or apparent regularities in the natural environment and in human cultures as responses to it. And instead of appealing only to traditional authorities, whether gods or ancestors, they insisted that a *logos*, a reason, argument, an account could be sought and found to enable them better to understand their collective social myths as well as those assumptions they already accepted when they said they understood common-sense reality. The discovery and account of what the basic laws of human nature are should explain not only how each and every society came into being but why they have the histories they have.

For some Greek thinkers, the *logos* discovers an objective and evident order in appearances. For others, the *logos* discovers a hidden order that is inaccessible to common sense, so that reality is to be sharply distinguished from appearance. Still others argued that human nature does not follow objective and independent laws at all, but rather results from arbitrary human customs and conventions and, therefore, our definition of human nature depends on culture and the processes of acculturation. On this view, there is no reason to prefer one moral outlook or one account of reality to another. Instead of there being a knowable and fixed truth about reality, how things are is a measure of convention; how things are is how they appear to any perceiver or thinker in a certain milieu in which he experiences what he experiences. These kinds of

discussions and the debates concerning how humans evaluate reality
and discover not only their moral convictions but the standards they use
in judging or criticising conventional norms, laws, structures of organised power, in their own society and in that of others, were central to
Greek political philosophy, that is, to their systematic accounts of the
social world. Variations on all these views still exist in our own world.

Here, however, we must pause. There is no Greek philosophy or
social discourse which presupposes or aspires to the idea that man is
self-made, an autonomous thinking 'I' whose cognition is culture-free.
No Greek claimed what Descartes was to claim later, in the seventeenth
century: that there was only one clear and distinct idea to which man is
inwardly compelled: *cogito ergo sum* (I think, therefore, I am), the
existence of the thinking, conscious self, an idea which is established
autonomously, privately, without any extraneous aid, and which transcends culture and its prejudices.[14] Culture for the Greeks was either
natural (for instance, divinely established or simply the result of natural
impulse), or conventionally established, but man was not usually conceived of as being capable of thinking without it. How humans classify
and handle the things to be known was discussed by the Greeks in terms
of an order that inheres in the culturally instilled manner of holding
shared conceptualisations, and these came about through society.
Greeks were prepared to admit that shared conceptualisations varied
from one society to another and that the content of concepts was socially
guided. But the boundaries of shared conceptualisations were understood to be acquired only by being part of a community, be that
community a naturally or a conventionally established one, and it is this
which defined man for them, as distinguished from beasts. A hypo-
thetical man who lived outside a law-governed social community was,
by definition, not a man at all but either a beast or a god. Man, for the
Greeks, was rational in the large sense, meaning that, generically, men
think in circumscribed, shared concepts that arise in them by means of
controlled and collective social habituation, be that acculturation
process a consequence of nature or of convention (*physis* or *nomos*).
Society, however it came about, through force, or through fear, or
through a kind of pragmatic utilitarianism, or as the consequence of
divine intervention, and however it was arranged, was sacred to them
because it was the context in which 'man' could be defined. 'Man' could
not be defined without it. This context comprised a shared history,
rituals, myths, religions, customs and norms. In considering man's
ability to reason, they situated him within a context where reason either

---

[14] See the discussion in E. Gellner, *Reason and Culture: the Historical Role of Rationality and
Rationalism* (Oxford, 1992).

lived side by side with Greek religion and myth or had to confirm religion and myth. Although some, namely the leading philosophers, came to depersonalise their conceptions of nature and they increasingly accounted for cosmic history without continual references to gods with human-like motives, they none the less did not separate nature from religion. They may have considered sense experience and human knowledge to be limited but they were not sceptical about the general orderly structure of the world or about the separate existence of gods and their general relation to humans.[15] Reasoned explanations were, for them, the means of rephrasing rather than replacing myth. This is a rationalism that is not the rationalism of modern analytic philosophy which begins, more or less, with Descartes, although elements of it can be found in Hobbes.[16]

What is often taken to be the modern notion of reason[17] assumes the existence of a generic faculty that is identically present in each human mind, capable of categorising and calculating, and it assumes a general criterion of truth applied to all cases, impartially and universally, without being tied to local circumstances. When the emphasis is placed on the general criterion of truth applied to all cases, this modern reason's method of discovering it is said to be detached, procedural, a rule-following logic that is meant to liberate from a specific culture each self-sufficient and autonomous mind that operates on its own. Indeed, this kind of reason is meant to transcend the natural in the sense that it requires that explanations be subject to tests which are not under the control of either a prevailing system of ideas, an orthodoxy, or a culturally-induced vision of the world. No world vision is allowed to dictate the rules of evidence. The truth this modern reason is said to establish is unified and systematic, external to and independent of any society's social requirements. Furthermore, and of great importance, a modern account of the truth is not meant to be stable; it is open to change and is ever revised. No stage in its progress is ever regarded as final so that the past and its truth are always viewed as provisional. Modern truth is, therefore, cognitively unstable. But the means to its achievement is methodologically orderly and fixed. Through its logic of

---

[15] E. Hussey, 'The Beginnings of Epistemology: From Homer to Philolaus', in S. Everson (ed.), *Epistemology. Companions to Ancient Thought* 1 (Cambridge, 1990), pp. 11–38.

[16] J. Cottingham, *A Descartes Dictionary* (Oxford, 1993), p. 5 on the slippery concept of modernity and Descartes as the 'father of modern philosophy'.

[17] See the co-authored introductory essay in R. Rorty, J. Schneewind and Q. Skinner (eds.), *Philosophy in History* (Cambridge, 1984); K. Popper, *The Poverty of Historicism* (London, 1957) and Popper, *Objective Knowledge: an Evolutionary Approach*, revised edn (Oxford, 1979); Gellner, *Reason and Culture*; J. Rawls, *A Theory of Justice* (Oxford, 1972).

proceeding it is said to owe nothing to community, or to one society or another, when it gives all and sundry *the* valid view of reality, a reality that is thought to be immune from the dominance of any collective 'illusion'.

This modern reason is not ancient Greek (Roman or medieval and Renaissance) reason in certain fundamental ways. For Plato, notably, the truth is not open to change and revision. It is not progressive. For Plato, the truth is cognitively stable and access to it is methodologically orderly. This is because of his assumptions about cosmic orderliness and his belief that human reason may obtain access to it in the here and now. Aristotle, too, provides a version of this cognitive and methodological stability. There is similarly a range of prior assumptions which need to be uncovered before we can assess the cogency of the arguments of many other political theorists in the tradition of Western political theorising.

How should we study the history of political thought?

The preceding paragraphs may appear rather abstract. But it is important that we consider the difference between 'ancient' and this type of 'modern' reason before studying the writings of earlier political theorists. The purpose of trying to draw a distinction between ancient and modern reason is to elucidate some of the consequences of studying the history of political thought in one way as opposed to another. Modern philosophers and political theorists have increasingly displayed an interest in ancient philosophy and have applied modern logical analysis to ancient Greek texts, thereby seeking to attract contemporary students back to the classics.[18] They tell us that they are not engaged in reconstructing the past ideas of political history and, therefore, are not interested 'simply' in what the ancient Greeks believed and why.[19] They confirm instead that their interest in the history of thought requires a selection of past beliefs and arguments which are of philosophical interest to *them*. Such a selection of interesting philosophical ideas is not largely concerned with those ideas which *in fact* influenced social organisation and behaviour in the past. Rather, modern philosophy is interested in the beliefs expressed in ancient philosophy for which a certain kind of rational argument has been provided and such rational arguments can then be assessed or evaluated *now* according to what *we* take to be the logical criteria of coherence and the cogency of inferences drawn, assuming that the logical criteria of coherence are themselves not

[18] S. Everson, 'Introduction', in S. Everson (ed.), *Epistemology*, pp. 1–10.
[19] See the introductory essay in Rorty et al. (eds.), *Philosophy in History*.

only timeless but the only criteria to be invoked in judging an argument. This philosophical approach has produced some stunning analyses and should be drawn on to help explain distinctive features of certain political theories of the past.

But let us consider the possibility that an ancient, medieval, Renaissance or early modern philosopher held the views he did because of *non*-philosophical or undemonstrable beliefs that were sustained in his religion, society and culture. That is, let us consider that his philosophical discourse and its logic actually begin in unexamined premises that are held not to be open to logical proof or philosophical scrutiny. These views sustained by non-demonstrable premises can be open to a kind of *historical* scrutiny of a tradition of enquiry and discourse, and this leads to another kind of investigation alongside the philosophical. This would not be, as some historians of philosophy seem to think, an investigation which 'merely' and uncritically reproduces arguments and conclusions as found in the original sources.[20] A 'mere' reproduction of original arguments is virtually impossible for us to achieve because a 'faultless reproduction' could only come about by doing no more than citing the text itself in its original language. And it would also require a 'perfect reader' who would have to be more 'perfectly receptive' than simply a contemporary of the author with whom the author intended to communicate, assuming the author knew how to achieve this.

Furthermore, students of the history of political thought today read ancient Greek and Latin texts in translation, and every translation is an interpretation. Indeed, every reading of a text is an interpretation. Once one re-presents an ancient, medieval or Renaissance argument cogently in *our* language, we require that an explanation be given concerning not only what we take to be the 'logic' of its argument, but why this kind of argument might have appeared plausible and sustainable to its original audience even if, and perhaps especially if, not to us. In other words, we would want to know what question these arguments were meant to answer in order to judge an argument both logically coherent and plausible *in given circumstances*. Only if we insist on the modern rationalist criteria by which we assess *all* past philosophical arguments for validity and universal truth claims achieved by a very specific (and narrow) understanding of reasoning can we dismiss certain past philosophical arguments as 'obviously fallacious'[21] and, therefore, take no further interest in them. In doing this we certainly extend our modern

---

[20] This is asserted in the introduction of Rorty et al. (eds.), *Philosophy in History* and similarly by S. Everson, 'Introduction', in Everson (ed.), *Epistemology*, p. 2.

[21] Everson argues, in contrast, that 'Some of the arguments preferred by even great philosophers are too obviously fallacious to warrant our attention'; *Epistemology*, p. 2.

philosophical brief, but we lose in the process our historical sense and see the Greeks or anyone else as interesting only in so far as we can make them at home in *our* world, always assuming that our world is 'the world', explained according to culture-free criteria of truth.

Hence, a history of political thought ought not to limit itself to setting past political theories in a philosophical context of other contemporary theories (e.g. Plato surrounded by Sophists who were his opponents) and thereafter, 'simply' assess them in terms of a universal, logical coherence and cogency appropriate to an autonomous mind operating on its own and divorced from local circumstances. The aim should be to examine the theories proffered against cultural norms and explicitly expressed, often theological or metaphysical premises which have not necessarily survived as our premises. In doing this, the Greeks no less than the Romans and medieval thinkers can be shown to have argued logically and coherently where they did so, given that we have grasped the questions *they* thought it important to answer. They can also be shown in important ways that were essential to their identity not to have been like us and necessarily so. A balance between trying to understand the cogency of ancient arguments on the one hand, and an elucidation of why Greeks, Romans, medieval and Renaissance thinkers, respectively, thought the ways they did (and why we often think differently) on the other, is central to a *history* of political theorising. It is, in other words, a history of sameness and difference.[22] Hence, a history of political thought must provide the socio-historical context from within which different political theories were generated, as well as often lengthy philosophical analyses of theorists' positions, and in so doing, attempt to satisfy some of the demands of modern philosophy without ignoring the claims of historians.

I hold to the view that we cannot always assume that the problems of political philosophy are eternal or subject to true solutions. To say this is not, however, to adopt the relativist position of the sort where anyone who happened to express a view can be defended across time. Nor is it the kind of historicism which thinks that human thoughts and beliefs are 'caged' by the context in which they were thought so that they perish with the leaving behind of the historical time in which they came to light. It is simply to observe that the political theorists we study in the history of political thought were not all answering the same universal questions. Their activities are, for us, arranged in a continuum of

---

[22] 'The artefacts of the ancient world stumble upon different meanings in new locations': James Davidson, 'To the Crows!', review of Bernard Knox, *The Oldest Dead White European Males and Other Reflections on the Classics* (London, 1993), in *London Review of Books*, 27 January 1994, p. 20.

changing problems in which the very questions that were asked changed over the course of time and culture. Therefore, we should not think that Hobbes's 'state' was his answer to Plato's question about the Greek political ideal, the *polis*.[23] From our point of view as readers of past texts who are interested in the evolution of political theorising as an activity, ethical and political questions and their answers are transitory and historical rather than permanent. We must always remind ourselves that the voices of ancient Greece and Rome came to be heard and understood through other mediations – most notably, that of the Bible and its commentators along with traditions of collective living that were modified in practice across the centuries. For this reason political theories or political philosophies must be embedded within socio-political history in order to elucidate why these texts ask and answer certain questions rather than others.

The Greeks and Romans, no less than authors of political theories in other ages, are to be viewed as representatives of groups, parties, all of them positioned in structures not of their own making. These theorists are not, then, to be treated simply as individual linguistic agents in speech situations; rather, they should be taken to be representatives of local kinds of arguments set in contexts that were not purely linguistic. The contexts survive for us through texts which re-present the non-linguistic circumstances in which concepts were developed and experiences had. Certain conceptual configurations may be revealed through languages used at the time in order to highlight numerous and simultaneous prejudices which were constitutive of ways of being in the world during the periods in which different political theories emerged. The multiple pre-judgements were embedded and passed on in the languages people used and these prejudices lay behind such people's more reflective judgements as we read them in their political theories. Indeed, all cultures are sustained by multiple prejudices which lie behind their more reflective judgements. When people are engaged in understanding, they are engaged in something other than, but inseparably achieved by means of, linguistic communication. It is less the case that we always possess our world linguistically than that we are possessed by language. In other words, our horizons are given us pre-reflectively by the languages we learn in a particular language community. But this does not mean that there is no way of mediating between different language games learned in different communities. This is because there is a reflexive dimension to human understanding that necessarily begins in

---

[23] Compare R.G. Collingwood, *The Idea of History* (Oxford, 1946), p. 229; G.W.F. Hegel, *Lectures on the Philosophy of World History*, trans. H.B. Nisbet (Cambridge, 1975), first draft, p. 21 .

an interpreter's immediate participation in a tradition of understanding, but such a tradition is only in part revealed in a present tradition of language use.

One of the things we observe in the study of the history of political theorising is the activity of integrating and fusing language games from the past and a theorist's present in order to achieve what *we* recognise, retrospectively, as changed socio-political concepts within their traditions. Through interpretative effort we observe theorists attempting to bridge the gap between their own familiar world with its own horizons and that of strange meanings with other horizons, notably from ancient Greece and Rome onwards. A history of political thought enables us to observe men doing more than learning their own first language; we observe them entering into dialogues and learning other languages, expanding their original horizons – without ever losing them – by confronting and interpreting past texts and other voices. It is this reflexive dimension in which we are ourselves engaged when we read and interpret their writings. This very activity of making texts intelligible to us when we read them ensures that what they had to say cannot be, and is not, completely lost to us. Not only has the past a pervasive power in the activity of human understanding but all interpreters are, and always have been, within their own historicity. This is as true for us as it was for the Greeks. For this reason some of their questions and answers still appear to be alive for us because they have entered our thought in an evolved state, a reconstructed state, having already been taken up, re-thought and re-interpreted by earlier thinkers who thought it important to keep *their* interpretation of the thought of 'their fathers' alive. The old questions and answers are part of our tradition of re-thinking, of making intelligible, in different intellectual and social contexts, these wide-ranging matters. In this way, the past necessarily penetrates our present lives. But ideas from the past are not universal or transhistorical; they have a history but not on their own. Their history is due to their having been re-thought, reconsidered and rendered intelligible by historically situated thinkers and we are the latest in the queue.

Today, what seems to hold this tradition of evolving thought together for us is our assumption that there is a universal logic of thinking as an activity. This is not a new idea by any means – Aristotle, in particular, works with this assumption. A thinking mind is assumed to have a nature that is expressed in the ways it functions as mind in general, and also as a particular mind with its dispositions and faculties which it exercises in contingent, historical circumstances to express its individual thoughts. But this does not mean that mind's activities lead, in specific past and future moments, to the same, unalterable, universally applicable conclusions so that how humans will think and act in the future may be fixed forever by laws that are determined on the basis of how minds have thought and men have acted in the past. Some of the thinkers we study in the history of political thought did, however, believe this to be the case. I have already noted that it was quite common for past European thinkers to assume that men of antiquity were just like them and that is why they believed they could imitate past actions by uncovering universal laws of human behaviour that operated in all circumstances.[24] Past concepts were not taken to be antiquarian curiosities. Unlike post-nineteenth-century historians, earlier Europeans looked for answers to what they took to be unchanging questions and they thought they could engage unproblematically in dialogues with philosophers across time and re-use their solutions to what they took to be eternal problems about human governance. Of course, from our point of view, what they did was construct continuities with their selected pasts while believing themselves to be able to learn from and indeed repeat the virtues of the past because they held that the past was filled with men who were just like them. Today, however, we would argue that they sustained this essential continuity by completely trans-forming past concepts to suit their own circumstances and experiences. They believed themselves to be living within a tradition but actually were in the extended process of constructing one. Where today some modern and postmodern theories insist on highlighting difference, premodern theories sought to mediate difference in order to transform it into an essential continuity of sameness. Today, we assume something a little different.

Today, psychologists and neuroscientists seem to assume that humans do share a general procedure in thinking, that mind is recognisably structured and it happens to function in ways determined by its structure. But what individual minds happen to think is dependent not simply on their functional capacities, but rather on function related to the determinate situations they are in. Such determinate, contingent situations are not repeatable over long tracts of time. *Types* of human behaviour may seem to recur when thinking humans are taken to be in the same kinds of situations, but when, with hindsight, we observe that the social structures and certain of men's values have changed, then the types of behaviour also change and men think and act in ways that respond to the collective and individual, historically transient circum-stances they are in. We recognise this when we say not only that ancient Athenian and Spartan societies were different from the societies of

---

[24] This is further discussed at length in Coleman, *Ancient and Medieval Memories*.

fourteenth-century Italian city-states and, in turn, all of these were different from our own society, but also that each society left evidence of substantively different behaviour and activity. This seems to be a relatively modern observation and one that matters to us today. But it is a perspective on the past that was not shared by medieval or Renaissance thinkers when they recorded their reflections on what they took to be the *essential similarity* between ancient Greek and Roman societies and their own.[25] For them, the basic situation between persons where virtue and vice were exposed remained always the same with every deed arising from this basis. The recurring occasions which gave rise to appropriate alternatives in human behaviour – courage or cowardice, truth or mendacity, moderation or excess – were considered the primordial conditions which were never superseded so that moral behaviour could be viewed as typical, and hence, it conformed to precedent. But for us, what might be considered acts of courage and cowardice, moderation or excess, even rational or irrational behaviour, are not taken to be essentially the same in all cultures or across time.

Therefore, the continuity between, say, Plato's thinking and ours has to be *established* by our thinking in a new context, ours, what he tells us in his texts he took to be, for instance, the components of the unchanging ideal of political life. But our understanding of it is as a Greek ideal and not as one of ours. The common ground we share with Plato is not, of course, context. Nor is it enough to say that we all share an ability to understand the logic of coherent expression so that we grasp Plato's meaning by doing no more than read his texts (in translation). To take Plato or any other past political theorist seriously we need, in addition, to situate Plato and attempt to recognise the range of his meanings, a range that is in part determined by his ancient Greek context and his ancient Greek language, so that we are aware, at least to some degree, of how this context places a limit on what he could *not* have said or meant.[26] This does not leave us without access to the logic of his communication. But the logic is insufficient to convey his meaning or the way in which his views were received when he communicated to his contemporaries.

---

[25] J. Coleman, *Ancient and Medieval Memories*, and J. Coleman, 'The Uses of the Past (14th–16th Centuriea): the Invention of a Collective History and its Implications for Cultural Participation', in A. Rigney and D. Fokkema (eds.), *Cultural Participation: Trends Since the Middle Ages*, Utrecht Publications in General and Comparative Literature 31 (Amsterdam, 1993), pp. 21–37.

[26] See P. King (ed.), *The History of Ideas: an Introduction to Method* (London, 1983), especially King's contribution, part I, pp. 3–65; Q. Skinner, part II, 'Critical Perspectives', part IV, 'Afterword', in J. Tully (ed.), *Meaning and Context: Quentin Skinner and his Critics* (Oxford, 1988).

We cannot, of course, crawl into Plato's psychology, but we can and do respond to the ahistorical logic of his various positions which speak beyond the text and beyond his age, and we also try to reconstruct his cultural premises in order to place this logic within a context of the underlying presuppositions and accepted principles he never argued for. In this way, we modify our own ways of thinking *and* the thought of the author we read without ever eliminating our modern overview. We achieve an awareness that past thinking and activity are both similar to and also different from present thinking and activity. We are unable to conceive of past political thinking as wholly alien and different from the present because if we did so conceive of it, we would have no means of making any sense of it. Some ways of thinking may no longer be current but they cannot be completely lost to us or we would have no access to them. But this does not mean that texts from the past do no more than present us with mirror images of ourselves. The history of political theorising is a history of changing but related ideals of personal conduct as well as of ideals of social organisation. And we make sense of these changing ideals by attempting to grasp something about what people of a certain time and culture believed about the nature of their world even if, or perhaps especially if, it is not what we believe about the nature of our world.

We can never re-present the past or past thinking in a pure form. These are always mediated through our present perspectives and orientations.[27] This was no less true of Romans reflecting on Greece, or of medieval churchmen reflecting on Rome. And this is precisely why in our reconstruction of past arguments we need to engage *both* a philosophical and a historical sense. Doing this we can assess a philosophical proposition in terms of what we take to be its logical cogency, *which is, in practice, how we first read any text*. But we must then go back and look at the argument as a historical phenomenon, as a local utterance, and try to place it in terms of the circumstances in which it emerged and to reconstruct plausible reasons as to why it was enunciated in a particular language. We must examine a text within the context of an author's contemporary world of meaning and distinguish, where we can, its differentness from ours, in order to show, at least minimally, what an author might have meant as well as what he could not possibly have meant. This language, as a social product, rather than as the author's private code, cannot but have been used by the author to argue his position with his contempor-

---

[27] See H.-G. Gadamer, *Truth and Method*, trans. J. Weinsheimer and D.G. Marshall, 2nd rev. edn (London, 1989), part II, i.1: 'Elements of a Theory of Hermeneutic Experience'.

aries.[28] But social codes or discourses, ways of speaking and using words, indeed, the concepts expressed by the words spoken, all have histories that are developed by the social groups that use these languages and who, inadvertently or consciously, change the previously accepted meanings of terms.[29] There are linguistic histories that are then situated in non-linguistic, socio-economic and political contexts which also have histories. Ideas, languages and customary non-linguistic behaviour all have histories, they all change, but not necessarily at the same rate.

We all need a 'crib' when we read Shakespeare today because we no longer speak that historically 'local' kind of English that was current in the sixteenth century. But with a little help with sixteenth-century definitions and information on how the constraints of sixteenth-century rhetorical and literary genres operated, along with information on the social and political life of his times and how this was discussed by the author and his contemporaries, we grasp a meaning that is coherent although it still will not be precisely a sixteenth-century meaning. We may not agree with the views expressed or we may even find some of them implausible. Some positions may appear very strange to us and we may not be able to sustain them in our own world with its current discourses. And yet some positions appear to have been sustained in languages other than the author's own. It is here, in the reconstructed *uses* made of earlier political theories by later generations and societies in different historical contexts, that we can observe how and why political theories are open to a kind of survival as intelligible, where practices as enshrined in particular institutions often are not.

With this in mind, we can point to a distinctive feature of the social context in which Greek political philosophy's discourse developed. Its systematic accounts of the social world became a kind of critical reflection on moral and political questions that was not confined to speculatively trained small groups of men. It was engaged in more widely, especially in fifth- and fourth-century BC Athens, where questions and

[28] See R. Ashcraft, *Revolutionary Politics and Locke's Two Treatises of Government* (Princeton, N.J., 1986), especially the introduction; J.G.A. Pocock, 'The Concept of Language and the *metier d'historien*: Some Considerations on Practice', in A. Pagden (ed.), *The Languages of Political Theory in Early-Modern Europe* (Cambridge, 1987), pp. 19–40; D. Boucher, *Texts in Context: Revisionist Methods for Studying the History of Political Thought* (Dordrecht, 1985).

[29] See the explanatory method of *Begriffsgeschichte* in R. Koselleck, *Futures Past: On the Semantics of Historical Time*, trans. K. Tribe (Cambridge, Mass., 1985); M. Richter, *The History of Political and Social Concepts: a Critical Introduction* (Oxford, 1995); and the various contributions to H. Lehmann and M. Richter (eds.), *The Meaning of Historical Terms and Concepts: New Studies on Begriffsgeschichte*, German Historical Institute Occasional Paper 15 (Washington DC, 1996); see J.G. Gunnell, 'Time and Interpretation: Understanding Concepts and Conceptual Change', *History of Political Thought* 19 (1998), pp. 641–58.

arguments concerning whether ethical values exist by nature or by convention were raised both for and against the prevailing democratic order. Indeed, the very conditions of Athenian democracy appear to have created a unique and fruitful, unresolved tension between social elites and the mass of people, a tension which seems to have been the very source of much of the Greek literature that Europeans take to have been foundational for their own intellectual identity. The democratic order allowed traditional elites and the ambitiously competitive within the society the scope for criticism and a valid place to express their values and their dissent from democracy. It has plausibly been argued that the educated elites were cast in the role of critics by Athenian democratic practice itself, which not only allowed forms of dissent but often actively provoked it from all quarters.[30] Precisely because the critical reflection on moral and political questions was not limited to debates between philosophers, the history of political thought in general, and its beginnings in ancient Greek culture in particular, pays attention to more than the writings of political philosophers in order to grasp the discursive context in which such philosophers said what they said. It takes into account other kinds of evidence such as contemporary drama, historical writings, or political speeches and legislation in order to assess what the surviving sources reveal about the business of conducting political affairs, especially in Athens.

The historian Herodotus (*c.* 484–*c.* 425 BC), for instance, not only provides a comparative description of Greek and non-Greek political systems, but also appeals (as did the pre-Socratic naturalists) to general laws which allow him to evaluate how people with certain customs and in distinctive environments may be expected to act in given circumstances. He explains the collective actions of Athenians and Spartans and attributes their respective success to their collectively held moral and political outlooks. For him, types of societies and specific social and political institutions produce expected effects on men's actions. Hence, history is, for Herodotus, a kind of enquiry, a methodological investigation of the relation between men and their environments which must be carried out *before* one composes one's narrative account of what happened, when, where and why. In explaining Athenian success he refers not only to the actions and decisions of aristocratic individuals but also to the collective behaviour of the people, the *demos*, in the growing democracy, which resulted in a greater sense of individual responsibility for the *polis* and its well being. Democratic Athens was not, for Herodotus, some happy accident; it was caused and the historian could

---

[30] J. Ober, *Mass and Elite in Democratic Athens: Rhetoric, Ideology and the Power of the People* (Princeton, N.J., 1989).

assert the consequent effects. Herodotus did not collect his empirical evidence uncritically. But his is an additional 'voice' to that of the philosophers Plato and Aristotle on the principles and practices of Athenian democracy.

So too, the 'voice' of the historian Thucydides (*c.* 460–*c.* 400 BC) must be added to that of the philosophers. His account of the Peloponnesian War (431–404 BC) was meant to illustrate how the basic *laws of human nature in collectivities*, once known, can explain social and historical processes and predict men's behaviour, especially in times of war and revolution. In the seventeenth century, Hobbes would provide the first English translation from the Greek and develop Thucydides' argument that a study of human nature in the conditions of peace and war leads to the conclusion that men are motivated to observe justice out of a more basic concern for their own power and from a fear of loss of security. (Thuc. III.82.1–2, 84.2).[31] Those who believe that men are motivated by moral considerations over and above a concern for power and fear are, according to Thucydides, deceiving others if not themselves as well. His views on the evolution of the democracy under Pericles, in mid-fifth-century Athens, provide a critical evaluation of the subsequent democratic populism (to 411 BC) when politics was no longer in the hands of his hero, Pericles, Athens' first citizen. Of course, Thucydides' laws of human nature are influenced by his political views and these colour his analysis of the events he narrates. But like Herodotus, he provides us with his version of the cultural ideal so that we can also add his 'voice' to that of the philosophers on the principles and practices of Athenian democracy.

Some of the thinkers who are best known to historians of political thought, such as Plato and Aristotle, and whose orientation was more or less anti-democratic in democratic Athens, persisted in their concentration on moral philosophy even to the extent of creating, as in Plato's case, a theoretical city that was in crucial ways the *opposite* of the classical, Athenian *polis*. Committed democrats, on the other hand, often responded to their attack simply by going about the business of conducting political affairs according to their own notions and established traditions without writing theoretical treatises. If this means for us that we lack contemporary writing of the kind *we* might call 'political science', we do, none the less, know something of the range of political ideals and behaviour on the ground. In so far as accounts of the ancient Greek practice of politics survived, along with the justifications for the

---

[31] E. Hussey, 'Thucydidean History and Democritean Theory', *Crux: Essays Presented to G.E.M de Ste. Croix on his 75th Birthday*, eds. P. Cartledge and F.D. Harvey, *History of Political Thought* 6 (1985), pp. 118–38.

developments of customs, laws and constitutions, in the writings of
dramatists or in the works of historians such as Herodotus and, even
more so, Thucydides, or in the accounts of those who made political
speeches in the Athenian Assembly (e.g. Demosthenes) along with the
more strictly political analysis provided by the 'Aristotelian' *Athenian
Constitution (c.* 320 BC),[32] the form of political organisation that evolved
in Athens over the course of the sixth to fourth centuries BC has come to
be better known. Indeed, from these additional sources a model of
democratic political behaviour and institutional practice became available to later, especially post-Renaissance generations, to supplement if
not to balance the accounts offered by Plato and Aristotle in their
philosophical works.

That later political theorists still remained more impressed by the
ancient political theory of the philosophers than by ancient political
practice tells us something about the later historical culture and its
perceived requirements. But from our point of view, which is concerned
to situate Plato's and Aristotle's theories in the context that helped to
generate them, we need to examine these other sources. If we can
construct a picture of what Athenian democracy was like it will help to
provide a background against which Plato's philosophical dialogues and
Aristotle's ethical and political philosophy can be set. It was, after all, to
their contemporaries that these philosophers addressed their works in
the first instance, Plato establishing a school known as the Academy
where Aristotle himself studied before he later came to set up his
Lyceum. In doing this we become more sensitive to the subsequent
mediations of later interpreters of their writings, becoming better able to
observe the changed meanings and uses of earlier ideas as later generations, including our own, came to accommodate past political theories
to their different intellectual and social contexts.

Perhaps one of the dominant observations we arrive at is that earlier
political theory texts suggest that the relations between the individual
and society are much closer than our contemporary liberal theory takes
for granted. This is because many early texts proposed that practices are
what enable us to give an account of what individuals are like and any
account of the individual cannot be prior to a theory of how they came
to be that way. Such texts propose theories of how one becomes a
person and they reveal no commitment either to a predetermined theory
of property as a philosophical concept, or to a predetermined theory of
the self that hovers above and is independent of social practices. Behind

---

[32] See P.J. Rhodes (trans. and ed.), *The Aristotelian Constitution of the Athenians*
(Harmondsworth, 1984) and Rhodes, *A Commentary on the Aristotelian Athenaion
Politeia with Addenda* (Oxford, 1993).

every individual is always a community. A *history* of political theorising enables us to examine a range of networks of explicit and interdependent social practices which the authors of premodern political theorising, beginning with the Greeks, describe as producing the person who is recognised as a *bona fide* member of a social whole. If nothing else, we become more sensitive to other ways of conceptualising 'being a person' which, in European political discourse, had a longer 'life' than that which became prominent in the discourse of the egoistic self that was said to be proper to civil society and would come to be described with ever-increasing certainty from the seventeenth century onward.

3   History of political theory in the Federal Republic of Germany: strange death and slow recovery

Wolfgang J. Mommsen

I

Intellectual developments in Germany during the period after the Second World War were overshadowed by the search for the causes for the rise of National Socialism and its ability to hold the Germans under its sway for more than a decade. The Allied policies of 're-education', attempting to bring about the intellectual re-orientation of the Germans away from their past nationalist tendencies, towards more Western-oriented political ideas were welcomed by many, as they seemed to offer a way out of the disaster, and all the more as they supported the Germans' very own liberal and democratic traditions, which had been long suppressed but which now experienced a quick recovery.

Even so, there was no sudden rupture with the past. Traditional authoritarian and nationalist views did not disappear overnight, neither in the public at large, nor among academics. Indeed, some of the dominant intellectual figures of the late 1920s raised their voices again, and initially there were but few others. The philosopher Arnold Gehlen propagated a social anthropology which lent intellectual support to the idea of an authoritarian society. Alfred Weber's cultural sociology was becoming very popular, even though it was strongly reminiscent of the intellectual climate of the 1920s. Its thrust was directed against modern technocratic society, which was allegedly about to destroy European individualistic culture as it was known. Its underlying cultural pessimism, reflecting Weber's regret of what he considered to be the progressive alienation in industrial society of the natural roots of human beings,[1] did not necessarily favour the emergence in Federal Germany of a Western-modelled democratic society. Despite his rather dubious role in streamlining German sociology in the early 1930s, Hans Freyer

---

[1] Alfred Weber's culture pessimism is particularly evident in his *Der Dritte und der Vierte Mensch* (Munich, 1953).

was also back in public favour. In 1955, he published his monumental study *Theorie des gegenwärtigen Zeitalters*, where he argued that modern technocratic society was about to make all traditional human values meaningless.[2]

Although only a few German historians had been active National Socialists before 1933, they had failed (for the most part) to see the writing on the wall. Many had initially welcomed Hitler, though only as a stratagem for the conservative reconstruction of the Weimar Republic. The moral responsibility of historians for not opposing the rise of Hitler to power and for their acquiescence (if not their active involvement) with the regime was widely acknowledged (notably in Friedrich Meineckes's *The German Catastrophe*, published in 1946). However, the initial shockwave caused by the realisation of the enormous brutality of the National Socialist regime gradually lost its momentum. In the 1950s more conservative assessments of Germany's history were again on the ascendancy. The older generation of historians had recovered their intellectual equilibrium. Few, if any, were prepared to submit to a thorough intellectual reckoning of what had gone wrong with the profession in the previous decades. Gerhard Ritter, foremost among others, struggled hard to rescue as much as possible from the wreckage of German history after the collapse of the National Socialist regime. Ritter argued that the roots of National Socialism were to be sought in modern mass society as it emerged during the nineteenth century, leading to the gradual erosion of effective traditional political authorities under the impact of emotive mass movements, and not so much in the peculiarities of German history, or, as it was put in the ensuing debate, the 'deutsche Sonderweg', the peculiarly German path towards modernity.[3]

Despite the initial predominance of more traditionalist views, pleas for opening up German society to the West rather than perpetuating the intellectual traditions of the Weimar period gradually won the day amongst academics. Political scientists such as Dolf Sternberger, Alexander Rüstow, Ludwig Bergsträsser and Theodor Eschenburg, assisted by Ernst Fraenkel and a small group of scholars who returned to Germany following their earlier emigration, exercised a substantial influence on the younger generation, who were ill at ease with the teachings of their elders who seemed to them to avoid the vital issues of

---

[2] H. Freyer, *Theorie des gegenwärtigen Zeitalters* (Stuttgart, 1955). See also Jerry Z. Muller, *The Other God that Failed: Hans Freyer and the Deradicalisation of German Conservatism* (Princeton, 1987).

[3] See, *inter alia*, Winfrid Schulze, *Deutsche Geschichtswissenschaft nach 1945* (Munich, 1989); Hartmut Lehmann and James Van Horn Melton (eds.), *Paths of Continuity. Central European Historiography from the 1930s to the 1950s* (Cambridge, Mass., 1994).

the day wherever possible, and to retreat into areas of 'objective research', devoid of direct relevance for current affairs. The idea of constitutional democracy based upon non-alienable natural rights gained ascendancy. Ernst Fraenkel's writings on representative democracy and the shortcomings of the German democratic tradition motivated Karl Dietrich Bracher to write his monumental study on the *Dissolution of the Weimar Republic*. This was not at first welcomed by the historical profession since it employed concepts peculiar to the science of politics. Moreover, his was a radical critique of German society during the Weimar Republic, which he thought was doomed from the very start because it lacked support from either the people or, more notably, the cultural elite.[4]

In a way, Bracher's *Dissolution of the Weimar Republic*, first published in 1955, broke the ice. It marks the take-off of a critical assessment of the traditions of German political theory and of German contemporary history, intent on laying bare their obvious shortcomings as seen from a democratic vantage point. Not surprisingly the reception of Bracher's book by the historical profession was initially rather cool. Werner Conze wrote a somewhat critical review (which he later disowned), objecting to the political science jargon used by Bracher, and to his theoretical, ahistorical approach to the subject. But Bracher had struck a new note in the discourse on the shortcomings and failings of Germany's path towards modernity, compared with those of the democratic societies in the West. Other authors followed suit. Kurt Sontheimer published a major study on anti-democratic thought in the Weimar Republic that laid bare the intellectual roots of the political Right in German politics.[5] Understandably, Carl Schmitt was singled out for bitter criticism, partly because he had appallingly and opportunistically associated himself with National Socialism, and partly because his friend–foe model of politics seemed to have contributed to the failure of the Weimar Republic, so paving the way for the rise of National Socialism, a view that, with hindsight, should be regarded with some qualification. My own book on Max Weber's political views (first published in 1959),[6] and, perhaps with a somewhat less critical approach, Erich Angermann's study of Robert von Mohl, who had been one of the intellectual pioneers of German constitutional liberalism,[7] demonstrated the fragility and half-

[4] K.D. Bracher, *Die Auflösung der Weimarer Republik* (Villingen, 1955).
[5] K. Sontheimer, *Antidemokratisches Denken in der Weimarer Republik. Die politischen Ideen des deutschen Nationalismus zwischen 1918 und 1933* (Munich, 1962).
[6] W.J. Mommsen, *Max Weber und die deutsche Politik, 1890–1920* (Tübingen, 1959); English edn, *Max Weber and German Politics, 1890–1920* (Chicago, 1984).
[7] E. Angermann, *Robert von Mohl, 1799–1875. Leben und Werk eines altliberalen Staatsgelehrten* (Neuwied, 1962).

hearted nature of German liberal and democratic traditions, and their readiness to embrace nationalist and even imperialist positions even though this compromised their credibility. A series of similar studies followed, also aimed at revisiting classic German political theory from the point of view of parliamentary democracy. Likewise a new generation of historians began to challenge traditional interpretations of recent German history including some of their theoretical presuppositions, notably the theory of the 'primacy of foreign policy', and the predominant concentration on the state as the agent of political change.

II

In view of these intellectual departures, the history of political theory came very much under the spell of the overriding issue of how to account for the rise of National Socialism in Germany, and also of how to assess its nature. In this regard two major political theories came to play a most significant role; the theory of totalitarianism and the theory of neo-liberalism. Each had been developed for the most part by political scientists and economists who had emigrated to Great Britain and the United States. Important groundwork had already been done in 1942 by Franz Neumann's interpretation of National Socialism in his *Behemoth*. In the Federal Republic it was above all Hannah Arendt and, in some respects even more persuasively, Karl Joachim Friedrich who introduced the model of totalitarianism into public discourse, as a conceptual tool by which to account for the rise and the nature of both National Socialism and Bolshevism. The theory of totalitarianism postulated a fundamental dichotomy between liberal and authoritarian societies. The former were built upon the spontaneous activity of the individual, while the latter tended to develop in fully totalitarian societies dominated by an omnipotent bureaucratic state and, eventually, by a single ideological party monopolising all political activities. This conceptualisation provided, or so it appeared at least, a most useful set of theoretical tools for assessing the nature of the Fascist and the Communist systems, and indirectly for the legitimisation of the new democratic order in West Germany.

The theory of totalitarianism took as its point of departure the role of the free, spontaneous individual, being the main source of dynamism and creativity in a liberal society, whereas in contrast totalitarian societies stifled individual initiative through oppressive state parties and bureaucratic institutions designed to impose the political will of either the state or a small oligarchy respectively. These assumptions corresponded to the basic tenets of neo-liberalism. Only an economy set free from governmental constraints of all sorts and regulated by the market-place, rather than by bureaucratic institutions, would be able to bring about an economic recovery of impoverished Europe, and notably of Germany. In the early years of the Federal Republic of Germany the theory of neo-liberalism was all the more attractive as it could build upon indigenous theoretical efforts as well. Many economists had worked during the last years of the 'Third Reich' for a return to a market-oriented economy. The neo-liberal ideals originating from the West, notably from the United States, were akin to the intellectual aims of German Ordo-Liberalism which had managed to survive under National Socialism and now raised its voice again. In the event, neo-liberalism came to be an important ideological force during the forma-tive years of the Federal Republic. It effectively pushed aside the socialist schemes harboured by various political groups, not only on the political Left. Admittedly it was presented to the public in a somewhat modified version, namely a 'social market economy' that would allow for a limited degree of state intervention in the economy in order to safeguard essential social objectives.

The impact of the theory of totalitarianism upon a whole generation of political theorists, but perhaps even more so of historians of very different persuasion, such as Karl Dietrich Bracher on the one hand and Ernst Nolte on the other,[8] cannot be overrated either. It provided an important point of departure for early research into National Socialism and its roots in Weimar and Imperial Germany, and, more importantly, an indirect legitimation of the new democratic order embodied in the Basic Law of the Federal Republic. More generally it has to be said that the influence of Western political theory was undoubtedly of major importance in re-establishing a democratic tradition in Germany. Like-wise it helped to revive the historiography of political thought that now came to be primarily concerned with the issues of democratic rule and its legitimation.

It is difficult to assess the impact of this intellectual constellation upon the development of political theory with precision. In the early years neither the political scientists nor the historians of political ideas were overly concerned with political theory, even though the classics of historical thought, notably the intellectual forerunners of constitutional democracy, were given a good deal of attention.[9] However, for a

[8] See Ernst Nolte's at the time path-breaking study, *The Three Faces of Fascism. Action Française, Italian Fascism, National Socialism* (London, 1965).

[9] See, for instance, the anthology *Klassiker des politischen Denkens*, edited by Hans Maier, Heinz Rausch and Christoph Denzer (Munich, 1967/8), which deals with the great classical thinkers from Antiquity to Nieztsche and Weber. It has a good survey of recent literature that drew heavily on French, English and American authors.

considerable period of time no new synthesis in this field was attempted. Intellectual discourse concentrated on political thinkers who could be considered forefathers of German democracy – there were after all not all that many – for instance, Hugo Preuss, Hans Kelsen, Friedrich Naumann, Alfred and Max Weber. Their intellectual opponents, such as the leading representatives of the so-called 'Conservative Revolution', were subjected to similar scrutiny. Carl Schmitt was given particular attention, in view of his dubious role during the Weimar Republic and the early years of National Socialist rule. Schmitt's theory of decisionism was subjected to stringent criticism, given the fact that the Weimar Republic had allegedly destroyed itself by adopting a false neutralist stance that was meant to treat with impartiality even its own enemies. In the background loomed a strong, though perhaps not very well articulated conviction that a democratic order will not survive unless it is grounded on a set of firm principles, such as the 'Rights of Man' in the American Constitution. However, the tradition of natural law was taken up in hugely different ways, ranging from the invocation of Locke and classic liberal theory, for instance by Dolf Sternberger, to the revitalisation of Aristotelianism and Catholic fundamentalist thought by Leo Strauss and Arnold Bergstraesser.

III

The 1960s and 1970s were dominated by the importation from the West of theories of constitutional democracy and, more generally, a multitude of middle-range theories related to the functioning and the regulatory principles of representative systems of government. The pragmatists and empiricists took over, whereas the generalists were pushed to the sidelines. Philosophies of history were considered dead, as they seemed to have provided the basis for ideological politics of different varieties. Karl Popper's famous *The Poverty of Historicism* had a far-reaching impact. Its message was to distrust holistic theories of whatever kind, as they appeared to be imbued throughout with ideologies of various sorts. This amounted to the abandonment of political and social theory in favour of short-range empirical analysis and 'piecemeal engineering'. In the 1960s and 1970s neo-Positivism dominated intellectual discourse, whereas traditional political theory was considered, if not outdated, at least less important. Daniel Bell forecast a new age beyond ideology, at any rate in the advanced industrial societies in the West; the age of grand theory seemed to be over. Hans Albert and Hans Topitsch rose to prominence, as standard bearers of the neo-Positivist message, and political scientists such as Rudolf Wildenmann at Mannheim or Peter Flora at Frankfurt who concentrated upon empirical research began to dominate their discipline. This situation was not propitious for the writing of histories of political theory. Even more so, since historiography itself was given less attention, whilst the analysis of present-day society and of its future was the main preoccupation. Empirical political science and notably the empirical social sciences rose to a hegemonic position in intellectual discourse, whereas the historians complained that society had cut itself off from its own past. Their diagnosis was that German society was suffering from a progressive 'loss of memory' (Alfred Heuss).[10]

Indeed, the battle cry of the moment was 'modernisation', whereas historicism was considered a methodology that had outlived its usefulness. For Friedrich Meinecke and Johann Huizinga historicism had been a kind of intellectual retreat providing a sort of shelter from the disturbing political events around them. The younger generation, however, no longer had confidence in the meaningfulness of the historical process. They saw this as an important reason why historians had failed in time to recognise the pernicious nature of National Socialism and why they had readily accommodated themselves within the regime. Historians reacted to this challenge in different ways. Many of them, notably those belonging to the older generation, clung to traditional research; others turned to themes of universal history and to the classical authors of the historical discipline, notably Leopold von Ranke and Jacob Burckhardt; yet others turned to social history. This seemed to provide an opportunity for side-stepping political history with its obvious ideological trappings, something which was explicitly welcomed by Otto Brunner. Historical inquiries into social reality below the level of state and governmental activities promised an opportunity for a new historiographic departure, not burdened by the ideological heritage of the recent past.

Even so, the shift towards social history became the basis for a remarkable innovation in the discipline. The Heidelberg 'Arbeitskreis für Sozialgeschichte' under the guidance of Werner Conze and Reinhart Koselleck gradually became a centre of considerable innovation in this field. The traditional concentration on the state as the key agent of social change here was abandoned in favour of a pluralistic approach that combined social history and *histoire des mentalités*, largely relying on the classic method of empathy, with, however, a new perspective. Werner Conze demonstrated, in what became a famous essay entitled 'Vom "Pöbel" zum "Proletariat"' (first published in 1954), that it was possible, via the analysis of the meaning of key concepts such as

[10] A. Heuss, *Verlust der Geschichte* (Göttingen, 1959).

pauperism, to gain new insights into the momentous changes of the social order during the crucial period of European history between 1750 and 1850.[11] Soon afterwards Reinhart Koselleck developed an elaborate model of the so-called 'Sattelzeit' between 1750 and 1830. He argued that this period not only brought in principle the breakthrough to modernity inasmuch as the key notions in usage in the political arena had gradually received new, modern meanings during this period of transition.[12] He emphasised that the concepts used in political and social discourse now took on a temporal dimension; all at once, the political language reflected a consciousness of being in a period of irreversible change. The analysis of the political and social language was used to measure social change and to ascertain its significance. Conze and Koselleck launched an ambitious project, consisting in the systematic analysis of changes in meaning and in the linguistic background of key concepts in German public discourse starting from the eighteenth century.[13] It took many years to complete the project of a multi-volume dictionary of political concepts, but this now stands as a very impressive document in its own right. Admittedly, the theoretical conception of 'Sattelzeit', developed by Koselleck in the first place and serving as a guideline for the various authors in writing their individual contributions to the encyclopaedia of political terminology since 1750, was gradually forgotten. The finished product does not qualify as the documentation of the origins of modernity in the eighteenth and early nineteenth centuries. Such a legitimation is no longer needed, though it was considered essential at the moment of its conception, when, according to Koselleck himself, German historiography was in dire need of theory.

Although the 'Heidelberger Arbeitskreis für Sozialgeschichte' has produced important contributions to historical research, at first it did not receive much public attention. The empirical social sciences still dominated public discourse throughout the 1960s and 1970s. More-

---

11 W. Conze, 'Vom "Pöbel" zum "Proletariat". Sozialgeschichtliche Voraussetzungen für den Sozialismus in Deutschland', in Werner Conze, *Gesellschaft, Staat, Nation. Gesammelte Aufsätze*, edited by Ulrich Engelhardt, Reinhart Koselleck and Wolfgang Schieder (Stuttgart, 1992), pp. 232ff; English edn, Georg Iggers (ed.), *The Social History of Politics, Critical Perspectives in West German History Writing since 1945* (Leamington Spa, 1985).

12 R. Koselleck, *Kritik und Krise. Ein Beitrag zur Pathogenese der bürgerlichen Welt* (Munich, 1959), pp. 8ff; English edn, *Critique and Crisis. Enlightenment and the Pathogenesis of Modern Society* (Oxford, 1985).

13 Otto Brunner, Werner Conze and Reinhart Koselleck (eds.), *Geschichtliche Grundbegriffe. Historisches Lexikon zur politisch-sozialen Sprache in Deutschland* (9 vols. Stuttgart, 1972–92). A brief description of the theoretical assumptions that motivated the authors in launching this project can be found in the introduction, vol. I, pp. XIV–XVI.

over, a group of younger historians broke with the Heidelberg model of social history (which was methodologically still fairly conventional and remained within the confines of historicism) and launched their own variety of social historiography that defined itself in somewhat provocative language as a historical social science. The protagonists of 'Historische Sozialwissenschaft', which from 1975 has issued its own journal *Geschichte und Gesellschaft*, notably Hans-Ulrich Wehler and Jürgen Kocka, intended to write social history no longer with the methods of empathy and linguistic analysis, but with the theoretical tools provided by the social sciences. To some degree, in doing so they adjusted to the trend of the time, carving out for historiography, however, an important niche in intellectual discourse. This was still dominated by disputes on neo-Positivism and its role within the social sciences themselves.[14] The Frankfurt School, and in particular Jürgen Habermas, fought a passionate crusade against the predominance of the seemingly almighty empirical social sciences in German scholarship. According to Habermas (and rightly so, I believe) neo-Positivists were unable to comprehend social systems in their entirety. They assumed their findings about social life to be indisputable matters of fact; but unwittingly they had become guardians of the existing social order. They provided instrumental knowledge for social engineering rather than insights into the fundamental nature of political systems and their far-reaching impact upon people's lives. Habermas's struggle against what he called 'ein positivistisch halbierten Rationalismus'[15] was, at the time, a rather rearguard action: its more positive aspect was to keep open the door for a fundamental investigation of industrial society and egalitarian democracy.

How far removed these discourses were from a genuine confrontation with the classics of political theory can be demonstrated by the extremely one-sided reception of Max Weber's methodological position and his political views by social scientists in the 1950s and 1960s.[16] For the most part they uncritically followed in the footsteps of Talcott Parsons who had emphasised Weber's role as a herald of modernisation. However, the disagreement between the Frankfurt School and the neo-Positivists referred largely to Weber's theory of abstention from value judgements, or, as it was seen at the time, of value-neutrality. The neo-Positivists invoked Weber's alleged demand of value-neutrality as a

[14] See, *inter alia*, Theodor W. Adorno et al, *Der Positivismusstreit in der deutschen Soziologie* (Frankfurt, 1972).

[15] J. Habermas, 'Gegen einen positivistisch halbierten Rationalismus', in Adorno et al. *Der Positivismusstreit*, pp. 235ff.

[16] Cf. W.J. Mommsen, 'Max Weber in Modern Social Thought', in Mommsen, *The Political and Social Theory of Max Weber* (Cambridge, 1989), pp. 169ff.

legitimation of their methodological approach. They totally failed to see that Weber's notion of value-relationship ('Wertbeziehung'), which plays a crucial role in the construction of ideal-types, meant something very different, a fact which Habermas was quick to point out. He in turn showed that Weber's methodology actually contained an element of decisionism inasmuch as reality can only be ascertained by means of ideal-types, and these are constructed in view of the cultural significance of the issues at stake.

The attribution of a neo-Positivist methodology to Max Weber was altogether beside the point. Nor, however, did his views support a fundamentalist social theory, such as those for instance embraced by Adorno and Horkheimer, as was later realised by Habermas himself. In fact, at the time, Max Weber's historical sociology was not given much attention by social scientists in Germany; at best it was used as a quarry for theoretical conceptualisations of the most diverse kinds. It is hardly surprising that Friedrich Tenbruch, a sociologist enjoying great authority at the time, could argue that Weber's methodological writings (which incidentally had been invoked by Dieter Henrich for a return to hermeneutics) had nothing to say whatever to contemporary social science.[17]

However, political scientists took an altogether different approach. They tried to stem the tide of what seemed to them meaningless political theorising with little empirical substance. They did so by paying little or no attention to either the role of values or the historical dimension of social reality. It was not surprising that after the débâcle of National Socialism, German political science experienced a sort of revival of fundamentalist positions, be it natural law or Catholic value theory. However, the trend of the time pointed in the opposite direction. Those political scientists who argued that a political order is, in the last resort, based upon fundamental human values and will only be sustained if those are not lost from sight, conducted a losing battle. Even Max Weber appeared much too technocratic in his reasoning. Arnold Bergstraesser attacked Max Weber for his allegedly technocratic notion of the state and his supposedly functionalist, value-neutral interpretation of constitutional democracy.[18] Wilhelm Hennis's essay 'Das Problem der deutschen Staatsanschauung' originally published in 1956 objected to Weber's reductionist approach to political theory that, as he put it, reduced political systems in the last resort to a set of naked power

[17] F. Tenbruch, 'Die Genesis der Methodologie Max Webers', *Kölner Zeitschrift für Soziologie und Sozialpsychologie*, 11 (1959), pp. 573ff.

[18] A. Bergsbraesser, 'Antrittsvorlesung in zeitgeschichtlicher Perspektive', *Vierteljahreshefte für Zeitgeschichte*, 5 (1975), pp. 217ff.

relationships.[19] The systematic elimination of fundamental political values, as a key factor of any political order, appeared to many German political scientists unacceptable; Hennis put it in the most strident language. To some degree the charge that Max Weber had been a protagonist of a mere technocratic or, at any rate, a mere legalistic notion of the modern state is corroborated by his well-known typology of 'three types of legitimate rule', a classification that deliberately side-stepped those types of reasoning in the natural law tradition. However, Hennis himself later revised this extreme interpretation, whilst in his recent publications he embraces a very different, if not altogether opposite, line of reasoning.[20]

In the wake of the so-called Student Revolution of the late 1960s, both political science and the social sciences were nearly swept away by a strong current of neo-Marxist thought. The ensuing endless debates about Marxist approaches to social and political issues in the universities paralysed serious research. For a while both disciplines were rendered ineffective in terms of their duty to provide intellectual guidance to society.

This intellectual constellation did not give encouragement to the writing of the history of political theory, except on Marxism. However, even in this field academic discourse took a turn towards increasingly dogmatic argumentation. Previously, scholars such as Iring Fetscher and Siegfried Landshut had paved the way for a rediscovery of the genuine Marx whose teachings had been manipulated beyond retrieval by official Marxist-Leninist doctrine in the USSR and the German Democratic Republic. In Marx's early writings they had discovered a far more humane and individualist approach than the bureaucratic Marxism that had become the new orthodoxy.[21] But now these new departures were again partially forgotten. A new dogmatic variety of Marxist thought was in the ascendancy, but now strangely mixed with the emotive anti-capitalism propounded in Herbert Marcuse's writings, which enjoyed an enormous popularity with the younger generation of students. Eventually, Che Guevara's altogether irrational anti-Imperialism prevailed. The theory of totalitarianism came under fire from the Left. The fact that it had put National Socialism and Soviet Communism on the same plane appeared no longer acceptable. The Left

[19] W. Hennis, 'Das Problem der deutschen Staatsanschauung', *Vierteljahreshefte für Zeitgeschichte*, 7 (1977), pp. 21ff.

[20] See W. Hennis, *Max Webers Fragestellung* (Tübingen, 1987); English edn, *Max Weber: Essays in Reconstruction* (London, 1988); W. Hennis, *Max Webers Wissenschaft vom Menschen* (Tübingen, 1996).

[21] See the introduction to Karl Marx, *Die Frühschriften*, edited by Siegfried Landshut (Stuttgart, 1953).

now gave preference to the concept of Fascism, as it symbolised, so it seemed, the allegedly intimate relationship between capitalism and National Socialism. In his turn, Ernst Nolte, who in his book *The Three Faces of Fascism* had initially introduced the concept of Fascism as covering diverse sorts of Fascist and National Socialist movements in Europe, now formally dissociated himself from the use of Fascism in this new sense, whilst Karl Dietrich Bracher put up a strong defence in favour of the theory of totalitarianism, despite growing doubts as to whether it could be maintained in view of new findings on the internal structure of the National Socialist governmental system.

Historiography was not affected to the same degree by the neo-Marxist currents of the 1960s. Here, a mêlée of social science empiricism and a Parsonite version of Max Weber's thought, with some elements of Marxist thought as additional ingredients, provided important intellectual stepping-stones for the new social history, somewhat euphemistically named 'Historische Sozialwissenschaft' – historical social science. In fact, unlike its Heidelberg rival, from the start it was social history with a strong political intent. It sought to substitute the traditional varieties of historiography with a social history approach that would lay open the social and institutional bases of authoritarian politics in Germany, in the study of the past as well as that of the present. Indeed, politically oriented social history, whose main intellectual headquarters came to be the newly founded University of Bielefeld, made such a strong impact upon historical scholarship that conventional history of political ideas was largely pushed aside, in favour of a new, explicitly theoretical approach to social reality. The key determinants of social change were sought in the socio-economic sphere and the conditioning factors of social and political processes. The 'Historische Sozialwissenschaft' deliberately opted for an explicitly theoretical approach to past history, by analogy with the methods used in the social sciences. A key role was assigned to theories of modernisation, sometimes taken at random. The result was that for almost a whole generation the history of political thought was considered to be of merely marginal importance; it almost disappeared from the curricula of the faculties of history at West German universities. It was left to the political scientists to deal with political theory, as far as it was still considered essential. Historians were preoccupied with theories and theoretical constructs directly applicable to the analysis of historical subjects. Medieval historians were operating with concepts such as feudalism, representing a particular model of social order; contemporary historians opted for middle-range theories concerning particular social formations, for instance the theory of 'organised capitalism'.

Ideal-typical models came to be used widely, for instance models of class divisions, social stratification or social mobility.[22]

IV

In the 1960s and early 1970s interest in political theory had been pushed to the margins of scholarship. Political science in Germany was dominated by various versions of Marxist thought that were not particularly conducive to a comprehensive historical analysis of political ideas. Historiography received important innovative impulses from the new social history, but at the expense of traditional history of political ideas. However, by the end of the 1970s fundamental change had got under way. The 'oil shock' in 1975 and the ensuing economic recession in Germany marked the end of a period of uninterrupted economic growth, during which social conflicts had been minimised thanks to the co-operation of entrepreneurs and trade unions. The 'Student Revolution' in 1968 had shaken the self-confidence of the older generation, and the universities had become, at least for some years, places of bitter ideological strife. The conflict between the generations which was widely attributed to a complete loss of historical consciousness seemed to endanger the social fabric. Apparently the confident forecasts, by Daniel Bell and other social scientists, that in advanced industrial societies the 'end of ideologies' was imminent had turned out to be false. Optimism and faith in the smooth working of the economy had given way to insecurity and irritation. People began to look for reassurance, not least by turning back to history. Historians were expected to end their critical assessment of Germany's recent past and come up with positive answers. This was supposed to be their contribution to a new national identity and to a revitalised idea of nation, compensating for insecurity and lack of orientation. This triggered off the so-called 'Historikerstreit', which centred on whether and how to write the history of Germany's most recent past. There also emerged a new interest in the question of German national identity, giving rise to a passionate debate on the notion of 'constitutional patriotism' and the other issues involved in the problem of nationality.

It had become obvious that empirical social science could not provide altogether satisfactory answers to the problems that had emerged after the end of a period of unprecedented economic growth. The pressing problems of the day could no longer be mastered merely by 'piecemeal

[22] For a good presentation of the objectives of the 'Historische Sozialwissenschaft' see Jürgen Kocka, *Sozialgeschichte – Begriff – Entwicklung – Probleme* (Göttingen, 1986). See also Hans-Ulrich Wehler, *Geschichte als Historische Sozialwissenschaft* (Frankfurt, 1973).

social engineering'. Practical direction on the global situation and on the likely long-term trends was in demand, not just instrumental knowledge. This necessitated, as it were, a return to social theory and, likewise, to comprehensive rather than middle-range theories, to theories taking into account the historical dimension of social reality. All of a sudden the social sciences and political theory stood in need of grand theory again.[23]

This may explain why there suddenly emerged a renewed interest in the sociological theory of Max Weber. He was now rediscovered not so much as a pioneer of empirical social research, as had been the case in the 1950s and 1960s, but rather as a social thinker who had combined detailed sociological and, indeed, political theory with a genuine historical perspective, or, more precisely, with a global historical model of social change which transcended the unintended 'presentism' of a great deal of recent empirical social research. Max Weber opened new ways for the interpretation of social and political processes in terms of a meaning-based analysis, taking into account essential human ideals and values, rather than mere instrumental knowledge. Notably his reconstruction of the development of Western civilisation (the 'occidental' world) as a process of progressive rationalisation (although eventually terminating in new irrationalities), and also his sociology of world religions which dealt with the non-economic motives for social and economic action, now received a great deal of attention again.[24]

Weber's sociological theories and political analyses were in the last resort motivated by the key issue of which types of human formations are likely to thrive best, or, conversely, worst under a particular set of social and political conditions. This refers in particular to modern bureaucratic institutions that, though they are more efficient than any other known form of social organisation, tend to stifle individual initiative and favour a mentality of passive adaptation to given conditions. Weber pointed in his studies to one central issue, namely the necessity of preserving a sphere of spontaneous action for the individual, even in modern bureaucratic society. His plea that research in the social sciences and in history alike must be anchored in cultural premises has by now found a large following.

In a way the two major ventures aimed at developing a comprehensive theory of modern industrial society, by Jürgen Habermas on the one

---

[23] See also Quentin Skinner (ed.), *The Return of Grand Theory in the Human Sciences* (Cambridge, 1985), pp. 5ff. and p. 14.

[24] Foremost in this respect is Wolfgang Schluchter's work, notably his study *Max Weber's Vision of History* (Berkeley, 1979), and his *Religion und Lebensführung* (2 vols., Frankfurt, 1988). See also Mommsen, *Political and Social Theory*, pp. 180ff.

hand and Niklas Luhmann on the other, were both inspired to a considerable degree by Max Weber's sociological theory, although in radically different ways. Luhmann took Max Weber's theory of bureaucracy – as a social formation that tends gradually to push all other types of social interaction aside, eventually creating a closed system of purely formal relationships, of purposes and means – as a point of departure for developing a formalist theory of systems of social interaction commonly known as 'Systemtheorie'.[25] However, he was not at all concerned with Weber's initial problem of how to maintain individual initiative under such conditions. On the contrary, he viewed the fact that for him modern social systems consist of a complex web of instrumental relationships that attain stability once the various social forces that interact with one another have reached a status of equilibrium; they are 'self-referential systems' that establish a relative degree of autonomy *vis-à-vis* their environment.[26] For the most part the behavioural patterns and the actions of the individuals are enforced by the systemic factors that determine their life conduct; spontaneous action by the individuals tends to be marginalised. It might be said that Weber's fear that some day 'Fachmenschen ohne Geist' – perhaps save a few intellectuals – would be predominant in the 'iron cage of future serfdom' has been turned from a mere perspective with apocalyptic undertones into a comprehensive theory of modern society. It goes without saying that in Luhmann's technocratic model of industrial society, politics is assigned only a subordinate role.[27]

A different path was pursued by Jürgen Habermas. Gradually emancipating himself from the Marxist premises of the Frankfurt School, from which he came, he developed a comprehensive theory of communicative action, amounting to a new grand theory.[28] In doing so he was heavily indebted to Max Weber, and the latter's key problem of defending the sphere of spontaneous creative action of the individual against the seemingly overwhelming collective pressures of bureaucratic society. Habermas's 'theory of communicative action' is guided by the regulative idea of a society in which domination is being progressively replaced by the interaction between individuals based upon free communication. Thereby it becomes possible, at least in principle, to arrive at a social order in accord with the old liberal ideal that the rule of man over men

---

[25] See N. Luhmann, *Zweckrationalität und Systemrationalität* (Frankfurt, 1973), pp. 23–5.
[26] Cf. N. Luhmann, *Soziale Systeme. Grundriss einer allgemeinen Theorie* (Frankfurt, 1984), p. 31.
[27] For an interesting encounter between Luhmann and Habermas see Jürgen Habermas and Niklas Luhmann, *Theorie der Gesellschaft oder Sozialtechnologie – Was leistet die Systemforschung?* (Frankfurt, 1971).
[28] J. Habermas, *Theorie des kommunikativen Handelns* (2 vols., Frankfurt, 1981).

ought to be replaced by the administration of things, via the intermediary agency of unrestricted communication. In this model the
classic Marxist postulate of the emancipation of the workers from
exploitation by the entrepreneurs has been twinned with the liberal
principle of self-determination. The social system operates without
conflict thanks to an ongoing process of free communication between
the individuals concerned, irrespective of their different social functions.
It goes without saying that the principle of 'Öffentlichkeit' (unrestricted
publicity) must be considered an essential element of a democratic
social order.

Although utopian in view of its ultimate objectives, Habermas's
theory of communicative action could serve as a point of orientation for
individual action in society. By and large a similar path was followed by
other authors such as Claus Offe or Klaus Eder. They aimed at keeping
alive the humanistic element of original Marxism without committing
themselves to orthodox Marxism-Leninism, which in any case had lost
its credibility long before the Soviet empire collapsed and deprived
Marxist-Leninist ideology of the institutional support that had kept it
alive in some intellectual quarters. Only authors such as Rudolf Bahro,
who combined a socialist, and at times anarchist, message with a strong
condemnation of the Stalinist variety of Marxism-Leninism, were taken
at all seriously, even though their impact upon political theorising was
slender.

V

These new departures in the wake of a renewed interest in Max Weber's
social theory may be taken as a signpost indicating that the trend that
discouraged all engagement within history of political theory had come
to an end. For one, macro-sociological theory was back on the agenda,
though hedged by caution as to the range of validity which can be
attributed to comprehensive theories of history. More importantly, by
now the emphasis on social history had given way to a plurality of
methodological approaches, governed by the notion that culture, in all
its different connotations, constitutes the centre of all disciplines
devoted to the study of 'la condition humaine', and not merely the
economy or the societal structure. This was bound to instigate a
renewed interest in political theory and the history of ideas. Mentality, it
would appear, is seen to be more than a mere reflection of reality; on the
contrary, it determines the ways in which human beings perceive social
reality. This is to say that in a way things have come full circle. The
representation of historical reality, in the perception of its contempor-

aries, is again considered the key to the analysis of social reality, whereas social and economic factors are ruled to be of secondary importance. Culture, in its various connotations, may be seen as the complex of world views and value attitudes shaping the perspectives through which reality is perceived and thereby constituted. Accordingly, culture has regained a hegemonic position in the social sciences and the humanities. This provided a new impetus to the study of the history of ideas, and notably to political theory. As recently pointed out by Ernst Nolte, this study was pursued by a number of scholars operating in relative isolation. These included, on the one hand, people such as Hermann Lübbe and Bodo Marquardt, who take a sceptical position *vis-à-vis* the race for modernity; and on the other, Hans Joas and Norbert Elias, who view the 'process of civilisation' in a somewhat more positive light.[29]

Right now there has emerged a new interest in the work of eminent German thinkers, among others Georg Simmel and his sociology of culture, Ernst Troeltsch's historicism, and Ernst Cassirer's neo-Kantian approach. Major new editions of the complete works of Simmel, Troeltsch and Cassirer are under way. Likewise the historiographical work of Friedrich Meinecke, long considered a representative of the old-fashioned history of ideas, has received a sympathetic reappraisal. New interest has also emerged in the 'political theology' of the 'bête noire' Carl Schmitt. It would be too simple to attribute this exclusively to political factors, although the revival of a new intellectual conservatism has something to do with it. According to Schmitt's most recent biographer, Heinrich Meier, the discourse between what the former called his 'political theology' and 'political philosophy' may well be carried on in our own day, without necessarily indulging in Schmitt's political views or value preferences.[30] This indicates that classic authors are again being read, in order to ascertain our own position in a rapidly changing world.

Not surprisingly after three decades of relative stagnation, all of a sudden anthologies of political theories abound. Iring Fetscher still feels obliged to justify the return to the classic texts and to unprejudiced biographical analysis: 'Possibly some will see in this option just indecision. However, in my view the history of political ideas is important because their scholarly presentation will re-ignite political controversies that are deemed to have long become insignificant. Their significance will however become apparent as soon as attempts to assign them a

[29] Ernst Nolte, *Geschichtsdenken im 20. Jahrhundert* (Berlin, 1991), p. 552ff.
[30] Heinrich Meier, *Die Lehre Carl Schmitts. Vier Kapitel zur Unterscheidung Politischer Theologie und Politischer Soziologie* (Stuttgart, 1994).

superficially topical relevance are avoided.'[31] Indeed, after years of lingering on the sidelines, the history of political thought is back at the centre of intellectual discourse.

It may be added in passing that historicism has recovered as well, albeit in a new, 'disenchanted' version (Thomas Nipperdey), no longer burdened with the idealistic and moral preconceptions of nineteenth century historicist thought.[32] This coincides with a new interest in hermeneutical theory, as the belated recognition of Hans Gadamer's *Wahrheit und Methode* may show.[33] Last but not least, Koselleck's historical analysis of the political language of the period of the Enlightenment is being seen in a new light. For a while his great venture of assessing the political terminology throughout Europe during a crucial period of its development since the Enlightenment in a seven-volume encyclopaedia appeared to some as a monumental document from a period of historical methodology about to vanish for good and to be replaced by theoretical social historiography. Today its light shines with brilliance again. It is likely, however, that future theoretical syntheses in the cultural sciences ('Kulturwissenschaften' is the phrase that has come once again into use) will focus neither on mental dispositions nor on social structure or class divisions, but on culture. As Max Weber pointed out long ago, the great cultural issues that constitute the perspectives of research in the cultural sciences are subjected to eternal change, and scholarship will have to reconsider its intellectual premises from time to time.[34]

---

31 'Einige werden dies vielleicht als Unentschiedenheit auslegen. Nach unserem Dafürhalten liegt die Bedeutung der politischen Ideengeschichte aber gerade darin, dass sich längst vergessen und erledigt geglaubte politische Debatten an ihrer wissenschaftlichen Darstellung neu entzünden, Aktualitäten auch und gerade dann sichtbar werden, wenn nicht vordergründig aktualisiert wird.' Cf. Iring Fetscher and Herfried Münkler (eds.), *Pipers Handbuch der politischen Ideen* (Munich, 1986), IV, p. 17.
32 Cf. Otto Gerhard Oexle, *Geschichtswissenschaft im Zeichen des Historismus* (Göttingen, 1996).
33 H. Gadamer, *Wahrheit und Methode. Grundzüge einer philosophischen Hermeneutik* 2nd edn (Tübingen 1965).
34 M. Weber, 'Die "Objektivität" sozialwissenschaftlicher und sozialpolitischer Erkenntnis', in Weber, *Gesammelte Aufsätze zur Wissenschaftslehre*, edited by Johannes Winckelmann (Tübingen, 1968), p. 214.

4   A German version of the 'linguistic turn': Reinhart Koselleck and the history of political and social concepts (*Begriffsgeschichte*)

Melvin Richter

I

Peter Burke has established three main approaches to the history of ideas, each of them dominant in a different language area. 'In Germany there is *Begriffsgeschichte*, a "history of concepts" on the border between the history of language and the history of society.'[1] Within this German style, there are significant variations in how this relationship between the histories of concepts and societies has been perceived and practised.[2] Although these differences will be discussed briefly, my concern here will be primarily with that theory of *Begriffsgeschichte* developed by Reinhart Koselleck in his writing on historiography, the theory of historical knowledge (*Historik*) and the history of concepts. His programme has been applied by himself and many other contributors in more than 7,000 pages of the great lexicon, *Geschichtliche Grundbegriffe* (*GG*), which he guided to completion after the deaths of its two other editors.[3]

---

[1] Peter Burke, *History of European Ideas*, 23 (1997), p. 55. So begins his review of Melvin Richter, *The History of Political and Social Concepts: a Critical Introduction* (New York: 1995) and Hartmut Lehmann and Melvin Richter (eds.), *The Meaning of Historical Terms and Concepts. New Studies on Begriffsgeschichte* (Washington, DC, 1996).

[2] Otto Brunner, Werner Conze and Reinhart Koselleck (eds.), *Geschichtliche Grundbegriffe. Historisches Lexicon zur politisch-sozialer Sprache in Deutschland* (hereafter *GG*) (9 vols., Stuttgart, 1972–95); Joachim Ritter and Karlfried Gründer (eds.), *Historisches Wörterbuch der Philosophie* (hereafter *HWP*) (8 vols. to date, Basel/Stuttgart: 1971–); Rolf Reichardt and Eberhard Schmitt, in collaboration with Gerd van den Heuvel and Annette Hofer (eds.), *Handbuch politische-soziale Grundbegriffe in Frankreich. 1680–1820* (hereafter *Handbuch*) (15 vols. to date, Munich, 1985–) (henceforth the editors are to be Reichardt and Hans-Jurgen Lüsebrink). Reichardt has disclaimed the term, 'Lexicon', and instead preferred to use *Handbuch* in his title. This is because of the relatively limited chronological coverage of this work as compared with the *GG* and *HWP*, which trace classical and medieval, as well as modern senses of concepts.

[3] The differences among these different styles have been charted and evaluated in detail by myself in the works reviewed by Prof. Burke. See n. 1, above.

This chapter will centre on the relationship of Koselleck's theory and practice of conceptual history to current controversies about language, meaning and the interpretation of texts. After having spread from literary criticism and philosophy to historiography and intellectual history, these disagreements are now moving on to centre stage in discussions of how the history of political thought ought to be written. It is thus worth considering the implications of the history of political language as treated in this German version of the 'linguistic turn'. Unlike French theory, whether in its structuralist, post-structuralist or deconstructionist variants, the principal challenge from German sources to *Begriffsgeschichte* in Koselleck's style has been posed by what he has called the 'radical hermeneutics' of Heidegger and Gadamer. His complex relationship to them needs explication.

From the beginning of his graduate training, Koselleck was involved with their problematics, Heidegger stressing the historicality (*Geschichtlichkeit*) and Gadamer the linguisticality (*Sprachlichkeit*) of being (*Dasein*).[4] But Koselleck had defined himself as a historian rather than a philosopher. He has developed his theories of historiography, historical knowledge and *Begriffsgeschichte* while contributing to, and editing, the *GG*. This has led him to break with his earlier philosophical mentors for reasons which will be developed more fully below. These changes derive in part from Koselleck's insistence on understanding in detail both the structure of the modern world and its distinctive conceptual vocabularies. This emphasis on the significance of social and economic history on the one side, and of *Begriffsgeschichte* on the other, was due to the decisive influence of participating in two projects organised by Werner Conze, and, after his death, headed by Koselleck. These were conducted by the same group, the *Arbeitskreis für Moderne Sozialgeschichte* (Working Group for Modern Social History). Its members produced both the on-going series of books, *Industrielle Welt* (The World of Industry), now numbering over sixty, focused on transformations of society and

---

4 Anthony Manser has commented that *Dasein* is 'an almost untranslatable term which refers to the way in which human beings, as distinct from things, exist'; *Dictionary of the History of Ideas* (5 vols., New York, 1973), II, p. 193. Manser describes Heidegger's concept of *Dasein* in terms of three important characteristics: '1) "Facticity," the fact that I exist in an already existing world, which is *my* world . . . Things in the world are not experienced as mere material objects but as tools, things "ready to hand" to be used in ways which are defined for me by the structure of this world . . . (*Geworfenheit*), "thrownness," the fact that I am born into a world which I did not make and which therefore sets limits on me. 2) "Existentiality": *Dasein* . . . is primarily possibility. I live my life as a series of "projects", and so in the future as much as in the present. My personal time is different from that marked by watches and calendars . . . 3) "Forfeiture," the way in which *Dasein* is distracted from the realisation of its true being by the claims of everyday life, of the trivial and the inessential . . . the inauthentic.'

economy during industrialisation, and the now completed massive nine volumes of the *GG*, covering the basic political and social concepts of German-speaking Europe.[5]

Koselleck was confronted by two challenges. *Qua* historian, he was responding critically to the hegemonic claims of social historians in West Germany during the 1960s and 1970s.[6] As against them, in his *Begriffs-geschichte*, Koselleck refuses to regard concept-formation and language as epiphenomenal, as determined by the external forces of social, that is, 'real history'. At the same time, he rejects the theory that political and social languages are autonomous 'discourses' with no reference to anything extra-linguistic. It is in this connection that Koselleck has dealt with those strong versions of discourse theory associated with French structuralism and post-structuralism, his view of which will be discussed below.

Koselleck's disagreement with radical hermeneutics arises from another set of considerations, deriving in part from his break with the older non-contextual German versions of intellectual history, and in part from his dissatisfaction as a working historian with the use of *Begriffsgeschichte* instrumentally to further the ontological and hermeneutic concerns of Heidegger and Gadamer. Thus Koselleck rejected both the unsituated quality of *Geistesgeschichte* and *Ideengeschichte*, and the older historicism based upon the qualitative distinction between the human sciences (*Geisteswissenschaften*) and the physical sciences (*Naturwissenschaften*). At the same time, he refused to subordinate the history of concepts to philosophy and to the history of philosophy as in the critiques of historicism by Heidegger and Gadamer.[7] In his work on the theory of historical knowledge (*Historik, Geschichtswissenschaft*), Koselleck defends this subject against Gadamer's general condemnation

---

[5] H. Lehmann and M. Richter (eds.), *The Meaning of Historical Terms and Concepts*, comprises papers from a conference held to commemorate the *GG*'s completion.

[6] A useful summary account is Georg G. Iggers, *Historiography in the Twentieth Century* (Middletown, Mass., 1998), pp. 65–7. Koselleck himself was the founding dean of the department at the University of Bielefeld, which became the centre of this circle of like-minded social historians. However, Koselleck thought its claims one-sided, and preferred the balance between the practices of conceptual and social history established by the groups formed around another Heidelberg teacher, Werner Conze. See Richter, *The History of Political and Social Concepts*, pp. 33–5.

[7] Charles R. Bambach, *Heidegger, Dilthey, and the Crisis of Historicism* (Ithaca, NY, 1995); Jeffrey Andrew Barash, *Martin Heidegger and the Problem of Historical Meaning* (Dordrecht, 1988); Leslie Paul Thiele, 'Heidegger, History, and Hermeneutics,' *Journal of Modern History*, 69 (1997), pp. 534–56. In addition to Gadamer's most extensive philosophical treatment of this subject, 'Hermeneutics and Historicism', in *Truth and Method*, 2nd edn (New York, 1975), pp. 460–91, see his 'Reflections on my Philosophical Journey', in *The Philosophy of Hans-Georg Gadamer*, edited by Lewis Edwin Hahn (Chicago, 1997), pp. 3–63.

of historical method, which has since been taken up by postmodernist theorists.[8] While one of the points of the *GG* is to demonstrate in detail just how political and social concepts became distinctly modern, Koselleck and his collaborators insist on being far more specific about the transformations of economy and society than the generalities which comprise the aesthetic and philosophical critique of modernity made by Heidegger and Gadamer.[9] What is at stake for the history of political thought in these disagreements between Koselleck and those he has chosen to answer?

II

Intense disagreements about the nature of language now divide those working in the humanities and social sciences, including those writing intellectual history and the history of political thought. The reception of *Begriffsgeschichte* in the English-speaking world may well be determined by the outcomes of on-going controversies about language, meaning and interpretation of texts. Some prominent versions of this theoretical discussion have been combined into a vulgate blending ideas taken from post-structuralist and postmodern theorists, including literary critics; from German hermeneutics; and from feminist theorists.[10] A new orthodoxy has arisen from these critiques of previous historians, including those of ideas and political thought. The principal issues have been summarised by a medievalist: 'Looking at the current critical climate from the vantage point of a historian, the dominant impression one takes away is that of the dissolution of history, of a flight from "reality" to language as the constitutive agent of human consciousness and the social production of meaning.'[11] At stake in this discussion is nothing less than the concepts hitherto used by historians to explain the past: 'causality, change, authorial intent, stability of meaning, human

---

[8] The Chair established for Koselleck in 1970 at the University of Bielefeld was called '*Geschichtswissenschaft*', focusing on the theory of history, study of (historical) methods and problems of teaching history (*Historik, Theorie der Geschichte, Methodenlehre, didaktische Probleme*). See *Historik*, in *HWP*, pp. 1132–347. The title of Koselleck's talk (discussed below) attacking Gadamer's position was 'Hermeneutik und Historik'.

[9] For a relatively clear but uncritical exposition of this anti-modern aspect of Heidegger, see Dana R. Villa, 'The Critique of Modernity', in Villa, *Arendt and Heidegger. The Fate of the Political* (Princeton, 1996), pp. 171–207.

[10] There are often sharp disagreements among the principal exponents of these sources of postmodern discourse. See, for example, the volume devoted to the inability of Derrida and Gadamer to find any common ground: Diane P. Michelfelder and Richard E. Palmer (eds.), *Dialogue and Deconstruction. The Gadamer-Derrida Encounter* (Albany, N.Y., 1989).

[11] Gabrielle M. Spiegel, 'History, Historicism, and the Social Logic of the Text in the Middle Ages', *Speculum*, 65 (1990), p. 2.

agency and social determination'.[12] How does *Begriffsgeschichte* fit into these present-day controversies, which are being conducted in terms of competing theories of language, meaning and interpretation?

Many English-speaking historians and meta-theorists of political thought continue to work from within the analytical philosophy of language still firmly rooted among anglophone philosophers. Until recently the mainstream of philosophy in the English-speaking world has had little to do with structuralism, post-structuralism, deconstruction, hermeneutics and postmodernity. English-speaking philosophers of language have tended to view such theories of language as encouraging the facile denial of a world made of 'independently existing objects'.[13] Although far from agreement in their theories of language and semantics, many anglophones maintain that an adequate theory of language must be capable of referring to a world outside language itself. Nor have many historians of political thought and intellectual historians contested the assumption that their objects of study exist or have existed in a world which was more than a topic of discourse.

Yet English-speaking intellectual historians and political theorists have been hearing increasingly urgent calls to reshape their subjects in the terms of language, interpretation, discourse or deconstructing the meaning of texts written in the past. In 1989 an article in the *American Historical Review*, David Harlan's 'Intellectual History and the Return of Literature', stated the case for applying to intellectual history the literary theory of those critics who challenge textual interpretations based upon the contexts or intentions of their authors. This theory, which Harlan calls 'postmodern literary criticism', is used by him to attack the 'most influential recent attempt to reconstruct intellectual history . . . made by Quentin Skinner and J. G. A. Pocock'.[14] 'Postmodern literary criticism', in Harlan's view, makes it impossible to apply to the writing of history any standard of correct epistemology or of method. 'Historians should simply drop the question of what counts as legitimate history and accept the fact that . . . they do not have and are unlikely to have, a formalised, widely accepted set of research procedures . . .'[15]

In the post-structuralist version of theory about the meaning and interpretation of texts, the first move is to invoke 'truths' said to have been established by Saussure or by 'modern linguistics' about the nature of language and meaning. First, in this view, language is a system of

---

[12] Ibid., p. 1.

[13] Michael Devitt and Kim Sterelny, *Language and Reality. An Introduction to the Philosophy of Language* (Cambridge, Mass., 1987), p. 219.

[14] David Harlan, 'Intellectual History and the Return of Literature', *American Historical Review*, 94 (1989), pp. 581–609

[15] Ibid.

interdependent signs, which do not refer to, represent or depict anything outside that system. Within it, the relationship of signifiers and signified is arbitrary. Language is constituted by its internal relations. There is no relationship between words and things. Language constitutes the world for humans; it does not refer to the world. Thus the meaning of a word, concept or any other element of a language has no extra-linguistic relations to the world outside the language. Such a theory leaves no room for the concept of truth in theories of language or linguistics, or in the practice of history.

Second, historical and contextual considerations are considered irrelevant to meaning and to the analysis of language, which is said to be a self-contained synchronic system. Although the interrelations and structures which make up that system have been created in the past, the story of its creation is irrelevant to the understanding of that system in the present. The writing of history itself is only a code-governed system of discourse. This view of language and linguistics is synchronic, and ahistorical, when it is not anti-historical.

Third, language as involved in all discourses is said to be a system determined by rules and deep codes unavailable to its users. Indeed, the human subject or self is said to be a recent invention, which produces misleading fictions when applied to language and texts. On this view, it is always a mistake for historians, intellectual or otherwise, to take seriously discourses purporting to narrate, describe or explain the past by concepts of intention, agency or will. As opposed to modes of thought dependent upon such erroneous subjectivism and individualism, language is said to operate behind the backs of those employing it. Rather than being a tool available to users, language, by its codes, shapes and acts through them.

Fourth, language is declared to be the source of authority and power. Discourse does not follow rules dictated by power, it is power. Phrased in one or another version of these contentions, and applied to the interpretation of texts, or to history regarded as itself a text, this set of views has gained many adherents. The principal theoretical sources usually cited are Foucault, Derrida, Lacan and, with less frequency, Althusser.

Fifth, the nature of modern European thought is said to have shifted at some point to a subject-orientated form of discourse. By combining the theory of a world external to the subject with the centrality of the subject or self, this move made possible later exaltations of the natural sciences, organised knowledge and technology. In addition, the new organisation of knowledge into such professions as psychiatry and penology served the purposes of those holding power by disciplining and controlling areas of behaviour hitherto unregulated. An important source of such attacks on the individual subject is the phenomenology of Husserl, and even more, the philosophies of Heidegger and Gadamer.

The central postulates of deconstructionist criticism, one variant of post-structuralism, include a number of the arguments summarised above. These have been usefully restated by Tzvetan Todorov:

(1) The world itself is inaccessible; discourse alone exists and discourse refers only to other discourse . . . 'There is no such thing as an outside-of-the-text.'

(2) Even so, we are not to believe that discourse is better endowed than the world; the latter may not exist, but the former is necessarily incoherent. Deconstructionist commentary always consists in showing that the text studied is internally contradictory, that its intentions are not carried out in actual practice . . .

(3) As no discourse is exempt from these contradictions, there is no reason to prefer one sort over another or to prefer one value over another . . . Any value-orientated behaviour (criticism, the struggle against injustice, hope for a better world) becomes subject to ridicule.[16]

III

Seen in the perspective of the challenges presented by post-structuralist, deconstructionist, hermeneutic and postmodern theories of language, the status of texts and meaning, what are the implications for writing *Begriffsgeschichte* in Koselleck's style, as distinguished from intellectual history, or the history of ideas? It has already been noted that the *GG*'s programme was designed to replace previous German work in *Geistes-* and *Ideengeschichte* which did not locate concepts within their contexts, political or social. The *GG* sought to combine the history of concepts with structural social history, a balance discarded in the *Handbuch* with its emphasis on *mentalités*. The *GG* also disclaimed any intention to draw philosophical conclusions from its work, and dismissed the possibility of using *Begriffsgeschichte* to attain ontological truths, as Heidegger and Gadamer claimed to do in their version of it. Thus the *GG*'s theory of language is better understood after discussing its relationship to the 'radical hermeneutics' of Heidegger and Gadamer, another major source for those attacking the project of analysing or explaining ideas, texts or actors in their historical contexts.

Although it is impossible here to do more than sketch that part of the history of hermeneutics relevant to this discussion, it is clear what Heidegger and Gadamer have contributed to the body of opinion

---

[16] Tzvetan Todorov, *Literature and its Theorists*, trans. Catherine Porter (Ithaca, 1987), p. 184. Todorov himself advances a number of arguments to confute the deconstructionist position.

sketched above.[17] Their mode of hermeneutic thought is clearly relevant to, although not identical with, the *GG*'s form of *Begriffsgeschichte*. Koselleck, long a student of Gadamer, knew Heidegger not only from reading him, but from Heidegger's frequent participation in Gadamer's Heidelberg seminar.[18] Throughout Koselleck's career, he has maintained close contact with Gadamer, and indeed was chosen as the speaker at the Heidelberg meeting commemorating Gadamer's eighty-fifth birthday.[19] On this occasion Gadamer replied at length to Koselleck's unusual commemoration in the form of pointed criticism. What are the main contentions of Heidegger and Gadamer's hermeneutics? First, hermeneutics is not, as nineteenth-century theorists held, a special way of determining the meaning of texts, but rather is essential to humans' 'being-in-the-world'. Hermeneutics is one part of the phenomenology of human existence, which is treated by philosophical ontology.

Second, the older hermeneutics associated with Schleiermacher, Droysen and Dilthey is held by Heidegger and Gadamer to have been vitiated by its emphasis on the transmission of meaning from one subject to another. In history, this entailed the attempt by later historians to reconstruct through empathetic understanding (*Verstehen*) what their subjects in the past intended by their actions or meant by their texts. But meaning, properly understood, transcends all such subjective and psychological categories. Interpretation, on this critical view, is a surrender to being, not to its conceptual or contextual shadow. 'When we are truly "seized" or taken by a meaning, we do not filter this meaning through the grid or intermediary categories which determine it as belonging to "art," "religion," or "history."' Meaning is not determined by us and our categories. Rather 'we belong to it'.[20]

Third, it is an error to regard hermeneutics as a method for grasping the meaning either of texts or of history. In the view of Heidegger and Gadamer, history is not an object of knowledge; it should not be confused with the so-called discipline or science of history (*Geschichtswissenschaft*). All these scholarly pursuits are obstacles to apprehending

[17] In addition to the references found in the Dominick LaCapra and Steven L. Kaplan *Modern European Intellectual History: Reappraisals and New Prospectives* (Ithaca, 1982), a remarkably clear article offers an entry into hermeneutic theory: Michael Ermarth, 'The Transformation of Hermeneutics: 19th-Century Ancients and 20th-Century Moderns', *The Monist*, 61 (1981), pp. 176–94. Another useful exposition is Georgia Warnke, *Gadamer: Hermeneutics, Tradition, and Reason* (Stanford, 1987).

[18] Personal communication from Professor Koselleck.

[19] Reinhart Koselleck and Hans-Georg Gadamer, *Hermeneutik und Historik*, Sitzungsberichte der Heidelberger Akademie der Wissenschaften, Philosophische-historische Klasse (Heidelberg, 1987).

[20] Paraphrased and cited by Ermarth, 'Transformation', p. 176.

the true status of history; such methods are symptoms of modern man's subordination of being to subjectivity. Heidegger argued that 'being itself is time'.[21] To recognise the bounds of human existence – birth and death, human temporality and finitude – is requisite to hermeneutic philosophy. As part of Heidegger's attack upon the method of the natural sciences, he insists upon the historicity of human understanding. Being is historical, finite and temporal. These qualities must be recognised as requisite to understanding, which is thus always historical.

Gadamer's hermeneutics is directed against any and all methodologies, including historiography and *Historik*, the study of what historical knowledge is.[22] Presenting his work as going beyond 'the restricted horizon of interest of scientific, theoretical methodology', which he wishes to discredit as a way to truth, Gadamer bases his own theory on the ontological structure of understanding as such.[23] He rejects the very possibility of understanding the meaning of a work by recreating its author's intentions: 'The meaning of a text goes beyond its author's understanding of it not just now and then but always. Understanding is not just a reproductive but a productive activity.'[24] Gadamer's version of hermeneutical theory identifies language with interpretation; he treats language not as an instrument, but as creating the horizon of humans' 'being-in-the-world'. 'We are always and already encompassed by the very language which is our own.'[25]

Hermeneutical thinking thus understood must take into account how all humans are bounded by their historical and existential situations. This is always given, rather than chosen. A proper hermeneutics, then, demonstrates how history operates within understanding itself. This is no new method, but rather a new consciousness of what occurs when we encounter the past. The hermeneutical situation, then, represents a standpoint which accepts limits upon the possibility of human understanding and vision. Gadamer uses the concept of 'horizon' to define what it means for human beings to be situated in the world. This is not a fixed or closed standpoint, but 'something into which we move and which moves with us'.[26] Our prejudices, a concept Gadamer seeks to rehabilitate in a positive sense, are necessarily brought with us and

---

[21] This is how Gadamer characterises Heidegger's position in *Being and Time*, cited in R.C. Holub, *Reception Theory: a Critical Introduction* (London, 1984), p. 40.
[22] See the helpful entry on *Historik* in the *HWP*.
[23] Cited in Holub, *Reception Theory*, p. 37, from the Epilogue of the 3rd German edn Gadamer, *Wahrheit und Methode* [*Truth and Method*], p. 514.
[24] Gadamer, *Truth and Method*, p. 280, cited in Ermarth, 'Transformation', p. 188.
[25] Hans-Georg Gadamer, *Philosophical Hermeneutics*, trans. David Linge (Berkeley, 1976), p. 62, cited in Ermarth, 'Transformation'.
[26] Gadamer, *Truth and Method*, p. 271.

represent the horizon past which we cannot see. Understanding is defined by Gadamer as a fusion of one's own horizon with the historical horizon.

What is the relationship between Gadamer's view and Koselleck's theory and practice of *Geschichtswissenschaft* and *Begriffsgeschichte*? Writing before Koselleck specified his disagreements with Gadamer, Paul Ricoeur emphasised their similarities. This account occurs in the final chapter of his *Time and Narrative*: 'Towards a Hermeneutics of Historical Consciousness', a major theme in the work of both Koselleck and Gadamer. Ricoeur made striking use of Koselleck's distinction in his historiographical theory between the categories of 'space and experience' (*Erfahrungsraum*) and 'horizon of expectation' (*Erwartungshorizont*).[27] Both these categories were inconceivable without Gadamer, but are modified by Koselleck in a way unacceptable to his teacher.

For Koselleck, experience (*Erfahrung*), whether referring to that of individuals or that of past generations, connotes something once foreign being incorporated into what is local and customary. In this connection, the German word *Raum* implies that there are many different possible paths for moving through the space constituted by experience of the past to expectations of the future. Both categories are temporal, and the relationship between them can vary greatly from period to period. As will be seen, Koselleck's hypothesis is that the political and social concepts of the *Neuzeit* (early modern period), which ushers in modernity in German-speaking Europe, were crucially shaped by the growing gap between past experiences embodied in traditions and belief in the transforming quality of the future. He conceptualised the period as characterised by a new quality of time, now regarded not as a neutral dimension common to all history, but as an unprecedented force driving history. Centuries were classified not as temporal markers, but rather as epochs, each of which possessed its own unique spirit (*Zeitgeist*). The unity of every such period was placed within an irreversible trajectory of progress. The present was conceived as new because opening the prospect of an altogether novel future. A crucial change had occurred in the relationship between the 'space of experience' and the 'horizon of expectation'.

As the sense of living in an unprecedented age grew, so too did the sense of accelerated change. Because progress was thought to be

---

[27] Paul Ricoeur, *Time and Narrative* (3 vols., Chicago, 1984–90), III, pp. 207–240, originally published as *Temps et Recit* (Paris, 1983–6). Koselleck's most detailed exposition of this distinction is in *Futures Past: the Semantics of Historical Time*, trans. Keith Tribe (Cambridge, 1985), pp. 267–88, originally published as *Vergangene Zukunft. Zur Semantik geschichtlicher Zeiten* (Frankfurt, 1979).

increasingly imminent, the space of experience seemed to contract. Traditions, customs and norms orientated to the past could be more easily denounced and abandoned; any resistance to rapid and unprecedented change was described as the reaction characteristic of groups which were mere survivals from the past. Thus one of the key concepts of this period was that of revolution, the meaning of which was now altered from its sense of repetition within a cycle to the appearance of a qualitatively new and better form of regime and society.

Still another aspect of what Koselleck calls the *Verzeitlichung* or temporalisation of history has been the belief that history can and should be actively made, rather than regarded as something to which humans must submit. Thus history was not only personified, but given an active role and made into a norm framed in terms of utopian expectations about the future. Moreover, when the past was regarded as surpassed, and the future, despite its promise, remained indeterminate, the present was often depicted in terms of 'crisis', another key concept of the new time, *Neuzeit*. Here again, the history of a concept indicates both how it registers a group perception of a situation and how it contributes to action, as in the Weimar period when philosophies of crisis led to definitions of the situation in 'decisionist' and existentialist terms.

Thus 'space and experience' and 'horizon of expectation' are regulative notions of Koselleck's *Historik*, conceptual semantics applied to the vocabulary of history and to the time of history. Indeed, Koselleck holds that it was during the *Neuzeit* that history (*Geschichte*) came to be used as a collective singular signifying at once events and narratives of these events. Earlier the term *Historie* had been used to describe histories of events. Now history (*Geschichte*) could be viewed as itself an actor. Similar changes in old concepts, such as 'revolution' or 'crisis', as well as the introduction of neologisms such as *Geschichte*, are used by Koselleck as indicators of the accelerated rate of change in the structure of politics and society during the *Sattelzeit*. *Begriffsgeschichte*, however, in his view, does not merely serve the purposes of 'real' political and social history. The history of concepts is an autonomous study best conducted in tension with structural social history. The concepts used by groups and movements frame their definitions of the alternatives open to them and hence help determine their action.

How is Koselleck's theory of *Begriffsgeschichte* related to his repeated critiques of Heidegger and Gadamer?[28] Here it must be recognised that

---

[28] Koselleck, 'Hermeneutik und Historik'; Koselleck, 'Sozialgeschichte und Begriffsgeschichte', in Wolfgang Schieder and Volker Sellin (eds.), *Sozialgeschichte in Deutschland* (Gottingen, 1986); Koselleck, 'Erfahrungswandel und Methodenswechsel: Eine

at one or another time both of Koselleck's targets regarded the history of concepts and the phenomenon of conceptualisation as crucial to their philosophical work. Heidegger, like Carl Schmitt, had been one of those who had aroused Koselleck's interest in the history of concepts. 'Heidegger impressed Koselleck . . . by his method of tracing concepts back to their roots: isolating the manner in which key categories shifted and transformed over time and highlighting the resonances present in the contemporary vocabulary of socio-political language.'[29]

As for Gadamer, in his 1997 'Reflections on my Philosophical Journey', he states what he takes to be the significance of concepts:

Language and words have a completely different place in the tradition of philosophy familiar to us than . . . in the Anglo-Saxon tradition of philosophy . . . [where] concepts have no different function than in . . . the empirical sciences . . . [The] project of phenomenology really entailed changing the meaning of 'concept' itself . . . towards a new discipline of thinking in which the concept is not merely an instrument . . . of understanding, but becomes the subject matter (*Sache*) of philosophy . . . [It] was a new experience for me when, in my first encounter with Heidegger, I heard the term '*Begrifflichkeit*' (conceptuality), and also when I learned, under the caption of '*Destruktion*,' a critical suspicion over against the concepts resident in philosophical terminology. This also involved a slow process of re-educating myself to a viewpoint in marked contrast to that found in the predominant theory of signs, with its instrumental view of their function.[30]

Gadamer has stressed the importance of concepts to his philosophy:

Hermeneutics is above all a practice, the art of understanding, and of making something understood to someone else . . . In it what one has to exercise above all is the ear, the sensitivity for perceiving prior determinations, anticipations, and imprints that reside in concepts. This goes for a good part of my work in the history of concepts . . . I organised a series of colloquia on the history of concepts . . . and these have triggered a variety of similar endeavours.

. . . A consciousness of the history of concepts becomes a duty of critical thinking.[31]

historisch-anthropologische Skizze', in Christian Meier and Jorn Rusen (eds.), *Theorie der Geschichte. Beitrage zur Historik. Historische Methode 5* (Munich, 1988), pp. 13–61; Koselleck, 'Linguistic Change and the History of Events,' *Journal of Modern History*, 61 (1989), pp. 649–50.

29 Keith Tribe, 'Translator's Introduction', in Koselleck, *Futures Past*, p. viii.
30 Gadamer, 'Reflections on my Philosophical Journey', pp. 20–21.
31 Ibid., pp. 17–18. It is perhaps of some interest that when Gadamer referred to enterprises affected by his work on the history of concepts, he did not mention either the *GG* or the *HWP*, to which he contributed the entry on 'Hermeneutics'. Instead Gadamer mentioned the working group on 'Poetry and Hermeneutics'. Although among its principal figures were Hans-Robert Jauss, the founder of reception theory, and Koselleck, the founder of *Begriffsgeschichte* in the *GG*, Gadamer in his 'Reflections' mentioned Jauss only as committing the same error as Derrida. Koselleck received no mention at all. There may be an implicit reference to Koselleck's lecture in the 'Reflections', at p. 55.

For both Heidegger and Gadamer, *Begriffsgeschichte* was a means towards attaining the purposes, both negative and positive, of their respective philosophies. One shared goal was to destroy the emphasis of the neo-Kantians on treating the history of philosophy in terms of allegedly unchanging philosophical problems (*Problemgeschichte*). Heidegger went on to develop a new philosophical language designed to restore being (*Dasein*) to the place it held for the pre-Socratics. Gadamer first developed his version of *Begriffsgeschichte* in order to argue that the *Geisteswissenschaften* (human sciences) are necessarily hermeneutical, and later, to support his theory of the fundamental linguisticality (*Sprachlichkeit*) of humans in their collective existence. In the 1950s Gadamer led a committee on the history of philosophical concepts, and was a founding editor of the *Archiv für Begriffsgeschichte*. Since the 1960s when his *Truth and Method* appeared, Gadamer has championed a theory of hermeneutic *Begriffsgeschichte* as an instrument through which understanding and interpretation can be practised by detecting changes in meaning against the background of that effective tradition (*Wirkungsgeschichte*) into which we happen to be born.[32]

Rejecting, as has been seen, Gadamer's subordination of *Begriffsgeschichte* to philosophical hermeneutics, Koselleck finds crucial defects in both Heidegger's and Gadamer's treatment of historical writing. These faults Koselleck attributes to their stopping at the vague rubric of the historicality of *Dasein*. Koselleck's critique partly hinges on his view that Gadamer's condemnation of any and all reflection upon historical method is overstated and mistaken. But his critique is also based on his own commitment to the necessary relationship between *Begriffsgeschichte* and the structural histories of government, society and economy. This relationship, in his view, leaves no room either for the ontological consequences drawn by the theories of language used by Heidegger and Gadamer in their version of *Begriffsgeschichte*, or for their assumption that language and history are identical. On the contrary, Koselleck holds that history and language must be distinguished. Neither one can be reduced to the other. Each of them, when considered in terms of its characteristics and functions, turns out to differ in significant regards from the other: 'All language is historically conditioned, and all history is linguistically conditioned. Who would want to deny that all the concrete experiences we have only become experiences through the mediation of language? It is just this that makes history possible. But at the same time I do not want to insist that language and history be kept separate analytically.'[33]

---

[32] H.G. Meier, '*Begriffsgeschichte*', in *HWP*, I, p. 806.
[33] Koselleck, 'Linguistic Change and the History of Events', pp. 649–50.

In the histories of political, social and economic structures, Koselleck finds further reasons both for denying that language is coterminous with history, and for asserting that there are extra-linguistic aspects of experience. Histories dealing with demographic changes, with basic alterations of governmental or social structures over the long term, with fundamental shifts in the nature of the economy – these cannot be treated as purely linguistic aspects of discourse. Any historian refusing to recognise that such developments are extra-linguistic will end up in some untenable form of idealism. To bracket everything that is not language is to substitute a linguistic idealism for that of Hegel. Long-term structural changes cannot be identified, described or explained by theories of discourse which exclude the possibility of referring to anything external to the system of signs or outside the dialogue said to constitute language.

Nor does Koselleck share the view held by Heidegger and Gadamer, as well as Foucault, along with other structuralists, post-structuralists, deconstructionists and post-modern theorists: that language is independent of subjects, that it works behind the backs of those who use it. Koselleck holds that 'there is no history which could be constituted independent of the experiences and expectations of active human agents'.[34] This assertion is supported, as will be seen, by reference to the political uses of language during the French Revolution. This discussion occurs in Koselleck's rejection of those strong forms of discourse theory which deny that there is anything external to language.

Crucial to Koselleck's critique of Heidegger's and Gadamer's treatments of historical writing is his own theory of *Historik*, defined as the conditions for the study of writing any possible histories. It takes into account the two sides of history, how events are connected and how they are represented. It asks which presuppositions, and which analytical categories are presupposed by anyone writing history.[35] All possible histories presuppose temporal distinctions between earlier/later; spatial distinctions between inside/outside boundaries; political distinctions based on authority from above and obedience from below.[36] These conditions Koselleck calls 'metahistorical', pre- and extra-linguistic. In his critique of Heidegger, he points out that the natural necessity of death, which Heidegger makes into one of the elements of being, is profoundly modified by the human capacity to kill others classified as

---

[34] Koselleck, *Futures Past*, p. 269; *Vergangene Zukunft*, p. 351. The German original as phrased by Koselleck includes not only the notion of human action, but that of human suffering: '*es gibt keine Geschichte, ohne das sie durch Erfahrungen und Erwartungen der handelnden oder leidenden Menschen konstituiert worden wäre*'.

[35] Koselleck, *Hermeneutik und Historik*, p. 11.

[36] Koselleck, 'Linguistic Change and the History of Events', pp. 649–50.

enemies: '[W]hen the inevitability of death is pre-empted by killing or self-sacrifice . . . there will then occur events, or chains of events, or even cataracts of events . . . to which we can only react with silence.'[37]

What of those histories concerned with events? In Koselleck's view, language is here a reaction to events but describes them inadequately. 'Language is never identical with events.' Some chains or cataracts of events are:

> beyond the pale of language, and to which, all words, all sentences, all speech can only react. There are events for which words fail us, which leave us dumb, and to which, perhaps, we can only react with silence. We need only remember the speechlessness of the Germans in 1945 when they were confronted with the catastrophe into which they had drawn such countless numbers of individuals and peoples. And every attempt to find a language adequate to mass extermination has up to now been a failure . . . It is this difference between history in the actual process of its occurrence and history in its linguistic elaboration that remains, in any case, fundamental for their relationship.[38]

Even when discussing the types of histories which deal with events, Koselleck does not deny the potentially constitutive aspects of language. These emerge from his distinction between language regarded as a pre-linguistic medium in the sense just discussed, and language taken as a spoken or written discourse that may actually contribute to bringing about events. Linguistic change occurs more slowly and over different intervals than does the sequence of concrete events which language helps call forth. This explains the relationship between the history of concepts and sequences of events, which are unique; the same is not true of the concepts used in language.

Koselleck's position on language treated in terms of discourse was most clearly articulated in his contribution to a discussion of 'History, Language, and Culture in the French Revolution'.[39] These comments focus on the relationship between revolutionary texts and events during the French Revolution, and were directed against the position taken by

---

[37] This passage is from Koselleck, 'Linguistic Change and the History of Events', p. 652. It continues the critique of Heidegger in 'Hermeneutik und Historik', pp. 11–21.

[38] Koselleck, 'Linguistic Change and the History of Events', p. 652.

[39] Koselleck's intervention occurred during a memorable conference organised at Bielefeld by Reichardt, who, with Koselleck, edited the proceedings. R. Koselleck and R. Reichardt, *Die Französiches Revolution als Bruch des Gasellschaftlichen Bewusstseins* (Munich, 1988), pp. 664–66. Another sustained example of Koselleck's method in action summarises a massive research project applying *Begriffsgeschichte* to a comparative study of the forms of address, the lexicography of the term bourgeoisie, and arguments for and against extending the franchise in nineteenth-century Britain, France and Germany: Koselleck, 'Linguistic Change and the History of Events', pp. 657–61.

Jacques Guilhaumou, who applied Foucault's theory of discourse.[40] Koselleck asks how best to conceive the theory of relationships between language and historical reality (*Wirklichkeit*) in general, with particular attention to the relationship between language and events during the French Revolution. He posits three possible such relationships:

(a) Language can be understood as basically instrumental. As such, its relationship to groups involved in action may be studied as part of the sociology of language. When so viewed, language always remains an epiphenomenon of so-called actual history [*Realgeschichte*].

(b) By specifying their differences, language and reality may be placed in a reciprocal relationship without altogether reducing one to the other. For example, Luckmann proposes the notion of a world in which linguistic meanings are created in a way that both frees and limits the possibilities of experience . . . reality is always mediated through language. To say this does not exclude non-linguistic conditions which affect how reality is constituted.

(c) The third of these possibilities is at the opposite extreme of the first: text is taken for reality itself: a position of Foucault, which Guilhaumou has radicalised. This is to neutralise the social context of texts, and to take the theoretical position that all possibilities of utterance are reducible to those offered by texts. Such a procedure makes it impossible to use texts as sources . . . In that case history is determined exclusively by language . . . Such history falls into the danger of being conceivable only as a history of consciousness. Texts then cannot be used in a semantic that refers to anything outside them . . .[41]

The historian must examine thoroughly what lies behind the evidence offered by language. For the units of political and social action (classes, groups, factions, institutions, peoples) cannot be adequately determined from a study of events and acts alone, even if they are speech acts. Long-, middle- and even short-term diachronic processes of basic structural changes cannot be detected from textual statements alone. Analyses limited only to what is stated in texts cannot provide what we need to know about the actors using them:

For example, how can Guilhaumou define certain texts as 'Jacobin'? These texts do not necessarily so define themselves. In this case, are not the criteria necessary for such an identification imported from outside the text? It is certainly possible that . . . [t]he language used by Girondins and Jacobins [as contrasted to their policies] was the same. Thus if only language is considered . . . real differences may disappear.[42]

---

[40] Guilhaumou's paper is in Koselleck and Reichardt, *Die Französische Revolution als Bruch des Gesellschaftlichen Bewusstseins*, pp. 358–78; his reply to Koselleck, pp. 666–8. His fullest recent statement of his position is his book, *La langue politique et la Révolution française. De l'événement à la raison linguistique* (Paris, 1989).

[41] Koselleck and Reichardt, *Die Französiche Revolution als Bruch des Gesellschaftlichen Bewusstseins*, p. 664

[42] Ibid., p. 665.

This statement about the relationship of the linguistic to extra-linguistic elements in history is a temperate reply to those who would reduce history to discourse. Koselleck, although thoroughly familiar with radical hermeneutics and its linguistic theory, insists that any account of language adequate to the practice of history must be referential, that is, placed within a plausible relationship to historical experience. Thus he calls attention to historical analyses of changing structures of government, society and economy which cannot be detected by analysis of texts alone.

In his statement of the *GG*'s programme, Koselleck has neither claimed to be contributing to questions posed by linguists, nor confined to techniques used in their works to linguistic methods. He has not attempted to use studies of conceptual history as foundations for political theories or as interpretations of history. His analyses are not claims to deeper knowledge as made in Foucault's 'archaeology', or amongst those practising semiotics. The contributions of the work directed by him are pragmatic, adapted to its subjects, problems and available materials. His standards of evidence are those recognised by historians as appropriate for dealing with those sources available to them.

The forms of *Begriffsgeschichte* applied in the *GG* are at once more modest in their claims and more substantial in their achievements than works on political language derived from either post-structuralism or 'radical hermeneutics'. These studies in conceptual history have shown in detail how, and with which sources, their respective styles of inquiry may yield the conceptual language actually used in politics in society during periods of rapid and often revolutionary change. With a precision and on a scale never before achieved, they have created a corpus of information, detailing over time the range of usages and functions of political and social concepts. The *Handbuch* has called attention to materials previously not utilised by historians: theories of language, semantic theory, and language planning and policy prior to, during and after the French Revolution.

These materials provide valuable new dimensions to the study of language during a revolutionary period. Perhaps language does ordinarily operate 'behind the backs' of its users, but during the French Revolution this rear-end view of language was not notably persuasive. In many cases, it was all too clear that political language was being altered at an unprecedented pace, sometimes purely manipulatively, sometimes registering the *faits accomplis* of fast-moving events. At still other times, political language was generated or constituted by institutions meant to apply general political theories, the practical effects of which were impossible to foresee. In such circumstances rival groups and interests attempted to discern and state the conventions of language, the language games, played both by their adversaries and by themselves. Theories of grammar, of semantics, meta-theories of language became indispensable to political controversy. So too were arguments *ad personam*, accusations of mendacity, as well as of linguistic manipulation on the part of one's adversaries. Such understandings of language (Koselleck's first category) should not be dismissed *a priori* as irrelevant to the politics of language.

Koselleck's second formulation is, however, even more important for investigating the possible relationships between language and what was happening in politics and society. By specifying their differences, language and reality may be placed in a relationship which does not reduce one to the other. In such a theory linguistic meanings both create and limit the possibilities of political and social experience, as well as of legitimation, a point also prominent in Skinner's theory of political language. This is a cautious but highly defensible view of the relationship between language on the one side, and political and social organisation on the other.

There are indubitable differences between the views of language held by Koselleck, and by English-speaking philosophers and historians of political thought such as Pocock, Skinner, et al. When Skinner contrasts Gadamer's position with his own, he is more concerned with the question of what authors may have intended or meant than with the relationship of linguistic to extra-linguistic dimensions of meaning.[43] Yet both Koselleck and Skinner resist the extravagant claims made by post-structuralist and radical hermeneutic philosophers who assert the dominance of language over human agency and projects. What are the principal objections to post-structuralist, postmodern and radical hermeneutic views of language?[44]

Both the German and English-speaking critics of these theories argue in their separate ways that such views of language do not satisfy the working assumptions historians share with non-historians – that their own speech, as well as the sources they use, refer to something extra-linguistic, outside the texts. And what distinguishes historians are their methods for dealing with sources and evidence for what has occurred in the past. As two Australian philosophers of language have argued, the

---

43 Q. Skinner, in J. Tully (eds.), *Meaning and Context: Quentin Skinner and his Critics* (Oxford, 1988), pp. 276–81, esp. pp. 279, 281.

44 For an attempt to link these three theories, see Richard Bernstein, 'What is the Difference that Makes a Difference? Gadamer, Habermas, and Rorty', in Brice R. Wachterhauser (ed.), *Hermeneutics and Modern Philosophy* (Albany, N.Y., 1986), 343–76. The same three theorists are treated in Warnke, *Gadamer: Hermeneutics*.

ontology of post-structuralist, postmodern and hermeneutic philosophers is based on 'a swift move from talk of the language-dependence of
theories to the language-dependence of reality. Constituting theories of
the world is one thing; constituting the world, a very different thing.'[45]
Or as has been remarked about deconstructionist theories, there is
something perverse in asserting 'that sign-systems affect perception but
that the world does not'.[46] While Koselleck is not directly involved in
the philosophical discussion of language, his comments, previously
cited, hold that to determine how meaning is in fact contested, it is
prerequisite for the historian of social and political language to determine the units of political and social actors (classes, groups, factions,
institutions, peoples). This cannot be adequately determined from a
study of events and acts. And long-, middle- and even short-term
diachronic processes of even basic structural changes cannot be detected
from textual statements alone. Analyses limited only to what is stated in
texts cannot provide what we need to know about the meanings attached
to these texts by those using them in political and social contestations.

If it is true that the relationship between language and extra-linguistic
reference is conceived of in approximately the same way by German
conceptual historians and by English-speaking philosophers of the
analytical school, then there may be a basis for relating the *Begriffsgeschichte* of Koselleck to the treatment of political language by Pocock
and Skinner. Elsewhere I have attempted to answer such questions as: to
what extent is their work compatible with that done in *Begriffsgeschichte*?
What would be the consequences of trying to combine the resources of
these two bodies of work in German and English on the language of
political and social thought? And what would be gained by doing so?[47]

IV

This set of questions has now been addressed by some of the major
theorists on both sides.[48] Koselleck has responded to objections by

---

[45] Devitt and Sterelny, *Language and Reality*, p. 219.

[46] Robert Scholes, *Textual Power: Literary Theory and the Teaching of English* (New Haven,
N.J. and London, 1985), p. 164.

[47] Richter, *The History of Political and Social Concepts*, pp. 124–42.

[48] In Lehmann and Richter (eds.), *The Meaning of Historical Terms and Concepts*, Pocock is
sceptical about this possibility (in his 'Concepts and Discourses: a Difference in
Culture? Comment on a Paper by Melvin Richter'), while Koselleck is not (in 'A
Response to Comments on the *Geschichtliche Grundbegriffe*'). For a summary of their
differences, see Melvin Richter, 'Opening a Dialogue and Recognising an Achievement', *Archiv für Begriffsgeschichte*, 39 (1996), pp. 19–26. Sandro Chignola argues the
thesis of ultimate irreconcilability in '*Storia dei concetti e storiografia del discorso politico*',
Filosofia politica, 11 (1997), pp. 99–122.

Skinner to the history of concepts in general, and by Pocock, to the *Begriffsgeschichte* of the *GG*. Koselleck sought to dispel some misunderstandings and to identify legitimate differences among alternative research strategies for studying political and social language historically. So many legitimate questions may be posed about language that, when treating any linguistic question, we must adjust the lens through which we view it. The choice of an appropriate research strategy will depend upon the investigation's focus, concepts, whole discourses or the entire language, whether considered synchronically or diachronically.

In one paper Pocock asserted that the history of concepts is dependent upon, and ancillary to, the history of multiple discourses. Therefore diachronic analysis must be subordinated to synchronic analysis. While conceding that concepts always function within a discourse, Koselleck disagrees that the history of concepts and the history of discourses are incompatible. Each depends on the other. A discourse requires basic concepts in order to express what it is talking about. And analysis of concepts requires command of both linguistic and extra-linguistic contexts, including those provided by discourses. In cases of conflict (according to both Pocock and Koselleck, the normal state of affairs in political discussion), discourse depends upon possession, by the parties involved, of the same shared basic concepts. Only when this is the case is it possible to understand and be understood, to persuade, to negotiate, or even to fight (which involves the concepts of 'peace' or 'war'). Although concepts always function within discourse, they are pivots around which all arguments turn. Hence Koselleck's definition of 'basic concepts': *Grundbegriffe* are inescapable, irreplaceable parts of the political and social vocabulary. Only after concepts have attained this status do they become crystallised in a single word or term such as 'revolution', 'state', 'civil society', or 'democracy'. Basic concepts combine manifold experiences and expectations in such a way that they become indispensable to any formulation of the most urgent issues of a given time. Thus basic concepts are highly complex; they are always both controversial and contested. It is this which makes them historically significant and sets them off from purely technical or professional terms.

As for the relationship between diachronic and synchronic analyses of political language, Koselleck argues that both modes are indispensable, and that the synchronic cannot be privileged. For in any synchronic exegesis of text, the analyst must keep in mind those criteria of selection which lead a writer to use concepts in one way and not otherwise, and to do so through a new rather than an older formulation. Every author must confront the relationship between the former meanings of a word or term and the author's own intended purposes. No author can create something new without reaching back to the established corpus of the language, to those linguistic resources created diachronically in the near or more remote past, and shared by all speakers and listeners. Understanding or being understood presupposes such prior knowledge of how the language has been used. Every word, term and concept thus has a diachronic thrust, against which anyone seeking to add a new meaning must work. This point is related to Koselleck's argument that linguistic change occurs more slowly and over different intervals than does the sequence of concrete events language helps call forth.

What is Koselleck's reply to the potentially damaging assertion by Pocock and Skinner that it is not, strictly speaking, possible to write a history of concepts? Perhaps surprisingly, Koselleck agrees with this statement of what he calls 'rigorous historicism'. But he distinguishes *Begriffsgeschichte* from the history of ideas. The *GG*'s project has been aimed against Meinecke's version of *Ideengeschichte*. In his work on the idea of *Staatsräson*, Meinecke presented it through several sets of paired concepts which he claimed were used for three hundred years. But a history of 'immutable' ideas cannot account for the entirely different functions performed by them in disparate contexts: that of religious civil wars, that of enlightened absolutism, and that of bourgeois nation-states. By contrast, the history of concepts deals with the use of specific language in specific situations, within which concepts are developed and used by specific speakers.

Thus Koselleck agrees that every speech act is unique. But does not this admission open the way to Pocock's second point, in which he invoked Skinner's maxim that for this reason; there can be no histories of concepts? Here instead of disagreeing with Pocock and Skinner, Koselleck affirmed his own rigorous historicism: all concepts are speech acts within a context which cannot be replicated. As such, concepts only occur once, they are not substances, quasi-ideas capable of leading a diachronic life of their own. Concepts can become outdated because the contexts within which they were constituted no longer exist. Thus, although concepts age, they have no autonomous history of their own. Such epistemological purism is required for any adequate analysis of how language may be matched to the contexts within which it functions. To that extent, a rigorous historicism registering the non-convertibility of what is articulated by language is the precondition of every conceptual analysis. But *Begriffsgeschichte* does not end there. The history of basic concepts cannot be reduced to instrumental speech acts by individuals.

Every reading by later generations of past conceptualisations alters the spectrum of possible transmitted meanings. The original contexts of concepts change, as do the original or subsequent meanings carried by concepts. The history of concepts may be reconstructed through studying the reception or, more radically, the translation of concepts first used in the past but then pressed into service by later generations. Therefore, the historical uniqueness of speech acts, which might appear to make any history of concepts impossible, in fact creates the necessity to recycle past conceptualisations. The record of how their use was subsequently maintained, altered or transformed may properly be called the history of concepts.

Once a concept becomes basic, that is, indispensable to discourse, it takes on a life of its own. It frames and restricts, it augments and limits the vocabulary available to subsequent generations. With more or fewer deviations from earlier meanings, concepts may continue to be used or re-used. Although such variations may be either marginal or profound, linguistic recycling ensures at least a minimum degree of continuity. To the extent that it records how component parts of older concepts continue to be reapplied, *Begriffsgeschichte* resembles the history of ideas. However, these components do not continue to exist in the sense of transcending experience. Any assertion about continuities in the use of concepts must be supported by evidence based upon concrete, iterative uses of the vocabulary.

Thus Koselleck's version of the linguistic turn marks a decisive break with the positions of Heidegger and Gadamer, whose formulations led him to begin developing his own theory and practice of *Begriffsgeschichte*. Crucial to these changes was the strenuous process of first formulating the programme for the *GG*, and then over twenty-five years implementing it in the huge lexicon that it became. Koselleck applied to his own work the programme and standards set for other contributors. The project took on a life of its own and with it, Koselleck developed his own *Historik* and theory of historiography. Thus the origins of his concern with the history of concepts did not determine the ultimate form of his theory, scholarly practice and methods. Once his programme of research had been stated, declaring publicly the standards by which this team of scholars asked to be judged, the practice of this new discipline of *Begriffsgeschichte* shaped and changed not only those enlisted as contributors, but also Koselleck himself.

5 One hundred years of the history of political thought in Italy

Angelo d'Orsi

A beginning: Gaetano Mosca

In 1896 – a crucial year in Italian history, with the failed attempt at colonialisation in Africa and the beginning of the long crisis of the end of the century – Gaetano Mosca published his masterpiece, *Elementi di scienza politica* ('Aspects of Political Science'), gaining a chair at the University of Turin in the same year. Mosca was to teach constitutional law, but it was a teaching focused on historical and political rather than juridical studies. Mosca's attention to ideas and political institutions was, however, focused on legislation with an eye to empirical and historical matters. Along with constitutional law, philosophy of law was the other subject that, more than any, formed the basis for the discipline of political studies, shortly to be introduced in Italian universities. Numerous legal philosophers contributed to the history of political ideas in the twentieth century, from Gioele Solari to Giorgio Del Vecchio, and from Adolfo Ravà to Alessandro Levi.

The philosophy of law is a typical borderline subject, concerned as it is with both positive law and abstract speculation. It was the historical approach to the latter that provided an important starting point for the history of political doctrines. The neo-idealists, starting with Croce and Gentile, developed a complex philosophical historiography. Gentile's school practised a history of thought centred on 'precursors', using a unidirectional temporal axis leading from the present to the past. Philology, chronology, and biographical and background reconstruction were given little attention, while the focus was solely on the construction of 'chains of concepts': an 'arrangement of connections of a super-temporal kind between the various links of these chains, for the exclusive clarification of logical connections'.[1] However, in those writings primarily devoted to Italian thinkers, Gentile himself practised the history of ideas in a way not entirely devoid of a certain philological

---

[1] Paolo Rossi, 'La storiografia dell'idealismo italiano' (1956), now in Rossi, *Storia e filosofia. Saggi sulla storiografia filosofica* (Turin, 1975), pp. 17–69, at p. 32.

and erudite taste, which partly made up for his speculative approach. The weight of history is even more apparent in Croce. In his own historical work, the role played by original historical research is greater than his theoretical assertions might lead one to believe. The speculative nature of some of his famous books, such as those devoted to Vico and Hegel, is not born out in the methodology he theorised and employed in many of his other writings. The rich variety of the interpretative methods employed is not limited to his remarkable ability both for textual reading and for establishing connections between abstract ideas. Moreover, in the 1930s and 1940s Croce seemed to distance himself from the kind of historiography of his former friend (but now political adversary and cultural rival) Gentile. Occasionally, he combined his repudiation of academic philology and neutral descriptivism with impatience for a history conceived purely as the actualisation of thought. It must, however, be remembered that both Croce and Gentile exercised their cultural hegemony not just with their writings, but through their wider cultural entrepreneurship, with their editorial work for periodical journals and publishing houses, and with the formation of their own academic (Gentile) or non-academic (Croce) circles.

Overall the influence of idealism (particularly of the Gentilian kind) on the history of ideas did not achieve particularly illuminating results. This is more striking when one considers the conceited arrogance adopted by Gentile's followers towards other historiographical schools, due mainly to their ill-concealed conviction as to the superiority of philosophical 'actualism'. Furthermore, they showed a certain disdain towards historical method. Their criticism of so-called 'philologism' – that is, an excess of philology, blamed for the abandonment of all efforts at either interpretation or comprehension – 'resulted in a total rejection of philology, in the absence of any philological method, in the ignorance of its rules and techniques.'[2]

On closer examination, however, the opposition between 'philosophical' and 'historical' ways of studying ideas is the result not necessarily of a difference between philological and philosophical approaches, but rather of the particular attitude and accuracy of individual scholars.[3] A monumental *Storia della filosofia* ('History of Philosophy' 1918–1947) was written by Guido De Ruggiero, 'one of the most

[2] Rossi, in 'La storia della filosofia: il vecchio e il nuovo', in Paolo Rossi and C.A. Viano (eds.), *Filosofia italiana e filosofie straniere nel dopoguerra*, special issue of *Rivista di filosofia*, 79 (1988), pp. 545–68.
[3] Cf. G. Sasso, 'Intorno alla storia della filosofia e ad alcuni suoi problemi' (1966), now in Sasso, *Passato e presente nella storia della filosofia* (Bari, 1967), pp. 11–67, at pp. 50–1.

prestigious figures in 20th century Italian culture',[4] and a follower of
Gentile. He was also the author of a classic work on political ideals,
the *Storia del liberalismo europeo* ('History of European Liberalism',
1925). This is one of the best examples of an idealistically inclined
history of ideas, but also a well-documented and well-argued piece of
research, which contributed, indirectly, to the formation of the anti-
fascist generation.[5]

However important the role played by the philosophy of law and the
history of philosophy in the prehistory of the discipline of political
thought in Italy, it was left to a constitutionalist, Mosca, to inaugurate
its academic teaching in the form of the history of political doctrines and
institutions. Even before taking up the new chair, Mosca contributed to
the blossoming of the new discipline. In 1923 he wrote:

The history of political doctrines, which has been studied extensively in France
and England, and also in Germany and the US, has been almost entirely
overlooked in Italy since the publication, more than half a century ago, of the
Storia degli Scrittori Politici Italiani ['History of Italian Political Writers'] by
Giuseppe Ferrari. This is deplorable because it is a subject destined to acquire
great importance if political science, or sociology as it has been called, is really
to become a science. Indeed, by looking at the development of political thought
through history, one may notice that contemporary political events have a great
influence on the development of a writer's ideas and theories, but that, in so far
as these very theories, once formulated, have a powerful influence on the
shaping of subsequent generations' political mentality, they also contribute to
determine future events.[6]

In fact, the beginning of a theoretical debate on the history of ideas
had already started. Maffeo Pantaleoni, an economist who rose to
public attention as a political commentator for the extreme Right,
maintained that the history of economic doctrines should exclusively
deal with theories that time had showed to be 'true', in so far as they
were still widely accepted, whilst 'false' doctrines had been condemned
to oblivion by history itself.[7] As for Croce, he distinguished the history
of political ideas from the history of political, moral and philosophical
sciences. The latter dealt with theories in the strict sense, whilst the
history of political ideas was only apparently concerned with them, but
instead consisted in the investigation of the practical proposals underlying political theories. The history of political ideas therefore coincided

[4] E. Garin, 'Guido De Ruggiero', in Garin, *Intellettuali italiani del XX secolo* (Rome,
1987), pp. 104–36, at p. 104.
[5] G. De Ruggiero, *Storia del liberalismo europeo*, with preface by E. Garin (Milan, 1962).
[6] G. Mosca, 'Il materialismo storico', *La rivoluzione liberale*, 2, 1 (11 January 1923),
pp. 1–2.
[7] Cf. M. Pantaleoni, 'Dei criteri che devono informare la storia delle dottrine
economiche', *Giornale degli economisti*, 2nd series, 17 (1898), pp. 407–31.

with the history of ideologies, being more concerned with their practical effectiveness than with their theoretical coherence.[8] In 1924, Croce returned to the same topic, further developing the distinction. The history of theory is one thing – he maintained – that is, the history of 'political philosophy' in its proper sense; a different thing is the history of 'political science', which is instead concerned with an empirical science devoted to understanding and classifying political and state institutions; yet another thing is the history of 'practical tendencies', namely political programmes and political ideals, whose status is that of pseudo-theories.[9]

In that same year, Mosca asked to be transferred to the University of Rome. Here he joined the newly founded School of Political Science, shortly to be given the formal status of a separate faculty, where Mosca became the first in Italy to teach the history of political doctrines and institutions. The universities of Padua and Pavia soon followed suit by instituting similar schools and eventually faculties. Yet, in the storm of the Fascist 'second wave', following the murder of Matteotti (one of the socialist leaders of the opposition), the new school was considered by the more radical supporters of the Fascist regime to be infected with liberalism if not outright anti-fascism. Since it regarded political science to be of great importance as an instrument for the formation of a new fascist ruling class, the regime could not tolerate university staff like Mosca: a self-confessed conservative, a 'gentiluomo' of recognised uprightness, but who had publicly criticised the process of fascistisation, besides having signed a *manifesto* promoted by Croce and many other intellectuals against Gentile, who by now was the official philosopher of Fascism. Mosca's new chair was therefore abolished from the school (now faculty), whilst the non-fascist or anti-fascist staff were moved to other posts, starting with Mosca himself, who returned to the faculty of law, within whose context his teaching of the history of political doctrines and institutions was clearly of reduced importance.[10]

In his 'faithful and extended account' of his lectures, published in 1932 after his retirement, Mosca explained his own conception of the new subject. In the introductory section, whose title reads 'Necessary connections between the study of doctrines and the study of political institutions', he argued that in societies with 'a certain degree of education' there are 'two kinds of forces' that guarantee, on the one hand,

[8] Cf. B. Croce, 'Intorno alla storia degli studii politici e sociali', *La critica*, 3 (1905), pp. 165–8; also published as 'La storia delle idee politiche', in Croce, *Conversazioni critiche* I (Bari, 1918), I, pp. 189–92.

[9] Cf. B. Croce, *Etica e politica* (Bari, 1967), pp. 196–203, 223–34.

[10] Cf. M. D'Addio, 'Gaetano Mosca e l'istituzione della Facoltà romana di Scienze Politiche (1924–1926)', *Il politico*, 58 (1993), pp. 329–73.

intellectual and moral, and on the other, material cohesion. The first kind comprises ideas and feelings shared by individuals as members of the 'political community'; these are ethnical consciousness, commonality of religion and loyalty to a dynasty. As part of the second kind of forces, one may find the influence exercised by 'the hierarchy of state officials who possess the necessary means of coercion, and know how to direct the actions of the masses towards the ends the masses themselves may desire, but, in any case, conforming to the ends of the ruling classes'. In highly educated societies, the material forces 'attempt to justify their own action by making appeal to the intellectual and moral forces', whilst these look for power in order to 'put into practice the kind of political organisation they favour'. It appears from this that, by 'moral and intellectual forces' Mosca means political ideas at large – doctrines, theories, ideologies and all those other ways in which political proposals and programmes can be formulated and the exercise of power justified – whilst by 'material forces' he means people, those groups, that is, whose aim is the conquest and exercise of power. In his own terminology, Mosca referred to the latter as 'the political class' (*classe politica*) and to the former as 'the political formula' (*formula politica*). Changes in the 'political formula' interfere with the recruitment of the political class. Conversely, changes and transformations in the political class have an effect on their choice and development of *ad hoc* 'political formulas'. From a historiographical and methodological perspective, Mosca concluded that 'it is impossible to study the history of political doctrines without simultaneously studying the history of political institutions'.[11]

Gioele Solari and his school

After completing his studies at the University of Piedmont, and graduating with the economist Salvatore Cognetti de Martiis, Gioele Solari at first specialised in the 'social question'. But, in contrast to many of his colleagues, he never became a socialist, remaining instead ideologically and politically autonomous. A Lombard by birth, Solari's academic career started at the University of Turin with the support of Giuseppe Carle, a jurist of positivist training, but with a historical sensibility and open-minded towards the new social sciences such as sociology. Giuseppe Carle, from whom Solari inherited his chair in 1918, maintained the need for the philosophy of law to abandon metaphysics so as to engage in the 'fertile terrain of science'.[12] Within the Italian context,

---

[11] G. Mosca, *Storia delle dottrine politiche* (Bari, 1966), pp. 7, 11–13.
[12] N. Bobbio, 'L'opera di Gioele Solari' (1953), in N. Bobbio, *Italia civile. Ritratti e*

this was an anomalous approach, which had some influence on Solari's own work. But both in his early writings and in a work which was to occupy him for most of his life, *L'idea individuale e l'idea sociale nel Diritto Privato* ('The individual and the social idea of the private law'), Solari was to develop his own version of a social philosophy of law in opposition to the individualist philosophy of natural jurisprudence.[13]

Luigi Firpo, who graduated in 1937 under Solari's supervision with a thesis on Campanella, and who was one of Solari's favourite students, had this to say of his teacher's didactic work: 'Recalling with vigorous analysis the eternal problems of political life during the twenty [Fascist] years, Solari broke with conformism and cultural isolation, arousing pangs of conscience, damaging the unrefined, reigning in dogmatism, thus revealing the dramatic complexity and deep historical roots of the greatest issues of civil life.'[14] In Solari's own teaching the historical and political dimension predominates over the more philosophical and juridical. Despite the title of his chair (philosophy of law), and a certain propensity for the speculative approach, Solari fulfiled his 'genuine vocation' of historian of political and social ideas.[15] To his work as a historian, he brought the same anti-individualistic approach characterising his philosophy of law. For him, even when elaborated by a single individual, theories are always, in some ways, 'the fruit of collective work, of century-old debates'. However, as both Firpo and Norberto Bobbio (the other of the Solarian 'Dioscuri') noticed, Solari arrived at history through philosophy and almost against his own will. Having been trained at the harsh school of the positivists' historical method, it was hardly possible for him to embrace idealist historiography. 'As a historian of ideas he showed a certain distrust for abstraction, dogmatism, and simplified schemes, whilst having an acute sense of the complexity of age-old debates, of their innumerable cross-references and influences, of the deep uncertainty of the questions arising from social life: an indignant aversion for all superficiality, which obliged him to engage both in a meticulous analysis of texts and in extended bibliographies searches.'[16] Such rigour and openness of mind towards the object of study resulted in substantive pieces of historical research

---

testimonianze (Florence, 1986), pp. 146–79, at p. 152. On the relationship between Solari and Carle, cf. G. Solari, *La vita e il pensiero civile di Giuseppe Carle* (Turin, 1928).

[13] Bobbio, *Italia civile*, p. 153. Cf. L. Firpo, 'Gioele Solari, maestro', in Firpo, *Gente di Piemonte* (Milan, 1983), pp. 271–92, particularly pp. 278–9 and the bibliography, at p. 344. Firpo's essay is an introduction to the collection of Solari's own studies, *La filosofia politica* (2 vols., Rome and Bari, 1974), I, pp. vii–xxxv.

[14] Firpo, *Gioele Solari*, p. 288.

[15] Ibid., p. 284.

[16] Ibid., pp. 279–80.

(he avoided methodological discussions), carried out in hundreds of lesser writings, articles, notes and reviews, rather than in massive, far-reaching works.

Amongst the first people to graduate with Solari in the inter-war period was one of the leading figures in the later methodological debate, Alessandro Passerin d'Entrèves, who graduated in 1922, and who, between 1946 and 1957, was a professor of Italian studies at Oxford. Piero Gobetti graduated in the same year and although he was drawn to the academic world (in 1922 he published his graduate thesis on the political philosophy of Vittorio Alfieri), he gave it up to enter the political, journalistic and editorial battle against Fascism, only to die at a very young age in exile in France. Gobetti's name is emblematic: the majority of Solari's best students gravitated, either directly or indirectly, around Gobetti's political world, starting with Passerin himself, who was a friend and colleague of his. So too did Norberto Bobbio, who graduated with Solari in 1931, before taking a second degree with the philosopher Annibale Pastore, and who outlined the exceptional genealogy of the 'Solarians'.

According to Bobbio, the combination of scientific interests and civil passions was their distinctive charateristic, even though their 'cultural awareness' did not always, nor automatically, marry with 'political intransigence'.[17] Their anti-fascism, it might be added, very often subsided when they were confronted by the demands of work or family. There nevertheless exists a clear link between the anti-fascist tradition of Croce and later Gobetti and Solari's teaching – bearing in mind that from his initial positivist position, he eventually adhered to some form of idealism. By listing the many jurists, historians, philosophers, sociologists and political scientists who were involved in the post-war political and cultural battles, often after having fought for the Resistance, Bobbio emphasised the 'civil function of university teaching' which a man like Solari exercised to the highest degree. It was this kind of didactic, scientific and above all intellectual work that, in the first half of the century, gave to the history of ideas (whatever academic labels this was given)[18] an indirect, but significant, political meaning. None the less, in the Mussolini years, this did not always imply an anti-fascist slant in teaching and research. There were also a number of scholars whose work as historians of political thought showed thematic preferences and, at times, ideological leanings more in line with the regime.

[17] Cf. N. Bobbio, 'Funzione civile di un insegnamento universitario' (1949), now published as 'L'insegnamento di Gioele Solari', in Bobbio, *Italia civile*, pp. 1124–31
[18] Solari himself, along with his chair in the philosophy of law, was also responsible for a few years for the teaching of the history of political doctrines.

Two (or three) ways: a methodological debate

Amongst those scholars closer to the regime was Rodolfo De Mattei, a colleague of Gaetano Mosca at the University of Rome, and the first, in 1927, to obtain the 'libera docenza' in the history of political doctrines and institutions. After Mosca's retirement, De Mattei, together with Alessandro Passerin d'Entrèves and Carlo Curcio, both of whom had some links with the Fascist regime (though the latter more so than the former),[19] won the first chairs established in the new teaching subject. All three, together with a few other scholars of the generation born within the century, were the protagonists of a new methodological debate, which was mainly conducted in the pages of the *Rivista Internazionale di Filosofia del Diritto* ('International Review of philosophy of law'), founded in 1921 by Giorgio Del Vecchio.[20]

Amongst the first to write on the subject were Carlo Morandi and Carlo Curcio. Convinced as he was that the history of political doctrines was mainly concerned with theories, and not facts, Curcio posed the question of 'what is a political theory?'. For him, the history of political philosophy (or of the philosophy of law) looks for absolute and universal truths, whilst the history of political doctrines deals with politics, which he regarded as the instantiation of particular values. Nevertheless, since the history of political doctrines also addresses fundamental issues such as power, freedom, revolution, etc., there remains an important link with philosophy. Curcio, however, criticised the idea that the theoretical core of the subject derived from its investigation of the state. Although often in a fragmentary fashion, political doctrines could be found, or so he maintained, in the works of non-political thinkers, writing literature, speeches, diplomatic and religious texts, etc. Only the sensitivity of the scholar, his instincts and his philosophical background can help him to discern such doctrines in them.

On his part, Carlo Morandi, a political historian in a more proper sense, emphasised the need to interpret political thinking in the light of both historical context and biographical evidence. There is, he wrote, a 'delicate moment', of which one needs to be particularly aware, when 'ideology becomes part of history itself . . . when political thought becomes action'. At such times, neither formal juridical principles nor abstract philosophical criteria are adequate instruments of investigation. The historian of political doctrines cannot limit himself to explore the

---

[19] Curcio collaborated with De Mattei and others on the *Dizionario di politica* ('Political Dictionary') published by the Partito nazionale fascista (PNF) in 1941.

[20] S. Testoni [Binetti], 'La storia delle dottrine politiche in un dibattito ancora attuale', *Il pensiero politico*, 4 (1971), pp. 305–80, at p. 318.

originality of the ideas or their inner coherence, but must concern himself with their efficacy and their duration within a society.

This debate was revived in 1932, probably because of the publication of Mosca's textbook, where he was insisting on the close connection between political doctrines and institutions. Adolfo Ravà, a philosopher of law, conceived the history of political doctrines in a broad sense, with direct links with the history of political events and drawing on a large variety of sources outside political texts.[21] Vittorio Beonio Brocchieri, a student of Gaetano Mosca and Gioele Solari at Turin, translator and scholar of Locke, Burke, Spengler, Hobbes and Nietzsche, and the editor of the Italian edition of Friedrick Pollock's *Introduction to the History of the Science of Politics*, followed a rather similar line,[22] looking at the history of political doctrines as both the assessment and the interpretation of those schools of thought that addressed the historical problem of the relationship between the individual and the community. But it is the historian's task to identify the 'political doctrines', those, that is, contributing to a 'political science', and undertaking enquiries 'aiming to establish a type of order that favours the maximum development of collective action, together with the minimum suppression of individual autonomy'. Political doctrines that do neither belong to 'political art'.[23] Beonio further developed his methodological approach in the introduction to the first volume of an unfinished and unsuccessful *Trattato di storia delle dottrine politiche* ('Treatise on the History of Political Doctrines'), from the Greeks to Christianity.[24]

Besides textbooks and methodological writings, a number of monographic studies were produced during the period. On the whole, these concerned Italian themes and authors as the effect of a certain nationalism pervading Italian universities, especially the faculties of political science. Partly influenced by Mosca, but mainly finding inspiration in a theme dear to the regime, De Mattei wrote a polemical work on democracy in post-unification Italy.[25] However, he also turned his

---

[21] Cf. A. Ravà, *Compendio di storia delle dottrine politiche con una introduzione sulla scienza politica generale* (Padua, 1933). Cf. Testoni Binetti, 'La storia delle dottrine', pp. 324ff.
[22] Amongst the essays, V. Beonio Brocchieri: *Federico Nietzsche* (Rome, 1926); *Studi sulla filosofia politica di Hobbes* (Turin, 1927); *Spengler. La dottrina politica del pangermanesimo post-bellico* (Milan, 1928). Amongst the translations: J. Locke, *Saggio sul governo civile* (Turin, 1925); E. Burke, *Riflessioni sulla Rivoluzione francese* (Bologna, 1931); O. Spengler, *Anni decisivi* (Milan, 1934).
[23] Cf. V. Beonio Brocchieri, 'La struttura dialettica nella storia delle dottrine politiche', *Annali di scienze politiche*, 3, 4 (1930), pp. 276–84.
[24] Cf. Beonio Brocchieri, *Trattato di storia delle dottrine politiche* (4 vols., Milan, 1934–51).
[25] Cf. R. De Mattei, *Il problema della democrazia dopo l'Unità* (Rome, 1934); De Mattei, *Cultura e letteratura antidemocratiche dopo l'unificazione* (Florence, 1937).

attention towards classical authors such as Campanella, Botero and, more surprisingly, to Petrarch, an author rarely if ever considered in a political context.[26] De Mattei placed his history of political ideas within a wider cultural context, in an effort to deal with doctrines together with institutions, events and biographical narratives.

The methodological writings of the time offered some valuable insight. It was maintained that the history of political doctrines could not be identified with the history of political philosophy. Contrary to the claims made by some historian-philosphers such as Felice Battaglia and Alessandro Passerin d'Entrèves, scholars should not limit themselves to studying the figures of the past. They must instead search for those glimmers of political insights that are harboured amongst the minor authors, so as to give the sense of an age or of a particular period. Nor should scholars rest content with discussing philosophical systems and abstract theory to the exclusion of political programmes, texts which are of vital importance, for they marry 'speculation and action'.[27] De Mattei was not interested in high conceptions of politics, which looked at this as either philosophy or science: 'a collection – that is – of constant and useful patterns' (here his polemical target was Beonio Brocchieri).[28] He was instead 'drawn by that more intricate intellectual underwood, whose intricacy makes distinctions harder to sustain'.[29] The boundaries between politics, on the one hand, and morals, culture, law and philosophy, on the other, become vague. The historian is an explorer, patiently and prudently searching for those materials documenting both the presence and the persistence of political reflection. So, according to De Mattei, the history of political doctrines is the history of the 'reflection on the general issues surrounding the state, and on political activity; a reflection that is perhaps non-systematic, casual, and subsidiary to other activities of the mind', comprising the economic, juridical and philosophical spheres, which should, in this connection, be considered not in their own specificity but in the way in which they affect political life.[30] The history of

---

[26] Cf. R. De Mattei: *La politica del Campanella* (Rome, 1927); *Studi campanelliani* (Florence, 1934); *Il sentimento politico del Petrarca* (Florence, 1944); *Il problema della 'ragion di stato' nell'età della Controriforma* (Milan and Naples, 1979); *Aspetti di storia del pensiero politico* (2 vols., Milan, 1980–82); *Il pensiero politico italiano nell'età della Controriforma* (2 vols., Milan, 1982–84).

[27] R. De Mattei, 'Sul metodo, contenuto e scopo d'una storia delle dottrine politiche', *Archivio di studi corporativi*, 9 (1938), pp. 200–36, at p. 204.

[28] Ibid., p. 203.

[29] S. Testoni Binetti, 'Dall'etica alla politica', *Trimestre*, 26 (1993), pp. 193–202, at p. 198. But cf. also Testoni Binetti, 'La storia delle dottrine politiche', pp. 345ff.

[30] De Mattei, 'Sul metodo', p. 203.

political doctrines is therefore no simple inventory, but a kind of study that is 'comparative, instructive and formative'.[31]

De Mattei's work points to an extended understanding of the history of 'political doctrines' as a history of 'political thought', comprising not only original, formalised and systematic theories, but all forms of political statement; hence his favourable view of the recently completed work of the Carlyle brothers. The *History of Medieval Political Thought in the West* offered a broad view of political thought, and therefore aroused the critical reservations of a scholar like Battaglia. The British historians were wrong, according to Battaglia, to paint too wide and generic a picture, whose foundations were empirical, without distinguishing political doctrines from institutions, and therefore failing to characterise political theory in some meaningful way and distinguishing it from practice.[32] In the same year as the appearance of the last volume of the Carlyle brothers, Battaglia published his *Lineamenti di storia delle dottrine politiche* ('Features of the History of Political Doctrines'). He saw the discipline as a revelation and a progressive clarification of politics. This was the embodiment of a category of spirit; this was the basis for the disciplinary autonomy of the history of political doctrines.[33] Only those theories endowed with a high degree of systematisation and formalisation, as well as autonomy and originality, should be taken into consideration by the historian, who should search for them only in the places they ought to be found – in treatises of political philosophy.

In his polemic against De Mattei, Battaglia found himself in the company of Alessandro Passerin d'Entrèves. Their agreement about the Carlyles' work is symptomatic. Passerin's opinion is particularly significant given his competence in medieval studies. Whilst appreciative of their work, he criticised it for failing to grasp the 'exquisitely speculative' nature of the continuity in medieval thought.[34] Passerin embraced a speculative conception of the history of political doctrines, which he found exclusively in philosophical formulations, particularly in the canonical works of the

---

[31] R. De Mattei, *La storia delle dottrine politiche* (Rome, 1938), pp. xix–xx, xxii.

[32] Cf. F. Battaglia, 'L'opera storica dei fratelli Carlyle' (1937), later published in F. Battaglia and A. Bertolini, *Problemi metodologici nella storia delle dottrine politiche ed economiche* (Rome, 1939), pp. 83–101.

[33] S. Testoni Binetti, 'La metodologia della storia delle dottrine politiche', in N. Matteucci and A. Pasquinelli (eds.), *Il pensiero di F. Battaglia* (Bologna, 1989), pp. 245–58; cf. also Testoni Binetti, 'La storia delle dottrine politiche', pp. 336ff.

[34] A. Passerin d'Entrèves, 'A proposito di alcuni recenti contributi alla storia delle dottrine politiche' (1936), now in A. Passerin d'Entrèves, *Saggi di storia del pensiero politico. Dal Medioevo alla società contemporanea*, edited by G. M. Bravo (Milan, 1992), pp. 227–34, at p. 230.

'authors who count'.[35] 'It is only by regarding the political doctrines as visions of the world, as philosophies in their own right, that one can, besides writing their history, examine their reasons and merits, and therefore judge them.' The scholar must therefore remove the doctrines from 'the progress of historical becoming', and consider them '*sub specie aeterni* and not merely in terms of their immediate contingency'.[36] No other author besides Passerin took such a clear-cut – and obviously disputable – view on the methodological questions asked about the new discipline. No one emphasised the philosophical specificity and the speculative character of the history of political doctrines in such terms.[37]

At the time, an attempt to reconcile idealism and anti-idealism was made by Mario Delle Piane, a young scholar who was to write his major works in the post-war period. He agreed with Battaglia that the history of political doctrines had a theoretical content with no necessary political and pratical ends. But he also acknowledged that theories and ideas can be found outside organic doctrinal systems, and hence in texts others than political treatises and works on political philosophy. More-over, his opinion on the importance of the influence that the context may exercise on political thought made his position close to De Mattei's. It was therefore of some importance for scholars of the doctrines of political thought to study the historical context in which a text was written in order to better understand the text itself.[38]

The post-war period

The discussion concerning the method, nature and object of the study of the history of political doctrines during the inter-war years seems rather detached and almost provincial when compared with contem-porary international historiographical discussions, but also within the context of the Italian historical debate. However, its importance is significant when related to the discipline's own development, and to its autonomy as an academic subject. Naturally the discipline's progress

---

[35] A. Passerin d'Entrèves, *La dottrina dello Stato. Elementi di analisi e di interpretazione* (Turin, 1962), p. x.

[36] A. Passerin d'Entrèves, *Il 'palchetto assegnato agli statisti' e altri scritti di varia politica* (Milan, 1979), p. 20.

[37] Testoni Binetti, 'La storia delle dottrine politiche', p. 334, but cf. also pp. 332ff. For Passerin see 'Giovanni Althusio e il problema metodologico nella storia della flosofia politica e giuridica' (1934), now in Passerin d'Entrèves, *Saggi di storia del pensiero politico*, pp. 243–58 and his *La filosofia politica medievale* (Turin, 1934), Introduction, pp. 3–14.

[38] Cf. M. Delle Piane, 'I problemi di metodo nella storia delle dottrine politiche (A proposito di alcuni recenti studi sull'argomento)', *Studi senesi*, 53 (1939), pp. 527–52; cf. Testoni Binetti, 'La storia delle dottrine politiche', pp. 355ff.

depended more on the proliferation of substantive pieces of research than on the methodological debate. Many of the new studies were written by authors who did not participate in the methodological discussion and who were not part of the new academic 'corporation'. Croce and Gentile were amongst these. Not only did they write essays that rightfully belong to the genre, but both contributed to the creation of a favourable cultural and historiographical climate with their vast historical output, their theoretical pronouncements and their work as cultural entrepreneurs.

Other prominent scholars, such as Delio Cantimori and Federico Chabod, produced noteworthy studies. Chabod deserves particular attention. In 1925 he began his studies on Machiavelli, a choice probably influenced by his teacher, Meinecke, who in 1923 had published an edition of *The Prince*, soon to be followed by *Die Idee der Staatsrason*, a work which the young Chabod used 'not only for the history of Machiavellism, but also for [his] interpretation of *The Prince* and of his thought'.[39] Following on the same line of enquiry on the 'reason of state', a decade later, Chabod turned his attention to Botero.[40] However, he refrained from engaging in the methodological debate, probably because he was rather suspicious of the abstract nature of such a discussion, but also because of the character of the discipline itself. Indeed, the works on Machiavelli and Botero both confirm Chabod's standing as a historian of ideas and of culture, and as a political historian *tout court*.

The post-war debate on the history of political doctrines was less lively than that in the two previous decades. Yet, the new generation of scholars appeared to have already absorbed the results of the earlier debates. The contrast between the historical and the philosophical approach persisted, though less acutely, partly through a more general increase in interdisciplinarity and partly because of a certain influence from abroad. The new debate that invested Italian historiography was rooted in the changing political and social context of the time. Idealism and Marxism – the former in retreat, the latter in ascendancy, thanks also to the publication of Gramsci's prison writings – were confronted by the emergence of analytical philosophy, neo-Positivism, pragmatism and the social sciences. Journals and publishing houses, as well as the universities and the few research institutions in existence, became the

[39] G. Sasso, 'La storia delle idee', in B. Vigezzi (ed.), *Federico Chabod e la nuova storiografia italiana* (Milan, 1979), pp. 247–93, at p. 252. Cf. also F. Chabod, *Scritti su Machiavelli* (Turin, 1964); Machiavelli, *Il Principe*, edited by L. Firpo, with introduction and comments by F. Chabod (Turin, 1961).

[40] Cf. F. Chabod, *Botero* (Rome, 1934).

centres of attraction for scholars and for their activity. Laterza in Bari, Einaudi and Utet in Turin, La Nuova Italia and Sansoni in Florence, the Editori Riuniti in Rome and Feltrinelli in Milan (which also created the eponymous institute, as part of its library, which soon assembled one of the richest collections on the history of the workers' movement), all showed an interest in political studies and political texts. In the context of this sedimentation of the discipline, it is worth noticing the debate that developed on the relationship between philosophy and historiography, especially historiography of ideas, between Eugenio Garin, Delio Cantimori, Furio Diaz, Paolo Rossi, Norberto Bobbio, Pietro Rossi, Pietro Piovani and others. Here too, one of the themes to emerge was whether historians of philosophy were to see themselves foremost as historians or as philosophers. It is true, as it has been noted, that traditionally there has been a 'marked historiographical interest'[41] in Italian philosophy at large, but it is equally true that the dominance of idealism in the previous fifty years had produced a reaction against historical and philological methods when applied to philosophers' work. The present debate, however, contributed to redress the balance, thanks also to a new dialogue with the physical and social sciences, and the emergence of Marxism and other trends of thinking more sensitive to the thematics of historical change.

The work of Pietro Piovani, philosopher and historian of philosophy, went in that direction. His approach was historicist rather than idealistic. Knowledge as a human activity requires putting into a historical perspective not only what one intends to know, but also who wishes to know. In a similar vein, Eugenio Garin asserted the historical character of the history of philosophy, insisting on the necessary link between 'conceptions' and 'situations'.[42] A historian of philosophy (his are the most important works devoted to Italian philosophy), but also an excellent cultural historian, Garin was influenced by Croce and Gentile, and yet maintained an independent position, refusing to play the game of constructing chains of ideas and the idealistic attempt to 'actualise' authors. The main interests of his vast scholarly production were humanism and Renaissance writings. His studies dealt with moral and civil literature, which was closely related to the political interests of the humanists. In this field of research he was influenced by Cassirer and, more generally, by the research and methodology of the Warburg Institute. Erudition and interpretation are compounded in his philoso-

---

[41] C.A. Viano, 'Il carattere della filosofia italiana contemporanea', in *La cultura filosofica italiana dal 1945 al 1980*, 2nd edn (Naples, 1988), pp. 11–62, at p. 51.

[42] E. Garin, 'Osservazioni preliminari a una storia della filosofia', in E. Garin, *La filosofia come sapere storico* (Bari, 1959), pp. 33–86.

phical historiography, sensitive to the lessons of positivism and imbued with civil passion, particularly attentive to those ideas capable of influencing events and political action. In this respect, his intellectual encounter with the main authors of Italian Marxism, from Labriola to Gramsci, was of great significance. In them, he found thematic and methodological stimuli, besides ethical and political inspiration. Perhaps from this also came his interest in the history of intellectuals, which he practised with sensitivity towards the new horizons that the social and institutional history of culture was disclosing: one need only think of the particular attention that he paid to the history of printing.

The debate on the history of philosophy therefore intersected with that on the history of ideas, with frequent references to the discussion on the methods and the study of political doctrines. The boundaries between these fields became blurred and the common ground was once again that of the history of ideas, in which political history was incorporated, along with the new, and self-confident, social history. The conviction began to prevail that the selection of ideas (especially political ideas) could be made on the basis not of their supposed originality, but of their efficacy, of the degree in which they permeated a culture, of their capacity for diffusion and permanence in a society. This favoured a switch of interest from 'high' to 'low' culture, in which is evident the influence of the *histoire des mentalités* that began to diffuse in the 1960s. As a consequence, the model of the history of 'doctrines' now appeared to be in decline. Greater emphasis was given to the need to reconstruct the process of the *circolazione delle idee* (the way in which ideas diffuse), so as to distinguish between continuity and discontinuity, between the way in which ideas are camouflaged and hidden, between their legacies and their persistencies, or their materialisation in facts and institutions, their temporary or sudden disappearance.[43]

In 1981, Norberto Bobbio attempted a balance sheet of post-war Italian philosophical culture. While sharing the widespread self-criticism at its lack of originality and its dependence on foreign influences, he also highlighted some positive elements since the end of fascism, which coincided with the collapse of the hegemony of idealism. He found 'a rapidly growing process of de-provincialisation', 'an increase in philological exactness' and 'a refinement in research methods and techniques'.[44] These characteristics also applied to the practice of the history of political thought. Bobbio himself, after all, can be said to have

---

[43] Cf. F. Venturi, 'La circolazione delle idee', *Rassegna storica del risorgimento*, 34 (1954), pp. 203–65.

[44] N. Bobbio, 'Bilancio di un convegno', in *La cultura filosofica italiana*, pp. 301–11, at p. 311.

contributed to the latter, even though he must primarily be considered a political scientist, interested in the double-sided nature of political studies: empirical on the one hand (political science) and theoretical and conceptual on the other (political philosophy). His background was mainly philosophical and juridical, but not without a historical dimension, partly originating from the influence of his first teacher, Gioele Solari. To this dimension also contributed his strong interest, typical of a 'militant intellectual', in civil society, and in political polemics of present and immediate concern. In his works on the vicissitudes of political ideas, Bobbio writes *philosophically*, without however denying himself to be a *historian*. He does this by treating political ideas through the history of men, themes and movements, assembling this material in an exceptionally lively mosaic, but keeping it under strict control, and looking at it from a supranational perspective with regard to both themes and approaches.[45]

As the years have passed, Bobbio, the philosopher of law and politics, has given himself more and more frequently to history, an exercise which became functional to the expression of his conviction on the civil role played by university teaching, characteristic for instance of the experience of Solari, and more generally of the academy in Turin, which Bobbio gradually rediscovered in a journey back to his roots, which was, however, devoid of provincialism. Throughout the same period, Bobbio has increasingly played the role of the lay, liberal-democratic guide within Italian political discussion. With reference to the study of political ideas, it is not wholly inappropriate to talk of the 'Bobbio method'. This is based on the individuation of conceptual dichotomies; on a prevalently typological approach to the reading of texts; on the research of themes common to different authors, even when these may be distant in time and space; on his persuasion that in political thought there are recurring themes which the historian must wisely identify, isolate and, eventually, compare.[46]

Other first-rate scholars came from the University of Turin. Although they cannot properly be categorised as historians of political thought, their work falls, in various ways, within the subject here discussed. Aldo Garosci, Alessandro Galante Garrone and Franco Venturi are amongst them, and they often combined a life as a scholar with one of political militancy and action. Bruno Leoni's is a case apart. A student of Solari and a cultural organiser with a keen curiosity for the philosophy, theory

---

[45] See C. Violi (ed.) *Bibliografia degli scritti di Norberto Bobbio. 1934–1993* (Rome and Bari, 1995).

[46] Cf. M.L. Pesante, 'La cosa assente. Una metodologia per la storia del discorso politico', *Annali della Fondazione L. Einaudi*, 26 (1992), pp. 119–80, at pp. 132ff.

and sociology of law, as well as for economic theory and the socio-political sciences at large, Leoni also wrote a work on the history of political and social thought. In it, he discussed many authors of the past two centuries through some broad conceptual categories from which he believed the main political and social ideologies of our time originated. He identified the latter as individualism and socialism, and to a lesser extent democracy, nationalism and internationalism, considering any other political tendency to be derivative of the first two. His was a broad-brush kind of research, whose impact was very limited, but which represented a new departure in the history of political thought. Perhaps his most enduring contribution was to have restarted the *Annali di scienze politiche* in Pavia (originally founded in 1928, mainly thanks to Beonio Brocchieri), under the new title of *Il politico*. Especially in its first years of publication, this became a meeting point for different and complementary disciplines, and its main aim was to fight 'the confusion of ideas in political studies' through conceptual clarification.[47]

Looking at the entire scientific output of the first twenty years after the war, one may on the whole agree with Federico Chabod when he remarked that the debate on the nature of the discipline did not end in 1945. In his view, the historiography of political thought was not 'at the level required by the methodological proposals that had been put forward'.[48] His own student, Vittorio de Caprariis, developed a similar line of criticism by promoting the historicist approach and distancing the history of political doctrines from both the speculative abstractions of philosophy and the technical aridity of law. It was not out of mere flattery that he praised Chabod's essays on Machiavelli as 'an extremely worthy example of how the historiography of political thought should be, a clear example of the need . . . to anchor political thinkers to history'. Reviving the polemical opposition against the use of abstract and doctrinal concepts, he stressed the need for the scholar to look at political events and institutions, at the economic and social factors, and at whatever else might contribute to give a better picture within which to place political ideas and their authors. Thus, historians of ideas cannot limit themselves to search for the sources of the authors they study amongst the 'greats', whilst neglecting the large field of minor writers; nor can they shy away from expanding the range of sources from which they may draw. To support his own conception of the history of political thought, De Caprariis quotes, besides his teacher Chabod, De Mattei

---

[47] B. Leoni, 'Il nostro compito', *Il politico*, vol. 1 (1950), pp. 5–9, at p. 9. See also B. Leoni, *Scritti di scienza politica e teoria del diritto*, Introduction by M. Stoppino (Milan, 1980).

[48] Cf. Testoni Binetti, 'La storia delle dottrine politiche', p. 364.

and Morandi.[49] Between 1948 and 1964, De Caprariis published copiously, offering a persuasive exemplification of his own way of conceiving the history of political thought. Unfortunately, his premature death aged 40 prevented him from exercising a greater influence on the subject.

The contribution of Luigi Firpo

Since the end of the 1940s, another of Solari's students, Luigi Firpo, had started making an important contribution to the study of the history of political thought, bringing to it a coherence of approach and a certain congruence between his theoretical and methodological stance, his scientific output, and his activity of cultural promotion. He graduated in 1937 with a thesis on Campanella and three years later demonstrated his philological precision and research passion with a bibliographic essay on Campanella. As Bobbio remarked, this is a work that has stood the test of time.[50] Several years later, in the introduction to his *Ricerche Campanelliane* ('Studies on Campanella', 1947) he stresses the value of 'obscure, but not arid' philological work. This he regards as a 'humble and thankless' task, since the researcher 'analyses and confronts, checks and investigates, repressing in himself any passionate urge for wide-ranging interpretations', while shouldering the burden of freeing the field of doubts, obscurities and uncertainties. Such a passionate defence of philology – which with the passing of time was to become a vehement *apologia*, risking sometimes becoming a mere love of philology for its own sake; the other great temptation, besides erudition, in Firpo's own work – remained central in Firpo's overall production, as he never tired of pointing out by remarking on the historical and philological character of the 'history of political thought', a locution that he preferred – and not by chance – to the 'history of political doctrines'.

Introducing the Italian edition of the work by the Carlyle brothers, Firpo turns into virtues what Battaglia and Passerin thought to be its defects: the combination, for instance, of the history of doctrines and the history of political institutions, which, if anything, ought even to have been more explicit,

because the relationship of reciprocal action and reaction between institutions and doctrines seems to be of real, primary interest to those who do not regard the history of political thought as abstract speculation, but wish to understand

---

[49] V. De Caprariis, 'Appunti sul metodo nella storia del pensiero politico' (1948), in De Caprariis, *Scritti. 1. Storia delle idee. Da Socrate a Mann*, edited by G. Buttà (Messina, 1985), pp. 13–30, at pp. 22, 27, 30.

[50] N. Bobbio, 'Firpo, l'utopia realista', *La Stampa*, 31 October 1989.

how the constructive reflection on the problems of social life may contribute to their effective solution, whilst conversely the concrete conditions of civil life continuously bring forward new themes for reflection, at the same time stimulating doctrinal evolution.[51]

As part of his general interest in utopian writings, which he intriguingly reconciled with an attention to political realism (starting with Machiavelli's),[52] Firpo developed a great love for Campanella's work. Bobbio, who was also directed to the study of Campanella by Solari (as it was Paolo Treves), observed of Firpo that he admired 'not only [Campanella's] strength of mind, his boundless erudition, his unrestrained passions, the universality of the philosophical, political, historical, literary and even scientific issues that he had addressed, but also his superhuman courage'.[53] In fact, Firpo appreciated precisely those aspects of Campanella that an authentic liberal (or rather democrat) such as Bobbio rejected in him, namely the tension towards socialisation, Campanella's conviction that individual needs ought to be adapted, or even subordinated, to the needs of the community.[54]

Despite the clear appeal that erudition and philology had for him, in both his scientific work and in university teaching, Firpo evidently always chose his authors carefully, with an eye to their civil influence, preferring those who favour political and social change, and who were prepared to pay personally in order to promote such transformations. This is the case with the utopian writers of the Renaissance and the Counter-Reformation period, who, besides having in common generous hopes and the dream of a perfect republic, also suffered personal setbacks, always paid for at a dear price. Outside the utopian literature, Firpo's other favourites were the victims of persecution in the name of freedom of thought, such as Bruno, Galileo and Francesco Mario Pagano, the martyr of the 1799 Neapolitan Revolution. All his authors were devoted to reflection and analysis, whilst directly or indirectly getting involved in the events, disputes, and the civil and political battles of their own time. Although Firpo's interests were broad, he 'concentrated his studies on a series of themes that connected them logically, ideally and chronologically'.[55] His conception of the historiography of

[51] L. Firpo, Preface to R.W. and A.J. Carlyle, *Il pensiero politico medievale*, edited by L. Firpo (Bari, 1956), pp. vii–xvi, at p. xv.
[52] Cf. N. Bobbio, 'Firpo in utopia', in L. Firpo (ed.), *L'utopismo del Rinascimento e l'età nuova* (Alpignano, 1990), pp. 63–91.
[53] L. Firpo, 'Firpo, l'utopia realista', in Firpo (ed.), *L'utopismo*.
[54] See the letters between Solari, Bobbio and Firpo. For a first discussion, cf. A. d'Orsi (ed.), *La vita degli studi. Carteggio Gioele Solari – Norberto Bobbio 1391–1952* (Milan, 2000).
[55] G.M. Bravo, 'Luigi Firpo uomo di cultura, studioso, accademico, scrittore', *Bollettino Storico-bibliografico subalpino*, 87 (1989), pp. 1–8, at p. 2. Cf. E.A. Baldini and

political thought was therefore historicist, philological and 'totalising'.[56] The dogmatic and selective character of the kind of research focusing on pure 'doctrines' becomes wider and more animated when looking at 'thought' or 'ideas'. The latter were the key words of Firpo's historiographic universe.

Indeed, in 1968 Firpo founded *Il pensiero politico* ('Political Thought'), a periodical with the subtitle 'Review of the history of social and political ideas'. Title and subtitle witness a broad conception both of the discipline, which goes back to Mosca and especially to De Mattei, and of the emphasis on the historical approach. Together with Firpo, the other founders were Mario Delle Piane, Salvo Mastellone and Nicola Matteucci.[57] De Caprariis had died four years earlier, but his view of the discipline also found some echo in the new periodical. *Il pensiero politico* nevertheless aimed to be open to different approaches, ideal tendencies and methodologies. It was meant to favour the 'co-operation between the most varied tendencies traversing the history of political ideas, as long as pursued in a lively and vigorous manner'.[58] But, to all intents and purposes, history and philology seem the dominant approaches characterising the journal. This is particularly true for the philological work, on which there is no dissenting voice; less so for the historical tendency, within which there is no such unanimity, although over the years there is a prevalence of what might be called 'historical history' over the history of thought as 'philosophical history'.[59]

The historical aspect of the discipline was vigorously defended by Firpo at the very moment of presenting the new journal at the first Congress of the Historical Sciences in October 1967.

All meditations on the problems of organised communities, whether they be philosophical speculations, ideological simplifications or plans for political action, seem to belong to the history of political doctrines, whose main task consists in the description, classification and interpretation of conceptual processes linked to the dynamics of human groups. Its methods cannot but be those of history: a rigorous philology in its broader sense, without which any reconstruction of the past – either the *res gestae* or the world of ideas – is both superficial and arbitrary. The scrupulous analysis of texts must go hand in hand

F. Barcia (eds.) 'Bibliografia degli scritti di Luigi Firpo', in S. Rota Ghibaudi and F. Barcia (eds.), *Studi politici in onore di Luigi Firpo* (4 vols., Milan, 1990), IV, pp. 563–789.

[56] Bravo, 'Firpo uomo di cultura', p. 3.

[57] See M. Delle Piane, *Gaetano Mosca. Classe politica e liberalismo* (Naples, 1952); S. Mastellone, *Victor Cousin e il Risorgimento italiano* (Florence, 1955) and *Mazzini e la 'Giovane Italia' (1831–1834)* (2 vols., Pisa, 1960); N. Matteucci, *Antonio Gramsci e la filosofia della prassi* (Milan, 1951) and *J. Mallet du Pan* (Naples, 1957).

[58] [The Editors], 'Premessa', *Il pensiero politico*, 1 (1968), pp. 3–5, at p. 5.

[59] Cf. S. Testoni Binetti, 'Riviste e storia delle dottrine politiche', in Ghibaudi and Barcia (eds.), *Studi politici in onore di L. Firpo*, IV, pp. 157–73, at p. 169.

with an in-depth study of the cultural and social foundation in which the individual doctrines have their roots, a study of the entire context to which political thought, more than any other form of human reflection, is closely and tightly linked. Authentic political thought is only to be found in the uncovering of the unceasing circulation between life, concrete problems, conflicts of power, of race, of class, and of States, and the continuous meditation of thinkers, co-participants, and the man of the street. Political thought cannot be reduced to abstract philosophical speculation, even though this sometimes represents its highest systematic formulation.[60]

This was a useful formulation of the issues involved in the discipline, aiming to foreclose the methodological debate. But it was not to be, partly in view of the very breadth of Firpo's definition. By the end of the 1960s, responding also to developments in the discipline outside Italy, 'political thought' (or 'political ideas') became a kind of passe-partout, whose main scope was to identify all that contributed to the political culture of an age. On the threshold of the social transformations, the political changes and the large and small cultural revolutions of 1968, the history of political thought, even though not entirely in the self-apologetic form claimed by some historiography, became a 'priviledged field' for multidisciplinary interests, with rich experimental potential.[61] There was, however, no lack of problems facing the discipline, especially in its relations with other branches of historiography. Because of its close proximity to cultural history and the history of ideas, there was the risk of losing that specificity (the *ubi consistam*) so laboriously, but perhaps only apparently, acquired in the course of the preceeding decades.

Yet, by the end of the 1960s there was a consolidation of the image of the discipline in both the universities and the publishing world. Here, Firpo's role was relevant. He put to use his exceptional talent as a cultural organiser by setting up, for instance, the collective work of the *Storia delle idee politiche, economiche e sociali* ('History of Political, Economic and Social Ideas'). Outlining the aims of the work, in 1966, he emphasised the discipline's 'immense tasks', and its emancipation from the hold that jurists and philosophers had on it. The scope of the work – in which some fifty specialists were involved – clearly shows Firpo's vision of the history of political thought, or, to be more precise, of the history of political, economic and social ideas. By assuming, on the one hand, the technical impossibility and the theoretical absurdity of separating political from social and economic discourse, he further enlarged the field of research. On the other, he fully recognised the historical

[60] L. Firpo, 'Storia delle dottrine politiche', in L. De Rosa (ed.), *La storiografia italiana negli ultimi vent'anni* (3 vols., Rome and Bari, 1989), II, pp. 1309–19, at p. 1309.

[61] V.I. Comparato, 'Vent'anni di storia del pensiero politico in Italia', *Il pensiero politico*, 20 (1987), pp. 3–55, at p. 6.

nature of the discipline, firmly distinguishing it from philosophical, literary and scientific history (with which it shares the privilege of dealing with written texts, and therefore the need for 'rigorous philological analysis'), but also from political science and political sociology (which are empirical in nature). None the less, he frankly admitted that in many cases the boundaries with political philosophy and the philosophy of law are blurred and that often the discipline worked alongside 'state doctrines', and the history of political and social institutions, 'in a relationship of firm and stimulating inter-dependence'.[62]

The age of maturity

Starting from the 1960s and 1970s – in connection with the political explosion provoked by the protest movements – numerous publishing houses issued, or re-issued, political texts. As part of the diffuse need for so-called 'immediate history', the political explosion also awakened demands for more contemporary relevance. Marxism played an important role in this. Its two defining moments in post-war Italy were the importance that Gramsci's writings were given in national culture (not just political culture) in the aftermath of the Second World War, and, indeed, the protest movements of the 1960s. Often reluctantly, given that the academic structure of the history of political thought traditionally encouraged studies on the remote and very remote past, themes, authors and ideologies of the nineteenth and twentieth centuries increasingly became the subject of research. This had a clear impact on both university courses, monographs, works of scholarly synthesis and textbooks. The study of political ideas became above all the study of ideology, that is, of systems of ideas whose scope was more immediately directed towards political action. The relationship between theory and practice was therefore perceived as being more stringent, while greater attention was devoted to mass and minority movements directly related to particular ideologies.

The influence that the *Annales* exercised on Italian historiography and culture in the 1970s brought the history of ideas closer to that of mentalities and of the collective imagination – sometimes to the point of confusion. Other strong influences came from European Marxism, especially the Frankfurt School, while instead, Lukàcs's fame, which had been considerable in the previous decade, rapidly waned. The flourishing of Hegelian and Marxist studies was partly connected to the

---

[62] L. Firpo, *Programma di una storia delle idee politiche economiche e sociali* (Turin, 1966), also published as 'Introduzione', in Firpo (ed.), *Storia delle idee politiche, economiche e sociali* (6 vols., Turin, 1972–87), I (1982), pp. v–xvi.

sudden and brief fascination with Marcuse. Adorno's and Horkheimer's work was equally influential for the critique of Enlightenment and (capitalist) rationality, also indirectly facilitating the introduction of entirely new themes into the more traditional panorama of studies in the history of ideas. A similar impact later resulted from the diffusion of the work of Michel Foucault, who was often acclaimed as an intellectual guru or a dramaturgic figure.

In general, whilst monographs address over-specialised audiences, publishers, rather than publishing classical texts, concentrate their efforts on 'great undertakings': collective works in either single volumes or as a series aimed at a wider public. Such collective works often widen and enrich the scope of the discipline, but are also the cause of some confusion. The *Dizionario di politica* ('Dictionary of Politics') supervised by Norberto Bobbio and Nicola Matteucci, and edited by Gianfranco Pasquino, deserves a particular mention. On the one hand, in scope and compass it is comparable to Firpo's *Storia delle idee* mentioned earlier. On the other, it has greater methodological imbalance and great uneven-ness of contributions, which tend to veer between the philosophy of law, political science, state doctrine, political philosophy, the history of doctrines, of institutions, of movements, of political parties and so on. The *Dizionario* lacks the historical grid that holds Firpo's *Storia* together, so that the contributions from the various disciplines tend to go in different directions.[63] Closer to Firpo's own approach is instead the collective work edited by two of his students, Gian Mario Bravo and Silvia Rota Ghibaudi, on the *Storia del pensiero politico contemporaneo* ('The History of Contemporary Political Thought'). This is an original (though debatable) work, where monograph studies are placed along with far-reaching analyses on particular themes. This produces an extremely varied picture of the political culture of the past two centuries, with the risk, perhaps, of losing its common thread.[64]

Together with the collective works, the publication of university text-books is a clear sign of the entrenchment of the discipline. But it also shows its academic vocation, detached from the discussions in both civil society and the intellectual world, still in search of its identity. Not many textbooks had been published. Mosca's venerable tome was still in use, together with the Italian edition of Sabine and Touchard, and other partial histories (Sinclair, Carlyle, Mesnard), and more interpretative works or works of synthesis only improperly described as textbooks. But

[63] Cf. *Dizionario di politica*, edited by N. Bobbio and N. Matteucci, with the collaboration of G. Pasquino (Turin, 1976).
[64] Cf. G.M. Bravo and S. Rota Ghibaudi (eds.), *Il pensiero politico contemporaneo* (Milan, 1985–87).

now, besides translations of works such as that of Prélot and Chevallier, second-generation scholars started to produce their own historical syntheses. Amongst those scholars one finds Paolo Alatri, who had strong interests in contemporary and modern history, and who published the first, serious Italian texbook,[65] Francesco Valentini, a historian of philosophy, whose work on political thought in the nineteenth and twentieth centuries, though a good synthesis of the subject, was overburdened with 'philosophical history',[66] and one of the founders of *Il pensiero politico*, Salvo Mastellone, who showed versatility in the genre, with several texbooks on European thought, the intention of which he later described as being a 'call to history'.[67] Following on De Mattei, De Caprariis and Firpo, Mastellone – although stating his dislike for abstract methodological statements (and indeed there are none in his texbooks) – clearly embraced the 'historical history' version of the study of political thought. His works have no evident philosophical components, being more narrative and denotative than interpretative and connotative in character.

A new line of enquiry, also evident in *Il pensiero politico*, and in a series of volumes linked to the journal, emerged at that time, showing a growing interest both in the nature of the 'political vocabulary' and in political and social 'models'. Such developments partly reflected an attention towards international debates and research such as those surrounding the 'new history of political thought' in Britain and *Begriffsgeschichte* in Germany. But there were also those who adopted more traditional stances. Mario D'Addio, a Catholic scholar, also on the editorial committee of *Il pensiero politico*, argued for a doctrine-based approach. As he stated, 'the expression "political doctrines" implies a systematic conception of politics orientated towards practical action'.[68] D'Addio restated his position more recently, warning against the risk of a lapse into political history, the history of movements, political parties and political ideologies. The discipline ought instead to deal, or so he maintained, with more systematic conceptions of politics aimed at practical political action. In short, his conception is therefore that of a

---

[65] Cf. P. Alatri, *Lineamenti di storia del pensiero politico moderno* (2 vols., Messina, 1973–75).

[66] Cf. F. Valentini, *Storia del pensiero politico contemporaneo* (Rome and Bari, 1979).

[67] S. Mastellone, 'Per una storia del pensiero politico europeo', in E. Guiccione (ed.), *Strumenti didattici e orientamenti metodologici per la storia del pensiero politico* (Florence, 1993), pp. 3–15, at p. 8. The author refers to his *Storia del pensiero politico europeo* (2 vols., Turin, 1989–90). By the same author, *Storia ideologica d'Europa* (3 vols., Florence, 1974–82), *Storia della democrazia in Europa* (Turin, 1986).

[68] Cf. M. D'Addio, *Appunti di storia delle dottrine politiche* (Genoa, 1980); the new edition was published as *Una storia delle dottrine politiche* (Genoa, 1984–85), from which I quote, I, p. 5.

'historical' discipline, but a selective one.[69] The diction of 'political doctrines' was also favoured in the works of Giorgio Galli[70] and Ettore Albertoni,[71] whilst the textbook of Firpo's previously mentioned student, Gian Maria Bravo, lay uncompromisingly on the historical and philological side of the classical divide within the discipline.[72] However, Bravo more fully embraced (together with the obvious risks of this) a 'totalising' view of history, which Firpo himself had implicitly practised but never fully supported.[73]

A borderline discipline

The widening of the historian's territory and a more open and frank relationship of the discipline with political science, philosophy, law and the study of general history seem to be common features of the history of political thought in recent decades. A third-generation scholar, Fulvio Tessitore, an expert on German historicism, conceives the history of political ideas as a borderline discipline, where historians meet philosphers, and the work of each is supported 'by the common reference to philology, meant not only as a method, but as the essence of history as a "new science"'.[74] Despite the ever-present methodological disputes about a discipline in perpetual search of identity and legitimation, this seemed now to be more firmly placed within that slightly undefined area in between political philosophy, on the one hand, and the history of political events, institutions, forms of government, and social and political movements, on the other. Thus, the kind of scholarship involved was that of ascertaining, narrating and explaining facts as well as discussing 'political values' and making value judgements.[75]

Even though the philological and historical aspects of the discipline

---

[69] D'Addio, *Una storia delle dottrine politiche*. I cite from my notes from his paper at the Conference on *Strumenti didattici e orientamenti metodologici per la storia del pensiero politico*, Erice, 17–19 October 1991.

[70] Cf. E.A. Albertoni, *Storia delle dottrine politiche in Italia* (2 vols., Milan, 1990), I, pp. 7–20.

[71] Cf. J.A. Pocock, *Politica linguaggio e storia. Scritti scelti*, edited by E.A. Albertoni (Milan, 1990).

[72] G.M. Bravo, 'Una storia del pensiero politico contemporaneo', in Mastellone (ed.), *Strumenti didattici*, pp. 37–48, at p. 41. Cf. G.M. Bravo and C. Malandrino, *Profilo di storia del pensiero politico* (Rome, 1994); G.M. Bravo and C. Malandrino, *Il pensiero politico del novecento*, Preface by M. Guasco (Casale Monferrato, 1994).

[73] Cf. Bravo and Malandrino, *Profilo*, pp. 15–21.

[74] F. Tessitore, 'Storiografia, filosofia e pensiero politico', in Tessitore, *Nuovi metodi della ricerca storica* (Milan, 1975), pp. 15–36, at pp. 16, 34; also in F. Tessitore, *Storicismo e pensiero politico* (Milan and Naples, 1974), pp. 291–326.

[75] D. Pasini, 'Problemi e finalità della filosofia della politica', *Storia e politica*, 22 (1983), pp. 543–53, at p. 543.

are now beyond dispute, in recent years there has been a renewed attention to its philosophical dimension, thanks also to a growing interest in problems of language partly derived from the influence of the Cambridge school, and the parallel discovery of Wittgenstein in the mid-1960s. Nicola Matteucci, more than others, has defended a more philosophical history of political thought. Although well aware of the dangers posed by such an approach, he has argued for a closer link with both political philosophy and the philosophy of law, besides expressing some concern that the domination of the historical over the philosophical and systematic approaches may be the sign of the discipline's *cupio dissolvi*. In his opinion, work in the discipline seems   to be concentrating on either the depiction of context or erudite essaying, risking reducing political ideas to their contingent and factual aspects, and obscuring them with too many philological details. Although Matteucci seems to take up where Battaglia left off, and he also claims to find inspiration in the *Geschichtliche Grundbegriffe* of Brunner, Conze and Koselleck,[76] he is none the less adamant about the historicity of the subject. The historians of political thought, he maintains, must pay attention to the personal, existential and psychological aspects of the authors they study; moreover, they must 'find a way between pure philosophers and pure historians'.[77] The new journal, *Filosofia politica*, founded by Matteucci and some of his and Battaglia's students, intends to follow this direction. Similarly, 'a strong demand for theoretical redefinition'[78] animates *Teoria politica*, another journal whose publication also started in the 1980s, and which groups together some of Norberto Bobbio's students. Its main aim seems to consist in neither constructing analytical categories nor suggesting new forms of conceptualisation. There seems to be no clear intention to distinguish the many aspects of political studies (theory, science, philosophy, and history of ideas), but rather to sum them up: 'the result is . . . the accumulation and reciprocal contribution to the deepening of already established themes as well as to the development of new directions of research'.[79]

In both the historical and the philosophical camps of the discipline, a certain need to 'think through models' has more recently begun to spread. This idea has been borrowed from the social sciences, and in the historiographic fields it relies to a great extent on analogical processes. In some way, this may bring together historians and philosophers, via

[76] N. Matteucci, *Lo stato moderno. Lessico e percorsi* (Bologna, 1993), p. 9.
[77] N. Matteucci, 'Introduzione: L'ordine politico', in Matteucci, *Alla ricerca dell'ordine politico* (Bologna, 1984), pp. 7–30, at pp. 11, 14, 16
[78] V.I. Comparato, 'La "politica" e la storia del pensiero politico', *Il pensiero politico*, 21 (1988), pp. 49–56, at p. 53.
[79] L. B[onanate], 'Il programma di "Teoria politica"', *Teoria politica*, 1 (1985), pp. 3–4.

the construction of general categories in which to fit particular examples. But there is the risk of sacrificing and devaluing the latter's specificity. Moreover, the introduction of models into the history of political thought may signal a partial retreat from the historical model. The answer to this has been a call to both caution and a renewed look at the historical nature of the discipline. But more than the debated and debatable use of models, more also than the generic and much repeated (perhaps to the point of tedium) appeal to 'interdisciplinarity', what currently seems to unite all the areas of study on political thought, is perhaps the issue of linguistics. To understand politics means, in the first place, to study its languages: to place them in their proper contexts, compare them by tracing the meaning of key words, identify the latter's transformation over time, and their distorted and sometimes reversed use, and also their return to prominence. All this allows the historian to continue being a historian, yet to work side by side with scholars in political science, in philosophy and in all those areas related to political action.

After the debates of the pioneering years, the post-war revival, the revolution of the 1960s and 1970s, the history of political thought in Italy has not stopped interrogating itself about its very nature and methodologies. This has not, however, prevented researchers from making progress – progress that is evident in the continuous production of texts, monographs, collective and wide-reaching research as well as textbooks and works of popularisation.

6   Discordant voices: American histories of political thought

Terence Ball

To survey the varied array of approaches to the history of political thought in the United States since the Second World War is too tall an order to fill in a single chapter. So I shall simply highlight a number of topics, themes, approaches and 'schools' that have been variously in vogue over the past half-century or so, illustrating each with especially noteworthy examples. I shall begin by considering the institutional site in which American historians of political thought typically work – namely, departments of political science – and how this has affected the approaches they adopt. I then consider a number of defining themes and moments, both inside and outside the American academy. Outside, the threats of fascist and communist totalitarianism, the Holocaust and the Cold War, the 'end of ideology' debate, the Vietnam War and the rise of the New Left, the black and women's liberation movements, and a resurgent conservatism; inside, the profound impact of European, and especially German-Jewish, émigrés, McCarthyism and the loyalty oath controversies, the 'behavioural revolution' in political science, the rise of positivism, the anti-behaviouralist and anti-positivist backlash, and the emergence of feminism, multiculturalism, postmodernism, and other influential perspectives.

I

As an academic subject, the history of political thought is typically studied in departments of political science, where it is classified under the larger heading of political theory – or, as the American Political Science Association designates it, 'Political Theory: Normative and Historical'. This designation separates and segregates this sort of political theory from 'Political Theory: Empirical and Analytic'. How the history of political thought came to occupy this marginalised position is

I am much indebted to Richard Dagger, Mary Dietz and the editors for commenting on an earlier draft of this chapter.

a long and rather convoluted story. As narrated by critics of 'traditional' political theory, the story goes something like this. In the United States the hope of making political science a truly 'scientific' discipline was advanced with a vengeance after the Second World War. And this is because there was amongst many American political scientists a sense of dissatisfaction with 'traditional' political thought that focused on the concepts of consent, citizenship, the state, obligation, authority, liberty and the like, and seemed more interested in prescribing how people ought to behave than in describing how they actually do behave, and explaining why. Traditional political theory also appeared to be more concerned with the past than with the present – with those 'old books' called 'the classics', than with pressing problems of the post-war period. Instead of consulting these old tomes political scientists should study the 'real world'. Instead of relying on the outmoded and pre-scientific theories of yesteryear, we should at least attempt to theorise about politics in a more modern, and preferably more scientific, fashion. We should take care to separate facts from values, description from prescription, ideas and ideals from interests, 'is' from 'ought'. We should discover and use universal laws of human behaviour in order to explain why people act as they do in political settings and situations. This was the impetus for, and the promise of, the post-Second World War 'behavioural revolution' in American political science. The revolutionaries were not hostile to all forms of political theory – on the contrary, they readily acknowledged that the analysis of political concepts such as 'power' could be very valuable – but they *were* hostile or at least antipathetic to the history of political thought, for this reason: if political science is to be a science in the fashion of physics or any of the other natural sciences, then there is no legitimate place for the history of earlier theorising. After all, aspiring physicists study physics, not the history of physics. One can be a very fine physicist and be utterly ignorant of the theories propounded by the Ionian nature philosophers, or by Aristotle or any other major figure in the history of science. Indeed, to study the history of science would be a distraction – interesting in its own right, perhaps, but irrelevant to current research and theorising. And, as in physics, so in political science: one need not study the theories of Aristotle or Plato or Cicero or Marsiglio in order to be a good political scientist; indeed, the time and effort spent in studying them would detract from research into, and theorising about, present-day politics.

Before the behavioural revolution of the 1950s and 1960s there was no strong and irreconcilable split between political 'science' and the historical study of political thought. Indeed, a number of eminent

American political scientists, including Charles Merriam, had themselves made conspicuous contributions to the history of political thought.[1] All the major departments of political science offered courses with titles such as 'the history of political thought: from Plato to the present'. Most of the first generation of behavioural revolutionaries – Robert Dahl, David Easton, Heinz Eulau, David Truman and others – had begun as students of political theory and some of their earliest published work dealt with thinkers in the tradition of Western political thought. As undergraduates and postgraduates they had read Dunning's *A History of Political Theories* (1902), McIlwain's *Growth of Political Thought in the West* (1932) and especially Sabine's *A History of Political Theory* (1937). But later, as budding behavioural revolutionaries, they rejected the backward-looking 'historicism' of their elders. 'Political theory today', Easton complained, 'is interested primarily in the history of ideas.'[2] If political science is to be a science, this preoccupation with the pre-scientific political thought of Plato and his progeny must cease.[3]

Briefly and crudely, the behavioural revolution drove a wedge between the 'scientific' study of political 'behaviour' and the 'historical' study of political 'thought' – as though thought and action are analytically separable or have nothing to do with one another.

The coming of the Cold War, the threat of nuclear omnicide, the search for 'subversives' in government and the academy during the McCarthy period,[4] the increasing prominence of logical positivism and the promise of 'value-free' inquiry, the rise of the large foundations (Ford, Rockefeller, Carnegie, Russell Sage and others) and their funding of 'objective' or 'non-ideological' empirical research in the behavioural sciences – these and other factors form the background against which the history of political thought became ever more marginalised within departments of political science. Whilst precious few funds were available for another book about Aristotle, the American academy was awash with money in the form of governmental and foundation grants to analyse the 'authoritarian personality', the psycho-

---

[1] C. Merriam, *A History of Political Theories* (New York, 1924).

[2] D. Easton, *The Political System* (New York, 1953), p. 236.

[3] This complaint is a common thread or theme running through interviews with behavioural-era American political scientists in M.A. Baer, M.E. Jewell, and L. Sigelman (eds.), *Political Science in America: Oral Histories of a Discipline* (Lexington, Ky, 1991).

[4] Amongst those driven out of the American academy during the McCarthy era was Moses Finley, the distinguished classicist who emigrated to England where he contributed greatly to our understanding of class structure, politics and slavery in ancient Greece. He ended his career as Master of Darwin College, Cambridge. Most left-of-centre American scholars were less fortunate. Too many lives ended in alcohol and suicide.

logical appeals of communism, attitudes towards communism and anti-communist 'counter-insurgency research', amongst others.[5]

The historical study of political thought could hardly remain aloof from or unaffected by the post-war and Cold War intellectual, political and cultural climate. The horrific legacy of fascism was fresh in many minds, and the threat of communism almost palpable. The history of Western political thought was told as a whiggish tale of the gradual if not inexorable triumph of liberalism over illiberalism, and individual liberty over collectivist tyranny.[6] The 'roots' and 'seeds' of totalitarianism were traced to a select few villains – to Plato, Machiavelli, Hobbes, Rousseau, Hegel and Marx, in particular – and the sources of democracy and individual liberty to Locke and Jefferson, amongst others.[7]

II

Unsurprisingly, American historians of political thought have long evinced an interest in American political thought from the puritans to the present. Attitudes towards the American national past have varied widely. Early in the twentieth century 'progressive' historians attempted, as did the muckraking journalists of the era, to expose error and denounce hypocrisy. And, by liberal-progressive lights, no group had been more mistaken or more hypocritical than the puritans. Historians of American political thought found puritan political thought peculiar and, indeed, something of an embarrassment. It seemed somehow an exception to, if not a blot on, the American past. Its illiberal communitarianism, its conformism, its emphasis on ortho-doxy and obedience stood in stark contrast to the exuberant optimism and individualism of America's liberal past and progressive present. In his now-classic study, *Main Currents in American Thought* (1930), Vernon Parrington viewed the puritans in much the same way one would view one's crazy aunt locked in the attic: not to be ignored, but

---

[5] See, respectively, T. Adorno et al., *The Authoritarian Personality* (New York, 1949); G.A. Almond, *The Appeals of Communism* (Princeton, 1954); S. Stouffer, *Communism, Conformity and Civil Liberties* (New York, 1955); H. Eckstein, *Internal War* (New York, 1964).

[6] See, e.g., G.H. Sabine, *A History of Political Theory* (New York, 1937; rev. edn 1950); F. Watkins, *The Political Tradition of the West* (Cambridge, Mass., 1948); W.Y. Elliott and N.A. McDonald, *Western Political Heritage* (New York, 1949).

[7] I am not, of course, suggesting that this was a uniquely American phenomenon; quite the contrary. See, e.g., R.H.S. Crossman's *Plato Today* (London, 1939), Karl Popper's *Open Society and its Enemies* (London, 1945) and Bertrand Russell's *History of Western Philosophy* (London, 1945). These last showed that great philosophers do not great historians make.

not to be brought downstairs and introduced in polite company, either.[8]

The progressive historians also sought to debunk national monuments and cut them down to size by 'following the dollar'. The greatest of these targets was the US Constitution which, as Charles Beard attempted to show, had intentionally created a government of the rich, by the rich, and for the rich. Its framers' inspiration was neither moral nor civic but basely economic. The Constitution was the creation of the wealthy for the protection of their entrenched economic interests, and its universal voice ('We the People . . .') merely a mask to conceal the tawdry contents within.[9] Progressives complained that the 'promise of American life' was being subverted by the residues of a repressive puritanical past and a constitutionally stifled present. Nine puritanical old men on the Supreme Court, worshipping the false idol of the American Constitution, were keeping much-needed reform at bay.[10]

These reformist impulses, at least in their more radical forms, peaked during the Great Depression and the New Deal, and largely disappeared during and after the Second World War. The rise of totalitarian regimes in Russia, Germany and Italy, the Holocaust, and the advent of the Atomic Age and the Cold War paved the way for a more sober, but peculiarly celebratory, view of the American past. America had escaped the horrors of war and genocide because of 'American exceptionalism'. Somehow Americans are different from other people, and America unique – a 'Citty Upon a Hill', as the puritan divine John Winthrop once put it. 'The genius of American politics' resides in the Americans' make-do pragmatism, their indifference to ideas, their immunity to ideology.[11] Americans are just puritanical enough to know that men are not angels, and our Constitution recognises – and wisely guards against – that fact. In post-war America the Constitution ceased to be the whipping-boy of progressive historians and was accorded renewed respect. Beard's economic interpretation of the Constitution was challenged and countered.[12] This rehabilitation and celebration of the American past was now extended even to the puritans. Through the eyes of Reinhold Niebuhr and Perry Miller the puritans were viewed as being very much in the American grain – sober, industrious, acutely aware of the faults and foibles of human nature, and appreciative of institutions that could check its excesses. Puritan communitarianism supplied a

---

8 V.L. Parrington, *Main Currents in American Thought* (New York, 1930).
9 C.A. Beard, *An Economic Interpretation of the Constitution* (New York, 1913).
10 H. Croly, *The Promise of American Life* (New York, 1909).
11 D. Boorstin, *The Genius of American Politics* (Chicago, 1953).
12 F. McDonald, *We the People: the Economic Origins of the Constitution* (Chicago, 1958).

much-needed bit and bridle to what might otherwise be the unbridled individualism of American liberalism.[13]

The liberal legacy in America was traced largely, though not exclusively, to one key figure – 'the great Mr Locke, America's philosopher'.[14] Locke was seen as the source of the concepts and categories that Jefferson had employed to justify the American Revolution.[15] Locke had defended individual rights, and in particular private property rights, against the encroachments of the state. He was an early and ardent defender of the religious toleration recognised and guaranteed by the First Amendment. On the *tabula rasa* of the new American society, Locke left a deep impression. By the mid-1950s Locke was deemed 'a massive national cliché', the *deus ex machina* of American politics. Politics in America are stable and appear to be non-ideological because of a long-prevailing 'Lockean consensus' about individual liberty, individual rights and the protection of property.[16]

This view soon came under stiff challenge. Bernard Bailyn's study of the pamphlet literature appearing before and during the American Revolution found remarkably few references to Locke, and many more to Bolingbroke, Trenchard and Gordon, amongst other English 'Real Whig' or 'commonwealth' propagandists of the early eighteenth century.[17] The emphasis on Locke and liberalism had layered over and obscured a strong 'republican' strain in early American political thought. Republican political thought emphasised the centrality of civic virtue, the dangers of internal 'corruption', the perils of a 'standing army' and so on. The rediscovery and recovery of republican political thought was begun by Zera Fink, whose 1944 study of *The Classical Republicans* had been largely ignored until its resurrection by 'republican' critics of Hartz's Lockean consensus.[18] These critics included, pre-eminently, Gordon Wood and J.G.A. Pocock.[19] I shall say more in a moment about Pocock's seminal contribution to the history of American political thought. Here it is enough to note that he helped move Locke from the centre to the periphery of early American political thought, which on their telling is less 'liberal' than 'republican'.

The so-called 'republican consensus' soon came under attack from

---

[13] R. Niebuhr, *The Children of Light and the Children of Darkness* (New York, 1944); P. Miller, *Errand Into the Wilderness* (Cambridge, Mass., 1956).

[14] M. Curti, 'The Great Mr Locke, America's Philosopher', *Huntington Library Bulletin*, 11 (April 1937), pp. 107–51.

[15] C. Becker, *The Declaration of Independence* (New York, 1942).

[16] L. Hartz, *The Liberal Tradition in America* (New York, 1955).

[17] B. Bailyn, *Ideological Origins of the American Revolution* (Cambridge, Mass., 1967).

[18] Z. Fink, *The Classical Republicans* (Evanston, Ill., 1944).

[19] G. Wood, *The Creation of the American Republic* (Chapel Hill, N.C., 1969); J.G.A. Pocock, *The Machiavellian Moment* (Princeton, 1975).

historians who emphasised the part played by 'Lockean' arguments in legitimising early American capitalism. They, like the progressives, proposed to follow the dollar, to see who lost and who gained in the fledgling capitalist order. Joyce Appleby (1992) and Isaac Kramnick (1990) viewed republican rhetoric as an ideological mask used by Jefferson and others to cloak and justify the emergence of a liberal-capitalist social order in late eighteenth- and early nineteenth-century America.[20] Although greatly diminished in intensity, this debate continues.

III

Until the Second World War Americans were accustomed to writing their own histories of American (and Western) political thought. Quite often these tended to be narratives about the emergence of liberalism and its hard-fought if still-tentative triumph over authoritarianism and intolerance. This rather rosy picture of the past, present and future of American and Western liberalism was soon to be challenged by foreign scholars who shared a decidedly less optimistic outlook.

Perhaps the single most important and influential development in post-war American political theory was the arrival in the late 1930s and 1940s of European, and more particularly German-Jewish, refugees. Hannah Arendt, Eric Voegelin, Leo Strauss and others left a lasting impression on American political theory and its view of the history of political thought.[21] The émigrés brought with them their own concerns and their own history, both philosophical and political. Philosophically, they were educated in the tradition of German idealism and its critics. Politically, and whatever their partisan allegiances, all were heir to the horrific history of twentieth-century Germany. The Weimar Republic had failed to stem the Nazi tide, not only because it was politically weak but, even more fundamentally, because it was philosophically bankrupt.

[20] J. Appleby, *Liberalism and Republicanism in the Historical Imagination* (Cambridge, Mass., 1992); I. Kramnick, *Republicanism and Bourgeois Radicalism* (Ithaca, N.Y., 1990).
[21] The contribution of émigré scholars is much broader and deeper than I can recount here. A fuller survey would include, *inter alia*, such social and legal theorists as Hans Kelsen, Otto Kircheimer and Franz Neumann; Frankfurt School critical theorists such as Theodor Adorno, Max Horkheimer, Herbert Marcuse and Erich Fromm; philosophers as different as Alfred Schutz, Hans Jonas, Herbert Feigl, Carl Hempel, Hans Reichenbach, Ernest Nagel, and Paul and Felix Oppenheim; social scientists such as Paul Lazarsfeld and Hans Morgenthau; the economist Fritz Machlup; the psychoanalytic theorist Otto Fenichel; and many others. For émigré scholars' contributions to political theory in particular, see J.G. Gunnell, *The Descent of Political Theory* (Chicago, 1993).

The watery, tolerant liberalism of Weimar was no match for the ferocity and fanaticism of fascists, communists and other extremists of the Left and Right. A regime armed only with a philosophy that professes political neutrality can stand for nothing and can tolerate almost anything, including its own demise. The lesson learned, and later taught, by the émigrés, was that liberalism is a singularly self-subverting political philosophy. In the weaknesses of liberalism are to be found the seeds of fascist and communist fanaticism – pseudo-philosophies that flourish where they are not checked and countered by a regime animated by and armed with a more robust and self-confident political philosophy. Wishy-washy by nature, modern liberalism cannot be such a philosophy. The twofold task of twentieth-century political thinkers must, accordingly, be to criticise liberalism root and branch, and to find or construct a more robust and well-grounded alternative philosophy.

It is against this political-philosophical background that the contribution of the European refugee scholars can best be understood. And nowhere is their contribution clearer or more evident than in their approach to the history of political thought. Very briefly, they all, in their often quite different ways – and quite unlike their American hosts – viewed the history of modern Western liberal political thought as a story of degeneration and enfeeblement.[22] They contrasted the vigour of classical Greek and Roman political thought with the resigned ennui of slack-minded modern liberal thinkers who preach tolerance and practise passivity.

Strauss in particular contended that modern liberalism is a philosophy without foundations. Having eschewed any grounding in nature or natural law, modern liberalism, from Hobbes to the present, is reduced to a spineless relativism and is therefore without the normative foundations and philosophical resources to resist the winds of twentieth-century fanaticism blowing from both Right and Left. The 'crisis of the West', as diagnosed by Oswald Spengler and Carl Schmitt, amongst others, has deep philosophical roots. 'The crisis of our time', Strauss announced, 'is a consequence of the crisis of political philosophy.'[23] His and his disciples' historical inquiries were accordingly attempts to trace the origins and diagnose if not cure the multiple maladies of liberalism, relativism and scientism that together make up 'the crisis of our time'. The present being bankrupt, students of political philosophy must look to the past for

---

[22] Strauss's and Voegelin's criticisms of modern liberalism, moral relativism and historicism were welcomed and embraced by Christian conservatives such as John Hallowell, Richard Weaver, Russell Kirk and William F. Buckley, Jr., all of whom supplied much of the intellectual arsenal of modern American conservatism. See also n. 35, below.

[23] L. Strauss, 'Political Philosophy and the Crisis of Our Time', in G.J. Graham and G.W. Carey (eds.), *The Post-Behavioral Era* (New York, 1972), p. 41.

guidance; they must be historians but not 'historicists'. Historicism and scientism are two sides of the same counterfeit coin. Historicism is the relativist doctrine that different ages have different, if not indeed incommensurable, *mentalités* and outlooks; accordingly, we moderns can hardly hope to understand, much less learn from, Plato and other earlier thinkers. The history of political thought, on this historicist view, becomes a vast burial ground instead of what it can and should be – a source of genuine knowledge and a reliable guide for the perplexed.[24]

Knowledge and guidance of the sort we require is not easy to come by, however. It requires that we read these 'old books' aright – that we decipher the real meaning of the messages encoded by authors fearful of persecution and wishing to communicate with *cognoscenti* through the ages.[25] For philosophy is dangerous; to espouse its truths in public – in that liberal oxymoron known as the 'marketplace of ideas' – is to risk ridicule and incomprehension, or even persecution, by the *hoi polloi*. To communicate with the great thinkers of antiquity is to appreciate how far we have fallen. The rot began in the seventeeth century, with the advent of modern liberalism, and that of Hobbes and Locke especially.[26] They disavowed the ancient wisdom and the older idea of natural law, favouring instead a view of politics founded on security and self-interest. The ancient 'philosophical' quest for the good life was transmuted into the modern 'scientific' search for safety, security and the accommodation of competing interests.

The 'Straussian' approach to the history of political thought requires the recovery of ancient, or at any rate premodern and preliberal, knowledge of 'political things'. And this in turn requires that one read not only the classics – Plato, in particular – but texts and authors who show us the way back into the labyrinth, e.g. Xenophon, Al-Farabi, Maimonides and others who are rarely (if ever) included in the non-Straussian curriculum.[27] In this way one is sensitised to, and initiated into the secrets of, political philosophy. Most philosophers have written two doctrines: an 'exoteric' one meant for consumption by the uninitiated, and a deeper 'esoteric' doctrine to be decoded and understood by those initiated into the mysteries. A 'Straussian' education consisted in considerable part in just this sort of initiation.

The decadence of the West was perhaps particularly evident in the United States, with its naïve faith in liberalism, democracy and the

---

[24] L. Strauss, *What is Political Philosophy?* (Glencoe, Ill., 1959).
[25] L. Strauss, *Persecution and the Art of Writing* (Glencoe, Ill., 1952).
[26] L. Strauss, *Natural Right and History* (Chicago, 1953).
[27] L. Strauss and J. Cropsy (eds.), *History of Political Philosophy* (Chicago, 1963); L. Strauss, *Studies in Platonic Political Philosophy*, ed. T.M. Pangle (Chicago, 1983).

common man. The truths of philosophy can be grasped only by the few; philosophy is therefore inherently anti-democratic – and democracy antithetical to philosophy. We must never forget that it was a democratic regime that condemned Socrates to death, and that Weimar was a democratic regime in which Hitler and the Nazis came to power by legal and democratic means.

To be sure, the European émigrés did not speak with a single voice. One singular and especially noteworthy voice was that of Hannah Arendt, whose star is perhaps now more ascendant than ever. In her first major work in English Arendt traced the origins of totalitarianism to European anti-Semitism and nineteenth-century imperialism.[28] She subsequently undertook an original inquiry into the *vita activa*.[29] But, insofar as she may be regarded as a historian of political thought, three other books are especially noteworthy: *Between Past and Future* (1961), *On Revolution* (1963) and *Crises of the Republic* (1972).[30]

Arendt was not first and foremost a historian of political thought. She was instead a political theorist who drew upon themes and topics taken from the history of political thought in order to illuminate the human condition in the modern world. The world in which we now live – disenchanted, scientised, bureaucratised, routinised – is indeed Weber's iron cage, in which modern men and women are largely confined. The affluence and comfort of modern consumer society masks and conceals our true condition, which is one of interconnected crises – political, educational and cultural.[31] We have failed to 'think what we are doing'. And one corrective to this thoughtlessness is to be found in the study of the past, and the history of political thought in particular. That history provides material for thinking about and reflecting upon our present predicament.

With some few exceptions, Arendt claimed, modern man has lost the sense of what it means to act politically.[32] The Greeks had a vivid sense of acting in public, of distinguishing oneself through words and deeds. The desiccated sensibility of modernity makes room only for for 'work' – the making of material things – or 'labour', i.e. attending to the endless cycle of biological necessity (eating, sleeping, procreating, etc.). To the

---

[28] H. Arendt, *The Origins of Totalitarianism* (New York, 1951).

[29] H. Arendt, *The Human Condition* (Chicago: 1958).

[30] H. Arendt, *Between Past and Future: Six Exercises in Political Thought* (New York, 1961); *On Revolution* (New York, 1963); *Crises of the Republic* (New York, 1972).

[31] Arendt, *Between Past and Future*, chs. 5 and 6.

[32] The noteworthy exceptions include the short-lived Paris Commune, the early soviets (workers' councils), the French Resistance during the Second World War and the abortive Hungarian uprising of 1955, but not, according to Arendt, those of the civil rights and women's movements of the late 1960s.

extent that our species' capacity for 'action' – that is, for acting politically – is what makes us uniquely human, we moderns suffer from the greatest loss of all: the loss of freedom, in the now largely forgotten sense of that term. The growth of science, and especially the behavioural sciences, has helped to further diminish our already much-diminished humanity. The 'social sciences', Arendt laments, 'have decided to treat man as an entirely natural being whose life processes can be handled the same way as all other processes'.[33] We are thereby led to view ourselves as so many quantifiable and interchangeable units, and not as unique human beings; as capable only of predictable 'behaviour' but not of inherently unpredictable 'action'; as parents, spouses and employees, but not as robust and active citizens.

One of the chief tasks of political theory is to help us to remember what we have lost. Arendt's 'historical' studies were, to a great degree and in different ways, concerned with loss. She laments the 'lost treasure' of the revolutionary heritage, the loss of (positive or political) 'freedom' ('What *was* freedom?') and 'authority' ('What *was* authority?'), and the loss of our capacity to act politically.[34] Those living in 'dark times' will seek illumination and light from other times. The history of Western political thought and action can be a source of such illumination.

IV

The German-Jewish émigrés made a deep and lasting contribution to American political theory. Of all these eminent émigrés, only Strauss can be said to have established a 'school'.[35] Although during her lifetime Hannah Arendt established no school, she nevertheless left her mark on one.

The 'Arendtian' approach to the history of political thought greatly influenced the so-called 'Berkeley school'. From the late 1950s to the early 1970s Sheldon Wolin, Norman Jacobson, John Schaar, Michael Rogin and Hanna Pitkin had a profound, if perhaps short-lived and indeterminate, impact on an entire generation of students of political theory.[36] If the Berkeley school can be said to have had a motto, or

---

[33] Arendt, *Between Past and Future*, p. 59.

[34] Arendt, *On Revolution*, ch. 6; *Between Past and Future*, chs. 3–4.

[35] Strauss's pupils and followers include such influential and prolific scholars as the late Allan Bloom, Joseph Cropsey, Herbert Storing, Martin Diamond, Harry Jaffa, Thomas Pangle, Harvey Mansfield, Jr., Timothy Fuller, Nathan Tarcov, and Catherine and Michael Zuckert, as well as such *engagé* neo-conservative intellectuals as Irving Kristol and Carnes Lord. Limitations on space preclude a discussion of other noteworthy 'schools' (save the Berkeley school, discussed below).

[36] Candour compels me to acknowledge that I, a graduate student at Berkeley from 1967 to 1971, was amongst those thus affected.

perhaps a preoccupation, it was this: 'the decline of the political' – and of political theory – in the modern age.[37] The once-vital Western 'tradition of political thought' had been enervated by liberalism, by the social sciences (and by behavioural political science in particular), by the modern administrative and organisational theory that underlay and legitimated the turn towards bureaucracy and the administrative state that Max Weber had called the 'iron cage' and 'the polar night of icy hardness and darkness'.

This concern was the Ariadne's thread that the Berkeley school followed back into the past, for two purposes. One was to recover what had been lost or discarded, that is, the robust outlook of earlier political thinkers before the ennui of the modern age set in. The second aim was to diagnose and trace the aetiology of this modern malady and, perchance, to find a cure in a reinvigorated 'participatory democracy'. This recovery of nerve required the rediscovery of 'epic political theory' – political theory in the grand manner of Hobbes and others who took a wide-ranging and synoptic view of the problems and possibilities of political life. Just as the great epic poets – Homer, Hesiod, Virgil, Dante – constructed grand narratives linking man, God and nature into an interconnected whole, so did the greatest political theorists aspire to 'epic' or 'architechtonic' theory which is god-like in the sweep and grandeur of its vision.[38]

If this aim now appears arrogant, or worse, we should remember the political and intellectual context within – and against – which the Berkeley school came into being. In the late 1950s the 'behavioural persuasion' was becoming increasingly prominent in political science. 'Grand theory' was being abandoned in favour of empirically testable 'middle range' theories. And, in the mid-1950s, the so-called 'consensus historians' were writing ideological conflict out of the American past even as the final 'end of ideology' was predicted by American academics associated with the Congress for Cultural Freedom, which itself enjoyed the (covert) financial support of the US Central Intelligence Agency.[39] The battle over political ideas and ideals, they claimed, was ending in the West; and it was only a matter of time until the tide reached Eastern and Soviet shores. The old ideological conflicts were now largely *passé*; eschewing extremes, a new-found, post-ideological consensus was

---

[37] S.S. Wolin, *Politics and Vision: Continuity and Innovation in Western Political Thought* (Boston, 1960), ch. 10.

[38] S.S. Wolin, 'Political Theory as a Vocation', *American Political Science Review*, 63 (1969), pp. 1062–83; Wolin, *Hobbes and the Epic Tradition in Political Theory* (Los Angeles, 1970); N. Jacobson, *Pride and Solace* (Berkeley and Los Angeles, 1978).

[39] See the contributions by Edward Shils, Daniel Bell and others in C. Waxman (ed.), *The End of Ideology Debate* (New York, 1968).

emerging and coalescing around 'the vital centre'.[40] A post-ideological politics of consensus was a pragmatic politics of technique, of the most efficient means to achieve unproblematic and uncontested ends. In this smugly consensual and self-congratulatory climate American-style democracy was declared to be 'the good society itself in operation'.[41]

In such a climate the history of political thought was widely perceived to be more *passé* than ever. Politics was no longer concerned with the competing visions, ideas and ideals described and defended by thinkers long dead. The past was well and truly past, and an interest in the history of political thought must perforce be a largely antiquarian interest in ideas no longer 'relevant' to the present. Students of political theory, who had long had a lively interest in utopian and unorthodox ideas, were admonished to turn away from the dead past and face the realities of a pragmatic present.[42] It was not long before obituaries for utopian thinking began to appear.[43] It was in this funereal atmosphere that Sheldon Wolin prefaced his *Politics and Vision* with a lamentation for the near-dead:

In many intellectual circles today there exists a marked hostility towards, and even contempt for, political philosophy in its traditional form. My hope is that this volume, if it does not give pause to those who are eager to jettison what remains of the tradition of political philosophy, may at least succeed in making clear what it is we shall have discarded.[44]

But political theory, and the history of political thought in particular, was not discarded. It was, like Lazarus, revived and brought back from the dead.

The revival of American political theory in the early 1970s was due to a number of factors outside and inside the academy. The civil rights, anti-Vietnam War and women's movements showed decisively that 'ideas' were not irrelevant and 'ideology' – and political theory – not dead. Quite the contrary, political philosophy flourished even as – and in part because – the ship of the republic rocked in stormy seas. Out of this widespread unease there emerged a large literature on the theory of violent and non-violent protest, civil disobedience, the sources and limits of obligation, and other pressing political concerns. Much of this had a historical slant, as politically engaged scholars re-read Sophocles' *Antigone*, Plato's *Apology* and *Crito*, medieval 'just war' theorists,

[40] A.M. Schlesinger, Jr., *The Vital Center* (Boston, 1949).
[41] S.M. Lipset, *Political Man* (Garden City, NY, 1960), p. 403.
[42] R.A. Dahl, 'Political Theory: Truth and Consequences', *World Politics*, 11 (1956), pp. 89–102.
[43] J. Shklar, *After Utopia* (Princeton, 1957); G. Kateb, *Utopia and its Enemies* (New York, 1963).
[44] Wolin, *Politics and Vision*, p. v.

Thoreau, Gandhi, and other theorists of non-violent resistance.[45] Hardly less important was that the behavioural revolution had largely ended, if not in the revolutionaries' defeat, then at least in a draw: the promise of a 'science' of politics had come a cropper, and some who had been associated with that movement had been discredited because of their complicity – via 'counter-insurgency' research, 'pacification' programmes and the like – in the government's war effort in Vietnam.[46] Logical positivism, which had supplied the philosophical *bona fides* for behaviouralism, had by the late 1960s come under withering attack from philosophers of science and political theorists alike, and was pretty well in tatters.

As the prosecution of the Vietnam War fuelled student protests, many of the protestors and their sympathisers sought guidance from a heretofore disreputable source – the thought of Karl Marx. Theirs was not the scientistic Marx of the rigidly orthodox Soviet variety – what Ernst Bloch once called the 'cold current' of the Marxian stream – but the 'warm current' of Western or 'humanist' or 'critical' Marxism. The 'young' or humanist Marx of the mid-1840s had written about 'alienation' and dehumanisation under capitalism. The mid-1960s to the late 1970s saw a veritable flood of books and articles about Marx and Marxism as well as by and about the 'critical theorists' of the Frankfurt School – Herbert Marcuse, Erich Fromm and others – and prominent twentieth-century neo-Marxists such as Georg Lukács and Antonio Gramsci, existential Marxists, and other varieties.[47]

Marx's presence was felt not only in the numerous books and articles about the thinker and his followers, but also in a recognisably 'Marxist' approach to the history of political thought. This was especially evident in C.B. Macpherson's inquiries into early modern anglophone political thought – that of Hobbes and Locke in particular. In *The Political Theory of Possessive Individualism* (1962) Macpherson espied early capitalist or 'possessive individualist' motivations in both thinkers, whose theoretical arguments aided in the legitimation of the coming capitalist order.[48] Perhaps the best that can be said about Macpherson's approach is that it inspired the more 'historical' refutations and critiques by Keith Thomas

---

[45] See, e.g., M. Walzer, *Obligations* (Cambridge, Mass., 1970) and *Just and Unjust Wars* (New York, 1977); E.M. Zashin, *Civil Disobedience and Democracy* (New York, 1972); R. Flathman, *Political Obligation* (New York, 1972).

[46] See J. Miller, *Democracy is in the Streets* (New York, 1987).

[47] See, respectively, B. Ollmann, *Alienation: Marx's Conception of Man in Capitalist Society* (Cambridge, 1971); M. Jay, *The Dialectical Imagination* (Boston, 1973); J. Miller, *History and Human Existence: From Marx to Merleau-Ponty* (Berkeley and Los Angeles, 1979); M. Poster, *Existential Marxism in Post-war France* (Princeton, 1975).

[48] C.B. Macpherson, *The Political Theory of Possessive Individualism: Hobbes to Locke* (Oxford, 1962).

on Hobbes and Alan Ryan, John Dunn and James Tully on Locke. It bears mention that Macpherson was a Canadian and his most astute critics Canadians and British.

Not that the Americans were all asleep at the switch. There also appeared in the early 1970s several seminal works of first-order political philosophy. The first and most influential was John Rawls's *A Theory of Justice* (1971), followed shortly by Robert Nozick's *Anarchy, State and Utopia* (1974).[49] Both were written by analytically minded philosophers, not by historically minded political theorists. Although one finds in their pages the names of earlier political thinkers – Locke, Rousseau, Hume, Adam Smith, Kant and Mill most notably – these figure mostly act as markers for doctrines whose historical origins and meanings are not called into question. Locke and Kant are treated pretty much as contemporary analytic philosophers and not as historically situated thinkers who faced problems quite unlike our own. Both books spawned an academic 'industry' whose workers were, by and large, hardly more historically minded.[50]

V

The women's movement in North America has had a profound and lasting impact on the way Americans approach the study of many subjects, and not least the history of political thought. A feminist perspective puts issues concerning gender front and centre, and from that vantage point one views the world anew and makes interesting – and by modern lights often appalling – discoveries. Such a sensibility injects a strong strain of scepticism into the study of 'classic' works. For, as Susan Okin observes, 'the great tradition of political philosophy consists, generally speaking, of writings by men, for men, and about men'.[51] To study this tradition from a feminist perspective is to be struck by the extent to which the civic and legal status of women was long considered to be a subject unworthy of theoretical treatment – or perhaps merely beneath the theorists' contempt, and therefore outside the purview of historians of political thought, most of whom happen to be male. The neglect of women in the history of Western (and indeed non-Western) political thought is a silence that, to modern ears, is deafening. Feminist re-readings and reappraisals of the 'canon' of 'classic' works have made, and continue to make, startling and often

---

49 J. Rawls, *A Theory of Justice* (Cambridge, Mass., 1971); R. Nozick, *Anarchy, State and Utopia* (New York, 1974).
50 See, amongst many others, N. Daniels (ed.), *Reading Rawls* (New York, 1975).
51 S.M. Okin, *Women in Western Political Thought* (Princeton, 1979), p. 5.

unsuspected connections between phenomena as apparently disparate as a thinker's view of the family and his (yes, his) view of liberty, authority, power, equality, obligation and other staples in the discourse of political philosophy.

A feminist or gender-centred approach to the history of political thought is not a single, stable thing. It has, on the contrary, gone through several phases. In the first phase, American feminists were looking for a 'usable past', a history that connected present struggles with previous ones largely neglected by historians – including historians of political thought. Feminist historians of political thought sought heroines – and heroes – who had championed the cause of women's rights and related causes. One early anthology included not only selections from Mary Wollstonecraft, Emma Goldman and others, but also a section on 'Men as Feminists', which placed Friedrich Engels, John Stuart Mill and other men in the feminist pantheon.[52] This transgender 'popular front', as it were, sought support from all available quarters.

Several specialised studies of particular thinkers appeared during this brief period. Thinkers who might roughly be labelled as 'liberal' were singled out for special homage. Melissa Butler found the 'liberal roots' of feminism in Locke's 'attack on patriarchalism'.[53] Jeremy Bentham was honoured as 'the father of feminism' and John Stuart Mill as its 'patron saint'.[54] This popular front was short-lived, however, for the father was exposed as a patronising patriarch and something of a misogynist and the patron saint as a closet sinner with feet of clay.[55] The differences between outright misogynists such as Aristotle and Rousseau and their more enlightened liberal brothers were merely matters of degree, not of kind: men will be men. Which is to say, men have heretofore taken (and if permitted, will continue to take) a patronising and patriarchal attitude towards women, putting them on pedestals, in the kitchen or nursery or bedroom, but in any case outside the public or civic sphere in which men move and act politically.[56] In the name of protecting the weak, men have by and large lumped women with children and idiots and have therefore accorded them decidedly less than the rights and obligations of fully-fledged citizens. And nowhere

---

[52] M. Schneir (ed.), *Feminism: the Essential Historical Writings* (New York, 1972).

[53] M.A. Butler, 'Early Liberal Roots of Feminism: John Locke and the Attack on Patriarchy', *American Political Science Review*, 72 (1978), pp. 135–50.

[54] M. Williford, 'Bentham on the Rights of Women', *Journal of the History of Ideas*, 36 (1975), pp. 167–76.

[55] Okin, *Women*, ch. 9; C. Pateman, *The Sexual Contract* (Stanford, CT, 1988) and *The Disorder of Women* (Stanford, CT, 1989).

[56] J.B. Elshtain, *Public Man, Private Woman* (Princeton, 1981).

are these nefarious moves more evident than in the so-called classics of political thought.

In this second, angrier – and arguably more accurate – phase, feminist scholars set out to expose and criticise the misogyny that occasionally leered from, but more often lurked in, the works of Plato, Aristotle, Machiavelli, Hobbes, Locke, Rousseau, Bentham, Mill and Marx, amongst many others. The public/private dichotomy and the concept of consent in liberal theory are a sham, the social contract a 'fraternal' construct, and the modern welfare state a decidedly patriarchal institution.[57] Not only are misogyny and patriarchy present in the history of political thought; they can be found in histories of political thought written by Wolin and other males whose interpretations of (say) Locke reproduce the latter's sexism by failing to detect or criticise its presence.[58]

A third phase followed in which the ostensibly civic virtues of men were turned into vices – the hunger for power, domination or simply showing off – that women singularly lacked. Men are domineering, women nurturing; men competitive, women co-operative; men think and judge in abstract and universal categories, women in concrete and particular instances; and so on. A new phrase – 'maternal thinking' – was coined to cover this gently militant momism.[59] On this view, men are absent fathers and domineering patriarchs; women are caring and concerned mothers speaking 'in a different voice'.[60] This represents something of a return to the 'biology-is-destiny' essentialism and 'functionalism' criticised so vigorously by Okin and others. It also accepts the public/private distinction criticised by Pateman and others, upending and reifying that dichotomy so that the 'private' realm of the family is taken to be superior to the 'public' area of politics, power, aggression and war.[61] Thus was Aristotle turned on his head, and *Antigone* re-read as a heroic defence of the family against an aggressive and anti-familial political realm.[62]

The new 'maternal thinking' – and the new maternalists' approach to the history of political thought, in particular – did not want for critics. Against the maternalists' valorisation of the private realm and the celebration of mothering, these critics held out the prospect of an active and engaged civic feminism, or 'citizenship with a feminist face'.[63] This

[57] Pateman, *Disorder*, chs. 2, 4, 6, 8.
[58] Ibid., ch. 5.
[59] S. Ruddick, *Maternal Thinking: Toward a Politics of Peace* (Boston, 1989).
[60] C. Gilligan, *In a Different Voice* (Cambridge, Mass., 1982).
[61] J.B. Elshtain, *Women and War* (New York, 1987).
[62] J.B. Elshtain (ed.), *The Family in Political Thought* (Amherst, Mass., 1982).
[63] M.G. Dietz, 'Citizenship with a Feminist Face: the Problem with Maternal Thinking', *Political Theory*, 13, 1 (1985), pp. 19–37.

prospect is precluded, or at least dimmed considerably, by inadequate interpretations of Aristotle and other seminal figures from whom feminists might yet learn something of value about politics and citizenship. A 'more generous reading' of Aristotle, Sophocles and others yields political insights and civic lessons that a cartoon-like inversion cannot hope to match. If feminists are to learn and apply these lessons, they must engage in more nuanced textual analysis and historical interpretation. The Western political tradition is not reducible to an abattoir or a sink-hole of misogyny and other vices; it can, despite its shortcomings and when properly understood, be an invaluable source of political wisdom, even – or perhaps especially – for feminists.[64]

Not the least of the considerable contributions made by feminist historians of political thought have been some striking reappraisals and reinterpretations of canonical thinkers.[65] No less valuable has been their role in the rediscovery, recovery and republication of overlooked and long-neglected women political thinkers, including Christine de Pizan, Mary Astell and Mary Wollstonecraft.

The women's liberation movement was followed shortly by the black, gay and lesbian liberation movements and a sometimes militant turn towards 'multiculturalism'. The curricula in American universities were either enriched or gravely threatened, depending on one's point of view, by the multicultural turn in the 1980s. Roughly, the argument in favour of a more multicultural approach amounted to this: the curriculum has for too long consisted of a 'canon' of works by 'dead white heterosexual European males'. It is high time to correct this oversight by omitting, or at least pushing to the margin, these works and thereby making more central works by women, gay men, lesbians, people of colour (i.e. non-whites generally) and other previously marginalised groups. By decentring the older conventional 'canon' and including these heretofore excluded voices we become aware of the richness and diversity of other, non-white, non-male perspectives on politics and allied areas.

As regards the writing and teaching of the history of political theory, the difficulties were both numerous and intractable. I have noted already the challenges that feminist scholars have posed. The challenge is further broadened when we add race and sexual preference to the criteria for selecting 'acceptable' authors. How then to teach, and write about, the history of political thought? The first – and by far the crudest – answer is that we should not consider seriously, much less teach, the political thought of 'misogynist', 'patriarchal' and perhaps 'racist' and

---

[64] Ibid., p. 29.
[65] M.L. Shanley and C. Pateman (eds.), *Feminist Interpretations and Political Theory* (Cambridge, 1991).

'homophobic' thinkers. But again the difficulty is evident: although we know the race and sex of (say) Plato and Aristotle, we have no way of knowing their sexual preference (much less what difference, if any, it might have made in their ways of thinking about politics).[66] Whatever his sexual preference, Plato wrote sympathetically (in the *Symposium*) about same-sex relations. And although Aristotle has little to say about these matters, he was something of a provincial – from Stagira, in northern Greece, and thus a metic, or resident alien, in Athens – and, probably, a heterosexual who was either amused or shocked by upper-class Athenian mores in these matters. But, granted even that bit of speculative licence, we would be on very shaky ground indeed if we tried to trace (much less reduce) the whole of his political philosophy to that biographical fact.

That 'white' authors are over-represented in the history of Western political thought is surely significant and easily explainable: until relatively recently, non-whites did not live in Europe, and the vast majority of black Africans in North America were until 1865 slaves, almost all of whom were illiterate. For every Frederick Douglass there were a thousand black slaves kept illiterate and ignorant by their white masters. Modern multiculturalists are surely right to remind Americans of this shameful fact. What then to do with the political thought of (say) Thomas Jefferson – a brilliant and articulate champion of human liberty, a critic of slavery, and himself the owner of more than two hundred black slaves? Should we overlook his shortcomings? Ignore him entirely? Expose his evident hypocrisy? Or mention him merely to chastise him and denigrate his thinking about matters political? How ought Americans now regard the author of their most sacred text, the Declaration of Independence? Multiculturalism was, and remains, a moral and intellectual minefield.

My own view is that the longer-term consequences of walking in this minefield are all to the good. We Americans do ourselves no favours by ignoring the seamier aspects of our history. And all the more so, since the consequences are with us still. Any adequate history of political thought – Western, European, American or whatever – must henceforth consider the ugly and the beautiful, the vices as well as the virtues. Only then can the history of political thought be genuinely historical, which is to say, truthful, insofar as we are able to discern and tell the truth. And, as that dead white English male John Stuart Mill famously put it, the

---

[66] John Searle has proposed the following thought-experiment. Suppose we were to discover that Plato was actually an Asian woman. What difference would – or should – that discovery make in the way we read and understand *The Republic* or any of Plato's other works?

cause of truth is best served by criticising the conventional wisdom. Challenges from all quarters – multiculturalism, 'queer' studies, subaltern studies – ought to be welcome.

The point is perhaps well illustrated by the sensation caused by Martin Bernal's *Black Athena: the Afroasiatic Roots of Classical Civilisation* (1987). Bernal contends that classical Greek thought was largely borrowed (or, as some Afrocentric scholars claim, 'stolen') from African and Asian sources. Therefore the 'genius of the West' and indeed the very idea of 'Western civilisation' itself is a non-starter.[67] Mary Lefkowitz and other critics have gone to great lengths to show the shakiness of the grounds upon which Bernal constructs his arguments, and the uses to which they have been put by Afrocentric scholars.[68] But who can doubt that this controversy, heated as it is, has made classical studies all the livelier and more interesting, not to say brought us closer to the truth? So it is as well with the recent work of Henry Louis Gates, Jr. and many other African-American scholars, of Froma Zeitlin and other feminist scholars, of the late gay scholar John Winkler, and others who approach 'the classics' from one or another subaltern standpoint.

The value of these varied approaches to the history of political thought is potentially very great indeed. To borrow a distinction drawn by Hans Reichenbach, the 'context of discovery' is wide open – claims and hypotheses can come from anywhere and (as Paul Feyerabend put it) 'anything goes' – but the 'context of justification' is rather more restricted. The unorthodox and unconventional perspectives brought by members of marginalised groups ought to be welcome. For they enrich and expand the context of discovery even as they are subjected to the stringent requirements of scholarly argument, evidence and justification.

VI

Of the various approaches to the study of political thought, perhaps the stiffest evidentiary challenges are faced by psychoanalytic interpretations. Psychoanalytic approaches to the history of political thought have been neither numerous nor notably influential. Erik Erikson's psychobiographical studies of Luther (1958) and Gandhi (1969) were widely read by the larger public, but little note was taken by historians of

[67] M. Bernal, *Black Athena: the Afroasiatic Roots of Classical Civilisation* (New Brunswick, 1987).

[68] M.R. Lefkowitz, *Not Out of Africa: How 'Afrocentrism' Became an Excuse to Teach Myth as History* (New York, 1996); M.R. Lefkowitz and G.M. Rogers (eds.), *Black Athena Revisited* (Chapel Hill, Ill., 1996).

political thought. Bruce Mazlish ventured bravely, if none too success-fully, into this territory with a psychobiography of James and John Stuart Mill, and a subsequent study of such 'revolutionary ascetics' as Cromwell, Robespierre, Lenin and Mao Zedong.[69] Mazlish saw the younger Mill as locked in an Oedipal struggle with his father who, he feared, had 'made' or 'manufactured' him in the elder Mill's own image. The twenty-year-old John Stuart Mill's 'mental crisis' was the product of, and the beginning of a solution to, his ambivalent feelings towards his father. Much, if not indeed most, of the younger Mill's mature writings – including *On Liberty* and *The Subjection of Women* – reflect the working-out of these feelings. More than that, the more shocking episodes in his personal life – particularly his open and scandalous liaison with, and subsequent marriage to, Mrs Taylor – can be similarly explained. Was not his father's wife, and thus his own mother, named Harriet? Was not Mrs Taylor also named Harriet? Did not John Stuart Mill therefore symbolically 'defeat' his father by marrying his own mother? Indeed, the incest theme can be carried still further, for J.S. Mill also had a younger sister named Harriet. By psychoanalytic lights, this is strong stuff. A more prosaic 'historical' approach might merely lead one to note that Harriet was a very popular name in nineteenth-century Britain, and no 'deeper' meaning need be sought or inferred.

Perhaps the two most notable and sophisticated attempts to psycho-analyse long-dead political thinkers were Isaac Kramnick's *The Rage of Edmund Burke* (1977) and Hanna Pitkin's *Fortune is a Woman* (1984). Kramnick takes careful note of the psychological pressures to which Burke was subjected by his outsider status: an Irishman in English politics, a commoner in the service of the aristocratic Marquis of Rock-ingham, a kept intellectual who had to defer repeatedly to his intellectual inferiors – all of which resulted in a 'rage' subtly if not always success-fully sublimated in an identifiably Burkean political philosophy.[70] Kram-nick, a sophisticated and prolific historian of eighteenth-century political thought, was careful not to press his case too far or to make too much of his findings, which he presents as suggestive and illuminating if not causally explanatory.

Pitkin's *Fortune is a Woman* – subtitled 'Gender and Politics in the Thought of Niccolò Machiavelli' – was informed both by psychoanalytic and feminist theory.[71] She takes her title from Machiavelli's infamous

[69] B. Mazlish, *James and John Stuart Mill: Father and Son in the Nineteenth Century* (New York, 1975) and *The Revolutionary Ascetic* (New York, 1976).

[70] I. Kramnick, *The Rage of Edmund Burke* (New York, 1977).

[71] H.F. Pitkin, *Fortune is a Woman: Gender and Politics in the Thought of Niccolò Machiavelli* (Berkeley and Los Angeles, 1984).

remark in *The Prince* (ch. 25) that 'Fortune is a woman, and the man who wants to hold her down must beat and bully her.' This misogynist sentiment supplies Pitkin with a point of entry into Machiavelli's mind and character, formed early in childhood, and carried over into his identity as an adult. Machiavelli the man was not whole, healthy and integrated; his personality was fractured and fragile, exhibiting a profoundly 'ambivalent' view of politics, citizenship and masculinity. A less 'psychological' and more 'historical' reading, as critics were quick to note, would show that the powerful Roman deity, Fortuna, was a woman – a goddess, indeed – and that Machiavelli's view of what is required to 'tame' her (if only temporarily) was wholly unoriginal and hardly unique to him, being something of a commonplace amongst earlier writers. Hence the details of Machiavelli's upbringing (suckling, weaning, toilet-training, etc.) that are apt to interest a psychoanalyst are neither necessary nor sufficient to account for political views that he articulated as an adult.

Although sometimes insightful, psychoanalytic interpretations are open to an array of criticisms – that they are speculative, impressionistic, non-falsifiable and so on – and it is perhaps these real or supposed shortcomings that account for the scepticism with which American (and other) historians of political thought have received them.

A rather different approach to textual questions is taken by the so-called 'new historians' of the 'Cambridge school' – Peter Laslett, Quentin Skinner, John Dunn and others – who, however, have met with some resistance in the United States. Their aim of recovering the original intentions of authors long dead and the 'historical identity' of their works has met with strong resistance from Straussians, the 'epic theorists' of the Berkeley school and assorted postmodernists, amongst others. There are, however, at least two notable exceptions to this rule. The first is J.G.A. Pocock, a transplanted New Zealander, who might be described as a fellow-traveller of the Cambridge school. In *The Machiavellian Moment* and other works Pocock traces the lineage of an 'Atlantic republican tradition' through its various guises and phases from Machiavelli to Harrington to the American founding. It is a dense and difficult book, baroque in its prose and sometimes oracular in its assertions; but it is for all that an original and occasionally brilliant book. Pocock charts changes and continuities in an identifiably republican *mentalité* that gives pride of place to the concept of time (conceived as a cyclical, not linear, process) and its role in the decay, destruction and reconstitution of republics. With his focus on temporality Pocock brings a wide array of apparently disparate phenomena into a more connected and coherent focus, enabling modern students of political thought to make sense of what might otherwise appear nonsensical or opaque.

Richard Ashcraft, once an acolyte of the Berkeley school, was at the time of his too-early death in 1995 the most unabashed American advocate of the 'new history' of political thought. His *Revolutionary Politics and Locke's 'Two Treatises of Government'* (1986) largely succeeds in its author's attempt to restore the political context in which Locke thought, wrote and acted.[72] Locke is revealed as a much more radical thinker than the standard 'liberal' interpretation recognises. More revealing of Ashcraft's own historiographical views is a little-known essay (1983), an angry and patricidal polemic written in his most caustic prose.[73] He likens students of his generation to 'privates' who were trained to be blindly obedient to the 'generals' – a thinly veiled reference to Wolin and other leading lights of the Berkeley school – who ordered them to attack the bastions of behavioural social science. Instead of teaching their students to be careful historians and sound scholars, these generals fed them fictions about an imaginary glorious cause they called 'epic theory' and an evil foe they called behaviouralism. Thus were the talents of a generation of young soldier-scholars squandered in futile battle. Ashcraft saw the methodological rigour of the Cambridge historians as an antidote to the ahistorical bent of the Berkeley school. A bracing dose of the new history will enable one to see clearly what the bay fog of Berkeley had long obscured: political theory is neither myth nor epic, but *political* theory, thought enlisted in this or that partisan cause, ideas immersed in the din and blood of battle.[74]

---

[72] R. Ashcraft, *Revolutionary Politics and Locke's 'Two Treatises of Government'* (Princeton, 1986).

[73] R. Ashcraft, 'One Step Backward, Two Steps Forward: Reflections upon Contemporary Political Theory', in J.S. Nelson (ed.), *What Should Political Theory Be Now?* (Albany, N.Y., 1983), pp. 515–48.

[74] Whether this is a fair criticism of the Berkeley school is surely open to question. For one, the 'school' was hardly monolithic; its faculty had diverse but complementary interests. Behaviouralism was but one of Wolin's many interests; Schaar and Jacobson were interested mainly, though not exclusively, in the history of American political thought; Rogin began as a student of modern American politics and became a leading figure in literary and cultural approaches to political theory; Pitkin was interested in applying 'linguistic' analysis (and later psychoanalysis) to problems in political theory. Moreover, the charge that the Berkeley school was somehow apolitical is clearly false. For example, Schaar's first book, *Loyalty in America* (1957), was inspired by the McCarthy-era loyalty-oath controversy at the University of California and elsewhere; Rogin's first book, *The Intellectuals and McCarthy* (1967), dealt with the same phenomenon from another angle; Pitkin's early essay on 'Obligation and Consent' (1965–6) was a critical-conceptual analysis of an increasingly urgent moral and political question. And, not least, the Berkeley theorists actively supported student dissidents during the Free Speech Movement of 1964, earning them the everlasting enmity of many of their more conservative colleagues.

Another approach, inspired in part by the Cambridge new historians and in part by the German school of *Begriffsgeschichte* ('conceptual history'),[75] emphasises the mutable meanings of political concepts. Conceptual history is not etymology, but, rather, the history of concepts in the changing contexts of their deployment in political argument. The concepts constitutive of political discourse – freedom, justice, power, property, equality, etc. – are also perforce partially constitutive of political life. These concepts have histories; their meanings change over time and as a result of contestations over their meaning. Who and what we are, how we arrange and classify and think about – and therefore act in – our world, are deeply delimited by the argumentative and rhetorical resources of the language we speak. But language – and political language in particular – changes. Changes in meaning can come about deliberately or accidentally. The task of the conceptual historian is to chart these changes and the actions and practices that brought them about.

In *Transforming Political Discourse* I attempted to defend and illustrate a conceptual-historical approach to the history of political thought.[76] Another work by many hands, *Political Innovation and Conceptual Change*, is a wide-ranging historical survey of key concepts – 'constitution', 'democracy', 'the state', 'representation', 'party', 'patriotism', 'public interest' and others.[77] And *Conceptual Change and the Constitution* attempts to apply the methods of conceptual history to the understanding of the US Constitution.[78] It is as yet too early to say how this approach will fare in the American academy.

VII

I turn, finally, to 'postmodern' approaches to the history of political thought. It would of course be a mistake to lump together all who call themselves postmodernists. There are important differences between those who follow in Foucault's footsteps and those who owe allegiance to Derrida and deconstruction. In their approach to the history of political thought, the former eschew 'history' in favour of 'genealogy' in something like Nietzsche's sense of that term. The latter, by contrast,

---

[75] For a useful explication of *Begriffsgeschichte*, see M. Richter, *The History of Political and Social Concepts* (Oxford, 1995).

[76] T. Ball, *Transforming Political Discourse: Political Theory and Critical Conceptual History* (Oxford, 1988).

[77] T. Ball, J. Farr and R.L. Hanson (eds.), *Political Innovation and Conceptual Change* (Cambridge, 1989).

[78] T. Ball and J.G.A. Pocock (eds.), *Conceptual Change and the Constitution* (Lawrence, Kans., 1988).

emphasise the deconstructive 'reading' of 'texts' in order to reveal their multiple and unstable meanings. Both approaches are alike, however, in several important senses. The first is that both focus on 'the project of modernity' launched by the thinkers of the Enlightenment and the importance of getting beyond the stifling limitations of that project (hence the term *post*modernism). This concern informs and perhaps indeed dominates postmodern approaches to the history of political thought. Everything is filtered through the lens of 'modernity'. Thus, despite their professed hostility to grand, sweeping 'metanarratives' – e.g. the Hegelian or Marxian philosophies of history – many postmodernists nevertheless invoke their own large and amorphous categories, constructed in hindsight, to classify and criticise earlier thinkers. This or that thinker is said to have contributed to 'the Englightenment project' or 'the project of modernity'. It matters not that these earlier thinkers did not, and indeed could not, have intended to contribute to 'projects' of which they were wholly unaware. What matters is that we can now see what they have wrought: for Foucauldian genealogists, the bureaucratised and routinised modern 'surveillance society' in which subjects are 'disciplined' and reduced to 'docile bodies' or objects of scientific study and analysis. For Derridean deconstructionists, the legacy is 'logocentrism' and 'the metaphysics of presence' – our tendency to think (mistakenly) that denotative language consists of stable signs or 'signifiers' that can call forth or 'represent' some equally stable entity beyond themselves.[79]

Both sorts of postmodernists also place considerable emphasis on 'reading' books, or rather, 'texts' from the vantage-point of the present. What the long-dead author of a text might have meant or intended to do merits little or no attention. The 'death of the author' does not refer to a biological fact, but to an artefact of postmodernist interpretation. What matters most is what a text means to the reader, with his or her own modern (or postmodern) preoccupations and concerns. In this sense the text is not a stable entity; its meaning or message changes over time and varies from one reader to another. A postmodern reading further destabilises the text by revealing its omissions or silences – what it does not say – and attending to the ambiguity of language. This ambiguity only increases with the passage of time and different readings, until – as Derrida famously puts it – a text's signifiers float freely and playfully apart.[80]

---

[79] See Quentin Skinner's contribution to the present volume.

[80] I must confess that this conjures, for me, the delightful image of bathers/readers batting brightly coloured beach-balls/signifiers floating freely in a sea of indeterminacy, playing a game without rules or referees in which any move is permissible and every player

The first[81] of these two postmodern approaches is well represented by William Connolly's *Political Theory and Modernity*. Connolly begins with the genial suggestion that one views earlier thinkers as collegial contemporaries residing down the hall from one's office. To read their works is like dropping by for a friendly chat.[82] (This is perhaps the amiably unbuttoned postmodern-egalitarian equivalent of Machiavelli's 'entering the ancient courts of ancient men', minus the Florentine's somewhat stringent dress code.) The reader's questions are posed, and criticisms made, from the perspective of the present – that is, of 'modernity' and the constitution of the modern 'subject'. Given this set of concerns we can now re-read the history of political thought in a new and presumably more fruitful way. That is, we can see who has contributed to or dissented from the project of constructing the modern surveillance society. A postmodernist re-reading relocates and realigns earlier thinkers along altogether different axes. A postmodernist reading of the history of political thought not only exposes heretofore unsuspected villains; it also reveals heroes who have dared to resist the pressures and processes of 'normalisation'. Amongst the former are Hobbes and Rousseau. That the historical Rousseau was exceedingly critical of the historical Hobbes does not matter for a postmodernist reading. For we can now see them as birds of a feather, each having extended 'the gaze' ever more deeply into the inner recesses of the human psyche, thereby aiding and abetting the subjugation of modern men and women. Amongst the latter, the Marquis de Sade and Friedrich Nietzsche are particularly prominent. 'We can', as Connolly contends, 'treat Sade as a dissident thinker whose positive formulations are designed to crack the foundations upon which the theories of Hobbes and Rousseau rest.'[83] Whether this design was consciously formulated and put into play by the aristocratic French pornographer is, at best, doubtful; but like other postmodernist interpreters Connolly eschews any concern with such historical niceties as authorial intention or with such petty logical questions as whether the reader might have committed the fallacy of *post hoc, ergo propter hoc*.

Despite their emphasis on 'identity' and 'difference', postmodernists

---

equally adroit. Since I am confessing I must also admit that the bubble bursts and my delight disappears when I bring this fantasy to bear on the reading of texts in political theory.

[81] Unfortunately, limitations on space preclude any discussion of the second or Derridian variant of postmodernism as found, for example, in Linda Zerilli's *Signifying Woman: Culture and Chaos in Rousseau, Burke and Mill* (1994) or Michael Shapiro's *Reading 'Adam Smith'* (1993).

[82] W.E. Connolly, *Political Theory and Modernity* (Oxford, 1988), p. vii.

[83] Connolly, *Political Theory*, p. 73.

are not at all concerned with what John Dunn has termed the 'historical identity' of works of political theory; nor are they concerned with the differences that earlier thinkers saw amongst themselves. Rousseau hardly saw himself as Hobbes's soulmate – quite the contrary, on Rousseau's own telling – but this does not deter postmodernists from lumping them together as fellow labourers on and contributors to a common project. Whether, or to what extent, such second-guessing is good history or bad remains a matter of considerable controversy.

I do not mean to suggest that postmodernism – or any of the other approaches I have discussed here – is misguided, mistaken or otherwise illegitimate. Quite the contrary, a postmodernist reading, like any other, can often be illuminating, leading us to see older works in a new and very different light. A plurality of interpretative voices is surely preferable to a hegemonic monologue. The danger arises when one voice, be it in a postmodernist or any other register, is believed to be the only, or the best, voice in what is or ought to be a chorus – or, better perhaps, a cacophony – of contending voices.

Robert Wokler

Introduction

The subject I mean to address here is the institutionalisation of political
thought in English universities in the twentieth century, and the establishment of its various identities, in the light of the most notable
professorial appointments which have been made in that field. In
seeking to identify an academic discipline's scope and trajectory by way
of the careers of scholars entrusted to define its purpose, I shall not at
the same time attempt to provide a historiographical survey of the major
writings devoted to it throughout this period, nor shall I consider the
ways in which political theorists in England interpreted their civic
culture or national crises. The differences between the themes pursued
in this chapter and those devoted to French and German political
thought may no doubt be partly characterised as differences of national
style, in so far as the extra-curricular prominence of intellectuals and of
their fashionable doctrines in France, and of ideological and bureaucratic regimes in Germany, lend themselves well to treatments of the
circulation of texts, on the one hand, and the social dimensions of
power, on the other. But I do not in these remarks wish to emphasise
such contrasts, since I have no doubt that there is ample scope for
textological or social scientific studies of English political thought in the
twentieth century, and room too for curricular histories of French and
German universities.

If I have here confined my subject to professorial appointments, it is
mainly because I believe that by this parochial route I can, in the limited
space available, trace both the birth and rise of the study of political
thought as a genuinely academic discipline in England in the course of

I am indebted to two anonymous commentators and grateful to both Dario Castiglione
and Iain Hampsher-Monk for various suggestions offered in the course of my revision of
this essay. For providing me with first-hand confirmation of Berlin's assessment of
Plamenatz, as reported here, I am also grateful to Gerry Cohen, the only holder of any
of the chairs at issue who has read this text before its publication.

its own practitioners' self-reflection in their choice of topics they believed that they were hired to teach. Professorial appointments often occasion debate about the nature of academic subjects, never more than when they are made to newly created chairs, with their attendant revisions of a syllabus, curriculum and examination papers. They carry seminal significance in mapping the anticipated future of a course of study and shed a special light upon it through which textological or social scientific interpretations of it can be filtered. They also indisputably reflect and diffuse the influence of these and other perspectives, which in each case, and hence for each chapter of this work, are at least as much matters of personal preference as of national style.

I thus propose to deal with the first holders of the main chairs of political thought in England, with the circumstances surrounding their appointments, their professions of what they took to be the subjects of their discipline, and the diverse institutional settings in which those subjects were nurtured and promoted in the teaching and training of several generations of students. Even in adopting this contextually delimited approach to my topic, I can only hope to carry conviction by entering into sufficient detail, that is, by being selective. With due deference, therefore, to pioneering studies and courses in political theory and the history of political thought launched at the universities of Exeter, Hull, Sheffield[1] and elsewhere, and mindful perhaps above all of the immense contribution made by Bill Mackenzie and his followers in the Department of Government which he inaugurated at the University of Manchester,[2] I should like here to consider three chairs in particular which, it seems to me, have shaped the directions taken by political thought in England more conspicuously than any others: the chairs of political science at the London School of Economics and at Cambridge, and the Chichele Chair of Social and Political Theory at Oxford.[3]

[1] By which I principally have in mind, in the first instance, the contribution made jointly by Janet Coleman, now at the London School of Economics, and Iain Hampsher-Monk in their launch and continuing editorship of the journal *History of Political Thought*; in the second instance, the work of W.H. Greenleaf, Robert Berki and Bhiku Parekh; and in the third instance, the writings and teaching of Howard Warrender and Bernard Crick.

[2] W.J.M. Mackenzie (1909–96) had first been a classics don at Magdalen College, Oxford, before changing to politics in 1936. In 1948 he was appointed Professor of Government and Adminstration at the University of Manchester, where he built up one of the largest departments of governnment or politics in the United Kingdom before returning to his native Scotland, in 1966, by way of the James Bryce Chair of Government at the University of Glasgow. It has been suggested that more professors of political science owed their initial appointment to him than to any other academic figure in the English-speaking world on this side of the Atlantic.

[3] For a comprehensive list of the incumbents of these chairs, see the appendix. In a recent essay on 'Contextual and Non-Contextual Histories of Political Thought', in Jack Hayward, Brian Barry and Archie Brown (eds.), *The British Study of Politics in the*

While the academic environment with which we are all too well acquainted today has no timeless significance, some of its currently most conspicuous features might nevertheless have seemed familiar to students of more remote epochs of the history of higher education, not only in Britain but on the mainland of Europe as well. Almost two hundred and fifty years ago Adam Smith contrived to take early retirement from his chair of moral philosophy at Glasgow in order to embark on *The Wealth of Nations*, perhaps having learned from his predecessor at Glasgow, Francis Hutcheson, who, on his own testimony, ceased after his appointment to produce work of such quality as had originally drawn him to the notice of his electors.[4] Alasdair MacIntyre, I believe, undermines his own case against what he has termed the *Enlightenment Project* when he commends the electors of the chair of moral philosophy at the University of Edinburgh in 1745 for turning down the application of David Hume,[5] since the subversive voice of cosmopolitan enlightenment that MacIntyre so much deplores might well have been silenced if Hume had conscientiously accepted the burdens of academic office encased within a straitjacket of a prescribed syllabus.

By way of official pensions and censorship, there were in the eighteenth century institutions and practices of a kind that would later provide warrant and sanctions for the research assessment exercises to which higher education is now so often prey, nowhere more conspicuously than in France, where the Faculty of Theology of the Sorbonne attempted to ban the *Encyclopédie* and later succeeded in prohibiting the sale or distribution of Helvétius's *De l'esprit* in 1758 and Rousseau's *Contrat social* in 1762. In an age when students paid their lecturers piecemeal, there were also teaching quality assessment exercises which effectively expressed consumer choice – at both Oxford and Cambridge sometimes articulated with remorseless disrespect of tutors, if their stagnant conversation with respect to 'college business . . . and private scandal' extinguished the hopes of such young sparks as Adam Smith or Edward Gibbon. 'The schools of Oxford and Cambridge . . . founded in a dark age of false and barbarous science . . . are still tainted with the vices of their origin,' remarked Gibbon in his autobiography, lamenting that professors at Oxford had for many years given up 'even the pretense

Twentieth Century (Oxford, 1999), ch. 2, pp. 37–62, P.J. Kelly focuses his attention on the contributions of the same professoriate, in his case with respect to the second generation in Oxford and London and the third generation in Cambridge, whereas here I concentrate mainly upon the first generation in each instance.

[4] See my 'Projecting the Enlightenment', in John Horton and Susan Mendus (eds.), *After MacIntyre* (Cambridge, 1994), p. 119.

[5] See MacIntyre's *Whose Justice? Which Rationality?* (London, 1988), pp. 286–7, and *Three Rival Versions of Moral Enquiry* (London, 1990), p. 224.

of teaching' and that the worst of his college tutors remembered the salaries they were owed but not the duties of their employment.[6] At least one of the reasons underlying the great flourishing of the five Scottish universities of the eighteenth century (at a time when England had only two) was the clerical hegemony and intellectual impoverishment which prevailed throughout the universities of England and France, driving such men as Smith, James Mill and Benjamin Constant to seek a better system of formal education in Scotland.[7] If the Enlightenment took root more deeply in France than elsewhere in eighteenth-century Europe, this was due in no small measure to the fact that most of its great luminaries were free spirits of independent means, either self-employed or sponsored by a patron or society, not subject to academic scrutiny or discipline.

In the course of the French Revolution and then throughout the nineteenth century, the worlds of higher education in France and England in particular were radically transformed, by the establishment of the *Institut national*, the *Grandes écoles* and the Napoleonic curriculum, on the one hand, and, on the other, by the creation of new civic universities in both countries, with different statutes and priorities. In part to appeal to new entrants, in part to escape political interference in the management of their internal affairs, Oxford and Cambridge underwent substantial reform as well, as clergymen were progressively transformed into dons and fresh academic disciplines began to acquire something approximating their current form and professorial appointments.[8] Chairs of modern history came to be established at both universities; the school of *Literæ humaniores* or 'Greats' in Oxford came to acquire a more philosophical focus with less emphasis on classical languages; a moral sciences tripos was created in Cambridge in 1851; and under the influence of such men as Freeman, Green and Jowett in Oxford, and of the likes of Seeley, Sidgwick and Marshall in Cambridge, the human sciences, including the study of politics, for the first time at

---

[6] For Gibbon's account of the indolence and prejudice of his Oxford tutors, see his *Autobiography*, edited by M.M. Reese (London, 1970), pp. 30–5.

[7] See ch. 1 ('The System of the North: Dugald Stewart and his Pupils') in Stefan Collini, Donald Winch and John Burrow, *That Noble Science of Politics* (Cambridge, 1983), pp. 23–61, and C.P. Courtney, 'An Eighteenth-Century Education: Benjamin Constant at Erlangen and Edinburgh (1782–1785)', in Marian Hobson, J.T.A. Leigh and Robert Wokler (eds.), *Rousseau and the Eighteenth Century* (Oxford, 1992), pp. 295–324.

[8] See especially A.J. Engel, *From Clergyman to Don: the Rise of the Academic Profession in Nineteenth-Century Oxford* (Oxford, 1983); Sheldon Rothblatt, *The Revolution of the Dons: Cambridge and Society in Victorian England* (London, 1968); and Rothblatt, 'The Academic Role', in *Tradition and Change in English Liberal Education* (London, 1976), pp. 174–94.

these two ancient establishments, came to acquire the status of properly accredited academic disciplines.[9]

The good and 'Greats' of Oxford

For my purposes here, the influence of the school of *Literæ humaniores* in Oxford is vital. The first professors of political thought at London, Cambridge and Oxford each read 'Greats' when they were students at Oxford, and in widely different ways they all reacted to the political ethos which informed its syllabus and style of teaching, as shaped above all by Benjamin Jowett, the Regius Professor of Greek and distinguished editor and translator of Plato, Vice-Chancellor of the University and Master of Balliol from 1870 to 1893. Under his guidance, Balliol's lofty pursuit of a life of the mind turned round a meticulous reading of the classics which had as its principal aim the fostering of a spirit, and preparation for the duties, of public office and service. To Florence Nightingale Jowett confided, only half in jest, that he would like to govern the world through his pupils,[10] which in a sense he accomplished through the Balliol political culture over which he presided, breeding, as it did, several generations of viceroys of India (including Lords Lansdowne and Curzon), not to mention Prime Minister Asquith. When Jowett and his successor, Edward Caird, reigned in Balliol, Oxford was truly, as it has been described, the great finishing school of the British Empire for pupils who had passed out of Eton.[11]

As the philosophical component of 'Greats' grew at the expense of its treatment of ancient literature, pressure was mounted by tutors both within the school and outside it to make it more accessible to students untrained in classics, and around the turn of the twentieth century the reformers began to advocate the establishment of a new school at Oxford, cast in the image of 'Greats' but addressed to more contemporary subjects. Ernest Barker, a Lancashire lad who after attending the

---

[9] On the establishment of chairs of modern history at Oxford and Cambridge, see especially Reba Sofer, 'Nation, Duty, Character and Confidence: History at Oxford, 1850–1914', *Historical Journal*, 30, 1 (1987), pp. 77–104, and Peter R.H. Slee, *Learning and Liberal Education: the Study of Modern History in the Universities of Oxford, Cambridge and Manchester, 1800–1914* (Manchester, 1986). On the subject of 'Greats' and its prominence at Oxford in the late nineteenth century, see especially Richard S. Symonds, *Oxford and Empire: the Last Lost Cause?* (London, 1986). On the moral sciences tripos and the academic study of politics at Cambridge, see chs. 10 and 11 ('Polity and Society in Marshall's Economics' and 'Political Science at Cambridge'), in Collini et al., *That Noble Science of Politics*, pp. 309–63.

[10] On Jowett and Nightingale, see Symonds, 'Prophets, Classics and Philosopher Kings', ch. 2 of *Oxford and Empire*, pp. 27–9.

[11] See Symonds, *Oxford and Empire*, ch. 2, p. 35.

Manchester Grammar School obtained a double first in both 'Greats' and modern history, came to promote just such ideals from the various posts he held in the Modern History Faculty at Oxford from 1897, and later his initiative was transformed into a campaign for 'Greats' without Greek and then 'Modern Greats', pursued along somewhat different lines, most notably by Sandie Lindsay, a Scot who had himself read 'Greats' at Oxford by way of the Glasgow Academy and subsequently took up a tutorial fellowship in 'Greats' at Balliol College in 1906. The scheme for a new school of 'Greats' without Greek failed in 1911, but by 1920 Lindsay and his associates had succeeded in establishing their programme of 'Modern Greats', that is, the now familiar school of philosophy, politics and economics, or PPE.[12]

In the course of these endeavours, highlighting academic needs which Oxford appeared unready to meet, it was agreed that a new chair of politics should be created, and this was duly achieved in 1912 with the establishment of the Gladstone Chair of Political Theory and Institutions, which by virtue of its title might well have become the first chair of political thought in England. If that appointment had been truly open to candidates with an interest in political theory in one form or another, it would almost certainly have been filled by Barker, on the strength of his first book, *The Political Thought of Plato and Aristotle*, published in 1906. Barker was drawn to that chair – to its official rubric, to its location in Oxford and thereby its connection with 'Greats' – more than he would be to any of the posts that later fell to him, but unfortunately this was to no avail, since by the terms of its endowment it was restricted to what was described as 'some able man from outside with practical experience'. Accepting that he was unlikely to be regarded as either an outsider or practical, Barker did not apply, and the chair was in due course filled by W.G.S. Adams, yet another 'Greats' scholar but one who fortunately did indeed possess the right qualifications, having been a lecturer in economics at Manchester and subsequently chief of intelligence at the Irish Department of Agriculture and Technical Instruction.[13]

Among the rejected candidates for the Gladstone chair was Graham Wallas, then a middle-aged lecturer in political science at the London School of Economics. Two years later, Wallas was promoted to the rank of professor and thereby came at the LSE to fill the first chair of political science in England, virtually stillborn at its inception, as it were,

[12] For a brief account of the establishment and early history of the PPE School in the wider context of social studies in Oxford, see Norman Chester, 'Modern Greats, 1920–39', ch. 3 of *Economics, Politics and Social Studies in Oxford, 1900–85* (London, 1986), pp. 30–45.

[13] See Julia Stapleton, *Englishness and the Study of Politics: the Social and Political Thought of Ernest Barker* (Cambridge, 1994), p. 44.

established without fanfare, advertisement or competition. Like Barker and Lindsay, Wallas had studied 'Greats' in Oxford – in his case as a classics scholar at Corpus Christi College. But he had scant interest in the textual scholarship which informed the school of *Literæ humaniores* and was never drawn to any notion of 'Modern Greats' cast in the same image. On the contrary, he rejected his undergraduate background and complained that reading Aristotle or Hobbes was inappropriate training for the administration of factory acts, the development of poor relief or the science of government in general. He greatly admired at least one political thinker – Jeremy Bentham – but that was because he appreciated Bentham's reforming zeal as a practically minded 'inventor of social expedients' whose statistical schemes facilitated, for instance, the exact measurement of health administration. Whatever 'the greatest happiness of the greatest number' might mean philosophically, Wallas was plainly attached to a science of politics that could nurture that cause institutionally. An evangelising Fabian socialist of deep Christian convictions who had been one of the founders of the LSE in 1895, he was to devote his life not only to teaching and writing but also to public service on the London School Board and London County Council, where he tried to promote what we might today term communitarian ideals of participatory democracy to combat the forces of social fragmentation generated by modern industrial society. If the syllabus of 'Greats' had not been for him, he was undeniably stirred by the public-spirited zeal kindled by both the teachers and reformers of that school.

Born in 1858, a year before the publication of Darwin's *Origin of Species*, he had first been educated at Shrewsbury, the town of Darwin's birth. Like Bagehot and Sir Henry Maine before him, he had been profoundly influenced by Darwinian conceptions of evolution and devoted much of his career as a scholar to the connection between biology and politics, particularly in his best-known work, *Human Nature and Politics*, which dates from 1908. More than anyone else in England in the early twentieth century who was academically employed in the teaching of political science, he was interested in techniques of applied social research and closely followed the experimental approaches to the study of political psychology practised first at the University of Chicago and then at New York's New School for Social Research. He was, if I may so put it, an Essex or Michigan man before his time, attached to the notion of a genuine and practical science of politics shared by none of the luminaries who taught 'Greats' in Oxford.[14]

The electors of the Gladstone chair, who had sought a candidate as

---

[14] For an account of Wallas's intellectual career, see especially Terence H. Qualter, *Graham Wallas and 'The Great Society'* (London, 1980).

uncontaminated by 'Greats' as they could possibly find, might well have regretted failing to appoint Wallas as their first professor, since after his accession Adams virtually sank without trace. But at the LSE, despite his much-commended skills as a lecturer, teacher and director of research, Wallas did not really flourish either, at least not in the manner of his most immediate successors to the chair of political science, Harold Laski and Michael Oakeshott. Laski, a fellow socialist who won Wallas's support when he retired, never emulated his friend's fascination with what another academic luminary of the LSE later described as a peculiarly *American* science of politics,[15] while Oakeshott may be fairly described as the negation of Wallas, espousing a spirit of pragmatism of an utterly distinct kind, conservative rather than socialist, sceptical rather than Christian, unevangelical, quietist and anti-rationalist. Above all, perhaps, Wallas at the LSE suffered almost the same fate as Adams in Oxford, because his academic interests fitted the rubric of his chair only too well. Uniquely among all the professors of political science whose careers I address here, he was wedded to a belief in his subject. Rather unfortunately for Wallas, his chair, after his retirement, though not redesignated and indeed now named after him, was transformed into a chair of political thought, unsatisfactorily for a good many other members of the Department of Government there, who have periodically campaigned for a politics specialist, if not necessarily of science then at least of institutions.

Meanwhile, beneath Oxford's gleaming spires, Barker's career in the Modern History Faculty was somewhat becalmed. For over twenty years he quite happily taught the paper in 'political science' which had been offered in the modern history syllabus since 1885, dealing with passages from Aristotle's *Politics*, Maine's *Ancient Law* and Bluntschli's once celebrated but now wholly forgotten *Theory of the [Modern] State*, described by its translators as 'an attempt to do for the European State what Aristotle had accomplished for the Hellenic'.[16] But among the constitutional historians who were prevalent in his faculty, that paper, and indeed the whole subject of political science as he understood it, was as irrelevant to the *real* study of history as it was to the real science of politics as conceived by Wallas at the LSE. The zealots of 'Modern Greats' were less conspicuous among Oxford historians than among classicists, and Barker's proposed reforms of the syllabus seemed a more

---

[15] See Bernard Crick, *The American Science of Politics: Its Origins and Conditions* (London, 1959).

[16] Johann Caspar Bluntschli, *The Theory of the State*, authorised English translation (by D.G. Ritchie, P.E. Matheson and R. Lodge) from the sixth German edition (Oxford, 1885), preface, p. v.

solitary affair than the efforts orchestrated by Lindsay and his circle which were eventually to lead to the creation of the PPE School. While he was a popular lecturer with a large student following, Barker appears to have made less of an impact upon the teaching of modern history at Oxford than he hoped, not least because, to his fellow historians, he was really a classicist with an enthusiasm for what passed for political science. He had just stumbled into his first teaching post because the prize fellowship in classics which he was awarded in 1899 paid an inadequate stipend for a don about to marry, and that post, a lectureship in modern history at Wadham, proved to be the only one available when he needed it.[17]

Unlike Lindsay and many of Lindsay's pupils, Barker was a Liberal or Whig rather than any kind of Fabian socialist, but he fell under the same influence of late nineteenth-century English Idealism as they did; he shared their respect for Maitland and Dicey;[18] and he was swayed by Caird, Jowett's successor as Master of Balliol, who preached a gospel of civilisation and Christianity which the chosen people of England had bequeathed to the world. Among the tutors of 'Greats' and then PPE he would have been more plainly in his element than proved to be the case in the Modern History School. Barker's career was not undistinguished, however, and in 1920 he was offered, and accepted, the post of Principal of King's College London, where he managed to acquire the skills necessary for college administration, even though, as a displaced northerner in London, he found the political and cultural circles of the nation's capital somewhat forbidding. When in 1927 a new chair of political science was founded in Cambridge, he seized the chance denied to him fifteen years earlier by his exclusion from the Gladstone chair at Oxford.

Unfortunately, as he admitted himself, that post proved quite the wrong chair for him, allowing for the fact that throughout the whole of its subsequent history there was never to be any consensus as to what field of academic expertise should be expected of candidates who presented themselves for consideration. It has often been remarked that no one scrutinising the careers or publications of its holders could possibly fathom what subject they might have in common, except perhaps by negation, in so far as not a single incumbent of this chair has practised political science as it has come to be exercised elsewhere. If the

---

[17] See Stapleton, *Englishness and the Study of Politics*, pp. 32–3.
[18] With regard to Maitland, see especially David Runciman, 'Maitland and the Real Personality of Associations', ch. 5 of *Pluralism and the Personality of the State* (Cambridge, 1997), pp. 89–123. With respect to Dicey, see Stapleton, 'Dicey and his Legacy', *History of Political Thought*, 16, 2 (Summer 1995), pp. 234–56.

benefaction from the Rockefeller Trust which established it had been honoured, the chair would have promoted empirical and applied research into politics and society along scientific lines such as was being pursued at the London School of Economics under the directorship of William Beveridge, and if the electors had been mindful of their brief, and he had been of the right age, Wallas would have made the ideal choice. Thanks to the endeavours of Marshall and other economists in Cambridge, a specialist tripos in political economy had long been separated from the moral sciences tripos, which had been judged too abstract and philosophical for an empirical discipline, and Cambridge scholars with an interest in comparative politics campaigned for a separate political science tripos as well, which would have accorded with the wishes of the Rockefeller Trust. But for several generations of undergraduates, the teaching of political science had come to be located within the historical tripos alone, where the appropriate examination papers, one devoted to 'Comparative Politics', the other to 'Analytical and Deductive Politics', were renamed, with all the clarity of purpose that informed the judgement of their tutors, as 'Political Science A' and 'Political Science B'.[19] The Rockefeller Trust could hardly have found a less suitable university anywhere in the world in which to promote its vision of political science.

In his inaugural lecture of 1928 entitled 'The Study of Political Science', Barker made plain his own misgivings about taking up the appointment. Observing that the subject of his chair was 'known in this place by the name of political science', he proceeded to explain why, as he put it, 'I am not altogether happy about the term *science*', accepting only Aristotle's conception of that subject and preferring instead, as a description of what he did, 'the name of political theory'. For good measure, he then sang the praises of the Oxford School of *Literæ humaniores*.[20] In 1945, his successor, Denis Brogan, who was to fill the same chair for almost thirty years, began *his* inaugural lecture in much the same spirit, with the remark that there was 'a pretension' in the title of his chair 'that many find repellent', since 'the direct connection of science with politics . . . may well be doubted'.[21] Being a political historian, Brogan could in no sense claim to follow Barker's preference for the title 'Professor of Political Theory', but by virtue of his background in history, albeit at Oxford, he had a great advantage over Barker in the domestic affairs of the Faculty of History in Cambridge.

---

[19] See Collini et al., *That Noble Science of Politics*, pp. 348–51.
[20] See E. Barker, 'The Study of Political Science', in his collection of essays entitled *Church, State and Study* (London, 1930), pp. 194–5.
[21] D. Brogan, 'The Study of Politics: an Inaugural Lecture' (Cambridge, 1946), p. 8.

As a student of 'Greats', Barker, by contrast, had only a meagre impact on the world which adopted him. He tried to set up a new tripos in 'social and political studies', but his greatest achievement was perhaps in renaming and recasting the two papers from the old moral sciences tripos he inherited. On his instigation 'Political Science A' became the 'History of Political Thought', while 'Political Science B' became 'The Theory of the Modern State', thus bequeathing to Bluntschli's book, which Barker knew so well from his days at Oxford, an abiding influence which had seldom penetrated to any of its readers. The last vestige of political science in Cambridge was thereby put to rest by its first professor, whose revisions to the political thought papers in the history tripos had just encapsulated an attempt to transport 'Greats' to the Fens.[22] Not once in the course of any of the elections to the chair has a candidate in possession of what might elsewhere be regarded as accredited standing in the field so much as managed to reach the final short list.

Douglas Cole, the first Chichele Professor of Social and Political Theory in Oxford, was fifteen years younger than Barker and in a sense – because he had been born in Cambridge – completed Barker's journey from the dreaming spires to the Fenlands in reverse. By temperament, however, he belonged to neither city, whose quadrangles and cloisters he found too parochial, too remotely scholastic, for his tastes. As a populist whose socialist philosophy had been inspired by William Morris's *The Earthly Paradise* which he had read while a pupil at St Paul's School in the borough of Hammersmith, he instead chose to live mainly in London. Unless it was his contemporary, Laski, whose comparable ambition to shape the direction of public life steered him even nearer to the Labour Party's seats of political power in Transport House and Whitehall, there has never been a professor of political thought, or indeed of political science, who was ever drawn closer to the pulse of British politics. Twice a candidate for Parliament and feeling more at home in Hampstead or Hendon than in any Oxford college, Cole inhabited the urban epicentre of the socialist movement. He was so wedded to a notion of *democratic centralism* that, even after Khrushchev's denunciation of Stalin in 1956, he seemed reluctant to accept that this ideal had been rather discredited by way of its long history of abuse in the Soviet Union.

Like Wallas, Barker and Lindsay, Cole also read 'Greats' at Oxford, in his case at Balliol College, where Lindsay himself had been his tutor. Yet as distinct from both Wallas and Barker, in particular, Cole lived, as

---

[22] See Stapleton, '"Continental" Political Science and the Cambridge Chair', ch. 6 of *Englishness and the Study of Politics*, pp. 128–53.

E.M. Forster described it, in a 'world of telegrams and anger',[23] framed by two global wars. During the first, he held a prize fellowship at Oxford's Magdalen College; towards the end of the second, in 1944, he was appointed to his chair and, with it, a fellowship of All Souls, which at least before the war had seemed to be Oxford's leading bastion of both privilege and appeasement. First elected to the Fabian Society Executive Committee in 1914, at the age of only twenty-four, Cole was to become deeply embroiled in the domestic political repercussions of those international conflicts. Hostile to militarism and all the forms of blind discipline upon which armies depend, he had been a conscientious objector at the outbreak of the Great War; but there was nothing pacifist about his perception of the class struggle, which in his mind had been merely obscured by the mobilisation of British troops against Germans. Together with other Guild Socialists, he greeted the Bolshevik Revolution of October 1917 with enthusiasm.

Nine years later, after he had become a Reader in Economics and Fellow of University College, Oxford, Cole set up a committee of the University to assist Oxford City's Trades and Labour Council in its workers' prosecution of the General Strike. The achievement of social upheaval in Britain by parliamentary means alone he deemed a pious illusion. If it had not been for the dictates and pretensions of Comintern, both he and his wife, Margaret, might well have joined the British Communist Party.[24] Sir Isaiah Berlin, his successor as holder of the Chichele Chair, could almost have intended his 'Two Concepts of Liberty',[25] the most celebrated of all the inaugural lectures of the professors of political thought in Britain, as a reply to a too-zealous Old Whig from a more sceptical New one, discreetly passing judgement on virtually the whole of Cole's career, while recognising the extent of his 'impact' and 'fame'.[26] In the course of two world wars and in the period between them both men had witnessed the most dismal face of modern totalitarian regimes, but aside from sharing a contempt for fascist governments of any complexion, they were in utter disagreement about the nature of those regimes and even their identity.

For much of his life, in addition to serving trade union causes as a middle-class activist, Cole was also a journalist, mainly as Labour

---

[23] Cited in Margaret Cole, *The Life of G.D.H. Cole* (London, 1971), introduction, p. 15. On Cole's career, see also Gerald Houseman, *G.D.H. Cole* (Boston, 1979) and A.W. Wright, *G.D.H. Cole and Socialist Democracy* (Oxford, 1979).

[24] Cole, *The Life of G.D.H. Cole*, ch. 10, pp. 123–4.

[25] Delivered at the University of Oxford on 21 October 1958, and first published by the Clarendon Press in the same year.

[26] For Berlin's appreciation of his predecessor in the Chichele Chair, see his 'Two Concepts of Liberty', in his *Four Essays on Liberty* (Oxford, 1969), pp. 120–1.

correspondent of the *Manchester Guardian* from 1925 and as a frequent contributor to the *New Statesman* from 1918 virtually until his death in 1959. In the 1930s he had been the principal founder first of the Society for Socialist Inquiry and Propaganda and then of the Socialist League. In 1941 he was appointed director of the Nuffield Reconstruction Survey, whose aims included the tracing of war conditions upon public services and their bearing on problems of the nation's social recovery. In the early 1950s he assumed a variety of responsibilities, through UNESCO and other organisations, in aid of workers' education.

The otherwise hagiographical account of his life produced twelve years after his death by his widow suggests that, largely on account of his preoccupation with day-to-day matters, Cole had published 'comparatively little' in book form until he became Oxford's professor of social and political theory.[27] But in the light of his earlier output – which included notable biographies of William Cobbett and Robert Owen, as well as a textbook in social theory, editions of selected writings of Rousseau and Morris, at least fifteen novels (mainly written jointly with Margaret), a three-volume not so *Short History of the Working-Class Movement* and, perhaps most notable of all, a still-celebrated study of *The Common People* (in collaboration with Raymond Postgate) – it is unclear just with whom such a comparison might have been meant. Bearing in mind as well his writings subsequent to 1944, including especially his five-volume or seven-part *History of Socialist Thought*, it remains the case that no holder of any of the chairs of political thought in Britain which are at issue here has, at least until now, published more.

To my mind, however, the most important figure in the academic world of twentieth-century British political thought is a man who never held a chair in the subject at all. Alexander Dunlop (or 'Sandie') Lindsay had an even greater impact than any of his colleagues on the establishment of the School of PPE in Oxford, for which several of the London and Cambridge professors of political science taught at various stages of their careers, as well, of course, as all the Chichele professors at Oxford. The PPE School stands to the second and every subsequent generation of professors of political thought almost in the same position as did 'Greats' to the first; more than any other course of studies it has nurtured the current discipline of political thought in Britain. In promoting the establishment of 'Modern Greats' in Oxford, Lindsay helped to open fresh avenues for the study of politics which were distinct from those available through the political science paper, offered in the School of Modern History, and in this way he steered

---

[27] Cole, *The Life of G.D.H. Cole*, p. 235.

reforms through Oxford boards on a scale that Barker was never really able to manage in dealing with the historians at both Oxford and Cambridge. The differences between the teaching of political thought as part of the PPE School in Oxford, on the one hand, and within the history tripos in Cambridge, on the other, have become crucial to the now widely divergent perspectives on the subject which are prevalent at both of these ancient universities. In Oxford, what are taken to be the central questions of political thought, and the correct ways of addressing them, are shaped by philosophers, and often by moral philosophers, who despite the great cuts of the Thatcherite era still congregate there in larger numbers than almost anywhere else in the world. In Cambridge, while political philosophers have a notable presence as well, the subject is mainly taught by historians of ideas, more likely to be specialists in certain periods than with respect to particular concepts. The students to whom they lecture, and whose dissertations they supervise, themselves have characteristically scant familiarity with the disciplines of philosophy. They instead read for degrees within the Faculty of History and write monographs, often based on archival sources, whose breadth and command of minute detail are generally scrutinised more closely than is the coherence of their arguments.

Lindsay himself was a philosopher by training, an admirer of Jowett and a disciple of Caird, both of whom had preceded him as Masters of Balliol. It was from this Olympian post that, over a period of twenty-five years, he was able to exercise a pivotal influence over some junior but above all several professorial appointments, and in no field was his power greater than in political thought. He was one of the electors who secured Barker's accession to the Cambridge chair of political science in 1928; and he supported Walter Gallie, the chair's third holder, who in the 1930s had been his pupil at Balliol and whose appointment in 1951 as the foundational Professor of Philosophy at the University College of North Staffordshire in Keele he engineered as well. Cole, who was his close friend and associate in the cause of democratic reform both within Oxford University and outside it, was to claim that it was Lindsay's example which mapped out his own life's way.[28] Berlin, after succeeding Cole, was to describe Lindsay as a great public figure of unusual moral power, who as a philosopher had perhaps missed his true vocation, since he might have proved an unforgettable public statesman of the highest order.[29]

Lindsay's most enduring monuments are undeniably the institutions that he helped to establish rather than any of his scholarly works, which

[28] See Druscilla Scott, *A.D. Lindsay: a Biography* (Oxford, 1971), p. 116.
[29] Ibid., p. 223.

to other Oxford philosophers seemed too much encumbered by a tradition of Idealism that by the 1920s had already fallen from grace. His democratic zeal and attachment to a 'collectivist spirit of the common life'[30] did not endear him to conservative elitists among his colleagues, and several thought it odd that his avowedly mundane faith in the intellect and virtues of ordinary men and women should be couched in the lofty terminology of Bosanquet's theory of the general will. A meticulous student of Kant's critical philosophy, Lindsay addressed that subject mainly in two books, one short and popular, the other weighty and learned, neither of which was to have much impact upon Kant scholarship. Students of early twentieth-century political thought still turn occasionally to his principal work, *The Democratic State*, but if he is consulted at all by the non-specialist reader today, it is as the editor of numerous Everyman classics, most of which he drafted while in his late twenties or early thirties, particularly Plato's *Republic* (which he also translated), Mill's *Utilitarianism* and Hobbes's *Leviathan*.

Yet Berlin's description of Lindsay is apt; he was one of the great public figures of his age. Not only did he devote much of his life to the Workers' Educational Association in that tradition of adult education so close to the hearts of Green, Toynbee and other Balliol luminaries. Not only, when already Master of Balliol, did he play a major conciliatory role both in the General Strike of 1926 and, four years later, by chairing the International Missionary Council's report into Christian higher education in India. In the autumn of 1938, just after he had served for three years as Oxford's Vice-Chancellor, he stood as the joint Labour and Liberal candidate against Quintin Hogg, the future Lord Hailsham, in an Oxford by-election in which he halved the Conservative majority, following a campaign uniquely addressed to the public disgrace, as he described it, of the policy of appeasement of Prime Minister Chamberlain.

Around the same time, he managed to persuade an exceedingly reluctant Lord Nuffield that the benefaction which he had in mind for Oxford so as to bring it closer to the practical world of business would be better served by a college of economics and social studies than by one devoted to engineering and industry. Having worn out Britain's leading capitalist with specious arguments about the use to which his gift would be put, he then contrived, after the war, to arrange for Nuffield College to be run by its sub-warden, that arch-enemy of capitalism, Cole.

---

[30] On the theological roots of Lindsay's philosophy, see especially ch. 10 ('Christianity') of Scott's (his daughter's) biography, *A.D. Lindsay*, pp. 173–89. For an assessment of the philosophical dimensions of his Christianity, see Dorothy Emmet's appendix, forming ch. 20 of the same text ('Lindsay as Philosopher'), pp. 389–415.

Thereafter Lindsay, who in 1945 had been made a life peer, showed the same energy in establishing at Keele the first new university in Britain for an age of mass education, which he anticipated and for which he planned with enthusiasm. Not since the thirteenth century had there been such an exodus of Oxford dons to form a new university in England. Among the men from Balliol that Lindsay took with him, in addition to Gallie, was Sammie Finer who, by way of the University of Manchester, would later return to All Souls College, Oxford, and the Gladstone chair (by then renamed) of government and public administration which sixty years earlier had escaped the clutches of Barker. In *Summoned by Bells*, John Betjeman recounts this move of Balliol's *aurora borealis* in verse:

> Sandy Lindsay from his lodge looks down
> Dreaming of Adult Education where
> The pottery chimneys flare
> On lost potential firsts in some less favoured town.[31]

In Lindsay's life was encapsulated the career of one of the Victorian era's last great public moralists and teachers, who also happened to be a scholar. Albeit timid in private and not a particularly eloquent speaker, he assumed his responsibilities with a swashbuckler's flourish, hurtling from each high office to the next like Errol Flynn passing through a crowded room by way of the chandeliers.

Misbegotten chairs and their succession

How are these developments to be interpreted? The history of the professorial appointments I have outlined here suggests that there has been fundamental confusion with respect to the remit of selectors, each committee proving uncertain of what it was seeking and many of the candidates in doubt as to whether they should even apply. The electors to the Gladstone Chair of Political Theory and Institutions in Oxford, and to the first chair of political science in Cambridge, were determined to strike out in fresh directions by appointing outsiders; but in both instances the outsiders were drawn into the byzantine network of already established committees and degree structures, and whatever expectations of radical change might have been envisaged by electors and candidates alike were quickly neutralised in the labyrinth of long-settled practices. At Oxford and Cambridge there have been dramatic changes to the syllabus of political thought and to the manner of its

---

[31] John Betjeman, 'Irregular Ode to Oxford', in ch. 9 ('The Opening World') of Betjeman, *Summoned by Bells* (1960), reprinted in *The Illustrated Summoned by Bells* (London, 1989), p. 130.

teaching, but by and large those changes came from pressures *within* the faculties, from reforms promoted by progressive dons who were already influential figures known to their colleagues, and who generally succeeded in their plans, first by revising the examination papers, then by making junior appointments to cater for a new syllabus and only finally by seeking a professorial rubric to lend official warrant to these changes. At the LSE, with looser internal structures, it was otherwise. New professors of political science could and did manage great upheavals, not least by encouraging the resignation or early retirement of colleagues appointed by their predecessors.

Second, I believe that the initial appointments to chairs of political thought which were made in English universities point as well to a crisis of identity as to the nature of their subject among the professors themselves at every one of its major centres. The fact that its first professors at London, Cambridge and Oxford all read 'Greats' at Oxford is of scant significance, to my mind, since they each formed a different judgement of that school, with Barker embracing it wholeheartedly, Cole determined to bring it up to date, and Wallas largely unimpressed by its charms and anxious to strike a fresh path. In the light of their perceptions of political theory and political science, I would even hazard the claim that each of their appointments proved to be a category mistake. Wallas, in his disdain for theoretical abstractions and the mere study of texts, and in his attachment to the most fashionable explanations of human behaviour of his day, was really a follower in the footsteps of Bagehot and of the Cambridge historians Cunningham and Seeley, showing none of Barker's hesitation in accepting *his* chair of political science. Cole, both in attempting to explain how modern political thinkers were also social reformers, and in devoting so much of his own life to popular causes, was most in his element when nearest the heart of British politics – that is, in London, to which even as a professor in Oxford he returned for at least half of each week. Barker was not at all displeased to be uprooted from London by a summons to Cambridge, but as a textual scholar and student of classics throughout his life he really was attached above all to the doctrines of Green and Bosanquet and to the tradition of scholarship which informed the teaching of *Literæ humaniores* that had served him so well. All of which is to say that Wallas should really have been the first professor of political science in Cambridge, Cole should have preceded Laski at the LSE and Barker should have been the first incumbent of the chair of social and political theory at Oxford.

Any doubts which these professors of political thought might entertain about their subject or the place in which they truly belonged were seldom matched by their opinions of one another or of each other's work – which they often articulated with a courteous smile through clenched teeth. Although Wallas had supported Laski, and Lindsay had sought the promotion of Cole, by and large each one of Britain's foremost professors or doyens of political thought lent virtually no encouragement to any other, including his successor in particular, and in almost every instance that succession was marked by what the French fondly call a 'rupture' or *décalage*, of which perhaps the most conspicuous quality was the new incumbent's departure from all the principles and interests which his predecessor had held dear. Nowhere have these somersaults been more conspicuous than at the London School of Economics, most famously when the whole character of the School was changed by Michael Oakeshott and his circle, and Laski's widow felt unable to set foot there again.[32]

In Oxford there has perhaps been more continuity, at least of a certain kind. Cole and Berlin, like Jowett several generations earlier, had been students at St Paul's School in London before obtaining their firsts in 'Greats' and thereafter becoming master or sub-master of an Oxford College; and All Souls or New College connections may at least have given occasion for the forging of genuine friendships that would enable Berlin to exercise some influence over the appointment, if not of his immediate, then of his subsequent, successors. Such links may have had some bearing on the fact that Oxford has maintained a certain consistency of perspective and method over the years – a relatively unbroken lineage of a kind absent from both London and Cambridge – despite the fact that not one of the incumbents of the Oxford chair throughout the past four decades has been a native Briton, whereas no one born outside the British Isles has ever held the chair of political science in either London or Cambridge.

Over the past eighty years there have of course been real differences of substance or principle which, in each generation as well as across them, distinguish the outlooks of these professors of political thought, and it is, moreover, striking, if not surprising, that proximity in age has only occasionally given rise to reciprocal esteem. Berlin frequently described John Plamenatz, who succeeded him in Oxford, as 'Montenegro's greatest political thinker',[33] and we have it on the testimony of Noel Annan that he once proposed that Oakeshott write a book on Hegel, in

---

[32] Maurice Cranston's and especially Brian Barry's subsequent appointments to the same chair have marked notable breaks with precedent as well.

[33] In his accession to All Souls College, Oxford, to which the Chichele Chair of Social and Political Theory is attached, Plamenatz, as son of the last premier and foreign minister of the Kingdom of Montenegro before its incorporation in Yugoslavia, may have appeared to possess an even more exotic background than Berlin, a Russian Jew.

so far as a book written by a charlatan would be better than no book at all. When Berlin subsequently gave one of the Auguste Comte memorial lectures at the LSE, Oakeshott, we are told, spun a web of silky treacle in introducing him as the virtuoso Paganini among the lecturers of his day.[34]

Yet even in the absence of clear identities, shared convictions, mutual respect or dynastic continuities among these professors of political thought, there have, I believe, been some discernible trends which the incumbents of the principal chairs have mapped out over the past eighty-five years or, in essence, three generations. With regard to the first professor in every instance at the three universities considered here, and including as well their chief mentor at Oxford and the second professor of political science at the London School of Economics – that is, Wallas, Lindsay, Barker, Cole and Laski – I would say of each of them that he was a public moralist in the sense attributed to this expression by Stefan Collini in his work bearing that title.[35] Collectively they professed civic ideals, advocated political programmes, and exhorted their readers and students to pursue and uphold noble causes. Their whole careers were bathed in an incandescent light of virtue. They were campaigners and activists, reformers, crusaders or conciliators, the *engagés volontaires* of political righteousness. They wrote tracts; they were journalists and broadcasters; they took part in public debate and took charge of the public conscience with regard to England's destiny and the character of the nation. Dispassionate objectivity had scant place in any syllabus of political science which was of interest to them, and neither were they drawn beyond any other calling to the reclusive attractions of the college senior common room or cloister.

With the accession to their chairs of Denis Brogan, Michael Oakeshott, Isaiah Berlin and their successors, that Victorian and Edwardian world of public engagement ceased to be the province of the nation's leading professors of political science and political thought, at least in so far as their predecessors had taken their civic responsibilities to be implicit in, if not entailed by, their academic duties. That Brogan, Oakeshott and Berlin held strong convictions themselves and at least in two cases possessed an intimate knowledge of the management of public affairs are facts whose significance I do not in any way seek to diminish; on the contrary, I acknowledge that each of these men may indeed have been in possession of a profounder and more sophisticated understanding of comparative politics and international relations than his

---

[34] See N. Annan, *Our Age: Portrait of a Generation* (London, 1990), p. 401.
[35] See S. Collini, *Public Moralists: Political Thought and Intellectual Life in Britain (1850–1930)* (Oxford, 1991).

already astute predecessor. What I am describing here – as, in effect, the depoliticisation of the incumbents of these chairs of political thought – may thus appear odd. Even if we make allowances for the essential quietism of both Brogan (who, despite occasional broadcasts and reviews in the popular press, never aspired to be anything other than a historian) and Gallie (whose philosophy of essentially contested concepts always made him see the merits of alternative views),[36] the relatively disengaged character of Oakeshott, Berlin and Berlin's successor, Plamenatz, when compared with the temperament of their precursors, needs some explanation.

I must not of course exaggerate the difference, since Berlin was deeply exercised by the conduct of British foreign policy during the Second World War and sought to exert some influence upon it, especially on behalf of Zionist causes of which he was a lifelong advocate; while Plamenatz, himself a victim of communist persecution, was an impassioned critic of both Stalin and Tito and played as active a political role in combating Yugoslav intolerance as was possible for a full-time professor in Oxford. And yet Oakeshott's, Berlin's and Plamenatz's perspectives on their office, by contrast with those of their predecessors, seem to me striking. Separately and collectively, they understood their station and its duties in a fashion distinct from that of Barker, Laski and Cole. At least as incumbent professors of political science or political thought, they were not fundamentally public moralists.

To my mind, an explanation for that change, if one can be found at all, would include the assessment of Enlightenment rationalism espoused by each of these men as a central feature of his own political philosophy. Oakeshott, Berlin and Plamenatz were in their different ways largely critical of the pretensions of the major eighteenth-century *philosophes* as they understood them – Oakeshott because he regarded them as the dogmatic authors of merely speculative systems of thought; Plamenatz because he held their notions of human nature to be too abstract and unsocial; and Berlin because he thought their doctrines monolithic and insensitive to the plurality of ends which individuals actually pursue. As against Enlightenment rationalists, all three may be said to have espoused the dictum which Berlin drew from Kant that 'no straight path may be drawn from the crooked timber of humanity'.[37] To this list of critics of Enlightenment philosophy I might add America's

---

[36] See W. Gallie, 'Essentially Contested Concepts', *Proceedings of the Aristotelian Society*, 56 (1955–6), pp. 167–98.

[37] See I. Berlin, *The Crooked Timber of Humanity: Chapters in the History of Ideas*, edited by Henry Hardy (London, 1990). The expression is inspired by a passage from Kant's *Idee zu einer allgemeinen Geschichte in weltbürgerlicher Absicht* of 1784. On the origins of Berlin's own rendition of the expression, cf. the Editor's Introduction, p. xi.

pre-eminent political theorist of roughly the same generation, that is, Leo Strauss, who identified an Enlightenment commitment to scientific objectivity as the principal source of the valueless and rudderless relativism prevalent in the modern world.

I hesitate to call Strauss, Oakeshott, Berlin and Plamenatz post-modernists on account of their joint hostility to a so-called *Enlightenment Project*, but it seems to me that their mistrust of and distaste for the political rostrum of public moralists were informed by, among other factors, their misgivings about the manner in which principles can be pursued in politics. Their subtly nuanced scepticism was in each case contrary to the spirit of Enlightenment as they understood it – at once more textured, more delicate and more hesitant, because of their appreciation of the complexities of political life on grounds that excluded any grand theory of comprehensive change. At any rate, with this new generation of professors of political thought, the advocacy of social and political reform ceased to be a professorial duty. Particularly over the past forty years or so, the holders of England's pre-eminent chairs in the subject have, from the point of view of public moralists, entered the age of the great slumber, even Marxists among them driven to reticence by the burdens of their office, as they sit upon their hands astride their chairs. The iron cage of professorial duty has, by and large, appeared to drive out the calling of politics, which, for political theorists and historians of political thought in England, and indeed our politics departments and social science faculties more widely, has become an inescapably extracurricular activity, marginalised from our professional lives, increasingly remote from, and potentially at variance with, our official responsibilities to both our students and employers.

These remarks with respect to the relative depoliticisation of the academic discipline of political thought in England since the 1950s are intended as descriptive and not as a lament. Several of the professors I have here described as constituting the second generation among titular holders of chairs in the subject were my teachers, three became my intimate friends, and I hold the achievements of almost all of them in higher esteem than those of their precursors of the first generation, none of whom I ever met or heard. I think it inconceivable that Laski or Cole, who combated fascism so vigorously in the 1930s, or Lindsay, who in his old age stood for Parliament to fight appeasement, would have permitted ethnic cleansing in Cambodia, Rwanda, Bosnia or Kosovo to pass with such little comment as was expressed from within university departments of politics in the 1990s, but in depicting this development as a generational change of temper I only wish to articulate some doubt as to whether it can be explained institutionally or in the light of the disciplinary history of political thought, as distinct, say, from an accidental conjunction of personal styles.

The change I have portrayed here, allowing that it has occurred at all, is to my mind not just a matter of the professionalisation of our subject, or of the progressive imposition of academic constraints which, in the teaching as distinct from the practice of politics, require a divorce of facts from values. I believe that Bernard Crick[38] among professors of political theory in England has always been a public moralist of the old school, and I suspect that so too, albeit more sceptically, is John Dunn;[39] Charles Taylor, who succeeded Plamenatz as the Chichele Professor in Oxford, may likewise be portrayed in this fashion, at least when he is on Canadian soil. Public moralists have remained conspicuous in our universities, even in the post-war period, when they disappeared from our main chairs of political thought. Some took up chairs of public policy, or government, or history, at other universities; some remained at Oxford or the LSE as professors of sociology. But by and large the tradition of *Literæ humaniores* which so inspired Lindsay and his followers was not so much extinguished as transported to other disciplines and departments at some distance from the social sciences – mainly to English and Comparative Literature, where F.R. Leavis, Richard Hoggart, Raymond Williams, George Steiner, Terry Eagleton and others have carried the different flags of the Great Society, as cast in the image of great books or classic texts, while so many of our leading professors of social and political theory have kept their heads below the parapets and slumbered through the long *durée*. However we explain it, I believe that England's own peculiar version of the *Enlightenment Project*, as institutionalised above all in the 'Greats' syllabus at Oxford, has since the 1950s ceased to be of relevance to the study of political thought.

I turn, finally, to the historical revolution in our subject, elsewhere termed the 'new history' by Richard Tuck, which has been described in detail by Dario Castiglione and whose fundamental character and implications are addressed by Iain Hampsher-Monk in his own contribution to this volume.[40] With respect to our discipline there have, as is

[38] Crick, the holder of various posts at the LSE from 1957 to 1965, was Professor of Political Theory and Institutions at the University of Sheffield from 1965 to 1971 and then Professor of Politics at Birkbeck College London, from 1971 to 1984. In connection with my thesis here, see especially his *In Defence of Politics* (first published London, 1962), and his *Political Theory and Practice* (London, 1972).

[39] Dunn, Reader in Politics at the University of Cambridge from 1977 to 1987, has since 1987 held the post there of Professor of Political Theory. With respect to my suggestion here, see especially his *Western Political Theory in the Face of the Future*, 2nd edn (Cambridge, 1993), and *The Cunning of Unreason: Making Sense of Politics* (London, 2000).

[40] See R. Tuck, 'The Contribution of History', in Robert E. Goodin and Phillip Pettit

widely acknowledged, really been *two* major revolutions since the late 1960s, splitting the Oxford nucleus that once gave it its predominant form, driving its atoms to Cambridge West, on the one hand, and Cambridge East, on the other. By which I mean of course that John Rawls's *Theory of Justice* and the writings of other authors which this work inspired have had at least as great an impact upon the teaching of political thought in the English-speaking world as the 'new history' of John Pocock and Quentin Skinner, in providing a genuine warrant for grand theory in the manner of Hobbes, Locke or Rousseau as distinct from a mere learner's licence to comment upon the meaning or relevance of their doctrines. No less a figure than Brian Barry has recognised the extraordinary leap into fresh territory, heralded by Rawls, as marking a transformation of the discipline; and ambitious political theorists today need a level of philosophical sophistication comparable to that of philosophers in other disciplines, just as historians of political thought now need to situate the writings which *they* seek to explain with such refined detail as is professionally required in other fields subjected to real historical scrutiny. These two methodological revolutions, moreover, may also be said to mark the advent, over the two following decades, of a third generation of professorial appointments to the principal chairs of political thought in England, first by way of Skinner's election to the Cambridge chair of political science in 1978, then Cohen's to the Chichele Chair at Oxford in 1985, followed by Barry's to the chair of political science at the LSE in 1987.

In so far as they apparently betoken qualitative changes of our discipline, those revolutions have, moreover, virtually compelled its current professional practitioners to aim for deeper levels of philosophical argument, on the one hand, and richer contextual descriptions of their meaning, on the other, than were prevalent before, even among the second generation of incumbents of the three leading chairs of political thought in England whom I have here identified. That development is, in principle, progressive; it points to higher standards of research; it should be welcomed. But I believe that we ought nevertheless to recognise the price paid to ensure the triumph of our new canons of political philosophy and the history of political thought, whose conquests of our discipline have been achieved by way of victories over a whole tradition dedicated to the interpretation of classic texts which merit critical scrutiny that once formed part – indeed, the most central part – of a humane and liberal education.

(eds.), *A Companion to Contemporary Political Philosophy* (Oxford, 1993), pp. 72–89, and D. Castiglione, 'Historical Arguments in Political Theory', in *Political Theory Newsletter*, 5 (1993), pp. 89–109.

That tradition was most evident in the 'Greats' syllabus at Oxford, of which Lindsay and Barker were both students and teachers, and in the PPE School, or 'Modern Greats' syllabus which was also offered in Oxford, by Cole. It was, moreover, also evident in Cambridge from the mid-nineteenth century in several papers pertaining to political philosophy and the history of political thought, first, in the moral sciences tripos as conceived by Sidgwick, then in the history tripos as constructed by Seeley, and, finally, in the economics tripos devised by Marshall. The same tradition, which drew much inspiration and a good measure of its style and language from late nineteenth-century English Idealism, was in essence embraced by Oakeshott, Berlin and Plamenatz as well, even though they often adopted alternative idioms and were not fundamentally public moralists themselves. Of a similar character, albeit different pedigree, were the approaches to the study of political thought adopted by Sheldon Wolin and Judith Shklar in the United States of America, where, indeed, an equally sharp separation of philosophical from historical treatments of political concepts has marked the relative demise of the 'Great Books' approach – America's main counterpart to the School of *Literæ humaniores* – bred in the late 1930s and 1940s at the University of Chicago by Robert Hutchins and Mortimer Adler.[41]

As distinct from the change of temper and style which in England marked the passage from the first generation of public moralists among professors of political thought to their less engaged and more sceptically minded successors, the two revolutions which have inspired the third generation are methodological and call for doctrinal rigour. Their success bifurcates a loosely defined field of political theory into two quite distinct disciplines of political philosophy and the history of political thought. Having entered our third age it has not only become impossible to revert to the first but also absurd to lament the loss of that immaturity. We are no longer so naïve as to examine classic texts critically in order to nurture our students' zeal and prepare them for public office. In interpreting political arguments we have become, both by choice and necessity, aloof from their prescriptions. We plainly inhabit a world strikingly different from that of Jowett, Barker and Lindsay, but what our pupils might reasonably expect to learn from their current teachers of political thought is less clear.

---

[41] See R.M. Hutchins and M.J. Adler (eds.), *The Great Ideas: a Synopticon*, forming vols. II and III of Hutchins and Adler (eds.), *Great Books of the Western World* (54 vols., Chicago, 1952).

Appendix

Professors of political science at the London School of Economics and at Cambridge, and professors of social and political theory at Oxford

LONDON	CAMBRIDGE	OXFORD
Graham Wallas 1914–23	**Ernest Barker** 1928–39	**G.D.H. Cole** 1944–57
Harold Laski 1926–50	**Denis Brogan** 1939–67	**Isaiah Berlin** 1957–67
Michael Oakeshott 1951–69	**W.B. Gallie** 1967–78	**John Plamenatz** 1967–75
Maurice Cranston 1969–85	**Quentin Skinner** 1978–96	**Charles Taylor** 1976–81
Brian Barry 1987–98	**Gareth Stedman Jones** 1997–	**G.A. Cohen** 1985–
David Held 1999–		

Studied at Oxford, 14; studied at Cambridge, 2; studied 'Greats' at Oxford, 4; studied modern history at Oxford, 5; studied PPE at Oxford, 4.

Received Oxford DPhil, 4.

Pupil of St Paul's School, Hammersmith, 3 (Cole, Berlin, Stedman Jones).

FBA 9 (Barker, Brogan, Oakeshott, Berlin, Plamenatz, Taylor, Skinner, Cohen, Barry).

Kt. 3 (Barker, Brogan, Berlin).

OM, 1 (Berlin).

Died in office, 2 (Laski, Plamenatz).

8 The history of political thought and the political history of thought

Iain Hampsher-Monk

This chapter is partly exegetical, partly analytical and partly critical. The exegetical part is in fulfilment of one of the aims of the collection which is to bring together what has been going on in the history of political thought in various national contexts over the past twenty or thirty years. It will start by presenting a terse reading of the two most influential methodologists (and practitioners) of the history of political theory in the English language, sharpening their differences whilst acknowledging their common aims. The analytical points are twofold – first to identify their illocutionary force by locating them in the context of those conventional, academic speech acts from which they might be seen to be departing, and second to draw out the implications of such a departure. The critical phase is concerned to confront the tensions which the author sees existing between the successful methodological revolution and recent practice in the field. First then, I will rehearse, briefly, a story the outlines of which will be well known to many readers.

In 1962 John Pocock published an essay entitled 'The History of Political Thought: a Methodological Enquiry'.[1] In 1968 John Dunn published 'The Identity of the History of Ideas'[2] and the following year Quentin Skinner published 'Meaning and Understanding in the History of Ideas'.[3]

The thrust of these three foundational works, taken together was clear. Invoking the key words of each title, what was being asserted was that the identity of political theory was historical, that the appropriate method to be deployed in its study was a historical one, and that the meaning to be derived from political theory texts which vindicated any claim to have understood them had to be, or be shown to be departing from, a historically identifiable meaning.

[1] J.G.A. Pocock, 'The History of Political Thought: a Methodological Enquiry', in Peter Laslett and W.G. Runciman (eds.), *Politics Philosophy and Society*, 2nd series (Oxford, 1962).

[2] J. Dunn, 'The Identity of the History of Ideas', *Philosophy*, 43 (1968), pp. 85–116.

[3] Q. Skinner, 'Meaning and Understanding the History of Ideas', *History and Theory*, 8 (1969), pp 3–53.

Quentin Skinner articulated his position at the outset through the application of a technically precise philosophical position – namely Austin's analysis of speech acts.[4] Pocock's initial work was, by contrast, grounded in a tradition of intellectual practice and he went on to explore a range of methodological underpinnings but with an underlying and increasingly precisely articulated commitment to the concept of language. It would be only slightly parodic to claim that, whereas Quentin Skinner started out with a starkly specific, challenging and even combative methodological position, to which only minor adjustments have been made,[5] Pocock at the outset engaged in a much more tentative internalist exploration, acknowledging the untheorised character of the practice of the study of the history of political theory. As he put it: 'Simply, there is a body of thinkers to whom we have grown into the habit of paying attention, and a number of viewpoints from which they appear interesting to us.' This Oakeshottian conception of a tradition of intellectualising, illumined both some of Pocock's subject matter and his recommendations about how to approach it. Theorising within a tradition seemed necessarily to involve an abridgement or abstraction from it. The confusion in the history of political thought which he identified consisted in the mixing of modes: the misguided attempt to present the history of a tradition of discourse not by establishing historical evidence for conceptual continuities, but by the speculative identification of connections or, worse, mere resemblances, arrived at by philosophical abstraction from canonical exemplars.[6]

For Pocock, following Oakeshott, a particular political theory might be approached in different moods or modalities. Whether thought of as modes of experience (the historical, the practical. . .) or as disciplinary rivals, this analysis highlights for us the primary tension in the field, namely that between the historical and the philosophical. In view of later observations in this chapter, it is worth remembering (as my parentheses in the preceding sentence is intended to signal) that, for Oakeshott, the

---

[4] Skinner articulates his debt to Austin at various points, e.g. in his 'Language and Political Change', in T. Ball and J. Farr (eds.), *Political Innovation and Conceptual Change* (Cambridge, 1989), p. 9 n. 4.

[5] Skinner, 'A Reply to My Critics', in James Tully (ed.), *Meaning and Context: Quentin Skinner and his Critics* (Cambridge, 1988), p. 288.

[6] Pocock, 'The History of Political Thought', pp. 184–5. 'In *illo tempore* then, the study of political thought was confused to the point where one did not know whether "political thought", "theory" or "philosophy" was the appropriate designation for the field one had chosen . . . Alone amongst the major branches of historical study in the middle of the twentieth century, the history of political thought was treated as the study of a traditional canon, and the conversion of the tradition into history was conducted by the methods of philosophic commentary on the intellectual contents of the tradition, arbitrarily defined as philosophy': J.G.A. Pocock, 'Languages and Their Implications', in Pocock, *Politics Language and Time* (London and New York, 1972), pp. 4–5.

practical too was a distinct mode of experience forming another tension or polarity within the field: history – philosophy – practice.[7]

Pocock's analysis possessed both sociological and linguistic dimensions; it was that stable societies developed discrete political vocabularies comprising concepts grouped together in an internally ordered domain with a grammar and syntax, and repertoire of associations – even a literature – which mimicked that discoverable in a natural language. Where occupational groups within a single society were sufficiently segregated, the same political society might contain two or more such vocabularies.[8]

Pocock's first major work had identified the conflict between two such languages – that of the Common Law – according to which the following of precedent meant the past was essentially unchanging – and that of the Feudal Law, which discerned a distinct and authoritative structure to the English past. For both of these languages the past was authoritative for the present, and so the exponents of each language sought to know the truth about the past as a means of establishing the legitimacy or otherwise of the present. He saw the primary interpretative task of the historian of political thought as that of identifying and reconstructing such languages and their mutation over time. Explaining a particular writer's production involved identifying its relationship with the language – or languages – being deployed by the writer.[9]

This second order presentation of a language always involved the danger that the exegete might present as coherent that which was not. By drawing attention to the difficulty of resisting the temptation to engage in (as opposed to write histories of) political theory, Pocock explained the lamentable but 'constant tendency [for the history of political theory] to become philosophy'.[10]

Escaping such pitfalls involved, amongst other things, correctly assessing the level of abstraction at which a given composition was intended to operate, as well as the extent to which it was intended as a reflective

[7] M. Oakshott, *Experience and its Modes* (Cambridge, 1933; repr. 1985) suggested a pretty stark division of experiences; Oakshott, *Rationalism in Politics* (London, 1962) made slightly less of the boundaries.

[8] 'When we speak of 'languages', therefore, we mean for the most part sub-languages: idioms, rhetorics, ways of talking about politics, distinguishable games of which each may have its own vocabulary, rules, preconditions and implications, tone and style': J.G.A. Pocock, 'The Concept of a Language and the *métier d'historien* . . .', in A. Pagden (ed.) *The Languages of Theory in Early Modern Europe* (Cambridge, 1987), p. 21.

[9] Pocock, 'Languages and Their Implications', p. 25; Pocock, 'The Concept of a Language', p. 23; J.G.A. Pocock, 'The State of the Art', in Pocock, *Virtue Commerce and History: Essays on Political Thought and History, Chiefly in the Eighteenth Century* (Cambridge, 1985), p. 7.

[10] Pocock, 'The History of Political Thought', p. 187.

or reconstitutive philosophical activity or a rhetorical exhortation to action.[11]

Thinkers at a high level of abstraction uncovered and sometimes sought to restructure basic linguistic relationships in a fairly self-conscious fashion, but the activities of less abstract thinkers worked within, rather than restructuring, political languages. Their productions could be explained by bringing to the reader's attention relationships between concepts and patterns of speech now lost, which the subject of the study had assumed rather than made explicit.

Pocock's claim that the appropriate level of abstraction for dealing with a text was a historical question, rather than a matter of choice for the investigator, suggested the priority of historical over philosophical moods of approaching texts; yet, whilst insisting on the distinction, he could be quite agnostic about their relative priority.[12] To Stanley Fish's sceptical 'Is there a text in the class?', Pocock's firm answer was that 'There is a text in the historian's class', whatever other practitioners find, or fail to find, in theirs.[13] Despite Pocock's commitment to 'present the text as it bore meaning in the mind of the author or his contemporary reader',[14] some critics have claimed that his narratives have operated at a level of abstraction 'far exceeding that attained by the writers he studied'.[15] However, his identification of languages as the appropriate transhistorical units of study provides him with some warrant for doing this. A language may be said to comprise a set of relationships – logical and associative – and potentials which, whilst they might be unrealised by its users, can nevertheless be transmitted by them and so remain available to subsequent users of the language.[16]

The work done by the concept of language in Pocock's thinking – despite his toying with the Kuhnian notion of the paradigm[17] – has

[11] There *were* such thinkers as Wolin's 'Epic Theorists': the 'fully self-conscious linguistic performer'; Hobbes was one such, but their identification was a matter of empirical historical research. Pocock, 'The State of the Art', pp. 16–17.

[12] See, e.g. Pocock, 'Languages and Their Implications', pp. 6–9; and Pocock, 'Political Theory, History, and Myth: a Salute to John Gunnell', *Annals of Scholarship*, 1 (1980). Revealing of the differences between Skinner and Pocock at this time about the priority of historical understanding is Skinner's observation about Pocock's 'surprisingly respectful discussion of Gunnell'. Skinner, 'Reply to My Critics', p. 326.

[13] Pocock, 'State of the Art', p. 21.

[14] Pocock, 'Languages and Their Implications', p. 6.

[15] A. Lockyer, 'Pocock's Harrington', *Political Studies*, 27 (1980), p. 485.

[16] See Pocock, 'Languages and Their Implications', p. 23–4: 'It is true that [a user of language] could not have meant to convey any message which the resources of language in his lifetime did not render it possible for him to have meant . . . but within these limits there is room for it to have happened to him (as it happens to all of us) to mean more than he said or to say more than he meant.' Also Pocock, 'State of the Art', pp. 20–1.

[17] See most enthusiastically, Pocock, preface in *Politics Language and Time* (repr. 1989),

increased over time, acquiring a deep Saussurian patina (and it is a patina, not a gloss).[18] Crucial to the viability of this exercise, he acknowledges, is the maintenance of the distinction between *lange* and *parole*; if the language cannot be identified independently of the text which exemplifies it, it can exercise no explanatory power.[19] Pocock even identified at one point what looked suspiciously like a series of verification criteria to test for the independent existence of a language.[20]

Nevertheless the concepts of tradition and practice have remained primary to his theoretical formulations or abridgements to which they have from time to time given rise.[21]

Indeed it is tempting – looking back at *The Ancient Constitution and the Feudal Law* – to see Pocock's method as immanent in one of his earliest and recurrent subject matters: the Common Law mind and the customary character of even the most theoretical performances. That is to say one is tempted to see Pocock's insight into the hermetic qualities of the constitutive rule of the Common Law tradition as a property which he generalised into all traditions: 'because our rule is always to follow precedent the past must have determined the present, and provides the only guide for action in respect of the future'.[22]

John Pocock's work was that of a master practitioner intermittently essaying methodological reflection. Skinner's earliest practice, by contrast, was already combined with some very precise methodological

---

p. x and the first and last essays in that volume: 'Languages and Their Implications' and 'On the Non-Revolutionary Character of Paradigms'; but note in 'The Concept of a Language': 'we may think of them as having the character of paradigms, in that they operate so as to structure thought and speech in certain ways and to preclude their being structured in others, we may not describe them as paradigms if the term implies that preclusion has been successfully effected.' p. 21.

[18] J.G.A. Pocock, 'The Owl Reviews his Feathers: a Valedictory Lecture', xerox, Johns Hopkins University, 11 May 1994: the history of political thought 'has been becoming all my life less a history of thought than of language, discourse, literature', p. 18.

[19] This is not quite the idiom in which Pocock puts the point (see 'The concept of a Language', pp. 26–7), but it seems concisely appropriate. For the superiority of such forms of 'explanation' over ubiquitous economic explanations on precisely this issue see my 'Reasons as Explanations, Prices as Descriptions' in J. Barry and J. Melling (eds.), *Culture Production and History* (Exeter, 1992)

[20] Pocock, 'The Concept of a Language', pp. 26–7. These criteria were: 1) different authors carried out a variety of acts within it; 2) discussing one another's use of it; 3) being able to predict the implications, intimations, entailed by its use in particular circumstances; 4) discovering its use in unexpected places; and 5) successfully excluding languages from consideration on grounds of non-availability. And similarly if less formally, Pocock, 'State of the Art', p. 10.

[21] For example in 'The Concept of a Language', where he proposes 'to let them [meta-theory, a general theory of language] arise, if they arise at all, out of the implications of what I shall be saying we as historians do. The *Métier d'historien* . . . is primarily his craft or practice', p. 19.

[22] J.G.A. Pocock, *The Ancient Constitution and the Feudal Law: A Study of English Historical Thought in the Seventeenth Century*, 2nd edn (Cambridge, 1997).

claims. The nub of his position is the idea that a work of political theory is a (linguistic) performance.[23] This is so in two specific senses. One is that explored by Austin and Searle. Austin had pointed out that, rather than referring (to things), linguistic acts (written and spoken) *perform*.[24] The notorious example is the first person use of the word 'promise' which performs what it designates. There are many others, a number of which are of huge importance in political language (and action). Consider for example the political implications in the use of verbs such as 'founding', 'banishing', 'abolishing' (monarchies, for example) or 'declaring' ('independence', for example, or 'the rights of men' or 'women').[25] In speaking or writing therefore we also often perform, and paradigmatically so in the case of political action. Allied to this notion of performance is the tricky notion of intention. Skinner couched his commitment to the historicity of an interpretation in terms of the recovery of authorial intention. Some critics complained that such an inscrutably private notion as an intention could not be used as a criterion of meaning. But intention is intended as a shorthand to indicate the existence of a convention or conventional repertoire of meaning within which intentions could be framed. As in the much beloved analogy of the game of chess – a move can only be made within the context of an established, rule-governed, framework – so, within a language comprising meanings, associations and expectations, a grammar and syntax, some locutions are more easily conceivable than others – and some are inconceivable. Consequently the ascription to an author of an intention to perform an inconceivable move (as judged by these public, recoverable, criteria) can rightly be judged improbable or impossible. This is clearest in the case of the ascription of genres which had not yet emerged, the deployment of which could not therefore reasonably be ascribed to the author. Thus, for example, the claim – periodically advanced – that Machiavelli's *The Prince* was a satire (in the eighteenth-century sense of that word) designed to expose, through exaggeration, the character of princely government, is to be ruled out. If Machiavelli's cultural repertoire did not include such a genre it was not open to him to frame an intention to write such a work.

---

[23] The theory of speech acts may be approached most easily in J.L. Austin's, *How To Do Things With Words*, edited by J.O. Urmson (Oxford, 1962) [delivered as the William James Lectures, Harvard, 1955]. A more developed account is John R. Searle, *Speech Acts: an Essay in the Philosophy of Language* (Cambridge, 1969). Skinner's major statement was 'Meaning and Understanding in the History of Ideas', reprinted with other essays by him and criticisms of his position in Tully (ed.), *Meaning and Context*.

[24] Austin, *How To Do Things With Words, passim*.

[25] Excellent historical accounts of such speech acts have recently been given; see, for example, the title essay in the collection by Keith Michael Baker, *Inventing the French Revolution* (Cambridge, 1990).

However, Skinner exploited the notion of intention in a distinct and more dynamic way to reveal the character of innovation.[26] In doing so he showed how his analysis might contribute both to the construction of a historical narrative concerning the development of thought *and* to our understanding of the *political* character of such change. Political writers commonly seek to persuade through exploiting different elements of ethically loaded terms. Two such elements are their commendatory character, and their role in referring. The political author, seeking to persuade an audience to accept a particular set of arrangements as eligible, will identify a term which has positive commendatory overtones and look for ways to insinuate that the arrangements he wishes to have accepted possess the relevant empirical features to which the term refers. One classic modern version of this, Skinner claimed, was the way that 'competing elite' theories of democracy managed to 'capture' the commendatory overtones of the term for a set of elitist arrangements which did not, at the outset, qualify as democratic at all.[27] It was precisely in this innovative or at least a-typical deployment of linguistic conventions that we could recover the political import in meanings, since the act of political persuasion most commonly involves the rhetori-cally innovative extension or restriction of conventional meanings or repertoires, as the author seeks to capture or deny the commendatory force of the term or particular application of it under discussion. This rhetorical device of using one set of (stable) meanings or associations as a hinge on which to swing valencies towards another set in a different direction exemplifies very clearly what political persuasion is often about, as well as revealing a major source of change in political theory.[28] It also provided a usable programme for researchers by giving them an agenda and criteria of significance in assessing what variations were important in an often bewildering range of locutions and material. [29]

---

[26] As Skinner pointed out in response to critics who thought his account precluded the possibility of innovation, it is only against a background of conventional locutions that we can even identify innovatory speech acts.

[27] Q. Skinner 'A Plague on Both your Houses. Empirical Theorists of Democracy and Their Critics', *Political Theory*, 1 (1973), pp. 287–306.

[28] Skinner has also explored the history of this as a recognised device of formal rhetoric and its perceived threat to moral stability in 'Thomas Hobbes: Rhetoric and the Construction of Morality', *Proceedings of the British Academy*, 76 (1990), pp. 1–61, and subsequently in the full-length study *Reason and Rhetoric in the Philosophy of Hobbes* (Cambridge, 1996).

[29] A strikingly successful example is the way Martin van Gelderen showed how, during the Dutch Revolt, publicists and pamphleteers continually extended the range of meaning and application of (for example) city charters granting or guaranteeing 'liberties' to their citizens so as to justify rights of political action on the part of individuals and eventually of independence and liberty for the Netherlands as a whole. Van Gelderen, 'Liberty, Civic Rights, and Duties in Sixteenth-Century Europe and the Rise of the

Deploying either of these notions of intention requires a knowledge, both of the general range of intellectual resources available to an author, and of the immediate controversial context in which he or she intervened. Hence for Skinner, as well as for Pocock, it was important to familiarise oneself with a much wider range of texts, not just as a focus of study in themselves but as an intertextual nexus from which to identify both stable context and innovatory linguistic moves. This stress on the moment of linguistic action originally differentiated his position from Pocock's diachronic stress on languages and their transformation as the unit of study.

In Skinner's account the recovery of *meaning* stresses 'conventional availability' as a criterion, and the moment of understanding stresses the identification of innovation and departure which is logically dependent on conventional meaning. Pocock has now endorsed this view.[30] Both moments (and both thinkers) emphasised the importance of the local historical meaning as, at the very least, a point of departure, and on some stronger readings as a necessary component of any plausibly ascribable meaning.[31] However, a number of critics charged that the new methodology – in insisting on the context-embedded meaning of political-theoretical utterances – was politically emasculating, since it rendered them so irretrievably historical as to make them unavailable for contemporary political philosophy or argument.[32]

It could not be said that the implications of which the critics complained were all in the minds of the readers. John Pocock in a muted and often less than explicit way, John Dunn and Quentin Skinner more explicitly, early insisted on drawing attention to the impropriety their reflections had led them to perceive in deploying historical locutions, arguments and concepts for the purposes of contemporary political argument.

Dutch Republic', in Janet Coleman (ed.), *The Individual in Political Theory and Practice* (Oxford, 1996), and at greater length in his *Political Thought of the Dutch Revolt, 1555–1590* (Cambridge, 1992).

[30] Pocock, 'The Concept of a Language', pp. 31–2, 34; Pocock, 'State of the Art' p. 14–16, 19.

[31] Cf. Mark Bevir, who lines Pocock up with Michel Foucault in viewing the author as 'mouthpieces of those scriptwriting paradigms that are constitutive of their conceptual frameworks'. Bevir, 'Errors of Linguistic Contextualism', *History and Theory*, 31 (1992), p. 278.

[32] Amongst those who develop this as an argument are Margaret Leslie, 'In Defence of Anachronism', *Political Studies*, 18 (1970), pp. 433–47; Charles Tarleton, 'Historicity, Meaning and Revisionism in the Study of Political Thought', *History and Theory*, 12 (1973); John G. Gunnell, 'Interpretation and the History of Political Theory: Apology and Epistemology', *American Political Science Review*, 76 (1982), pp. 317–27; Howard Warrender, 'Political Theory and Historiography', *Historical Journal*, 22 (1979), pp. 931–40.

Amongst the propositions controversially advanced by Skinner was that there were no enduring political ideas such as could properly be the subject of historical enquiry. (It was, as he put it, 'not that such histories can sometimes go wrong, but they can never go right'.) And even if there may, at a suitable level of abstraction, be enduring questions in political theory (which he doubted), the necessarily historically specific answers given to them could not be relevant to our present concerns, so that, more generally, we should not expect to learn anything directly applicable and relevant to our own political situation from the proper (i.e. historical) study of political theory.[33] Indeed given the impressive theoretical structure of Skinner's argument it might not be too much to say that the disqualification of any diachronic deployment of political concepts or theories was not only an intention of the complex set of speech acts comprising his methodological offensive, but that it was a strict and logical entailment of them.

None of this was equivalent to denying that there were things to be learnt from history. However, the kind of learning that was held to be possible was firstly that of an anthropological and culturally mind-broadening character gained by insights into that which was strange and other, rather than knowledge providing direct tools for immediate political employment

Nevertheless the strangeness was bought at a price. To be truly strange was surely to be incapable of being used in our own world. It seemed to many that the effort involved in recovering the strangeness of the writing of Locke or Rousseau rendered it, like Azande Witchcraft in Peter Winch's famous account, an activity which could hardly be translated into our terms at all. The more historically specific a speech act was, the more unavailable it must be to its modern investigators. Unavailable that is, not to the sensitised understanding, but as a component of action. Indeed, some joyfully celebrated the caesura which a proper understanding of them created between even the Greatest Texts and the present.

In the introduction to what remains an epochal study of Locke, in this or indeed any other context, John Dunn remarked, 'I simply cannot conceive of constructing an analysis of any issue in contemporary political theory around the affirmation or negation of anything which Locke says about political matters.' And although he has subsequently expressed regret at what he very candidly called the 'dismayingly unequivocal' character of the remark, his more recent attempt to distinguish what is still living in the philosophy of John Locke seems to

---

[33] Skinner, 'Meaning and Understanding', pp. 54, 66, 65.

me to have salvaged very little.[34] The tremendous strength of the contextualist case – as a technical philosophical argument – seemed to have been bought at the cost of the contemporary political availability of past political theory or propositions or concepts within it. One could not, it seemed to many, gain on the swings of historical context – and there were very real gains – without losing on the political roundabouts.

One of the persistent criticisms of the 'historical revolution' has been that it detached the history of political thought from the activity of political theorising, by seeming to fix exclusively limited historical meanings on texts which we had been used to treat as open and available. Recently, however, members of the historical school have been displaying signs of wishing to evade these strictures – if strictures they be. For Pocock that discourse which first identified land as the guarantor of stability of interest in the citizen, and then saw the endowment first of a national church and then of a cultural clerisy as a necessary means of superintending the volatility of a commercial and increasingly private virtue, was not only a discourse by which eighteenth- and early nineteenth-century political thinkers accounted for their own reality;[35] the authority of it reaches to the present, enabling Pocock to observe acidly on its final destruction, by neo-Jacobins masquerading as conservatives, using the device of 'a state claiming to limit its own powers to destroy the independence of the universities, motivated by a contempt for their nature and function.'[36] If a theory is an abridgement of a practice – even an intellectual one – one could still pursue the present intimation of that practice or its abridgement. Yet whilst he acknowledges that the study of political thought 'belongs both to the discipline of history and to that of political theory (political theorising?) and philosophy' the relationship of either, or both, to practice is unclear. In occasional review articles, on Europe, on the condition of Anglo-American political life and discourse, the vitality of some of those languages is celebrated or deprecated, and contemporaries situated within them – identified as inheritors or linguistic variants of radicalism in that past of which they are a linguistic product.[37] Even more strikingly in his writing on Burke we find the

---

[34] J. Dunn, 'What is Living and What is Dead in the Political Theory of John Locke', in Dunn, *Interpreting Political Responsibility* (Cambridge, 1990).

[35] On the eighteenth-century 'landed interest' sources of Coleridge's argument for the establishment of a standing, cultural clerisy see John Morrow, *Coleridge's Political Thought* (London, 1990).

[36] J.G.A. Pocock, 'A Discourse of Sovereignty', in Nicholas Phillipson and Quentin Skinner (eds.), *Political Discourse in Early Modern Britain* (Cambridge, 1993), p. 424.

[37] Thus, for example, 'Richard Nixon was a figure of the Old Whig political imagination . . . America may have guaranteed the survival of the forces of corruption it was created to resist.' J.G.A. Pocock, '1776: the Revolution Against Parliament', in Pocock (ed.), *Three British Revolutions: 1641, 1688, 1776* (Princeton, 1980), p. 286.

direct leap to the present: it would, he writes, be wrong to criticise Burke's admittedly overdrawn picture of the French Revolution, for Burke 'seems to have known more about what revolution could become than what it was yet like . . . we may protest that in 1797 France was in full retreat from Jacobinism: but the emergence of the Nazis, the Red Guards and the Khmer Rouge in our time suggests that Burke's last work was the *1984* of its generation. He had discovered the theory of totalitarianism and was enlarging it into prophecy.'[38] Prophecy is, of course, one language or idiom of the repertoire furnished by our inheritance. Yet what distinguishes the kind of observation Pocock makes here is the shift from identifying the idiom, to endorsing the claims made through its deployment. It is almost as though revolution were the only trans-historical entity, breaking, as it would claim to, the continuity of language which constitutes our political identity, and so everywhere and always ushering in disaster and moral chaos.

In Pocock's writing this threat of linguistic and therefore political discontinuity constitutes the crisis of our time, threatening first from the left, now from the right: 'the Ogre may wear a different face'. Pursuing an awareness of the history of our political language in all its richness, right through to the present, is therefore presented as both an urgent and a civic task, and an absolute prerequisite for making its intimations available in the present. The values of the academy are not the values of the market or of the state. Yet its civilising function is vital to each, and vital to maintaining the bleak but not unhopeful conviction that although 'things fall apart the centres somehow hold'.[39] The clearest statement of this is made by Gordon Schochet in the epilogue to *Varieties of British Political Thought*, the essays written by the directors of the various seminars held at the Folger Institute's Center for the History of British Political Thought and edited by Pocock, who himself was, with Schochet, largely responsible for the Center's massive, and impressive, total output.[40] Schochet interestingly both poses and sets out

---

[38] J.G.A. Pocock, 'Editor's Introduction' to Edmund Burke, *Reflections on the Revolution in France*, edited by J.G.A. Pocock (Indianapolis, 1987), p. xxxvii; and 'Burke would have known what to say about the Great Cultural Revolution and the evacuation of Phnom Penh': Pocock, *Virtue Commerce and History*, p. 191.

[39] See the preface to the second edition of Pocock, *Politics Language and Time* (1989), pp. xi–xii.

[40] Gordon J. Schochet, 'Epilogue: Why Should History Matter? Political Theory and the History of Discourse', in J.G.A. Pocock (ed.), with Gordon J. Schochet and Lois G. Schwoerer, *The Varieties of British Political Thought 1500–1800* (Cambridge, 1993), pp. 321–57. The trajectory of the Folger Library's operation can be followed in the six volumes of published papers under the general editorship of Gordon J. Schochet: *Proceedings of the Center for the History of British Political Thought* (6 vols., Washington DC, 1990–3).

to answer the question 'Why should history matter?' His answer is that 'the past and the present of a civil society must be held together if that society is to survive at a level of consciousness in which its members can participate'. The goal, therefore, 'is to create and even sanctify, a tradition that tells a people who they have been and are and allows them to ponder who they might become . . . discursive continuity and academic history can stand as partners in the same enterprise'.[41]

Yet there are here, as so often in the case of a sceptically based procedural conservatism, serious equivocations. They lie in issues such as whether linguistic continuity is a contingent or a necessary feature of politics, in whether it is the whole of our tradition, or only the self-consciously conservative elements of it that continuity requires us to sustain. If linguistic continuity is a (logically) contingent feature of political communities, sustained by some, destroyed by other languages, then the imprecation to maintain it, and as a means to favour some languages – those of a Hume, a Smith, or even a Burke, over those of Price or Paine or even Godwin – becomes a political and very contestable choice, not a philosophical observation emanating ineluctably from our present or the human condition.[42] Alternatively if linguistic continuity is a (logically) necessary condition of political community this will be true of all the political languages comprising it and there will be no need to favour one over the other.

John Dunn, Quentin Skinner and their students, too, have for some time now been deploying the historical understanding of political theory for contemporary purposes. John Dunn's edited book of essays – interestingly published by Oxford University Press not Cambridge – about an idea, 'Democracy', subtitled 'The Unfinished Journey 508 BC to AD 1993', is, in as much as a collective endeavour can be, a history. In it, despite drawing our attention to the massive differences between Greek and modern democracy, the editor asserts the existence of clear continuities of meaning between them[43] and indeed the persistence of at least one perennial problem, namely whether 'in the life that human beings live together, the balance between arbitrary external constraint

---

[41] Schochet, 'Epilogue', p. 323
[42] If the issue is taken to be – as Burke does and Pocock may – one between the privileging of rational abstraction as against embedded experience, it has been pointed out that the disposition to abstract from experience and to privilege the insights of reason over inherited tradition lies at the heart of both Greek science and democratic politics, and so must, far from representing its overthrow, in some sense be central to our culture. G.E.R. Lloyd, 'Democracy, Philosophy, and Science in Ancient Greece', in John Dunn (ed.), *Democracy: the Unfinished Journey, 508 BC to AD 1993* (Oxford, 1992), pp. 52–3.
[43] J. Dunn, 'Conclusion' in Dunn, (ed.), *Democracy: the Unfinished Journey*, p. 256.

and reasonable personal choice can be decisively shifted towards the latter'.[44]

In that same book, David Wootton ironically, as it eventually appears, points out that the whiggish perception of Levellers as having anticipated twentieth-century liberal society means that 'we are still waiting for a satisfactory account of the Levellers which will succeed in making their apparent modernity seem no more than an illusion of perspective'. He seeks to 'restore the Levellers to their age by showing that unlike moderns they were not democrats, that they were essentially religious, not secular thinkers and actors, that they were nostalgic not forward looking and that they had no conception of modern political processes – in particular party government'. But this turns out to be devil's advocacy: the Levellers, on investigation, *were nearly* democrats, strikingly secular, appealed against history – 'we are men of the present age' – to universal standards and abstract principles, and, if they would have been uneasy at the sight of the modern party's 'queasy mixture of principle, interest, and expediency', then this, as Wootton remarks, 'hardly marks them out as visitors from another culture'.[45] It turns out that the major feature that separates the Levellers from us is their 'extraordinary faith in the power of words'.[46] But this difference itself overcomes the gap between us and them. Almost magically, when we read them, 'we seem to achieve the impossible: we seem to hear the dead speak . . . To our surprise, the language that they speak is sometimes indistinguishable from our own.'[47]

Richard Tuck prefaces his new study of early modern philosophy and government by claiming that 'The point of studying the seventeenth century . . . is that many of the conflicts which marked its politics are also to be found in some form in the late twentieth century, and indeed, the better our historical sense of what those conflicts were, the more often they seem to resemble modern ones.'[48] James Tully expresses similar if less explicit hopes in his collection of essays on Locke.[49]

Finally, Quentin Skinner himself, in another chapter of Dunn's *Democracy*, devoted to Italian City-Republics, pursues a theme explored in a number of his articles going back to the early 1980s. Whilst warning against assuming any easy identification of city-republics with democracy, he states that they nevertheless contributed to the 'history of

---

[44] Ibid., p. 259.
[45] D. Wootton, 'The Levellers', in Dunn (ed.), *Democracy: the Unfinished Journey*, p. 79.
[46] Ibid., p. 85
[47] Ibid., p. 88. The hope that the Levellers might speak to us, no less than the content of their message or their distaste for the politics of interest and compromise, is one also expressed in the recent past by Tony Benn MP.
[48] Richard Tuck, *Philosophy and Government 1572–1651* (Cambridge1993), p. xi–xii.
[49] J. Tully, *An Approach to Political Philosophy: Locke in Contexts* (Cambridge, 1993), p. 2.

modern democratic theory and practice' and specifically 'engendered a rich political literature in which a number of arguments in favour of government by the people were articulated for the first time in post-classical thought'.[50] More specifically, what Skinner elsewhere discusses under the rubric of the debate between negative and positive liberty, and here, less technically, as 'the unfamiliar connection drawn by ideologists of the city-republics between freedom and [the obligation of] participation', represents, he claims, 'the most significant lesson we can hope to learn from them', namely 'that we must never put our trust in princes. If we wish to ensure that governments act in the interest of the people, we must somehow ensure that we the people act as our own government.'[51] Indeed, the strategy of reviving classical ideals crops up in unlikely places: Michael Mansfield QC on prime time television invoked Greek and Roman conceptions of the value of public space in his opposition to the Major administration's public order bill.[52]

More dramatically, in his inaugural lecture for the Regius Chair of History at Cambridge, Skinner sought to demonstrate – *and recover* – a pattern of argument he calls neo-Roman, which, he hoped, would enable us to see how individual liberty (in a negative sense) is not only consistent with a republican concern for the sustenance of the republican state, but indeed requires it. One does not have to be skilled in the nuances of context to catch the political significance of advancing a republican argument in a Regius inaugural address. Not only does Skinner there pursue these longstanding republican themes in his work, he addresses head on, and seeks to counter, the claim that insisting on the historicity of political thought robs it of contemporary relevance. Becoming aware of our political pasts, he urges, is part of understanding our political selves. Recovering the way in which concepts and arguments still in use have been defined in the past is a way to escape being 'bewitched by our own intellectual inheritance'.[53]

None of these aspirations is uncongenial to me, either in a political or an academic sense. Quite the contrary: I have elsewhere expressed a diffident combination of appreciation of the intellectual results of the new methodology and wariness about its potentially depoliticising character.[54] Nevertheless these developments cannot be – or at least

---

[50] Q. Skinner, 'Italian city-republics', in Dunn (ed.), *Democracy: the Unfinished Journey*, p. 60.

[51] Ibid., pp. 68–9.

[52] *The Moral Maze*, BBC1, 15 October 1994.

[53] Quentin Skinner, *Liberty Before Liberalism* (Cambridge, 1998); see further my review, in *The Historical Journal*, 41, 4 (1990), pp. 1183–8.

[54] I. Hampsher-Monk, 'Political Languages in Time: the Work of J.G.A. Pocock', *The British Journal of Political Science*, 14, 1 (1984).

have not been – reconciled with the philosophical foundations on which at least one – and the most rigorous – version of the historical revolution was built, and I see no methodological revisions in train, let alone any of a comparable degree of technical sophistication to those which established the original position.[55]

There are, however, historical precedents. The early Renaissance humanists pursued an increasingly historically sophisticated understanding of their Latin stylistic models in a range of fields. They set out to recover ancient meanings in the hope of embellishing their contemporary world with the results of their research, only to discover that the meanings were so strange that they could not be applied.[56] Yet, again and again significant numbers of them turned to exploit the political importance of the content of their material when the loss of political liberty threatened.[57] Hans Baron, one of the greatest historians of the most celebrated of such episodes, the Florentine resistance to Visconti, wrote his account of it in circumstances where that history itself cannot but be seen as a contemporary political act intended to warn Germans of the imminent loss of their own liberty and of what must be done to preserve it.[58] Ernst Cassirer too sought, in his study of the Enlightenment, to recover for his German readers a sense of German thinkers' integral involvement in that movement, at least in part in order to repudiate a growing political movement which sought to define a blood-based nationalism in conscious opposition to the values of enlightenment.[59]

In the absence of philosophical help, perhaps these models provide for the moment the best way of reading the recent re-application of historical material to our contemporary world by those who have been foremost in insisting on its irreducibly historical character. Margaret Thatcher was neither Gian Galeazzo Visconti nor Adolf Hitler, yet her own and ensuing governments during the period I am discussing were

---

[55] Sympathetic practitioners seem to share my sense that there is a problem; see David Miller, 'The Resurgence of Political Theory', *Political Studies*, 38, 3 (1990), pp. 424ff; Dario Castiglione, 'Historical Arguments in Political Theory', *Political Theory Newsletter*, 5, 2 (1993), esp. pp. 95–6, 98.

[56] See Pocock. *The Ancient Constitution*, pp. 9–11, and the story recounted there of the great French jurist Cujas who was asked to apply his understanding of Roman law to the considerable problems of late sixteenth-century France, and replied: 'Quid hoc ad edictum praetoris?' ('What does this have to do with a Praetorian Edict?').

[57] Q. Skinner, *Foundations of Modern Political Thought* (2 vols., Cambridge, 1978), vol. I, pp. 28ff.

[58] Hans Baron, *The Crisis of the Early Italian Renaissance. Civic Humanism and Republican Liberty in an Age of Classicism and Tyranny* (Princeton, 1966).

[59] Ernst Cassirer, *Die Philosophie der Aufklärung* (Tubingen, 1932); see R. Wokler, 'Multiculturalism and Ethnic Cleansing in the Enlightenment', in Ole Grell and Roy Porter (eds.), *Toleration in Enlightenment Europe* (Cambridge, 1999), p. 79.

perceived by many to have presided over an unprecedented deconstruction of those structures of civic independence and representative institutions which provided citizens with the possibility – I do not say they guaranteed it – of controlling those who exercised power over them. Perhaps, like the sceptical Hume, whose doubts about induction could not persuade him to believe that the bread which had nourished him in the past could be presumed to do so in future, but whose nature supervened on his reason, enabling him to fall to and eat, perhaps like him, in appropriate circumstances, our political natures overcome our philosophical or historical propriety and we fall to and act.

9 The rise of, challenge to and prospects for a Collingwoodian approach to the history of political thought

Quentin Skinner

I need to begin by sounding a sceptical note. It makes little sense to speak of a British – still less an English – style of writing the history of political thought, if only because the English language is the principal medium of communication in Australasia and North America, two places in which this kind of history has recently been vigorously practised and very ably discussed. It is certainly possible to say, however, that within these anglophone intellectual communities a particular style has been developed in the course of the present generation which stands in strong contrast with a number of European approaches to the study of political thought, including the current German preoccupation with *Begriffsgeschichte*[1] and the continuing French passion for post-structuralist and especially deconstructionist methodologies. My focus in the following remarks[2] will accordingly be on this anglophone intellectual community rather than on the idea of national contexts and traditions of thought.

It likewise makes little sense to speak of the approach I wish to consider as an approach specifically to the history of political thought. It is true that some of the most interesting contributions to the theoretical debate have been made by practitioners of this particular sub-discipline, as the names of John Dunn, Peter Laslett, John Pocock and James Tully sufficiently attest. But the questions they have raised are questions about how best to set about interpreting any kind of text, and in discussing their views I shall not limit myself – any more than they do themselves – to specifically political examples. The merits of their approach to the

---

[1] But for a valuable attempt to reconcile the genre of *Begriffsgeschichte* with what I am calling a Collingwoodian approach, see Melvin Richter, *The History of Social and Political Concepts: a Critical Introduction* (Oxford, 1995).

[2] What follows is a revised version of an article I have already published under the title 'From Hume's Intentions to Deconstruction and Back' in *The Journal of Political Philosophy*, 4 (1996), pp. 142–54. I am grateful to the editors and to Blackwell Publishers Ltd for permission to incorporate much of my earlier article into my present text.

history of political thought need to be assessed by way of assessing their programme more generally.

I

Within the anglophone community of which I have spoken, perhaps the most influential pioneer of the approach I want to discuss was R.G. Collingwood, although he in turn owed much of his inspiration to Hegelian views about the philosophy of history, especially as developed and popularised by Benedetto Croce in Italy.[3] Collingwood's ideas initially fell on stony ground, but in the late 1950s his work began to be discussed by a growing band of philosophers and intellectual historians broadly sympathetic to his cause. Some of the earliest signs of this interest came from Australasia, where John Passmore and John Pocock both published classic papers on intellectual history in the early 1960s in which they spoke in partly Collingwoodian tones.[4] Shortly afterwards a similar approach began to be extensively discussed and practised in England, and particularly at the University of Cambridge, where the new impetus chiefly stemmed from the work of Peter Laslett, John Dunn and their numerous associates and followers,[5] among whom I would wish to number myself.[6]

If these scholars have anything methodologically in common, it might be summarised as a desire to stress the historicity of the history of political theory and of intellectual history more generally. Collingwood

[3] For the most succinct statement of his general position see R.G. Collingwood, *An Autobiography* (Oxford, 1939), ch. v, pp. 29–43 on 'the logic of question and answer'. There is an interesting (and surprisingly appreciative) account of this aspect of Collingwood's philosophy in Hans-Georg Gadamer, *Truth and Method*, 2nd English edn (London, 1979), pp. 333–41.

[4] See John Passmore 'The Idea of a History of Philosophy', *History and Theory*, Beiheft 5 (1965), pp. 1–32, especially his discussion of Collingwood's views at pp. 8–13. See also J.G.A. Pocock, 'The History of Political Thought: a Methodological Enquiry' in Peter Laslett and W.G. Runciman (eds.), *Philosophy, Politics and Society*, 2nd series (Oxford, 1962), pp. 183–202. Pocock's essay was published while he was Reader in Political Science at the University of Canterbury, Christchurch, New Zealand.

[5] John Dunn has recently surveyed this movement, to which he has contributed so notably. See John Dunn, *The History of Political Theory and Other Essays* (Cambridge, 1996), esp. pp. 11–38. Some of the finest statements and exemplifications of the approach discussed by Dunn have centred on the political theory of John Locke. See for example Peter Laslett's Introduction to John Locke, *Two Treatises of Government*, edited by Peter Laslett, student edition (Cambridge, 1988), pp. 3–122. See also the Introduction ('John Locke in History: the Problems') to John Dunn, *The Political Thought of John Locke* (Cambridge, 1969), pp. 5–10 and the Introduction to James Tully, *An Approach to Political Philosophy: Locke in Contexts* (Cambridge, 1993), pp. 1–6.

[6] I first discussed Collingwood's approach in an article published in 1969. See Quentin Skinner, 'Meaning and Understanding in the History of Ideas', reprinted in Skinner, *Meaning and Context*, edited by James Tully (Cambridge, 1988), esp. pp. 55–6, 64–6.

himself expressed this commitment by demanding that we should aim to recover the precise questions to which the philosophical texts we study were designed as answers,[7] while Pocock analogously spoke of the need to distinguish the various levels of abstraction at which different writers work.[8] Passmore emphasised the importance of recovering the intentions of authors and their underlying purposes,[9] while Dunn went on to defend a 'realist' aspiration to recover and describe past intellectual projects in the terms in which their exponents conceived of them.[10]

These injunctions and others like them have helped to generate a large and still-growing body of distinguished scholarship in intellectual history – and perhaps above all, as I have already noted, in the history of political thought. But times change, and the question that now needs to be addressed is whether this approach can still be given an effective theoretical defence in these avowedly postmodern days. How far can we continue to uphold the belief that we can usefully speak of recovering the projects and intentions of authors, of ascribing particular meanings to their utterances, of distinguishing right from wrong interpretations of complex philosophical texts?

II

These questions were made to seem urgent in the 1970s and 1980s by an increasing number of critics who argued that the very idea of textual interpretation is a mistake, since there are no such interpretations to be gained. There are only misreadings, since it is an error to suppose that we can ever arrive unambiguously at the meaning of a text. If we ask who attacked the traditional idea of interpretation in these terms, one obvious answer is that this was the sort of scepticism propagated by the vogue for deconstruction. It is true that there is a certain difficulty about interrogating deconstructionist critics about the reasons for their conclusions. It is part of their case that they are not available to answer such traditional humanistic questions, since this would be to co-opt them into the very style of discourse they repudiate. It is not clear, however, that they repudiate it consistently. Derrida, for example, has felt able to

---

[7] Collingwood, *Autobiography*, pp. 29–43.

[8] Pocock, 'The History of Political Thought', esp. pp. 185–8.

[9] See Passmore, 'The Idea of a History of Philosophy', esp. pp. 8–13.

[10] See in particular Dunn's essays 'The Identity of the History of Ideas' (first published in 1968) and 'Practising History and Social Science on "Realist" Assumptions' (first published in 1978) both collected in John Dunn, *Political Obligation in its Historical Context* (Cambridge, 1980), pp. 13–28 and 81–111. See in particular the discussion of Collingwood's views at pp. 102–3.

complain that Searle misreads him,[11] while Harlan has not hesitated in attacking my own views about interpretation to impute to me an identifiable set of intentions which he goes on to criticise in humanistic vein as inadequate to the realisation of my declared purposes.[12] I do not feel, accordingly, that we need feel unduly apologetic about making such writers part of our critical discourse, and I shall not hesitate in what follows to ask why they reject the possibility of recovering meanings and intentions, while attempting at the same time to assess the merits of their arguments.

It is in fact fairly clear, at least in Derrida's earlier writings, what reasons he has for rejecting traditional hermeneutics. He associates the project of interpretation with what he calls logocentrism, by which he means (roughly) the belief that meanings originate in the world and are conveyed to us by the capacity of words to refer to things. This belief is said to give rise, in Derrida's Heideggerian phrase, to a metaphysics of presence, to the illusion that the truth about the world can be made present to the mind through the medium of a denotative language.[13]

This assumption had of course been under attack long before Derrida questioned it. The worry about the tendency of signifiers to equivocate, and hence about the very idea of denotation, had featured in many nominalist philosophies of the early modern period, most notably in that of Hobbes.[14] The suggestion that meanings may amount to nothing more than conventional usages circulating within a particular form of life was similarly an important element in many holistic philosophies of language from the earlier part of the twentieth century, most notably those of Quine and the later Wittgenstein.[15] There can be no doubt, however, that Derrida carried the attack a long step further with his apparent commitment to the view that the terms we use to signify not only fail to do so univocally but float apart from what is purportedly signified until they come to exist in a state of free play.[16] Derrida went

---

[11] Jacques Derrida, *Limited Inc* (Chicago, 1988), esp. pp. 79–85.

[12] David Harlan, 'Intellectual History and the Return of Literature', *American Historical Review*, 94 (1989), pp. 581–609, esp. pp. 583–9.

[13] See Jacques Derrida, *Of Grammatology*, trans. Gayatri Chakravorty Spivak (Baltimore, 1976), esp. Part I, pp. 6–100. Cf. also Jacques Derrida, *Writing and Difference*, trans. Alan Bass (London, 1978), esp. ch. 10, pp. 278–82.

[14] See Thomas Hobbes, *The Elements of Law Natural and Politic*, edited by Ferdinand Tönnies, Introd. M.M. Goldsmith (London, 1969), esp. pp. 20–4. I have drawn attention to this aspect of Hobbes's philosophy of language in my recent book, *Reason and Rhetoric in the Philosophy of Hobbes* (Cambridge, 1996), esp. pp. 316–26.

[15] See especially the discussion of meaning and forms of life in Ludwig Wittgenstein, *Philosophical Investigations*, trans. G.E.M. Anscombe, 2nd edn (Oxford, 1958), esp. paras. 132–50, 217–43, pp. 51–9, 85–8.

[16] I speak of this as Derrida's apparent contention, since this is how his references to the element of 'play' (*jeu*) have generally been understood. It sometimes seems, however,

on to conclude that the alleged sense and reference of such signifiers are invariably deferred until they ultimately disappear, to be replaced by a state of pure intertextuality.[17]

It is true that Derrida sometimes modifies this anarchistic stance. He does not always seem to say that the free play of signifiers abolishes the referential capacity of language altogether. Rather he maintains that it prevents unambiguous reference, thereby deferring to the point of absence our capacity to be sure of any ascriptions of intended meanings to utterances. This certainly seems to be his position in his much-cited discussion in *Éperons* of the fragment, found among Nietzsche's papers, which reads: 'J'ai oublié mon parapluie' ('I have forgotten my umbrella').[18] As Derrida observes, everyone knows what these words mean;[19] the problem is that we can never know *'for sure'* what Nietzsche may have meant by writing them.[20] Derrida still wishes to insist, however, that the misguided figure whom he labels the hermeneut[21] faces an insuperable difficulty. The difficulty is that language in its inherently polysemic state of play inevitably writes itself over any intention to communicate any determinate meaning, leaving us to experience the exhilarating if unsettling absence of any such meanings at all.[22]

Derrida's has by no means been the only voice raised in recent times against the project of ascribing intentions to authors and meanings to texts. At least two further schools of thought may be said to converge upon the same point. We first need to take note of the assault on equating the intentions of authors with the meanings of texts which Paul Ricoeur mounted in his *Hermeneutics and the Human Sciences*,[23] and which Stanley Fish and others developed into a 'reader-response' approach to hermeneutics.[24] Ricoeur concedes that texts may well have

that his metaphor merely refers to the phenomenon of free movement around a fixed point, as when we speak of there being an element of play (*jeu*) in the operation of a machine. If this is the source of Derrida's metaphor, it implies a much less radical doubt about the capacity of words to denote effectively. I am indebted to Ian Maclean for this point.

17 See Derrida, *Of Grammatology*, esp. Part I, chs. 1 and 2, pp. 6–73; see also Derrida, *Writing and Difference*, esp. ch. 10, pp. 278–93.

18 Jacques Derrida, *Éperons: les styles de Nietzsche*, trans. Barbara Harlow (Chicago, 1979), p. 122.

19 Derrida, *Éperons*, p. 128: 'Chacun comprend ce que veut dire "j'ai oublié mon parapluie".'

20 Derrida, *Éperons*, p. 122: 'Nous ne serons jamais *assurés* de savoir ce que Nietzsche a voulu faire ou dire en notant ces mots.'

21 See for example *Éperons*, pp. 130, 132, 138.

22 *Éperons*, pp. 130–2; Derrida fearlessly applies the point to his own text at pp. 134–8. Cf. also Derrida, *Writing and Difference*, ch. 10, pp. 278–93.

23 Paul Ricoeur, *Hermeneutics and the Human Sciences*, edited and translated by John B. Thompson (Cambridge, 1981).

24 See especially Stanley Fish, *Is There a Text in This Class?* (Cambridge, Mass., 1980),

pristine intended meanings, but stresses that over the course of time, as well as because of the polysemic and metaphorical character of language, any text will acquire 'an autonomous space of meaning which is no longer animated by the intention of its author'.[25] Ricoeur's principal suggestion is that interpreters should concentrate on these changing public meanings of texts, rather than on the meanings that their original authors may have intended to assign to them. 'What the text says now matters more than what the author meant to say',[26] so that the act of interpretation should be seen as equivalent to that of appropriating the text for our own purposes.[27]

The other and contiguous school of thought I need to mention has gathered around Hans-Georg Gadamer's account of interpretation, especially as outlined in his *Wahrheit und Methode*. One of Gadamer's contentions is that the attempt to recover authorial intentionality presupposes that we can realise the goal of what he calls 'romantic hermeneutics', the goal of re-creating or re-thinking the thoughts of others.[28] Gadamer sees this aspiration as an obvious absurdity, assuming as it does that we can lay aside our position within our own traditions of thought and the prejudices – in the sense of the unavoidable pre-judgements of meaning – that inescapably result.[29] Gadamer's claim is not just that these prejudices help to shape whatever meanings we find. He is also making the Heideggerian point that, without such prejudging, we could never aspire to identify any meanings at all.[30] The only meanings we can hope to find are those which our traditions permit us to see. The most we can aspire to do is to bring other horizons together with our own; we can never hope to reach the end of other people's rainbows.[31]

The question I want to raise about these varying but convergent shools of thought is how far they force us to abandon the belief – the belief I have characterised as Collingwoodian – that one of the central goals of interpretation should be that of seeking to understand the intentions of authors and what they may have meant by what they

---

p. 3: 'the reader's response is not *to* the meaning; it *is* the meaning.' Fish tells us in his Introduction, however, that he has now abandoned this position in the light of the still more radical epiphany that 'interpretation is the source of texts, facts, authors and intentions' (p. 16).

[25] Ricoeur, *Hermeneutics and the Human Sciences*, p. 174.
[26] Ibid., p. 201.
[27] On 'interpretation as appropriation' see ibid., ch. 5, pp. 145–64.
[28] Gadamer, *Truth and Method*, esp. pp. 153–214. Harlan, 'Intellectual History', pp. 583–9 stigmatises my own approach in the same terms.
[29] Gadamer, *Truth and Method*, esp. pp. 235–40, 244–5.
[30] Ibid., esp. pp. 245–74.
[31] Ibid., esp. pp. 267–74.

wrote. It appears to be widely accepted that the combined force of the arguments I have been citing is enough to discredit any such attempt. But this is far from having been demonstrated. If we now return to Collingwood's *Idea of History*,[32] or to a sympathetic critique and development of Collingwood's position such as one finds in Passmore's classic essay, *The Idea of the History of Philosophy*, one meets with almost nothing that, in the light of recent discussions, one feels bound to admit is straightforwardly misconceived.

III

I shall seek to develop my case for the defence in two connected steps. My first rejoinder is that someone of Collingwoodian allegiances can perfectly well accommodate many of the alleged objections typically raised by the schools of thought I have singled out. Consider, for example, Derrida's insistence that traditional theories of interpretation underestimate the extent to which we can know 'for sure' what someone may have meant or intended by what they said. Historians of philosophy have generally taken care to concede this point, and to stress that any interpretation has the status merely of a hypothesis, instantly liable to be discarded in the light of new information or more nuanced readings. As Passmore puts it, for example, whatever interpretations we offer may always be wrong, and this is 'a risk we always have to take'.[33] Obsessed as he appears to be by Descartes's equation between knowledge and certainty, Derrida seems not to have noticed that this is a concession that almost every traditional theory of interpretation has been prepared to make.

Nor need a philosopher of Collingwoodian commitments feel any anxiety in the face of Ricoeur's analogous insistence on the need to distinguish the public from the intended meanings of texts. It is true that some theorists of interpretation – notably Hirsch and Juhl[34] – have sought to argue that the meanings of texts must be equated with the meanings intended by those who wrote them. But this is not a position that Collingwood ever adopted, and many of those sympathetic to his general argument have explicitly repudiated it. Passmore, for example, concludes his *Idea of a History of Philosophy* by stressing that our interpretations often have it as one of their specific aims to arrive at an

[32] R.G. Collingwood, *The Idea of History* (Oxford, 1946), esp. Part v, section 4, 'History as Re-enactment of Past Experience', pp. 282– 302.

[33] Passmore, 'The Idea of a History of Philosophy', p. 10.

[34] See E.D. Hirsch, *Validity in Interpretation* (New Haven, 1967), esp. pp. 12–13; E.D. Hirsch, *The Aims of Interpretation* (Chicago, 1976), esp. pp. 79–80; P.D. Juhl, *Interpretation* (Princeton, 1980), esp. pp. 16–44.

understanding of past writers and their works 'in a sense in which they did not understand themselves'.[35]

This seems an important point to underline. It will surely be a fact about any of the texts in which philosophers and political theorists take a professional interest that what they can legitimately be held to mean may differ from what – if we could get at it – their authors may have intended. It would certainly be amazing if all the allusions, connotations and resonances that an ingenious interpreter might properly claim to find in such texts could be shown to reflect the intentions of their authors at every point. But it would be a very crude mistake to suppose that this gives us any reason for excluding such elements from an account of the meaning of the *text*. If these elements of meaning are present, then they are present whether or not the author intended to put them there. If, as our culture increasingly urges us to acknowledge, almost all of what we dignify as thinking in fact takes place at an unconscious level, we shall be acting foolishly if we find ourselves defending any theory of interpretation which opposes this insight in a purely *a priori* way, even if it remains true that those interested in interpretation may still be mainly concerned with whatever thin trickle of thinking may properly be said to go on at a purely conscious level.

The second and principal point on which I wish to insist is that recent anti-intentionalist theories of interpretation have given us scarcely any reason for concluding that we must abandon the quest for authorial intentionality in the sense in which Collingwood and his admirers have been interested in it. Rather it seems to me that many commentators who invoke Derrida's and Gadamer's theories with the aim of discrediting the study of meaning and intentionality have misunderstood the way in which these concepts enter such theories as those of Collingwood and his followers (including myself).[36] The confusion derives, I think, from the fact that there are two separable senses in which we may be interested in the meanings of utterances. We may be interested in the dimension of linguistic meaning, in the sense and reference conventionally supposed to attach to words and sentences. Or we may be interested in the dimension of linguistic action, in the range of things that writers and speakers may be capable of doing in (and by) the use of such words and sentences. As ill-luck would have it, we use the word *meaning* in English to cover both these interests. (They manage these things better in France.) Referring to the first, we speak of understanding the mean-

---

[35] Passmore, 'The Idea of a History of Philosophy', p. 32.

[36] The misunderstanding seems to me particularly evident in Harlan, 'Intellectual History', esp. pp. 583–9. But see also the commentators cited in Quentin Skinner, 'A Reply to my Critics' in Skinner, *Meaning and Context*, pp. 272, 278–80.

ings of words, of statements, of entire texts. Referring to the second, we speak of understanding what someone may have meant by issuing a statement or composing a text. But it is unfortunate, and has certainly proved a source of confusion, that we happen to talk in this way. For when we ask about the meanings of utterances, it is far from clear that we are talking in effect about the intentions of language-users. It would require a powerful theory to persuade us of this suggestion, and Grice's repeated efforts to formulate such a theory encountered notorious difficulties. When, by contrast, we ask what people mean by their utterances, it is surely uncontentious that we are talking about intentionality. For in asking what they mean in this latter sense, we are asking about the meaning of their act of issuing their utterance. And in asking about the meaning of such linguistic acts, we are asking – as in the case of all voluntary acts – about the nature of the intentions embodied in their performance.

To bring out the significance of the distinction, consider again the Nietzschean fragment discussed by Derrida in *Éperons:* 'I have forgotten my umbrella.' We may wish to know what Nietzsche's words mean. But as even Derrida allows, this scarcely seems a problem in this case. Alternatively, we may wish to know what Nietzsche may have meant (that is, intended) by writing just those words. We may wish to know, that is, what he was doing in writing them, what linguistic act was being performed. Was he merely telling someone? Or was he perhaps reminding them, or warning them, or reassuring them? Or was he instead explaining something, or apologising, or criticising himself, or simply lamenting his lapse of memory, or what? Perhaps, as Derrida himself suggests, he meant nothing at all.

Generalising this point about the understanding of utterances, I can perhaps best put it as follows. The sort of texts in which historians and philosophers are interested usually embody – indeed consist of – arguments. But to argue is always to argue for or against some particular assumption or conclusion or course of action. Derrida insists in his *Grammatology* on a contrast between writing and dialogue,[37] but writing of the kind I am describing is always dialogue, since it always takes the form of an intervention in a pre-existing conversation or debate. It follows that, if we are to understand this kind of writing, we shall have to find means to identify the nature of the intervention it may be said to constitute. The same point can be put in a different way by noting that there is a sense in which we may need to understand why a certain proposition has been put forward if we wish to understand the propo-

---

[37] Derrida, *Of Grammatology*, esp. pp. 39–44.

sition itself. We may need to see it not just as a proposition but as a move in argument. To understand it, we may need to grasp why it seemed appropriate to make just that move, and hence to issue just that utterance.

An example may help to clarify the point and at the same time to reveal what difference it makes to the writing of intellectual history if we take it seriously.[38] Consider the fact that in the *Meditations* Descartes thinks it important to vindicate the idea of certain knowledge. If we are interested in the dimension of linguistic action, we shall want to ask what he was doing at this stage in his argument. This was not a question ever addressed in the older secondary literature. The view appears to have been that, since Descartes was an epistemologist, and since scepticism is a central problem in epistemology, there is no particular puzzle about his having examined it. But as Popkin, Curley and others have shown, such an answer discloses what one might call an inadequate level of puzzlement. They *have* in effect gone on to raise the question of what Descartes was doing, and have answered that, among other things, he was responding to a new and corrosive form of scepticism stemming from the rediscovery of Sextus Empiricus's texts in the latter part of the sixteenth century. They have established that Descartes was replying specifically to this argument, repudiating its presuppositions and seeking to reconstruct in the face of it a more traditional link between knowledge and certain truth.[39]

It will be obvious what general conclusion I wish to draw from the example. The example itself is of course concerned with meaning and intentionality. But in speaking here about meaning, we are asking what a particular author may have meant by arguing in a particular way. And in speaking about intentionality, we are asking what the author may have been doing in developing his particular line of argument. I take it, moreover, that this is what writers such as Collingwood had in mind when they spoke about the recovery of authorial intentionality. But if this is so, then their concerns wholly escape the strictures recently levelled against the study of meanings and intentions. For these strictures have largely been directed against those who have wished to advance a completely different thesis, namely that any text may be said to bear a single intended meaning which it becomes the business of the interpreter to recover.

These observations certainly apply to a number of the intellectual historians I cited at the outset, including both Pocock and Passmore.

---

[38] I adapt the example from Skinner, 'Reply', pp. 282–3.
[39] See Richard Popkin, *The History of Skepticism from Erasmus to Spinoza* (Berkeley, 1979) and E.M. Curley, *Descartes against the Skeptics* (Oxford, 1978).

Passmore in particular has always made it clear that his interest in intentionality has very little to do with recovering the purportedly pristine meanings of texts, and almost everything to do with character- ising the projects they may be said to articulate. This is especially evident in his early and coat-trailingly entitled book, *Hume's Intentions*.[40] From this we learn that, so far from being an increasingly sceptical though recognisable follower of Locke and Berkeley – as scholars at the time had generally maintained – Hume was far more affected in shaping his *Treatise* by his critical engagement with Bayle and especially Male- branche.[41] Although these writers make little appearance in Hume's text, Passmore's achievement was to uncover the extent to which it nevertheless makes sense to say that Hume's *Treatise* is in part *about* them.

IV

There is one point, however, at which the objections raised by recent anti-intentionalist critics seem to me justified. As we have seen, many of these critics have complained that the traditional idea of hermeneutics asks for the impossible if it asks us, in Collingwood's phrase, to think other people's thoughts after them. This objection certainly seems to me well taken: we can surely never hope to abolish the historical distance between ourselves and our forebears, speaking as though we can spirit away the influence of everything that has intervened, empathetically reliving their experience and retelling it as it was lived. But Colling- wood's admirers have often spoken as though they believe in such a possibility. Passmore, for example, remarks that the 'problematic' approach to intellectual history which he wishes to commend is 'well described' by Henry Jones when he declares that 'to understand a philosophical system we must retrace the steps of its construction, and accompany the mind of its author in its quest for the truth'.[42]

These are vulnerable *façons de parler*, but my defence of the Colling- woodian approach at this juncture would be to say that there is no need to invoke them, nor to rely on the dubious doctrine of other minds on which they seem to depend. Of course we cannot hope to re-enter the minds of historical agents. But in order to recover the kinds of intentions in which we are interested we are not committed to performing any such conjuring trick. We are speaking of intentions embodied in acts of linguistic communication. But these intentions, including as they do the

40 John Passmore, *Hume's Intentions* (Cambridge, 1952).
41 Ibid., esp. pp. 86–91.
42 Passmore, 'The Idea of a History of Philosophy', p. 27.

intention to communicate and be understood, will *ex hypothesi* be publicly legible, at least to any scholar learned enough to recover the relevant contexts of debate. Consider, for example,[43] the man in the next field, who is waving his arms in a manner which, I come to see, is not intended to drive off a wasp as I had initially supposed, but rather to warn me that the bull is about to charge. To recognise that he is issuing a warning is to recognise the communicative intentions embodied in his act of waving. But to recover these intentions is not in the least a matter of successfully re-creating the ideas inside his head at the moment when he first began to wave. It is rather a matter of understanding a particular convention and recognising its deployment in the given case. It seems a mistake to suppose that any act of empathetic re-creation is required, and equally a mistake on Gadamer's part to suppose that those who speak about the recovery of intentions must be committed to any such 'romantic' belief.

Let me generalise and at the same time underline this Wittgensteinian point, since although Gadamer makes occasional (if slightly patronising) nods in Wittgenstein's direction,[44] he appears not to have come to terms with the pivotal role of Wittgenstein's doctrine about forms of life. I have been arguing that texts are acts. To understand texts, one of the things we need to recover is the intentions with which they were written, and thus what their authors were doing in writing them. But this is not the mysterious empathetic process that traditional theorists of interpretation and their adversaries have alike supposed. For acts are also texts. They embody conventional meanings which, when we know the language involved – whether the moves in a natural language or a language of gesture – we can hope to read off. When we claim, that is, to have recovered the intentions embodied in texts, we are engaged in nothing more mysterious than this process of placing them within whatever argumentative contexts make sense of them.

There remains the doubt of which Derrida has made so much: that we can never say 'for sure' what lingistic code is being followed in any given case. To revert to his example from Nietzsche, we can never know whether the statement 'I have forgotten my umbrella' may have been intended as a reminder, a reassurance, a warning, an apology, or what, so that there can never be any prospect of performing the act of 'reading off' in which Collingwood and his followers are interested.

Derrida's example is certainly well chosen. There will undoubtedly be cases in which we cannot hope to recover the explanatory contexts necessary for making sense of particular utterances. And it certainly

---

[43] I adapt the example from Skinner, 'Reply', p. 279.
[44] See for example Gadamer, *Truth and Method*, p. 500.

looks as though the Nietzsche fragment is one such case.[45] But this is hardly a concession of a very substantial kind. What Derrida's example shows is that, if we cannot construct such an explanatory context, we cannot hope to give an account of the significance of the utterance or say what its author meant. But what the example obviously cannot show is that we can never hope to construct such explanatory contexts. Nor could such a hyperbolically sceptical position be readily sustained. It would involve claiming that it is impossible to issue any unambiguous communicative sign of any kind – so that, for example, it would become conceptually impossible to respond to an argument by shaking one's head in disbelief.

It must further be conceded that, even when we feel we can point to an explanatory context which helps to make sense of a given text, we are not of course claiming to know 'for sure' what the author in question meant by issuing a given utterance. As I have already acknowledged, when we are told, for example, that Hume is responding to Malebranche, and thus that there is a crucial sense in which his philosophy is about his great predecessor, what we are being offered is simply a hypothesis. As such, it will always be subject to challenge and revision from those who read the explanatory contexts differently, as well as from those who succeed in uncovering new and different explanatory contexts. To concede all this, however, is by no means to affirm that we cannot hope to construct more or less illuminating hypotheses. Of a given interpretation we can never say that it is unquestionably correct, and thus that debate is at an end. But we can often say of a proposed interpretation that it is unquestionably incorrect. For example, we may never know whether the Nietzschean fragment was intended as an apology or a warning, but we definitely know that it cannot have been intended as an instruction or a question, simply because it is in the wrong grammatical mood. To accept that the process of interpretation may be never-ending is by no means to say that it is wholly open-ended. As Nietzsche himself observed, there is an art of reading, and like any other art it can be practised badly or well.[46]

Friendly critics of the argument I have been putting forward are apt to retort that, even if it is not actually wrong-headed, it hardly seems of much importance. When we learn, for example, that Descartes's *Meditations* contains a critique of Pyrrhonism, or that Hume's *Treatise* embodies a commentary on Malebranche, what more are we being

[45] As Derrida himself observes, *Éperons*, p. 124, it lacks any 'contexte significant'.
[46] Friedrich Nietzsche, *On the Genealogy of Morality*, edited by Keith Ansell-Pearson, trans. Carol Diethe (Cambridge, 1994), p. 10.

offered (one critic has asked) than meagre and jejune summaries?[47] The right way to answer this doubt, it seems to me, is to revert to Collingwood's original emphasis on the importance of recovering underlying purposes. If, for example, Passmore's contention about Hume's intentions is correct, what we learn from his characterisation of the *Treatise* is something crucial about Hume's own conception of his project. But this is to acquire far more than a characterisation of Hume's text; it is to acquire at the same time a means of accounting for many of its detailed arguments. We may now be able to explain, for instance, why the *Treatise* is organised in a certain way, why it employs a particular vocabulary, why it concentrates on specific lines of argument, why in short it possesses its distinctive shape and character. These are hardly meagre results: rather they lie at the heart of the hermeneutic enterprise. It is true that this enterprise itself is widely thought to have been discredited. I have sought to argue, however, that while this belief is widely held, it is much less firmly grounded than it is currently fashionable to suppose.

[47] Graham Hough, 'An Eighth Type of Ambiguity', in David Newton-De Molina (Ed.), *On Literary Intention* (Edinburgh, 1976), p. 227.

10 Towards a philosophical history of the political

Pierre Rosanvallon

I

For the past twenty years or so we have been witnessing a 'return to the political', a phrase now hackneyed by use. Such a return can be explained by the concurrence of two factors. First, it belongs to a moment in history when, simultaneously, we are rediscovering the centrality of the issue of democracy and of its problematic nature. Until the end of the 1960s, the vision of a central ideological divide served to organise intellectual space around the opposition between the two prevailing visions of the world: the Marxist and the liberal. The advocates of classical parliamentary democracy and the champions of 'real' democracy each for their part believed that the model whose merits they proclaimed corresponded to a fully realised ideal. In the 1970s, a new version of the critique of totalitarianism challenged such convictions, thus leading to a deeper analysis of the problem of democracy. Since the end of the 1980s, the need for a new social contract, in a context characterised by the rise of nationalism and the crisis of the welfare state, has prolonged this search, thus contributing to making questions of politics central once again. But the 'return to the political' has also a methodological dimension. It goes hand in hand with the disenchantment with the social sciences that became apparent in the 1980s. With sociology or anthropology somewhat played out, philosophy seemed to some to offer a better way of both understanding and formulating the problems of contemporary societies. Within such a context one may better appreciate the emergence of what I call the philosophical history of the political.

In this essay[1] I tackle this question by making explicit the methodological approach and the underlying intentions of a number of my own publications, in particular *L'état en France: de 1798 à nos jours* as well as

---

[1] This contribution clarifies and develops thoughts set out in the article by P. Rosanvallon, 'Pour une histoire conceptuelle du politique (note de travail)', *Revue de synthèse*, 1–2 (1996), pp. 93–105.

Le sacre du citoyen.[2] One preliminary point, however, needs emphasising. The identification of a new philosophical history of the political rests on a definition of the political domain different from the one generally assumed by political science, according to which politics constitutes a subset of the social system as a whole. Max Weber, for instance, considered the political order, understood as the exercise of the monopoly of legitimate violence, to be in opposition to the economic and the social order. Each sphere of activities is subject to institutions and regulatory principles of its own. One could mention many other definitions of what politics is. But what characterises the social sciences is that they view it in terms of its specificity: the coherence inherent in the political domain emanates from the particular quality of power as a means of shaping the organisation and the hierarchy of the social fabric.

Running counter to this definition, the philosophical history of the political 'implies on the other hand the notion of a principle or a set of principles generating the relations that people entertain between one another and with the world'.[3] Seen from this angle, it is not simply a matter of drawing a line between what is political and what is social, taking the symbolic dimension characteristic of society as the point of reference. If setting the political within this symbolic framework is uncontested (and let it be noted in passing that that is what leads to the relationship between what is political and what is religious being considered as fundamental), one does need to be more precise. Here we can make reference to the very illuminating observations by Claude Lefort who defines the political as the set of procedures out of which springs the social order. Interpreted in this way, the political and the social are indissoluble, the latter deriving its meaning, its shape and its reality from the former. This definition of the political rests on a double premise. The first is the classical acknowledgement of the problematic nature of drawing up the rules whereby the community can live in peace, thus avoiding discord and its own ruin in the shape of a civil war. Aristotle's classic definition in his *Politics* is appropriate here: 'When there is a case for equality and a case for inequality, then we enter the realm of doubt and of political philosophy.'[4]

Understood in this way, the political can be defined as a sphere of activities characterised by irreducible conflicts. The political stems from the need to establish a rule outside the ordinary, and which cannot in

[2] P. Rosanvallon, *L'état en France: de 1789 à nos jours* (Paris, 1990); Rosanvallon, *Le sacre du citoyen, histoire du suffrage universel en France* (Paris, 1992).

[3] Claude Lefort, *Essai sur la politique, XIXe–XXe siècles* (Paris, 1986), p. 8.

[4] Aristotle, *Politics* (III, 1282, B 21) [author's own rendition; cf. Aristotle, *The Politics and the Constitution of Athens*, edited by S. Everson (Cambridge, 1996), p. 79].

any way be derived from something natural. The political can therefore be defined as the process that allows the constitution of an order that everyone signs up to, through deliberation of the norms of participation and distribution. 'Political activity', as Hannah Arendt observes in like vein, 'is conditional on the plurality of human activity . . . Political activity is concerned with the community and with how being different affects respective parties.'[5]

II

We can always start from such a classical definition of the political. But it should also be stressed that this acquires a new meaning in modern society. Indeed, the problematic character of participation and distribution is kept within bounds in Aristotle's concept by the belief in a certain natural order of things and of society. In this case the system of differences is in part something already given. Conversely, the political in modern society is being extended, one might even say is being unleashed. There are two reasons for this. The transition from a corporate society to a society of individuals gives rise, in the first instance, to a kind of deficit of representation. So the political is called upon to be the agent that 'represents' a society to which nature does not give immediate form. According to Marx, in the Middle Ages the social classes were immediately political.[6] In modern societies, on the other hand, positive steps have to be taken in order to provide representation for society. What is needed is for a society of individuals to be made visible and conspicuous, for a people to be given a face. This imperative of representation therefore distinguishes modern from ancient politics. At the same time, one must draw attention to a second fundamental difference, the difference which stems from the principle of equality linked to the advent of a vision of the social order as a product of conventions (which implies the equality of individuals as subjects of the law). In modern society there are no longer fixed limits that either nature or history can impose against egalitarian processes. Equality subverts all attempts to legitimate differences by reference to some form of natural order. Social life is characterised by two processes, consisting in new claims for economic equality and in the narrowing of anthropological differences. These two aspects of modernity lead thus to a considerable enlargement of the practical domain of politics when compared with the Aristotelian vision.

[5] Hannah Arendt, *Qu'est-ce que la politique?* (Paris, 1995), p. 31.
[6] Cf. K. Marx, *Critique of Hegel's 'Philosophy of Right'*, edited by J. O'Malley (Cambridge, 1970), pp. 72–3.

Seen from this perspective, the aim of the philosophical history of the political is to promote an understanding of the manner in which representative systems, which are instrumental to the way individuals or social groups may conceive communal life, are designed and evolve.[7] Given that these representations are born of a process whereby society is constantly re-examining itself, and that they are not exterior to the consciousness of the actors, the philosophical history of the political aims primarily to relate how an epoch, a country or a social group may seek to construct responses to what, with greater or less precision, they perceive as a problem. Second, it seeks to provide a historical account of the labour occasioned by the permanent interaction of reality and its representation, by defining historico-conceptual fields. Its objective therefore is to identify the *historical clusters* around which new political and social rationalities organise themselves, representations of public life undergo change in keeping with the transformation of institutions, and of the forms of social control and bonding. It is a philosophical history because it is around concepts embodying society's self-representation, such as equality, sovereignty, democracy, etc., that one can organise and verify the intelligibility of events and their underlying principles. Such a definition explains the privileging of two great historical moments: that of the loss of autonomy of the social order understood as a corporate body – the history of the political in so far as this is bound up with the loosening up of the organic representation of the social order – and the subsequent democratic period. These two great moments are very different from each other. One is the history of the birth of contemporary forms of politics, of the State, together with the emergence of the individual; the other is the history of what one may call the 'democratic experience'.

Contrary to the classical history of ideas, the material for this philosophical history of the political cannot be limited to an analysis of and the commentary upon the great texts, even though these, in certain cases, can justifiably be considered as focal points testifying to the questions raised in a period of history and to the answers that it sought to offer. The philosophical history of the political borrows from the history of mentalities its concern to incorporate the entirety of those elements which make up that complex object that is a political culture. This will certainly include the manner in which great theoretical texts are read, but also an attention to literary works, the press and movements of opinion, pamphlets and formal speeches, emblems and signs. More broadly still, the history of events and institutions must be apprehended

---

[7] The term political history is preferred to that of intellectual history because the term intellectual history has a very narrow sense in the Anglo-Saxon world since it treats history as separate from intellectual output or from intellectual circles.

as something always in the making, so that, to such an extent, there is no subject matter that is exclusive to this type of history of the political. It consists in gathering together all those materials drawn upon, each in separate ways, by the historians of ideas, of mentalities, of institutions and of events. For example, the relationship between liberalism and democracy during the French Revolution cannot be resolved in a kind of high-level debate between Rousseau and Montesquieu. One must make the effort to grasp what those who used these authors as authorities actually read in their works, study the mass of petitions sent to the National Assembly, immerse oneself in the world of pamphlets and satirical tracts, re-read parliamentary debates, become acquainted with the practices of clubs and committee. It is also necessary to study the history of words and the development of language (democracy did not mean the same thing in 1789 and in 1793, for example). This history is naturally multifaceted.

How does one analyse the multiplicity of these various levels? This is an important question because often the history of the political (when this is confused with the history of ideas) is reproached for being just a history of the great major writers. How does one deal with this question of history seen from the top down or from the bottom up? Here one must once again get to grips with the meaning of the classical texts. If a certain number of texts appear to be crucial, it is not just as expressions of thought, but because they represent a philosophical and conceptual formalisation of a specific historical, political or philosophical moment. It is not simply a question of carrying out a reading of the *Contrat social* in the style of Leo Strauss – *Du contrat social* as a philosophical contribution – something that is interesting in itself – but to show how *Du contrat social* represents one of the ways of expressing the question of the construction of the social order in the eighteenth century. If great texts may enjoy a particular status in this history, it is because the peculiar quality of great texts is precisely to establish a connection between a text and a problem. But obviously one cannot restrict oneself to the great texts. If, for instance, one wants to understand how a vision of modern political representation originates, one cannot undertake this exercise just with reference to Sieyès or Barnave, or even to the opposition between an old vision of representation, as in Montesquieu, and its radical critique, as in Rousseau. It is also necessary to analyse the way a society at large poses the same question, looking at pamphlets, iconography and songs. When I wrote *Le sacre du citoyen*, I therefore tried not to separate the use of classical texts from that of material of a less noble intellectual origin. I sought to place the analysis of iconographic documents alongside a classical commentary on different texts.

In this sense, the philosophical history of the political represents an attempt to give new meaning to Fernand Braudel's project of *a total history*. One must in fact move in the direction of a total political history in order to make sense of the political in all its complexity. Today the avenues by which history renews itself are many. In this respect, contemporary debates on the frontiers between history and fiction, on the renewal of the biographical approach to a knowledge of the social order and on the renewal of micro-history are all significant. History lives off these questions and such changes. The new philosophical history of the political must be understood within the framework of these major innovations within the discipline. It is this new history that takes over, in a different form, the old project of a total history; a history which in principle does not separate the different instruments of historical specialisms. In this sense, the history of the political can draw from cultural history, social history, from the classical history of political institutions and from the history of ideas, but what gives it coherence is not just the variety of instruments that it can bring to bear, but its very object; it is the peculiarity of its object that distinguishes it from the other fields of history.

The originality of this philosophical history of the political lies in both its approach and its content. Its approach is at the same time interactive and comprehensive. Interactive, since it consists in analysing the way in which a political culture, its institutions and events interact jointly to establish more or less stable political forms. This is done by charting the overlaps, the divergences, the twists, the convergence and the gaps that characterise the formation of the political forms and determines what is equivocal or ambiguous about them, or indeed their accomplishments. This philosophical history is also comprehensive, because its central objective is to apprehend an issue by placing it within the context of its emergence. Under these conditions it is impossible to keep to an objectivist approach which presupposes that the historian can survey and control a passive object from without. The comprehensive approach seeks to apprehend history in the making, whilst it remains within its potentiality, before it becomes actualised in its passive status of something necessary. In Max Weber's sense, understanding in the field of history implies reconstructing the way in which actors understand their situation, rediscovering the affinities and the oppositions from which they plan their action, drawing the genealogies of possibilities and impossibilities that implicitly structure their horizon. It is a method based on empathy, because it presupposes the ability to address an issue by putting oneself within the situation from which it emerged. But it is naturally a form of empathy limited by the very distance that may allow one to understand the blind spots and the contradictions of actors and authors: a controlled empathy, so to speak.

III

These general comments on the definition of the content and the approach of a conceptual history of the political are meant not as a rejection of the traditional methods of the histories of ideas, of events and of institutions – nor of the more recent history of mentalities – but to reassess their subject matters from a fresh perspective. Such a reassessment may in some instances entail the risk of making a return to the past. This is particularly true with respect to the history of ideas. This field was for so long forsaken by French academics that it was often necessary to start from the most traditional historical reconstruction before attempting a more conceptual account of it. It is important here to understand the connection between this history of the political and what is seen broadly as the *Ecole des Annales*. The distance between the two that occurred in the 1980s had an exaggerated appearance that derived from the inevitable sense of rediscovery that came from the reappraisal of a field of scholarship that had been neglected for far too long, with the result that the return to an earlier tradition of the history of ideas was briefly thought to be identical to a new approach to the political. The moment when the sense both of recovery and of innovation seemed to be superimposed is now at an end, and it is clear that the history of the political is one that fits into a perspective of extension and renewal of the French historical school rather than breaking away from it. The way forward is still uncertain and experimental. I can therefore well understand that this attempt can sometimes give the impression that it is one that opposes a top-down history to a bottom-up history. There, in terms of both its aims and methods, lies the obstacle in the path of this ambitious project. A path needs to be taken between what could become a simple history of ideas, albeit an improved one, and what would merely be political philosophy.

Far from being isolated from other fields of historical research, the history of the political is, on the contrary, easily reconciled with them. Moreover, certain historians have themselves discovered the political dimension, starting from their own historical perspective. This is so in the case of social history, if one considers for example the work of Jacques Julliard.[8] It is also so for the history of symbols, as is revealed by

[8] J. Julliard, *Autonomie ouvrière. Etudes sur le syndicalisme d'action directe* (Paris, 1988).

the undertaking of Pierre Nora in *Les lieux de mémoire*.[9] *L'histoire de France*, published by Le Seuil and edited by André Burguière and Jacques Revel, has also made for a fruitful exchange.[10] The conditions for a productive dialogue, indeed for collaboration between historians, philosophers and sociologists, have thus steadily emerged. Work with jurists has widened still further the possibilities for exchange. By its very nature, the study of the political requires taking diverse paths and the dismantling of narrow disciplinary boundaries.

Taking the argument further, the aim of this enterprise is to break the divide between political history and political philosophy, so as to arrive at a point of convergence between the two enterprises. The reasons for this ambition are founded on the important presupposition that history must be considered as a material for political philosophy, an object upon which it reflects. Hannah Arendt takes this line and in *Between Past and Future* observes that 'thought itself arises out of incidents of living experience and must remain bound to them as the only guideposts by which to take its bearings'.[11] Here emerges one of political philosophy's major features: it can be characterised primarily by its relationship at once necessary, insurmountable and for ever problematical with the experiences and the opinions present at any given time in the real politics of the community at large.[12] Thus in no way can political philosophy be viewed as a province of philosophy. Rather, it constitutes a particular *way* of philosophising, since its issues arise directly from the life of the community, along with the totality of the arguments and controversies that run through it. From this perspective, it is necessary to insist on the fact that no political concept (be it democracy, liberty or others) can be disentangled from its history.

Understood in this way, political experience is indeed the subject matter of political philosophy, but it therefore also follows what could be called its movement. It entails considering the history of politics as a form of research in which we are, to all intents and purposes, immersed. In fact, democracy is always at one and the same time the apparent solution to the modern problem of the constitution of the social order as well as a question for ever left unanswered, in the sense that no perfectly

---

[9] P. Nora, *Les lieux de mémoire* (Paris, 1984–6), cf. especially book I, 'La République' and volume II, book II, 'La nation', where politics occupies a very sizeable place.

[10] André Burguière and Jacques Revel (eds.), *L'histoire de France* (Paris, 1989–93).

[11] H. Arendt, 'Preface', in *Between Past and Future. Eight Exercises in Political Thought* (Harmondsworth, 1978), p. 14.

[12] Cf. H. Arendt, 'Truth and Politics', in Arendt, *Between Past and Future*. On this point I go along with the excellent comments by Philippe Raynaud in the article 'Philosophie politique', in Philippe Raynaud and Stéphane Rials (eds.), *Dictionnaire de philosophie politique* (Paris, 1996).

adequate response can ever be provided. Such a philosophical history of the political involves, therefore, a constant reworking of the antinomies constitutive of the modern experience. What is called for is an attempt to unravel the historical thread of questions, perplexities and innovations, so as to understand history in-the-making as part of experience. It boils down to writing a history that could be qualified as comprehensive.

The comprehensive approach may be justified by the presumption that there is an *invariance* between the situation of the author or actor who is being studied and our own. For the Weberian sociologist, such an invariant is that of human nature. In the case of a conceptual history of ideas, it is a function of our self-conscious immersion in the very questions investigated by the authors themselves. The work of the historian can thus open the way towards a new type of intellectual commitment. This does not involve investing our ideas, preferences or *a priori* assumptions into a text or a position; nor for that matter is it the representation of social groups or writers with whom the interpreter may readily sympathise. The aim is to turn conceptual history into a resource for understanding the present. It will be said quite justifiably that this is a commonplace: what is interesting about the history of the past is its capacity to throw light on the present. Looking at this closely, however, things are not quite so straightforward. Many history books seek in fact rather to reinterpret history in terms of the present or even of the future as they imagine it will be. Such an inversion of the terms of comprehension seems to me to be particularly striking in the field of political history.

Let us take as an example the political history of the French Revolution. Aulard's book,[13] which still remains the classic work of reference on the subject, produces an analysis of the political movement of the Revolution by constantly relating speeches and political institutions of the period to what he judges to be the fixed and established democratic idea.[14] Thus he traces the advances and the setbacks of democracy between 1789 and 1799 by reference to his own vision of democracy (government for the people and through universal suffrage). He makes judgements on this period by taking the present as the fixed point of reference. This sort of history, at once gradualist and linear, views as a given and a fact beyond dispute (universal suffrage = democracy) what is in fact the location of a problem (the gradual reduction of the idea of democracy to the idea of the vote). Aulard acts as if the democratic idea was there *from the outset*, prevented only from coming fully into effect by

---

[13] A. Aulard, *Histoire politique de la Révolution française* (Paris, 1901).
[14] The subtitle of Aulard's book – 'Origines et développement de la démocratie et de la république' – is in itself an illustration of this point of view.

circumstances, the insufficient discernment of the actors involved or the impact of the class struggle between the people and the bourgeoisie. History read this way is always simple: it is the territory where opposing forces clash (action and reaction, the progressive and the reactionary, the modern and the archaic, the bourgeois and the popular), the outcome of which explains the advances and the setbacks of the idea. The past is judged from the standpoint of a present which is not itself thought through. Under these conditions, history becomes a genuine obstacle to the understanding of the present. The philosophical history of the political in its comprehensive form allows us, on the other hand, to get rid of the barrier separating political history from political philosophy. Understanding the past and investigating the present are part of the same intellectual process. Besides this, philosophical history provides a meeting ground between interpretation/commentary (*essayisme*) and erudition, things which are often portrayed as mutually hostile. Erudition is the vital condition for understanding the work of history (the amount of information to be gathered and of texts to be read is, indeed, considerable when carrying out a comprehensive study), whilst commentary as a form of intervention on the present is the motor underpinning the questions lying behind the desire to know and to understand. This is not an 'engaged' history (where the writer might project his personal preferences and passions), nor is it a whig history, whose key and intelligibility we possess. Rather it is a history of the *resonances* between our experience and that of the past.

This way of conceiving the activity of the historian leads us therefore to reconsider *the relationship between intellectual labour and civic and political involvement*. The strength of this history of the political lies in considering academic life in such a way that it becomes an integral part of the civic experience. This leads to a new form of civic commitment. Commitment is no longer determined by the *position* of the intellectual (the authority conferred upon him by his specialised knowledge); it is of a more *substantive* kind. In a certain sense, it is the very nature of intellectual labour that produces political commitment. If concern with civic life may take forms other than ordinary political combat, or the adherence to certain values or utopias, then it can also be thought of as the capacity lucidly to apprehend the antinomies emerging from the circumstances in which people find themselves, and the questions that from them may arise. If so, the work of the political historian is part and parcel of this civic process. Knowledge thus becomes a form of action. To such an extent, intellectual labour *per se* is a form of political practice. It is a form of political understanding that, by its contribution to the elucidation of the antinomies, participates in the attempt at defining what properly belongs to the political domain. What is at stake here is the connection between erudition and involvement, between the work's commitment and commitment in the work. The philosophical history of the political is able simultaneously to forge instruments of understanding and tools for practical involvement. The aim is to reach the point where the distinction between knowledge and action vanishes. It means participating in the process through which society comes no longer to separate knowledge of the action itself from the knowledge of the causes that contributed to it.

The project for a philosophical history of the political is thus based on a strong thesis. It claims to rebuild the relationship between intellectual labour and politics along new lines. Intellectual labour is not a form of capital available for reinvestment in another field thanks to the degree of visibility secured by academic fame (which by itself confers credibility to political discourse). Rather, it is the very content of the intellectual labour that has a civic dimension. Speaking more personally, this is why I do not detect any clear difference between what I write as part of a more direct political or social involvement and my more academic publications. Of course, there is a difference between a specialist work and an essay. But the essay is informed by the serious intellectual investment of the former. Naturally there are very different levels and forms of writing. One can write as a scholar or as an essayist; one can also express oneself at different levels of complexity, by handling a very varied range of sources. But my contention is that one should not consider the short interpretative essay as too different from the thick scholarly tome with the stamp of erudition, since, to be sure, they flow from the same source of learning. For myself I endeavour to mix both genres. In this respect there is an experimental nature to my work. But, above all, I try to write books about politics of a different kind to find ways of drawing together an interested concern for civic matters and academic work. This position, I readily acknowledge, is that of a small minority within academia, but this does not seem to me to make it less worthy of defence.

IV

Having outlined the programme, one may now attempt to answer a certain number of objections often aired against this approach, and to try to define with more precision the relation between it and other approaches. One of the main objections against the philosophical history of the political is that put forward by the historian Roger Chartier, who has criticised the return to the political as a trite, idealistic attempt to restore the old philosophy of the free subject, whose lustre had been somewhat tarnished by the social sciences.[15] In his judgement, the philosophical history of the political fails mistakenly to distinguish between the discursive and the non-discursive. Such a criticism would appear justified if one tried to set up the social sciences against the old conception of the history of ideas. But it is precisely of the essence of the philosophical history of the political to consider that social representations cannot simply be assimilated to the order of ideology; nor can they be reduced to categories of prejudices reflecting a given state of social relationships. The philosophical history of the political maintains that beyond ideologies and prejudices there are positive representations organising the intellectual field within which lie a certain range of possibilities in a given historical moment. These representations need to be taken seriously: they constitute real and powerful infrastructures in the life of societies. In contrast to an idealist vision, which disregards the economic and social determinants structuring the field of human action, this approach sets out to enrich and render more complex the notion of determination. Alongside passive representations, it is consequently necessary to take into account all those active representations that shape action, enclose the field of possibilities by reference to what is thinkable, and determine the questions of the moment.

Far from taking a principled stand against social history, this philosophical history of the political follows its very same programme but tries to go beyond it. The ideas that it takes into account constitute an important part of reality, provided these ideas are defined as we have attempted to do so. One may even take the view that it incorporates what is in substance most intimate and most decisive about the social experience. Indeed, in modern society the forms of communal life ineluctably register a permanent tension with their own representations, since social structure is no longer a product of either nature or history, but needs to be continuously constructed and criticised.

I do not reject the approaches used in social history, preferring instead to deal with great writers or parliamentary orators rather than the silent and long-suffering masses. Nor do I disdain material history (which indeed I practise in my work). For example, it is important to trace the history of the hand-written ballot paper or to develop an interest in the voting booth (the Australian Ballot). But the facts of social history only reveal their meaning when they are placed within a context, or inserted into a more conceptual history, which for its part is not just an analysis of the great writers, even though the latter often represent an ideal

---

[15] Cf. Jeremy Jennings's discussion of Chartier's position in his chapter of this volume.

avenue into the political culture of their time. Social history and conceptual history have the same kind of relationship to that enjoyed by ordinary times with revolutionary periods. The conflicts between the forces of progress and reaction, between the people and the elite, between the ruled and the rulers, the clash of vested interests and prejudices, constitute as it were the everyday side of history, an everyday scenario tirelessly repeated and revisited through succeeding forms of obedience and domination, freedom and oppression. But this ordinary pattern only acquires a meaning when relocated within the process of transformation of institutions and ways of thinking. Otherwise, there is an ever-present threat of anachronism, which may creep in and unsettle our judgement. The philosophical history of the political aims to keep a hold of both ends of the chain. By seeking throughout to identify the intersections between human conflicts and their representations of the world, this philosophical history conceives politics as that terrain where society transforms itself. Let us recall that aims and methods cannot be dissociated. It is not therefore just a matter of doing a simple history of ideas, but rather of understanding the background against which the categories that reflect action are both constructed and transformed, to analyse how issues come about, how they impact on the social order, tracing a framework of possibilities, delineating systems of opposition and types of challenges. In fact, political history should not be understood as a more or less linear development, featuring a succession of conquests and defeats before leading to the end of history, with democracy celebrated or freedom organised. In a sense, there is no Hegelian history of the political. This approach is not only called for by what could appear to be a requirement of method; it is also congruous with the very essence of the political, which is defined by the interrelationship between the philosophical and events, the effect of the social upon the conceptual, and the attempt to invent the future by distinguishing the old from the new.

The question of the relationship with the work of Michel Foucault can also be raised. On this point I wish to be very clear: the project of the philosophical history of the political recaptures Foucault's own original intention, as it was manifested clearly, or so it seems to me, both in *Histoire de la folie* and perhaps even more so in *Les mots et les choses*.[16] Foucault is also interested in capturing political rationalities (cf. his notion of *épistémé*) from a total perspective. But, to my mind, Foucault's understanding of the political is too limited. He understands the political in physical or biological terms: opposing forces, processes of

---

[16] M. Foucault, *Histoire de la folie à l'âge classique* (Paris, 1972); Foucault, *Les mots et les choses* (Paris, 1966).

action and reaction, etc. In this respect, Foucault remains prisoner of an approach to the phenomena of power which is too narrow. For him the political consists in the struggle for emancipation. He presupposes a rationality of domination. The issue of power therefore sums up the question of the political, which is almost entirely apprehended in terms of strategic action. Although this aspect of the political cannot be neglected, it is not perhaps the most important. The political field is not only organised by clearly determined forces (passions, interests). It is also the territory of experiments and exploration. In sum, it may be argued that democracy is not just a solution, whose history can be reduced to a confrontation between progress and reaction that is at times brutal and at times subtle (Foucault has done a great deal to throw light on the subtle aspect); democracy is also a *problem*, felt as such by the social actors.

Although I share Foucault's interests – his concern to cut himself free from the narrow limits of his discipline, his concern for being at one and the same time historian, philosopher and citizen – my work is set within the framework of a different understanding of the nature of political experience.

Finally, one may try to clarify the approach of the philosophical history of the political by reference to the contextual history of ideas as defined by Quentin Skinner. Skinner, the author of the excellent *The Foundations of Modern Political Thought*,[17] has sought to go beyond the conflict, particularly pronounced in the Anglo-Saxon countries, between a philosophical reading of the major authors, based on a view of texts as something both complete and self-sufficient,[18] and a historical reading, smacking of Marxist undertones, and tending to turn political writings into mere ideological products, born of definite circumstances and fully determined by them. Skinner, on whom J.L. Austin's work made a strong impression,[19] besides his concern not to restrict himself to the major authors, sought to read the texts as linguistic acts set in conventionally recognisable fields of meaning. Texts are read as discourses whose aim cannot be understood unless their authors' intentions are contextualised within the prevailing conventions. This is an approach which has led to a major renewal of the history of ideas and which has made possible a dialogue between historians and philosophers, but whose innovatory character, in my view, has been limited by

[17] Q. Skinner, *The Foundations of Modern Political Thought* (2 vols., Cambridge, 1978).

[18] Cf. in particular as representatives of the text school, Leo Strauss and J. Cropsey who sum up their point of view well in their *History of Political Philosophy* (Chicago, 1963).

[19] Cf. John Austin, *How to Do Things with Words* (Oxford, 1962). For Austin, let us recall, language is an activity which accomplishes something; it is not just a passive operator of meaning.

the lack of distinction between the problem of the eternal issues of philosophy and that of working out the relevant contemporary questions. The terms within which the methodological debate on the history of ideas has been carried out in the United States and in England[20] have led Skinner to make too systematic a connection between attempts at a *philosophia perennis* and all other philosophical attempts to see the relationship between present and past issues.[21] The conditions under which he developed his criticism of the traditional history of ideas have prevented him from taking the decisive step towards embracing a philosophical history of the political. His contribution however remains invaluable and I readily acknowledge my debt to him.

A final word of conclusion. The philosophical history of the political has no recipes that can be mechanically applied in order to write a book illustrating the aspirations underlying the programme, at least, no better than can be done by a necessarily clumsy declaration of intention. Every piece of work is no more than a fragile attempt to produce, through *writing*, additional means towards rendering matter intelligible – in this subject perhaps more than in any other.

[20] There is a huge bibliography on this debate which has not produced much in the way of an echo in France. To appreciate this, two fundamental articles may be read: J.G.A. Pocock, 'The History of Political Thought: a Methodological Enquiry', in Peter Laslett (ed.), *Philosophy, Politics and Societies*, 2nd series (Oxford, 1962); Peter L. Janssen, 'Political Thought as Traditionary Action: the Critical Response to Skinner and Pocock', *History and Theory*, 24, 2 (1985); and see chapters 8 and 9 of this volume.

[21] Which raises the problem, let it be noted, of how to deal with modernity as an area of issues with relatively constant features. This question would justify a debate being devoted to the pertinence of the concept of modernity in political philosophy.

11 'Le retour des émigrés'? The study of the history of political ideas in contemporary France

Jeremy Jennings

I

Writing in the *Revue de synthèse* in 1988,[1] Stefan Collini remarked that it was 'the area of the history of political thought' in English-speaking countries that marked 'the point of greatest contrast with intellectual developments in France'. However, he went on, there were 'signs that a re-alignment of the intellectual field . . . may give political thought greater prominence'. This possibility he attributed to 'the recession of Marxism' and to what he described as 'a disenchantment with some of the major systematic theoretical constructions of recent decades'. Collini's suspicions have proved to be well founded. Since the beginning of the 1990s alone France has seen the creation of three reviews devoted, in different ways, to the study of the history of political thought: *Philosophie politique*, first published in 1992; *La pensée politique*, in 1993; and the *Revue française d'histoire des idées politiques*, in 1995.[2]

What has undoubtedly been the case, therefore, is that the much-vaunted 'return to politics' that had begun to take shape in the 1970s has now been bearing fruit. Indeed, it has had its own manifesto in the shape of René Rémond's edited volume *Pour une histoire politique*[3] and its own institutional locations: the Fondation Nationale des Sciences Politiques and the Université Paris X Nanterre as opposed to the Ecole des Hautes Études en Sciences Sociales (EHESS) of the *Annales* school. From 1984

---

[1] S. Collini, '"Discipline History" and "Intellectual History": Reflections on the Historiography of the Social Sciences in Britain and France', *Revue de synthèse*, 3–4 (1988), pp. 387–99.

[2] For a more detailed discussion of the content of these reviews see my 'The Return of the Political? New French Journals in the History of Political Thought', *History of Political Thought*, 18 (1997), pp. 148–56.

[3] R. Rémond (ed.), *Pour une histoire politique* (Paris, 1988). For the response of *Annales* see the review by Pierre Laboire in *Annales*, 6 (1989), pp. 1369–70. For another programmatic statement by Rémond see *Notre siècle* (Paris, 1988), pp. 7–15.

onwards it has had its own review, *Vingtième siècle*,[4] and its own subject, 'le temps présent', now recognised as a legitimate field of inquiry.[5]

Part and parcel of this 'return' has been a re-kindling of interest in political ideas and what has been increasingly termed 'intellectual history', a discipline which Olivier Mongin, the editor of *Esprit*, has commented is still 'in the process of construction'.[6]

Yet, as Collini's remarks imply, these developments have to be set in a much broader context.[7] In the same year as he published his article, the journal *Annales* (clearly panicked by the appearance of François Dosse's far from complimentary *L'histoire en miettes: des 'Annales' à la 'nouvelle histoire'*)[8] published an editorial that, in 'a time of uncertainty', placed the study of history at a 'critical turning point' and which, it admitted in a later issue, entailed 'a re-definition of its goals and methods'.[9] Identified as a cause of concern were what it stigmatised as 'the re-employment of old motifs – the return of narrative, the event, politics, biography'. Also in 1988, the influential *Le débat*, edited by a member of the 'third generation' of *Annales* historians, Pierre Nora, devoted a whole issue to the intellectual history of France since 1953, concluding with the hypothesis, 'brutally advanced' by Marcel Gauchet, that the previous decade had seen a 'radical change in the paradigm' that had placed linguistics, sociology and ethnology, supported by Marxism and psychoanalysis, in a position of hegemony. Dismissed, in other words, was the whole structuralist edifice and with it, according to Gauchet, 'a quantitative history wedded to social and economic formations' which had integrated itself 'without difficulty into this scheme of things whilst not playing a leading role'. Here had been a conception of history that had preferred 'the anonymity of large numbers to the point of view of privileged actors, the weight of the long term and the limitations

---

[4] For a statement of the place accorded to 'politics and ideology' in what was seen as 'a new history' see 'Déclaration de naissance', *Vingtième siècle*, 1 (1984), pp. 3–4.

[5] See here Denis Peschanski et al., *Histoire politique et sciences sociales* (Brussels, 1991).

[6] Olivier Mongin, *Face au scepticisme: les mutations du paysage intellectuel ou l'invention de l'intellectuel démocratique* (Paris, 1994), p. 55. Two institutional examples of this development can be cited. One is the creation of a 'groupe de recherche sur l'histoire intellectuelle' by the CNRS and the *Institut d'Histoire du Temps Présent*: the second is the review *Mil neuf cent*, first established as the *Cahiers Georges Sorel* and subtitled *Revue d'histoire intellectuelle*.

[7] Readers restricted to English-language texts should consult the excellent collection provided by Jacques Revel and Lynn Hunt (eds.), *Histories: French Constructions of the Past* (New York, 1995).

[8] François Dosse, *L'histoire en miettes: des 'Annales' à la 'nouvelle histoire'* (Paris, 1987).

[9] 'Histoire et sciences sociales: un tournant critique', *Annales*, 2 (March–April 1988), pp. 291–3 and 'Tentons l'expérience', *Annales*, 6 (November–December 1989), pp. 1317–23.

imposed by material conditions to a mistaken sense of the freedom of action'.[10]

The debate has subsequently continued with vigour. Published in the spring of 1996 by Jacques Revel and Nathan Wachtel, *Une école pour les science sociales: de la VIe section à l'Ecole des Hautes Etudes en Sciences Sociales*[11] is essentially a work of self-publicity on the part of what has been one of the most powerful and influential academic institutions in post-war France. Yet beneath the justified pride in an institution that, as the intellectual home of the *Annales* school, succeeded in shaping the research agenda of a whole generation of French historians is disclosed a doubt and uncertainty that are easily discerned. The EHESS's preoccupation with an 'interdisciplinarity' that located and confined history firmly within the social sciences no longer secures automatic assent and throughout the essays that make up the volume there is therefore an awareness that both methodologies and subjects of research have been subject to detailed revision and scrutiny. If this figures in the late Bernard Lepetit's assessment of the *Annales* historians themselves, it is even more evident in the articles of Jacques Revel and Roger Chartier.[12] Revel, referring back to the 'tournant critique' that from the early 1970s onwards had challenged the Braudelian vision of 'une histoire globale', acknowledges that the outcome has been the emergence of 'a multiplicity of particular histories'.[13] Chartier, in a typically incisive essay, recounts the demise of the once-dominant 'quantitative method' and the manner in which this has allowed the emergence of a cultural history devoted to the study of 'tastes, sentiments, sensibilities'.[14] Both recognise that the watchword is now 'diversity'.[15]

[10] See 'Notre histoire', *Le débat*, 50 (1988), pp. 165–70. For a detailed examination of this 'paradigm' shift see François Dosse, *L'empire du sens: l'humanisation des sciences sociales* (Paris, 1995). Interestingly, Dosse characterises this movement as the means through which France can escape her intellectual 'provincialism'.

[11] Jacques Revel and Nathan Wachtel (eds.), *Une école pour les sciences sociales: de la VIe section à l'Ecole des Hautes Etudes en Sciences Sociales* (Paris, 1996).

[12] Bernard Lepetit, 'Les Annales. Portrait de groupe avec revue', pp. 31–48, Jacques Revel, 'L'histoire sociale', pp. 49–72, and Roger Chartier, 'L'histoire culturelle', pp. 73–92, all in Revel and Wachtel (eds.), *Une école pour les sciences sociales*.

[13] See also another recent article by Revel, 'Micro-analyse et construction du social', in Jacques Revel (ed.), *Jeux d'échelles: la micro-analyse à l'expérience* (Paris, 1996), pp. 15–36.

[14] See also Roger Chartier, 'Philosophie et histoire: un dialogue', in François Bédarida (ed.), *L'histoire et le métier de l'historien en France, 1945–1995* (Paris, 1995), pp. 149–70 and *Au bord de la falaise: l'histoire entre certitudes et inquiétude* (Paris, 1998). The title of the latter, placing history 'at the edge of the cliff', is itself sufficient to indicate the theme pursued by Chartier.

[15] See also 'Gens à histoire, gens sans histoire: dialogue entre Pierre Bourdieu et Roger Chartier', *Politix: travaux de science politique*, 6 (1989), pp. 53–60. In this discussion Bourdieu and Chartier identified the supposed rigid distinction between explanations

Similar themes, with similar conclusions, have recently been explored in Bernard Lepetit's *Les formes de l'expérience: une autre histoire sociale*,[16] Jean Boutier's and Dominique Julia's *Passés recomposés: champs et chantiers de l'histoire*,[17] François Bédarida's *L'histoire et le metier de l'historien en France, 1945–1995*[18] and Gérard Noiriel's *Sur la 'crise' de l'histoire*.[19] The latter, for example, situates his entire argument in the context of what he describes as 'le temps des doutes'.[20]

What this move away from 'the great paradigms' has meant can be easily illustrated by reference to the intellectual evolution of the late François Furet. In a well-known essay published in Jacques Le Goff and Pierre Nora's *Faire l'histoire*, he characterised *l'histoire sérielle* (serial history) as 'one of the most fruitful ways of developing historical knowledge' and later, in an interview with Françoise Mélanio, he admitted to having been 'a defender – and practitioner – of the quantitative in history'.[21] Yet by the time he published his *La Révolution: 1770–1880* in 1988,[22] the emphasis had shifted dramatically from social statistics to ideology and 'politics' as 'the guiding thread' of his account. The 'confused notion' of 'mentalities' was cast as a 'degraded form' of the claims that sought to deny historical actors knowledge of the events in which they participated.[23]

More specifically, the sense of dissatisfaction or disappointment with the project of a scientific history inspired by the models of the natural

in terms of 'structure, hierarchies . . . objective relations' and those that made reference to the 'role of the subject', 'the social agent, the individual', as 'a false problem'. There were many styles of writing and these, they agreed, were decided as much by the intended audience as the demands of the discipline and the subjects under discussion.

16 Bernard Lepetit (ed.), *Les formes de l'expérience: une autre histoire sociale* (Paris, 1995).

17 Jean Boutier and Dominique Julia (eds.), *Passés recomposés: champs et chantiers de l'histoire* (Paris, 1995).

18 Bédarida, *L'histoire et le métier*.

19 Gérard Noiriel, *Sur la 'crise' de l'histoire* (Paris, 1996).

20 For Roger Chartier's appreciative, but critical, review of Noiriel's book see 'Entre Clovis et Lavisse, de nouveaux espaces à créer', *Le monde* (4 October 1996). 'For my part', Chartier writes, 'I cannot endorse the view which disqualifies as useless and dangerous questions taken to be "philosophical".' Historians, he concludes, need 'a little philosophy'. The debate about the status of history, in fact, precedes these volumes by some years, even if the books that raised the issue, as is now recognised, did not receive the attention they deserved. See especially Paul Veyne, *Comment on écrit l'histoire* (Paris, 1971) and Michel de Certeau, *L'écriture de l'histoire* (Paris, 1975). Significantly Veyne's book was republished by Editions du Seuil in 1996.

21 François Furet, 'Le quantitatif en histoire', in Jacques Le Goff and Pierre Nora (eds.), *Faire de l'histoire: nouveaux problèmes* (3 vols., Paris, 1974), vol. I, pp. 42–61 and Furet, 'La Révolution', *Mesure*, 1 (1989), pp. 163–70.

22 François Furet, *La Révolution: de Turgot à Jules Ferry, 1770–1880* (Paris, 1988).

23 For a brief assessment of Furet's overall achievement and significance see Tony Judt, 'François Furet (1927–1997)', *New York Review of Books* (6 November 1997), pp. 41–2.

sciences has opened up a renewed interest in the function of narrative in history. Encouraged by a faith in Febvre's central concept of *l'histoire problème* (problem-oriented history), it had previously been a 'commonplace' to be suspicious of *l'histoire récit* (narrative history).[24] Now, 'like it or not', history is seen to be inextricably wedded to 'the narrative form'. A key text in the re-assessment of narrative has undoubtedly been Paul Ricoeur's *Temps et récit*.[25]

Further, as Jacques Revel, the current President of the Ecole des Hautes Etudes en Sciences Sociales, has acknowledged, one example of the renewed interest in the possibilities of narrative has been a concern to re-assess the potential of biography. This too is a change that was much commented upon in the late 1980s and it is a trend that has since led to the publication of a spate of biographies, many of them in the field of intellectual biography and some of them, ironically, of those only too willing to have announced the death of the subject.[26] Foucault, Lacan, Althusser, Albert Camus and Raymond Aron amongst others have been the subjects of biographical studies,[27] as have such lesser-known figures as Jacques Rivière, editor of *Nouvelle Revue Française* between the wars.[28] There is no sign that this trend is abating.[29]

It was, moreover, this 'return' to a form of 'traditional biography' that was described as 'superficial, anecdotal, straightforwardly chronological [and] incapable of revealing the overall historical significance of an individual life' that led a 'desolate' Jacques Le Goff to wonder if something akin to the 'return of the émigrés' after the French Revolution of 1789 was not being witnessed. 'Nothing had been learnt and nothing

[24] Jacques Revel, 'Ressources narratives et connaissance historique', *Enquête*, 1 (1995), pp. 43–70.

[25] Paul Ricoeur, *Temps et récit* (3 vols., Paris, 1983–5). This is a view confirmed by Jacques Revel: see 'Au pied de la falaise: retour aux pratiques', *Le débat*, 103 (1999), pp. 154–61 and also by Chartier in his *Au bord de la falaise*.

[26] See for example Pierre Bourdieu, 'L'illusion biographique', *Actes de la recherche en sciences sociales*, 62–3 (June 1986), pp. 69–72; Giovanni Levi, 'Les usages de la biographie', *Annales ESC* (November–December 1988), pp. 1325–36; D. Madelenat, 'La biographie aujourd'hui', *Mesure*, 1 (1989), pp. 47–58; J. Lacarme and B. Vercier, 'Premières personnes', *Le débat*, 54 (1989), pp. 54–67; and Philippe Levillain, 'Les protagonistes de la biographie', in Rémond (ed.), *Pour une histoire politique*, pp. 121–60.

[27] See Didier Eribon, *Michel Foucault* (Paris, 1989); Elisabeth Roudinesco, *Jacques Lacan, esquisse d'un vie, histoire d'un système de pensée* (Paris, 1993); Yann Moulier Boutang, *Louis Althusser* (Paris, 1992); Olivier Todd, *Albert Camus. Une vie* (Paris, 1996); Nicolas Baverez, *Raymond Aron* (Paris, 1993).

[28] Jean Lacouture, *Une adolescence du siècle: Jacques Rivière et la NRF* (Paris, 1994).

[29] See Philippe-Jean Catinchi, 'Des nouvelles de "l'homo biographicus"', *Le monde* (19 February 1999); Guillaume Piketty, 'La biographie comme genre historique?', *Vingtième siècle*, 63 (1999), pp. 119–26; Bernard Pudel, 'Biographie et biographique', *Le mouvement social*, 186 (1999), pp. 3–8.

forgotten' as historians appeared again to be rallying to the discredited 'positivist historiography' associated with Ernest Lavisse and Charles Seignobos.[30]

Le Goff's point was twofold. First, the *Annales* school was not opposed to biography *per se*, only to certain forms of biography. He himself was writing, and has since completed, 'a life of Saint-Louis'.[31] Second, and more importantly, the historian was now 'scientifically and mentally better-equipped' to write biography because of the impact of *Annales* methodology. Le Goff's fear, in short, was of an indiscriminate backlash and of a headlong return to an earlier age before the *Annales* revolution.

II

The central question to be answered in this chapter is whether Le Goff is right to feel such concern and to fear a return of the émigrés. In short, his remarks highlight a set of pertinent questions that have arisen out of recent methodological doubts and uncertainties. When the range of questions is extended beyond the narrow confines of history to related questions in the study of politics, the issue is raised of what sort of return to politics is there to be? How is its history to be written? More specifically, what shape and form are its intellectual history to take?

Our starting point, however, is to recognise that, for all the hostile rhetoric, the history of politics and of political thought has always had a place, however marginal, in France. Texts such as Albert Thibaudet's *Idées de Charles Maurras* and more obviously Daniel Mornet's *Origines intellectuelles de la Révolution française* come to mind as too does Robert Derathé's classic *Jean-Jacques Rousseau et la science politique de son temps*, published originally in 1950.

Moreover, to the pioneering work in the study of politics of André Siegfried and François Goguel can be added that in the history of political ideas of both Jean-Jacques Chevallier and Jean Touchard, both of whom, as professors at the *Institut d'Etudes Politiques*, saw their subject as an indispensable part of the civic education required by those about to enter the service of the state.

Chevallier's *Grandes oeuvres politiques de Machiavel à nos jours*,[32] in its

---

30 Jacques Le Goff, 'Comment écrire une biographie historique aujourd'hui?', *Le débat*, 54 (March–April 1989), pp. 48–53. For a brief discussion of the 'positivist' school see Guy Bourdé, 'L'école méthodique', in Guy Bourdé and Hervé Martin (eds.), *Les écoles historiques* (Paris, 1997), pp. 181–214.

31 See Jacques Le Goff, *Saint-Louis* (Paris, 1996). In his introduction to this text, Le Goff affirms his intention to write 'a "total" life of Saint-Louis'.

32 Jean-Jacques Chevallier, *Grandes oeuvres politiques de Machiavel à nos jours* (Paris, 1996).

first edition prefaced by Siegfried and lauded as an example of how to teach 'political culture' as opposed to political 'technique', is undoubtedly the best and most typical example of this tradition. 'A great work', according to Chevallier, was one that 'had profoundly marked the mind of its contemporaries or that of subsequent generations'. They were defined, therefore, not merely by their 'intrinsic' qualities of 'construction, clarity and force of argument' but also by their 'historical *resonance*', by the fact that they had found a response in the 'preoccupations, the political passions of the moment or of a moment'. By this token, as Chevallier readily admits, he excludes Cournot's 'intrinsically great' *Considérations sur la marche des idées et des événements dans le temps modernes* but includes Hitler's *Mein Kampf*. Likewise his emphasis falls not upon what he describes as 'local colour' but upon what a text 'contributes to the clarification of the principal political problems posed to the human mind for centuries'. Accordingly, the text itself is sub-divided into four parts describing the advance of modern states towards monarchical absolutism; the ultimately victorious reaction against monarchical absolutism; the 'immediate' consequences of the French Revolution; and the long growth of socialism and nationalism. If the last text chosen dates from 1927, Chevallier remarks, it is because no book since then has been decisively marked with greatness.[33]

Yet in the 'French historical revolution'[34] that got under way from the late 1920s onwards, it was undoubtedly political history that, in the words of René Rémond, proved to be 'the favourite target and the first victim'.[35] The grounds of the objection to politics were, in fact, first formulated by François Simiand's famous programmatic statement of 1903, 'Méthode historique et science sociale', where, alongside 'l'Idole individuelle' and 'l'Idole chronologique', it was dismissed as 'l'Idole

---

[33] The best examples of Touchard's work are *L'histoire des idées politiques* (2 vols., Paris, 1959) and *La Gauche en France depuis 1900* (Paris, 1977). Touchard shifts the emphasis away from 'great texts', partly because he acknowledges Chevallier's 'livre excellent', but also because he wishes to study what he describes as 'ideas' rather than 'doctrines'. 'The historian of ideas', he writes, 'ought for each epoch to ask himself what are the political ideas of peasants, of workers, of civil servants, of the aristocracy, etc.'

A more recent example of the emphasis on texts can be found in F. Chatelet, O. Duhamel and E. Pisier, *Dictionnaire des oeuvres politiques* (Paris, 1986). The stated aim is to contribute to 'contemporary debate in political thought' and to do this they examine 125 texts, ranging from Hegel's *Philosophy of Right* to (again) Hitler's *Mein Kampf*. The 'civic tradition' element is continued in M. Prélot and G. Lescuyer, *Histoire des idées politiques* (Paris, 1990), where, through explicit acknowledgement of Chevallier, it is argued that, 'faced with a work, the political scientist asks himself less how it is situated in the past than what it still has to say to us today'.

[34] This is Peter Burke's phrase: see P. Burke, *The French Historical Revolution: the Annales School 1929–89* (Oxford, 1990).

[35] R. Rémond, 'Une histoire présente', in Rémond (ed.), *Pour une histoire politique*, p. 13.

politique'. 'It does not mean', Simiand wrote, 'that political facts should be ignored but they must lose the pre-eminent and unjustified place that they retain even in the researches of the other branches of history.'[36] Summarised by Jacques Julliard in 1974, the complaints went as follows:

political history concentrates on psychology and ignores conditions; it is elitist, even biographical, and ignores society as a whole and the masses who make it up; it is qualitative and ignores the serial; it concentrates upon the particular and ignores the comparative; it is narrative and ignores analysis; it is idealist and ignores the material; it concentrates on the specific and ignores the long term . . . in a word . . . it is *événementielle* [a history of events].[37]

Accordingly, when Jacques Le Goff, Roger Chartier and Jacques Revel published their compendium *La nouvelle histoire* in 1978 there was no entry under 'politics'.[38] The same line of criticism can be found as late as 1986 in André Burguière's *Dictionnaire des sciences historiques*. The entry on political history, written by Pierre Lévêque, repeats almost word for word the earlier characterisation by Julliard. 'The apparent objectivity [of political history]', Lévêque writes, 'hides an arbitrary choice which values individual psychology and the decisions of "great men" to the detriment of collective mentalities, systematically empha- sises "great events" and the short term without giving the attention they deserve to slow and deep movements, treats the study of economic and social structures as a poor relation.' If there had been a 'rehabilitation' of political history, Lévêque observed, it had been made possible because it had absorbed the principles and methods of the 'new history'. Hence- forth, the *événementielle* fact was to be better understood by its insertion within *la longue durée*.[39]

Within this methodological framework there was little or no room for the study of the history of ideas. Again the *locus classicus* of its denuncia- tion is to be found in François Simiand. In the same year that he published 'Méthode historique et science sociale' he also published a short two-page note entitled 'A propos de l'histoire des idées'.[40] When people speak of 'explaining an idea', Simiand wrote, they generally mean 'the task of finding all the forms, all the outlines, all the parts or elements of an idea that can be found in some earlier author or in an

---

[36] F. Simiand, 'Méthode historique et science sociale: étude critique d'après les ouvrages récents de M. Lacombe et de M. Seignobos', in Simiand, *Méthode historique et sciences sociales* (Paris, 1987), pp. 113–69.

[37] J. Julliard, 'La politique', in Le Goff and P. Nora (eds.), *Faire de l'histoire*, II, p. 229.

[38] Jacques Le Goff, Roger Chartier and Jacque Revel, *La nouvelle histoire* (Paris, 1978).

[39] Pierre Lévêque, 'Politique (histoire)', in André Burguière (ed.), *Dictionnaire des sciences historiques* (Paris, 1986), pp. 515–22.

[40] The importance of Simiand's remarks is best illustrated by the fact that they were reprinted in a special issue of *Politix: travaux de science politique*, 6 (1989), p. 6, devoted to 'Les liaisons dangereuses: histoire, sociologie, science politique'.

earlier text' and 'that is all'. But what, he asks, has this explained? Has this work of 'erudition' shown 'how an idea is really born, how it is formed and how it establishes itself . . . Have we left the false world of ideas taken in the air, apart, as sufficient to themselves, so as to place this intellectual function in the totality of human and social life where alone it can be properly understood?' His answer was clearly in the negative.

Lucien Febvre, armed with the concept of *outillage mental*, only added to the opprobrium when he later argued that those who engaged in intellectual history should be denied 'the generic title of historian'. The subsequent predominance of social, economic and anthropological history, deeply imbued with the principles of Febvre's *Annales* school, left little room for the study of such disembodied and abstract entities as ideas. Moreover, the hostility towards intellectual history remained even after the *Annales* school made its famous transition 'from the cellar to the attic'. The study of 'mentalités', in Chartier's words, 'constituted as the fundamental historical object an object which was the very opposite of that of classical intellectual history'. To the 'idea', seen as the conscious construction of the individual mind, was counterposed the 'collective mentality' which controlled the representations and judgements of social subjects. 'What it was important to understand', Chartier comments, 'was no longer the innovations of thought but rather the limits of the thinkable.'[41] Summarising these developments, François Azouvi, writing in *Le débat* in 1992, commented: 'It is outside France that to be a historian of ideas does not imply national dishonour.'[42]

[41] Roger Chartier, 'Histoire intellectuelle et histoire des mentalités', *Revue de synthèse*, 111–12 (1983), pp. 277–307. See also Roger Chartier, 'Intellectuelle (histoire)', in Burguière (ed.), *Dictionnaire des sciences historiques*, pp. 372–7. Whilst Chartier develops the arguments directed against 'intellectual history', he also recognises that the relationship between the history of mentalities and the history of ideas is more complicated than originally recognised by early proponents of the former. On 'mentalités', see Jacques Le Goff, 'Les mentalités: une histoire ambiguë', in Jacques Le Goff and Pierre Nora (eds.), *Faire de l'histoire*, III, pp. 76–98 and Jacques Revel, 'Mentalités', in Burguière (ed.), *Dictionnaire des sciences historiques*, pp. 450–6. 'The level of the history of mentalities', Le Goff writes, 'is that of the everyday and the automatic, it is that which escapes the individual subjects of history because it is revelatory of the impersonal content of their thought' (p. 80). Revel is equally forthright about its meaning: 'Today, as yesterday, with few exceptions, the history of mentalities privileges the collective over the individual, impersonal cultural processes rather than the culture of authors and works, the psychological rather than the intellectual, the automatic rather than the self-conscious' (pp. 455–6).

[42] François Azouvi, 'Pour une histoire philosophique des idées', *Le débat*, 72 (1992), pp. 17–28.

III

How and why politics, and specifically the history of political thought, re-emerged from its 'long eclipse'[43] is itself a complicated story for which many explanations have been provided. Amongst the more representative have been Pierre Nora's description of the 'event' as the 'wonder of democratic societies'[44] and René Rémond's characterisation of the twentieth century as 'the century of contingency'.[45] Whatever the truth of the matter, as the revival of interest (after years of neglect) in the work of Paul Ricoeur indicates,[46] recent years have seen an acceptance of a conception of history that is more open-textured and indeterminate than that which had previously prevailed.

To fully understand how politics made its entry into the sacred site of the *Annales* school, the Ecole des Hautes Etudes en Sciences Sociales, we can do no better than to turn to Pierre Rosanvallon's essay in the previously mentioned volume edited by Revel and Wachtel.[47] Long the subject of undisguised contempt, it was, according to Rosanvallon, in the early 1970s that the 'study of politics' began to take a 'significant place' at the EHESS. Rosanvallon attributes this to a variety of factors within the EHESS itself: the arrival of historians such as Jacques Ozouf, Pierre Nora and Jacques Julliard with a strong interest in politics; the impact of the house philosophers Claude Lefort and Cornelius Castoriadis, both of whom, through their analysis of totalitarianism, contributed much to the renaissance of political philosophy in France; and the intellectual re-orientation of certain individuals, most notably François Furet (himself President of the EHESS from 1977 to 1985). In the purely institutional terms of the EHESS, from 1977 onwards this produced the seminar that brought together, amongst others, Furet, Julliard, Nora, Marcel Gauchet, Pierre Manent and Rosanvallon himself and which, in 1985, led to the creation of the Institut Raymond Aron. Rosanvallon's own account of their work sub-divides into four sections: the 'political history' of the French Revolution; the intellectual history of liberalism; the attempt to define the 'constitution of modern politics'; and philosophical and historical reflection upon contemporary issues. The same group was behind the publication of *La pensée politique*.

---

43 René Rémond, 'Postface' to Pascal Ory (ed.), *Nouvelle histoire des idées politiques* (Paris, 1987), p. 763.
44 Pierre Nora, 'Le retour de l'événement', in Le Goff and Nora (eds.), *Faire de l'histoire*, I, p. 215.
45 René Rémond, 'Le siècle de la contingence', *Vingtième siècle*, 1 (1984), pp. 97–103.
46 See, for example, Olivier Mongin, *Paul Ricoeur* (Paris, 1994).
47 Pierre Rosanvallon, 'Le politique', in Revel and Wachtel (eds.), *Une école pour les sciences sociales*, pp. 299–301.

More broadly, Rosanvallon situates this development in what he describes as 'the general intellectual context of the period'. Often referred to in the stark terms of a 'paradigm shift', the wholesale abandonment of Marxism combined with a growing 'epistemological doubt' about the social science status of history created an atmosphere where superstructures could be regarded as being as important as substructures and where there was an acknowledged place for the role of ideas.

To take one important example from Rosanvallon's list of the work carried out through the Institut Raymond Aron: this approach is most clearly reflected in the fundamental reinterpretation of the French Revolution effected by François Furet and his former associates. It is best embodied in the emphasis given to ideas in Furet and Mona Ozouf's *Dictionnaire critique de la Révolution Française*.[48] The Revolution is no longer to be seen in terms of the economistic and reductionist categories of Marxism but as a struggle between competing political arguments and philosophical positions that produced not the dominance of the bourgeoisie but rather a new and distinctly modern form of politics. In purely historiographical terms, the 1989 *bicentenaire* was Furet's triumph, the crowning of a new political interpretation of the Revolution.[49]

Of almost equal significance has been the second area of inquiry highlighted by Rosanvallon: the rediscovery of the much-neglected liberals of the nineteenth century, most notably Benjamin Constant and François Guizot. So, for example, Rosanvallon published *Le moment Guizot* in 1985, Pierre Manent published his two-volume *Les libéraux* a year later and *Histoire intellectuelle du libéralisme: dix leçons* in 1987, whilst Françoise Mélanio published her *Tocqueville et les Français* in 1993. This process of re-evaluation culminated in the publication of Lucien Jaume's magisterial *L'individu effacé ou le paradoxe du libéralisme français* in 1997.[50] Jaume, acknowledging Furet as 'le maître irremplaçable',

[48] François Furet and Mona Ozouf, *Dictionnaire critique de la Révolution française* (Paris, 1989).

[49] For a discussion of the political significance of this immensely important debate see S.L. Kaplan, *Farewell Revolution: the Historians' Feud, France, 1789/1989* (Ithaca and London, 1995). Note also that towards the end of his life Furet turned his efforts towards a re-interpretation of the other great event of modern politics: the Russian Revolution. See F. Furet, *Le passé d'une illusion: essai sur l'idée communiste au XXe siècle* (Paris, 1995). The linkage is obvious. Both enterprises were concerned to demolish what Furet for long characterised as the Leninist and communist 'vulgate'. Both are part of an attempt to bring 'the Revolution to an end'. Since Furet's death, the analysis of the French Revolution has been continued in the work of such brilliant young historians as Patrice Guennifey.

[50] Lucien Jaume, *L'individu effacé ou le paradoxe du libéralisme français* (Paris, 1997). Not insignificantly, this volume was awarded the Prix Guizot. See also Jaume's brilliant *Le discours jacobin et la démocratie* (Paris, 1989).

establishes a threefold typology, dividing liberalism into a 'libéralisme du sujet' (principally Mme de Staël and Constant), a 'libéralisme élitaire' (Guizot and the *doctrinaires*) and 'le catholicisme libéral' (Lamennais and Montalembert). Not only does he demonstrate that French liberalism, in the main, was ready to sacrifice the claims of individual liberty to those of state sovereignty, but he does so with the clear recognition that his subject matter is constituted as 'l'histoire des idées politiques'.

The past decade or so, therefore, has seen a quite astonishing upsurge in what we can conventionally describe as political studies, much of it concerned with the nineteenth and twentieth centuries, a period largely overlooked by the *Annales* school.[51] For the most part this has not entailed a simple return to the ephemeral, the short term, the political 'event' nor has it involved an abandonment of the goal of multi-disciplinarity. Gérard Noiriel, responding specifically to the publication of Rémond's *Pour une histoire politique*, called for the development of what he termed 'a social history of politics'.[52] Others have argued for a 'new political history' which itself has aspirations to become 'total history'. New methods, the reply goes, are appropriate to a new, and much-enlarged, subject matter and in this way a history of politics written from top down, concentrating on 'great men' and 'great texts', is to be avoided.[53]

IV

As a focus for research the key notion has been that of 'culture', an idea that owes much to Maurice Agulhon's concept of 'sociability' first formulated in his work on communal life in the Var and which found early expression in Annie Kriegel's writings on the French Communist Party.[54] Attention has thus turned to cultural practices and their symbolic representation. How people lived, worked, dressed, consumed and spoke – *l'histoire des choses banales* – opened up the way for ground-

[51] The work of Marc Ferro is an important exception.
[52] Gérard Noiriel, 'Une histoire sociale de la politique est-elle possible?', *Vingtième siècle*, 24 (1989), p. 86. See also Noiriel's 'Pour une approche subjectiviste du social', *Annales*, 6 (1989), pp. 1435–60.
[53] See Pascal Balmand, 'Le renouveau de l'histoire politique', in Bourdé and Martin (eds.), *Les écoles historiques*, pp. 363–89, and Denis Peschanski, Michael Pollak and Henry Rousso, 'Le temps présent, une démarche historique à l'épreuve des sciences sociales', in Peschanski et al., *Histoire politique*, pp. 13–36.
[54] See A. Kriegel, *Communismes au miroir français: temps, culture, et sociétés en France devant le communisme* (Paris, 1974), and *Les communistes français: essai d'ethnographie politique* (Paris, 1968); cf. also *The republic in the village: the people of the Var from the French Revolution to the Second Republic* (Cambridge, 1982).

breaking studies of the press, book-selling and readership, education, religious rituals, public festivals and celebrations, and sexual habits as well as attitudes towards illness and death. Again, the practitioners of such a 'social history of culture' were clear that they were engaged in something different from a traditional 'history of ideas'. So, for example, by moving away from the great texts of the eighteenth century towards the actual diffusion and vulgarisation of books, pamphlets (including those pornographic) and ideas, it has been possible to provide an entirely different account of the cultural origins of the French Revolution.[55] Likewise, the work of Daniel Roche has completely reshaped our understanding of the France of the Enlightenment. His *La France des Lumières*,[56] for example, begins by looking at the 'perceptions and conceptions, customs and practices' of the 'people of the eighteenth century', before moving on to discuss 'the relation of the monarchical state to subjects and corporations', in order, finally, to re-interpret 'the relations among the essential and the biological, production, and material civilisation in an age that believed in prosperity as the basis of universal enlightenment'. Another example would be the recently published four-volume *Histoire culturelle de la France*, a lavishly illustrated attempt to synthesise much of this earlier work.[57] The publication of a key programmatic volume, *Pour une histoire culturelle*, occurred in 1997, with contributors drawn from an array of France's cultural historians.[58]

This in turn has opened up new areas of inquiry in the field of political culture. Frequently cited as an early example of innovation is the work of Jean-Jacques Becker on public opinion in France during 1914, but to this can be added a whole body of work that has sought to unravel the imagery, myths and symbolic representations that have served to fashion French political sensibility. Again we could cite the work of Maurice Agulhon, most notably his analyses of the visual representation of the Republic during the nineteenth century. But best of all is the recently completed multi-volumed series 'Les lieux de mémoire', edited by Pierre Nora. It would be difficult to do full justice to the richness of this collection in its exploration of the French collective memory. It is not just the Republic, with its symbols, monuments, educational institutions

[55] See Roger Chartier, *Les origines culturelles de la Révolution française* (Paris, 1991). It would, of course, be an error not to recognise the important impact in France of those American historians most associated with the *new cultural history*.

[56] Daniel Roche, *La France des Lumières* (Paris, 1993).

[57] See especially Antoine de Baecque and Françoise Mélanio, *Histoire culturelle de la France: vol. III Lumières et liberté* (4 vols., Paris, 1998).

[58] Jean-François Sirinelli and Jean-Pierre Rioux (eds.), *Pour une histoire culturelle* (Paris, 1997). The latter, with contributions from an array of France's best cultural historians, is a product of a seminar devoted to 'l'histoire culturelle de la France au XXe siècle' begun in 1989.

and celebrations that is placed before us but the multiple traditions, groups, professions, locations, buildings, texts and personalities that have forged the national consciousness in what Nora himself describes as 'the era of commemoration'. Parallel studies have approached the Vichy regime, the Algerian War and May 1968 in similar vein. In recent formulations political culture has been redefined so as to redirect inquiry towards an examination of the 'locations, environments and networks' that are deemed to be of vital importance in determining political affiliations and patterns of behaviour.[59]

Less obviously, the past decade has seen the emergence of the intellectual – and specifically the twentieth-century intellectual – as a major object of interest.[60] It would be inaccurate to say that the latter was entirely new – in the 1960s Jean-Louis Loubet del Bayle produced his study of *Les non-conformistes des années 30* and later Michel Winock gave us his account of the left-Catholic review *Esprit* – but it is only in recent years that the subject has risen to prominence.[61] In our context the principal significance of this development is that it provides us with an important insight into how political culture at this level has been approached. What is reflected is the desire to study the producers of ideas as much as the ideas themselves. What are further revealed are the conceptual instruments that have been developed in order to describe and analyse intellectual activity as social activity.

Here it is useful to say something about the work of Pierre Bourdieu, especially given his now immense influence in France. At its simplest, Bourdieu's prodigious output can be seen as an attempt to preserve the insights of structuralism and to prevent a headlong rush towards methodological individualism. This he has sought to achieve primarily through the utilisation of the twinned notions of *habitus* and 'field', both of which are intended to express the objective conditions through which the practice of individual agents is mediated. Frequently reworked to meet the comments of his critics, the emphasis in the past decade or so has shifted increasingly to the idea of 'strategy' as 'an orientation of practice'. This has been used to give a sociological underpinning to what might otherwise have been regarded as purely ideological or political debates. So too – as with recent innovations within the *Annales* school – it has redirected analysis away from the macro-social to the micro-social,

[59] We will return to this later when we examine the work of Jean-François Sirinelli but see the special issue of *Les cahiers de l'Institut de l'histoire du temps présent*, 20 (March 1992), devoted to 'Sociabilités intellectuelles: lieux, milieux, réseaux'.

[60] For a recent example see Jacques Julliard and Michel Winock, *Dictionnaire des intellectuels français* (Paris, 1996).

[61] See, for example, Pascal Ory and Jean-François Sirinelli, *Les intellectuels en France de l'affaire Dreyfus à nos jours* (Paris, 1986).

from society to the subject, and this, viewed more generally, has meant the reintroduction, whether it be for the study of individuals or groups, of politics into social reality.[62]

The most formulaic example of the study of intellectuals is to be found in Rémy Rieffel's *La tribu des clercs: les intellectuels sous la Ve République*,[63] published in the autumn of 1993. Here we are presented with a 're-reading of French intellectual life' resting upon a 'thorough sociological study'. This is done via an inventory of intellectual practices organised around three thematic categories defined by Rieffel as processes of 'affiliation', 'legitimation' and 'consecration'. The book begins therefore with where intellectuals eat, sleep and drink before moving ever upwards to where they buy their books, attend conferences, are educated, publish their work, are employed, teach, and eventually reach out to a wider public and see their endeavours sanctified by such great institutions of French intellectual life as the Sorbonne and the Académie Française. The almost-obligatory note of late twentieth-century pessimism is struck in Rieffel's conclusion that the hierarchy of intellectual legitimation has been radically revised in favour of the mass media.

All of this is undoubtedly fascinating and as a form of academic voyeurism is immensely enjoyable, but the reader is left with a picture of the intellectual that is curiously one-dimensional and which ignores the all-important ingredient of the intellectual's relationship with the world of ideas. The emphasis falls resolutely upon structures and conditions of intellectual production. And here, thinking back to Stefan Collini's remarks, it is difficult not to make the comparison with a recently published British treatment of the same period of French intellectual history. If Sunil Khilnani's *Arguing Revolution: the Intellectual Left in Postwar France* has a fault, it derives from telling us, perhaps too often, that political thinking should be characterised as 'a form of agency within a given context, rather than a reified outcome of social processes'.[64] In Rieffel's case, all we have are social processes!

Amongst the critics of Rieffel's book has been Christophe Charle, now professor at the Sorbonne and the author of *La République des universitaires, 1870–1940*, *Les intellectuels en Europe au XIXe siècle* and, most recently, *Paris fin de siècle*.[65] Writing in *Le débat*, he commented

[62] There is now an abundance of Bourdieu's work available in translation but beyond this an excellent guide to his work and that of his admirers is the journal *Actes de la recherche en sciences sociales*.

[63] Rémy Rieffel, *La tribu des clercs: les intellectuels sous la Ve République* (Paris, 1993).

[64] Sunil Khilnani, *Arguing Revolution: the Intellectual Left in Postwar France* (New Haven and London, 1993).

[65] Christophe Charle, *La République des universitaires, 1870–1940* (Paris, 1994), *Les Intellectuels en Europe au XIXe siècle* (Paris, 1996) and *Paris fin de siècle: culture et politique*

that Rieffel's 'falsely theoretical and artificial' framework succeeded in effacing important dimensions of the 'identity of intellectuals' in France.[66] Yet Charle's own work on intellectuals, heavily influenced by the theories of Pierre Bourdieu, is itself another example of what might be termed the sociological turn in the history of ideas. In the same article, for instance, he makes plain his own opposition to the 'essayism' that had for too long characterised approaches to his subject.

The application of Bourdieu's theories to intellectual history had been tried prior to the publication of Charle's work – most notably by Anna Boschetti in her analysis of *Les temps modernes*[67] – and now it is much in vogue,[68] but Charle had the originality of taking one of the most important events in modern French political history – the Dreyfus Affair – so as to rework it in terms of Bourdieu's notions of the 'dominant' and 'dominated' poles of the 'intellectual field'.[69]

To explain in detail how this is done is not necessary for our purpose. It is sufficient to note that Charle focuses his attention upon the emergence within the 'dominant' class of three distinct elites – politico-administrative, academic and business – during the period 1880–1900, concentrating upon the 'social' and 'career strategies' that determined their education, employment, marriage, family size, finance and invest-ment, styles of life and so on. Charle's conclusions are both far-reaching and original but crucial to his argument is the claim that the academic elite became progressively distanced from the other two, thus providing 'one of the objective foundations of the birth of "intellectuals"'. Having set the scene and laid out the conditions which would predispose individuals to become either Dreyfusards or anti-Dreyfusards, it is Charle's second volume, *Naissance des 'intellectuels'*, which presents a re-reading of the Dreyfus Affair, the different political positions adopted by opposing camps being explained not so much by reference to competing ideologies and values – the rights of the individual against those of the nation, truth and justice against the superior claims of the army – but in terms of divisions within the 'intellectual field' and the dissimilar relationship of each group with the dominant class. As Charle remarks:

(Paris, 1998). With regard to the subject of this chapter, the latter is the most interesting.

[66] Christophe Charle, 'Trop près, trop loin', *Le débat*, 79 (1994), pp. 31–7.
[67] Anna Boschetti, *Sartre et 'les temps modernes'* (Paris, 1985).
[68] For a very good example of this approach see the doctoral thesis of Gisèle Sapiro, 'Complicités et anathèmes en temps de crise: modes de survie du champ littéraire et de ses institutions 1940–1953', submitted to the Ecole des Hautes Etudes en Sciences Sociales in 1994, see *La guerre des écrivains* (Paris, 1999).
[69] Chrisophe Charle, *Les élites de la République 1880–1900* (Paris, 1987) and *Naissance des 'intellectuels' 1880–1900* (Paris, 1990).

These theoretical justifications certainly contributed towards mobilising the two groups of intellectuals. But they are insufficient in themselves and need to be given greater depth by reference to their social resonance. If formally identical individuals found themselves to be attracted to one or other system of values it is because it expressed their vision of the world, itself fashioned by their social trajectory plus the relative position in the field to which they belong and their relationship to the field of power.[70]

Charle's text explains precisely what he means by this and does so with great intelligence and erudition.

At least two objections can be raised to this approach. First, when it comes to the type of decision that Charle examines can there not be an element of contingency, the unexpected or chance? The painter Edgar Degas, for example, became an anti-Dreyfusard largely because of his anti-Semitism whilst his friend, the writer Octave Mirbeau, joined the other camp out of a sense of guilt for the anti-Semitism of his youth.[71] Second, can the complex relationships that make up an intellectual environment be reduced to a single mechanism, in this case that of strategies within fields characterised by dominant and dominated poles? Raised by Jean-François Sirinelli these questions lead to the conclusion that other conceptual 'tools' – and especially the notion of 'structures of sociability' – might better enable us to grasp 'the field of forces which structure and polarise French intellectual society'.

The work of Sirinelli – most notably *Génération intellectuelle: Khâgneux et Normaliens dans l'entre-deux guerres*[72] and *Intellectuels et passions françaises: manifestes et pétitions françaises au XXe siècle*[73] – is broadly representative of a much wider body of scholarship in France that seeks to write intellectual history whilst avoiding what he himself has described as 'a pure history of ideas'. Outlined in a series of articles during the 1980s and then put into practice in the two volumes cited, Sirinelli's contention is that 'a history of the *clercs*' can best be written through 'the study of itineraries, the observation of structures of sociability and the bringing to light of generations'. If the notion of itineraries should be reasonably clear in meaning, then the second two elements of this equation are there precisely to indicate that what is not intended is straightforward intellectual biography. So Sirinelli's highly impressive *Génération intellectuelle* is a study of the uniquely French institution of the *khâgne*, the

---

[70] Charle, *Naissance des 'intellectuels'*, p. 184.

[71] For an analysis of this issue much less indebted to the theories of Bourdieu see the special issue of *Mil neuf cent*, 11 (1993), devoted to the theme of 'Comment ils sont devenus dreyfusards ou anti-dreyfusards?'

[72] Jean-François Sirinelli, *Génération intellectuelle: Khâgneux et Normaliens dans l'entre-deux guerres* (Paris, 1988).

[73] Jean-François Sirinelli, *Intellectuelles et passions françaises: manifestes et pétitions françaises au XXe siècle* (Paris, 1990).

preparatory classes for entry into the *Ecole Normale Supérieure* and through it the reconstruction of the cultural and political world of what he has identified as 'the generation of 1905'. Aware of the problems that the concept of generation engenders, it is nevertheless Sirinelli's opinion that the 'intellectual milieu' is structured in part by patterns of 'solidarity' brought into existence by common origins, age and education and, in effect, that the birth and evolution of these generational groupings can be traced. In Sirinelli's terms we are talking of a 'microclimate' that 'characterises a particular intellectual microcosm'. Sirinelli's second volume, *Intellectuels et passions françaises*, turns its attention to the third element of his formula, structures of intellectual sociability; in this case, the petitions signed by intellectuals in the twentieth century. The justification is that these petitions – of which France has had an abundance – provide an 'observation point' through which the existence of intellectual 'networks' can be identified, the intervention of intellectuals in political debate explored, and finally the movement of ideas assessed. Less successful, it should be noted, is Sirinelli's application of the notion of 'trajectory' to his comparative study of Sartre and Aron.[74]

What we have in the work of Sirinelli is an approach that escapes the sociological reductionism of Bourdieu's disciples and which clearly owes much more to the emphasis on sociability and memory characteristic of recent research by Agulhon and Nora. In this it is typical of a growing trend in intellectual history in France. If, in Sirinelli's second volume, he chose the petition as an example of sociability then a far more obvious choice would have been the periodical review, in France the most central location for the formulation of new ideas, the fighting of ideological battles and, just as importantly, the creation of intellectual friendships as well as antagonisms. Here early work on the fascist journal *Je suis partout* has been supplemented, for example, by analysis of the far more prestigious *Nouvelle revue française*.[75]

Yet attention has also turned to other structures or 'networks' of intellectual sociability – the salon, the café, the publishing house, the international congress, literary institutions such as the Académie Goncourt and the Comité National des Ecrivains, as well as personal correspondence. One case where the study of these various aspects of intellectual sociability has been brought together in one volume would be Christophe Prochasson's *Les années électriques 1880–1910*.[76] Pub-

---

[74] Jean-François Sirinelli, *Deux intellectuels dans le siècle, Sartre and Aron* (Paris, 1995).
[75] P. Hebey, *La nouvelle revue française des années sombres, 1940–1941* (Paris, 1992).
[76] Christophe Prochasson, *Les années électriques 1880–1910* (Paris, 1991). Another example would be Géraldi Leroy and Julie Bertrand-Sabiani, *La vie littéraire à la Belle Epoque* (Paris, 1998).

lished as part of a collection devoted to *L'aventure intellectuelle au XXe siècle*, the introduction quotes Simiand's denunciation of the history of ideas at length whilst itself defining intellectual history as 'the history of intellectuals and their works'. The chapters therefore invite the reader on an 'excursion' into 'the mysteries of Parisian intellectual life'. 'The actors in this history', Prochasson explains, 'do not disappear immediately after they have been conjured up. They loiter, *with their ideas*, in drawing rooms as much as the offices of some review, in a bookshop as much as during a visit to an exhibition.' If they impact upon the environment then that environment in turn leaves its impact upon them. 'Let us therefore', Prochasson writes, concluding his introduction, 'follow these men, these women, and their ideas, from place to place.' And this is precisely what is done in the following pages. Moving beyond texts, 'the representation of an epoch' takes us to the theatre, the cinema, the art exhibition, the publisher, the academic institution and so on. Intellectual history thus 'intertwines', as Prochasson remarks, 'with the history of mentalities and with social history'.

V

Reference to the history of mentalities takes us to what will be the final part of our assessment of current trends in the study of the history of ideas in France. There is no need to rehearse the criticisms made of what has gone under the name of 'the third level of serial history' by Robert Darnton and others or to assess in detail the response of *Annales* historians such as Roger Chartier. In short, by shifting the concerns of cultural history away from the quantitative and towards the triple themes of 'representation, practice [and] appropriation' the latter has done much to neutralise the force of Darnton's remarks. Where we (like Prochasson's intellectuals) might choose to loiter, however, is upon Chartier's continued criticisms of the 'linguistic turn', voiced, for example, at the end of September 1994 in his commentary upon the posthumous publication of four volumes of essays by Michel Foucault and which figures at the heart of a volume of collected essays published in 1998.[77]

The substance of Chartier's hostility was made clear in an exchange of views with Keith Baker in response to the publication of the French edition of the latter's *Inventing the French Revolution: Essays on French*

[77] Roger Chartier, 'Au bord de la falaise', *Le monde des livres* (30 September 1994), p. x and *Au bord de la falaise*. In the latter volume Chartier repeatedly returns to a critique of Hayden White's *Metahistory*. See especially the essay 'Figures rhétoriques et représentations historiques', pp. 108–25.

Political Culture in the Eighteenth Century.[78] Citing the influence of Pocock and Skinner specifically, Chartier accused Baker of failing to distinguish the discursive from the non-discursive. Baker was thus committed, Chartier contended, to accepting that the only limitations upon the possible are 'linguistic and conceptual', a position which Chartier rejects, following Foucault, in his insistence upon the distinction between discursive practices and non-discursive systems. Baker's reply was to deny this characterisation of his position, seeking to situate himself (as he sees it) somewhere between Foucault and the Cambridge School whilst reducing his own disagreement with Chartier to a 'difference of intellectual strategy'.[79] 'What I want to emphasise', he argues, 'is that the social is discursive; what Roger Chartier for his part wishes to emphasise is that the discursive is social.' What for his part the author of this chapter would like to emphasise is that the views of Baker are close to the position advanced by what is now, in institutional terms, the most dominant school in French historiography, that associated with the late François Furet and his former colleagues at the Institut Raymond Aron.

How can Furet's achievement be summarised? Here we can turn to the opening chapter of the text that caused Chartier's annoyance, Baker's *Inventing the French Revolution.* 'Furet's analysis', Baker writes, 'has had the great value of redirecting historians' attention to the fundamental character of the French Revolution as a political phenomenon, a profound transformation of political discourse involving powerful new forms of political symbolisation, experimentally elaborated in radically novel modes of political action that were as unprecedented as they were unanticipated.'[80] Amongst the consequences of this programme, Baker makes clear, was 'a new creative synergy between French historiography of the revolutionary and post-revolutionary periods and an English-language historiography in which politics, political theory and the history of ideas had remained a matter of more vital concern'.

To illustrate this – and also to indicate where divergences between the two schools might exist – I intend briefly to examine the writings of Pierre Rosanvallon. As examples of practice we have above all *Le moment Guizot,* published in 1985, *Le sacre du citoyen: histoire du suffrage universel en France,* published in 1992, *La monarchie impossible,* published in 1994, and, most recently, *Le peuple introuvable: histoire de la représenta-*

---

[78] 'Dialogue sur l'espace public', *Politix. Travaux de science politique,* 26 (1994), pp. 5–22.

[79] To gauge the difference between Chartier and Baker it is interesting to compare their respective assessments of Foucault as a historian of the French Revolution to be found in Jan Goldstein (ed.), *Foucault and the Writing of History* (Oxford, 1994), pp. 167–205.

[80] Keith Michael Baker, *Inventing the French Revolution: Essays on French Political Culture in the Eighteenth Century* (Cambridge, 1990), p. 7.

tion démocratique en France. For a programmatic statement we need look no further than an article published in the *Revue de synthèse* in 1986 entitled 'Pour une histoire conceptuelle du politique'.[81] To this can be added the text of an interview published in the February 1995 edition of *Esprit*, his article 'Le politique' to be found in the Wachtel and Revel volume, as well as his chapter in this collection.

Distancing himself from both a sociological approach and the history of mentalities, Rosanvallon's intention is to outline what he terms a 'conceptual history of the political' that avoids what are in his opinion the faults of 'the history of ideas traditionally conceived'. These faults he identifies as various but in essence he says much the same thing as François Simiand in 1903. We have catalogued texts, classified them, compared them, reconstructed them and placed them within traditions but all in such a way as 'not to help us understand history even if we learn lots of other things'. The purpose of a conceptual history of the political, on the other hand, he defines as 'understanding the formation and evolution of *political rationalities*, the systems of representation which govern the way in which an epoch, a country or a social group carries out its actions and envisages its future'. Importantly these representations are judged not to be exterior to the consciences of the actors themselves and are rather seen as attempts by these actors to construct responses to what are seen by them, more or less clearly, as problems. It is conceptual history precisely because the focus falls upon the concepts – equality, sovereignty, democracy and so on – that give intelligibility to these situations. Less obviously, Rosanvallon further argues that this 'conceptual history' will always gravitate around one 'central issue', an examination of the 'advent, development and meaning of *political modernity*'. This in turn he characterises as the progressive emergence of the individual as 'the generator of the social', a circumstance which ensures that the relationship between liberalism and democracy will be at the heart of the 'dynamic of the evolution of societies'.

The purpose of this conceptual history of the political is therefore unambiguous. It is to be, Rosanvallon states, 'a means of understanding the present'. If, therefore, in *Le moment Guizot* Rosanvallon chooses to study the political thought of the Restoration it is not simply because it has been unduly ignored. It is, he argues, first because this particular period is of critical importance in the emergence of 'new political realities' and second because, like our own, it too sensed 'the limits of the democratic model'. 'To that extent', Rosanvallon comments, 'the

---

[81] Pierre Rosanvallon, 'Pour une histoire conceptuelle du politique (note de travail)', *Revue de synthèse*, 1–2 (1986), pp. 93–105; see also Rosanvallon's chapter in this volume.

debates and thinking which took place under the Restoration and during the July Monarchy have again become of major importance for us.'[82]

It is this second dimension that comes even more to the fore in *Le sacre du citoyen* and *Le peuple introuvable* and which allows us to discern more clearly the political project that unites Rosanvallon with Furet and his liberal friends.[83] In essence what is being explored is a failure of the French properly to conceptualise the nature of democratic representation. The charge is that the aspiration towards social unity or inclusion combined with the principle of equality has produced what is termed 'a democracy of integration' that is both incapable of perceiving the merits of pluralism and profoundly illiberal. 'If the French in 1789', Rosanvallon writes, 'invented equality, they subsequently established however a catalogue of the diseases and problems of modern democracy rather than their solutions. It is a specific form of universalism that is put forward by French democracy: far from constituting a model it is better seen as an inventory of the profound difficulties associated with political modernity.' Rosanvallon's conceptual history of the political is then quite definitely not identical to what he himself describes as 'a contextual history of ideas'.

VI

Where does this leave us in answer to our original questions? Stefan Collini was undoubtedly correct to suggest that the study of political thought in France was about to be given greater prominence. But does this mean, as Le Goff feared, that there has been a return of the émigrés? A return there has been but it has never been either simple or straightforward. The revival of narrative and the return to politics has not meant, on the whole, an abandonment of the goal of multi-disciplinarity nor a naïve concentration upon events and great texts. Nor, within this revised perspective, is politics often perceived as an 'autonomous' activity radically separated from and prior to social and cultural configurations and practices.

We have certainly seen a reduction in the differences of approach towards the study of political thought between the French- and English-speaking worlds. Collaborative work between British, French and American historians of ideas is evident not just in the multi-volumed series

---

[82] The context in which the French have apparently become aware of the limitations of the democratic model are explored in Rosanvallon, *L'état en France* (Paris, 1990).

[83] For an explicit statement of this project see François Furet, Jacques Julliard and Pierre Rosanvallon, *La République du centre* (Paris, 1988).

exploring 'The French Revolution and the Creation of Modern Political Culture' but also, for example, in Biancamaria Fontana's *The Invention of the Modern Republic*[84] and *Le siècle de l'avènement républicain*, edited by François Furet and Mona Ozouf.[85] Informal and institutional contacts now abound.[86]

Yet the contrasts and divergences should not be overlooked. They appeared starkly, for example, in the exchange of views that occurred between Yves Charles Zarka and Quentin Skinner at a conference on Hobbes which took place in Amsterdam in May 1996.[87] Zarka is the author of two major works on Hobbes[88] as well as the director of the Centre Thomas Hobbes in Paris, a CNRS-funded body engaged in the publication of a critical edition of Hobbes's work. Defending resolutely what he describes as a 'philosophical' approach to the texts of Hobbes, he not only contended that all attempts to understand the past by divorcing it from the present were 'illusory' but that the principal interest of the philosophy of Hobbes lay in its capacity to aid our 'understanding of modernity'. Skinner's 'contextualism' is accordingly cast as a form of 'historicism' which 'reduces' Hobbes's thought 'to the status of the vestige from a former epoch' and which also misleads through its 'scientific pretension' to appear as a true reading of Hobbes rather than as an 'interpretation'. On this view, it is the 'philosophical system' rather than the 'rhetoric' of Hobbes that should command our attention.[89]

Rosanvallon's original programmatic essay also recognises that important differences still remain. Acknowledging his debt to Quentin Skinner and his admiration for the 'très beau' *Foundations of Modern Political Thought*, Rosanvallon nevertheless remarks that 'the conditions in which [Skinner] developed his critique of the traditional form of the history of ideas led him not to take the step which would have pushed him very naturally towards a conceptual history of the political'. 'He wished, or was obliged', Rosanvallon concludes, 'to limit his role to that of a Cambridge professor.' For him, if not for Skinner, in short, 'the work of

---

[84] Biancamaria Fontana (ed.), *The Invention of the Modern Republic* (Cambridge, 1994).

[85] François Furet and Mona Ozouf (eds.), *Le siècle de l'avènement républicain* (Paris, 1993).

[86] One significant example would be Quentin Skinner's invitation to lecture at the Collège de France in 1997.

[87] See 'Aux origines de la politique moderne: Hobbes', *Le débat*, 96 (1997), pp. 89–120.

[88] See *La décision métaphysique de Hobbes* (Paris, 1987) and *Hobbes et la pensée politique moderne* (Paris, 1995).

[89] Skinner's response to Zarka's at times intemperate comments was typically measured but, nevertheless, succeeded in conveying the message that he and Zarka were engaged in two quite different intellectual enterprises. 'I am a historian, not a philosopher,' Skinner remarked.

the historian' can open up the way to 'a new kind of intellectual engagement'. In the more recent essay, he again refers to parallels with the Cambridge School as well as with the work of Pocock and Keith Baker but on this occasion makes the different point that, despite early appearances to the contrary, 'the history of the political is situated more in terms of a perspective of the prolongation and renewal of the French historical school than in a logic of rupture'.

Equally, it has to be recognised that the group broadly associated with Furet and the project to define in a French context the nature of a liberal polity do not survey the field unchallenged. Pierre Bourdieu, for example, has spoken of his aim to 'facilitate the emergence of a unified social science, where history would be a sociological history of the past and sociology a social history of the present'.[90] In addition, there are others, less sociologically inclined and less engaged in the analysis of Bourdieu's 'intellectual field' who, in their examination of patterns of intellectual sociability and their hostility to the 'linguistic turn', continue in a much-modified form the *Annales* tradition.

Does this mean that Jacques Le Goff can rest easy? Probably not. Were he to pick up a recent issue of *Vingtième siècle* he would find an article whose contents he would no doubt find deeply worrying. There for all to see is an article by eminent historian Antoine Prost telling us that Charles Seignobos, the very embodiment of all that the *Annales* had rejected, was not as bad as he had been made out to be.[91] It remains to be seen, in other words, just how far the return to politics will go.

[90] See, for example, Pierre Bourdieu, 'Sur les rapports entre la sociologie et l'histoire en Allemagne et en France', *Actes de la recherche en sciences sociales*, 106–7 (1995), pp. 108–22 and 'Dialogue sur l'espace public', *Politix. Travaux de science politique*, 26 (1994), pp. 5–22.
[91] Antoine Prost, 'Seignobos revisité', *Vingtième siècle*, 43 (1994), pp. 100–18.

Victor Neumann

I

The genesis of modern states in Eastern and Central Europe was no
linear process. Whilst enlightened political literature in the last decades
of the eighteenth century and the first decades of the nineteenth century
was sympathetic to imperial power, things changed during the romantic
period, when well-meaning scholars shaped the modern idea of nation-
hood. They regarded linguistic unity as both demonstrating the existence of a national spirit and contributing to the very formation of the
nation-state. National identity was asserted in opposition to the thin
cosmopolitanism encouraged by imperial administration and the Habsburg tradition of political thought was ignored. Austrian cosmopolitanism of the eighteenth and nineteenth centuries, which had helped to
avoid inter-confessional and inter-ethnic conflicts, lost its cultural and
political role. In its place, there emerged nationalist doctrines, which
were seized upon in the newly consolidated nations of the 'Dual Empire'
in the hope of reasserting their own separate dignities. All modes of
cultural expression, from sciences and literature to journalism and art,
were influenced by this 'nationalist turn'.

Linguistic borders, always hard to define, were to generate many
misunderstandings among the states emerging from the ruins of the
empires that had for so long dominated the region. All nations tended to
assert their own identity by denying it to others, particularly to the
nations in close proximity. The cultural and national identity of the
Greeks was constructed by denying it to the Turks. Bulgarian national
consciousness was asserted against that of Greece and Turkey. The
Romanian, Serbian, and Croatian nations considered the Magyar nation
to be the main enemy of their own development. Russo-phobia was, and
still is for many of the nations of Eastern and Central Europe, a natural
reflex of both the intelligentsia and the people. This 'neighbour' cliché
has been operating since 1850 and is no less active nowadays, as attested
by current history textbooks.

II

Of the dominantly nationalist and ethnic ways of political thought emerging in the nineteenth century, Hungary is a perfect example for at least two reasons. Like Poland, Bohemia and Moravia it strove to acquire independence and political self-determination, while, at the same time, it harboured in its midst a diversity of nations speaking different languages and with different religions and customs.

Nineteenth-century Hungarian nationalism was both ideological and cultural. The revolutionaries of 1848 perceived the problem of founding a modern Hungary as a matter of establishing state sovereignty against the Habsburg Empire. Progress towards modernity and self-determination became inseparable issues for them. The Austro-Hungarian compromise of 1867, establishing a dual leadership, with two capital cities, two territorial administrations, but a single foreign policy and a united army, can be seen as following directly from the 1848 revolution. But 1848 proved also that historical Hungary was an illusion, as the fight of the Magyar nation for its independence from the Habsburgs coincided with the formation of separate nations within its own borders: Croatia, Serbia and Romania. As István Bibó has shown, Magyar politicians drew from this two conclusions which had an enduring impact over a long historical period:[1] first, that their country had been abandoned by Europe during its fight for national independence; second, that the non-Hungarians would use democratic liberty in order to create their own political and administrative states. The policies that resulted – which did not match the lessons gained during the catastrophe of 1848–9 – consisted in maintaining the dualism with Austria, while resisting the claims of those peoples who had gained their own national consciousness.

The problem of founding an independent state is thus absent in the Magyar national consciousness. The process of structural modernisation, however, generated an important debate in which prominent

---

[1] István Bibó, *A kelet-európai kisállamok nyomorúsága* [Misery of the Small States of Eastern Europe], in Bibó, *Összegyűjtött Munkái* [Complete Works], vol. I, prepared for publication by István Kemény and Mátyás Sárkozi, with a foreword by Arpád Szölösi and an introduction by Zoltán Szabó (Berne, Munich, 1981), pp. 202–52. See also the French edition: István Bibó, *Misère des petits états d'Europe de l'Est*, translated from Hungarian by György Kassai (Paris, 1986). Bibó was one of the most important characters of the intellectual and political life of East-Central Europe. From the perspective of the history of political thought it can be said that he was the personality who most contributed to political thinking in Hungary. He was and still remains a central figure in Hungarian political culture. For work in English on Bibó, see R.N. Berki, 'The Realism of Moralism: the Political Philosophy of István Bibó', *History of Political Thought* 13, 3 (1992).

political thinkers such as István Széchenyi, József Eötvös and Ferenc Deák took part. Ferenc Deák, the architect of the 1867 compromise with Austria, was the first politician who recognised Hungary's vulnerability as a small nation within the Danube basin. For the first time in East-Central Europe, the need for the transformation of the institutions of both the state and society was realised. Whilst Széchenyi laid stress on the social and ethnic issues, Eötvös concentrated on the role of the state. The latter was preoccupied with reconciling the liberty and the equality of the citizens. He championed the non-discriminatory treatment of ethnic and religious minorities, and truly believed in the possibility of realising high and ennobling ideals.[2] Many of his contemporaries were not ready for this, however, and his aspirations were only taken up much later by some twentieth-century thinkers such as Ady Endre, Oszkár Jászi, Attila József, Imre Csecsy and István Bibó.

The political liberalism championed by Ferenc Deák was another important contribution to the debate of the time, but it remained a minority position. Closely linked to Herder's and Fichte's romantic nationalism, the idea of 'national construction' advanced by Sándor Petöfi and Lajos Kossuth proved instead to be more influential. Nationalist propaganda mainly rested on such a conception, whilst also reflecting the modernising features of a 'closed' conception of nationality.[3] This found expression in István Tisza's policies of defensive state nationalism. As Gábor Vermes has rightly argued:

The sacred cause which Tisza had embraced as a young man and had served according to his own convictions for over three decades was Magyar nationalism. His unwavering dedication to this cause infused Tisza's political career with a profound sense of mission. Although his zeal often limited his perception of the relationship between short-term tactical options and long-range policies, it also generated the supreme self-assurance which attracted followers, impressed foreign statesmen, and drove political opponents to distraction. Tisza's passionate Magyar nationalism included a profound attachment for the liberal heritage of Hungary, as he defined it. He viewed this heritage as the source of his nation's greatness in the past and the pre-requisite for its meaningful existence in the present and future. His strong commitment to the tradition of liberal Magyar nationalism and his anxiety about the future of the Magyar nation fuelled the sense of mission with which he approached issues of domestic and foreign policy.[4]

---

[2] Cf. J. Weber, *Eötvös und die ungarische Nationalitätenfrage* (Munich, 1966).

[3] For the typology and the meaning of nationalism, see M. Winock, 'Nationalisme ouvert et nationalisme fermé', in Winock, *Nationalisme, anti-Semitisme et fascisme en France* (Paris, 1990), pp. 11–40. The French political model was influential in Hungary, Romania and Poland.

[4] G. Vermes, *István Tisza. The Liberal Vision and Conservative Statecraft of a Magyar Nationalist* (New York, 1985), p. xx.

Tisza's nationalism originated as a reaction to an unfavourable context, but it was also an ideological position, which he first assumed in his youth and renewed in different forms throughout his career. One of its consequences was his refusal to take into serious consideration the national claims of the non-Magyar populations living under Budapest's administration: the Slovaks, the Romanians, the Ukrainians, the Serbs, the Croatians and the Ruthenians.

The complex of superiority cultivated by Tisza – also emphasised by Gábor Vermes – was a trait characteristic of the majority of the Hungarian cultural and political elite. Even Ady Endre, a famous Magyar writer whose attitude towards other ethnic groups was broadly tolerant, was none the less deeply impressed by Tisza's nationalism. Hungarian politicians were either unable or unwilling to separate the rightful claims of non-Magyar linguistic communities from their own fear of losing the Hungarian-speaking regions to secessionist movements.[5]

The confusion in which the Great War ended, if anything, increased the problems besetting both the 'Dual Empire' and, as a consequence, Hungary. The economic difficulties and the military defeat were the results of unrealistic political programmes. The controversies over the reconciliation of the various nationalities were widely debated in a climate dominated by ethno-nationalism.

A Hungarian political figure of the beginning of the twentieth century, Oszkár Jászi wrote:

In these weeks of supreme national excitement only children or fools could fail to realise that the 'Dual Empire' was ended and that an independent and thoroughly democratic Hungary had become an urgent and inexorable necessity. Yet in this condition of childish folly the Hungarian parliament and the dominant political groups remained up to the last. On October 22 [1918] they foolishly voted down Michael Károly's motion for a declaration of independence. There was only one way in which the old regime could have done anything to calm down the menacing waves of popular fury: by appointing a popular government and announcing without further delay a series of real and substantial national reforms. Instead of this, its one concern was to keep the king from appointing the Károly government, something which every progressive element in public opinion demanded with remarkable unanimity. This frantic reaction had the most fatal results. Had the Károly government being appointed six or even four weeks earlier, events in Hungary would have taken a very different course.[6]

---

[5] Cf. Bibó, *A kelet-európai kisállamok nyomorúsága.*

[6] O. Jászi, *Revolution and Counter-Revolution in Hungary*, with an introduction by R.W. Seton Watson (London, 1924), p. 16. Jászi was born at Nagy Karoly in 1875. He studied philosophy and political science at Budapest University and became one of the founders and most active leaders of the Hungarian Sociological Society. He edited its

Jászi was speaking here as both a political thinker and a man of action. He supported federalism or, at least, favoured fundamental change in Hungary's relations with its neighbours; hence it was no accident that he invoked Kossuth and his idea of confederation. It took a lucid analyst to realise not only that the empire was at an end, but that its component parts could affirm themselves as nations only by embracing democratic forms of governance. However, the Hungarian political elite's detachment from the people led to the revolutionary developments of 1918–19. Exasperated by the awful suffering and the unfairness of the war, and under the influence of the Russian Revolution, the people of Budapest were yearning for more radical reforms.

The loss of territories that had been under Hungarian rule for hundreds of years led the Trianon Peace Treaty to be viewed as unjust both by ideologists and later by the whole Hungarian population. Anti-liberal doctrines prevailed throughout the 1920s, glorifying both Magyar Christianity, against the Jews, and the culture of pure ethnicity as an alternative to capitalist corruption. In his book, *Három Nemzedék* ['Three Generations'], published in 1920, the historian Gyula Szekfű became the main spokesman of radical anti-Semitism and anti-liberalism.[7] In Szekfű's view liberalism was simply Jewish ideology. As did the jurist A.C. Cuza in Romania, he questioned the sincerity of the assimilated Jews, and justified anti-Semitism by making appeal to historical events of the twentieth century, cultural issues and the role played by Jews as industrialists, merchants and bank-owners during the 'Dual Empire'. The *Volkisch* ideology of populist nationalism inspired by German Romanticism re-emerged in the support it provided for Nazism. In the case of both Hungary and Romania the poor social condition of the majority, economic backwardness, and the reverberation of Nazism and Fascism, were all prominent features of inter-war politics. Yet Vera Ránki has argued that:

Hungarian fascism was racist only inasmuch as it was influenced by Nazism. Racism was not really indigenous. The legacy of the Monarchy still persisted, not only within the fossilised feudal structures and value systems, but also in the perception and articulation of social problems and ideologies. Hungarian fascists such as Gömbös and Szálasi, did indeed use Nazi, racist terminology,

---

organ, *Huszadik Század* ('The Twentieth Century'). This was 'a monthly review of advanced opinions, wich soon acquired a high reputation for its thorough analysis of social and economic problems and its courageous advocacy of political reform . . . Jászi and his group pled for justice for the non-Magyar nationalities of Hungary, and the fullest possible linguistic and cultural liberty in local administration, education and justice' (Seton Watson's 'Introduction', p. xvii).

[7] G. Szekfű, *Három Namzedék és ami utána következik* ['Three Generations and What Comes After'] (Budapest, 1989).

but the Hungarian middle classes filtered this through their Monarchy-nurtured perceptions.[8]

This is an important consideration, differentiating Hungary from neighbouring countries. However, Ránki probably overestimates the role of the Magyar middle class at a time when the *Volkischkultur* was gaining ground through the formation of the first generation of intellectuals of rural origin such as Szekfű and Szabo.

It was at this time that once again ethnic issues gained prominence in political thinking. They played an important role in fostering the myth of the great historical Hungary, pushing the country towards the catastrophe of 1940–4 by encouraging its commitment to Nazi ideology and the alliance with Hitler, through which it was hoped to restore the country to its former imperial power. As the tragedy unfolded, political thought became mere cultural propaganda, marked by a persistent sense of nostalgia, whilst impervious to any form of liberal rationalism. This was not an exclusively Hungarian phenomenon, but it illustrates how a fixation with ethnic themes generated confused and ultimately destructive ideologies.

III

There are similarities between the development of the Magyar and the Slav national consciousness. The doctrine of Austro-Slavism initiated by Palacky at the 1848 Congress in Prague, calling together the representatives of the entire Slav world, lasted well into the first two decades of the following century. Austro-Slavism was the attempt to keep the Slavic people of the Habsburg Empire united. On the one hand, it meant the abandonment of pan-Slavism as developed in Tsarist Russia so as to mark their separation from the Eastern Slavic world. On the other, it was meant to promote the representation of the Slavic-speaking population within the administrative bodies of the empire. Thus, Austro-Slavism was the attempt to guarantee Slavic unity without prejudice for the empire.

Many Czech, Slovak, Croatian and Serb intellectuals and political figures adhered to such an ideology. This fact may need some explanation. As with Magyars, so in the case of the Slavs, it was the aristocracy more than an over-cautious bourgeoisie who seemed keener to modernise. The various national groups saw in Austro-Slavism the opportunity to develop their own civil societies and to industrialise. Thus radical nationalism was slow to develop, as in the case of the Serbs, where it was

[8] V. Ránki, *The Politics of Inclusion and Exclusion. Jews and Nationalism in Hungary* (Sydney, 1999).

eventually triggered off by the occupation of Bosnia-Herzegovina by Austria–Hungary.[9] But for many years during the nineteenth century during which the 900,000 Serbs were under the rule of the 'Dual Empire', they were able to pursue successful public and private careers in Budapest and Vienna.

Within such a context, and in spite of the increasing dominance of ethno-nationalism, it was not surprising that federalisation projects were still much discussed at the beginning of the twentieth century. Amongst the proponents of federalism were the Austrian Karl Renner, the Czech Joseph Pekar, the Hungarian Oszkár Jászi and the Romanian A.C. Popovici.[10] Prince Franz Ferdinand himself supported such an approach. Because of this he was the object of intense lobbying by members of the Austrian military, by Czech aristocrats, by Romanian political figures, and by pro-Habsburg Hungarian representatives, all of whom subscribed to various shades of nationalism. The prince instead clearly disapproved of nationalism and of the attempts to establish German supremacy in Central and South-Eastern Europe.

The persistence of federalist projects is partly explained by the good relationships that Czechs, Romanians and Serbs maintained with Vienna, and also because many scholars continued to be educated in the Austrian capital. This ensured that throughout the period of 'dual rule' they were imbued with the liberal culture and the ethical and social ideas associated with the cosmopolitan empire. At the death of the emperor, in 1916, despite the precarious future of the empire, the Czech intellectual Joseph Pekar unhesitatingly reviewed the unprecedented progress of his own nation under Franz Joseph's rule. 'The difference between what we were in 1848 and what we are today it is absolutely remarkable. The majority of those things we are proud of nowadays, as a civilised nation, were created during this time, namely, the consciousness of our great past and our national ideas.'[11] But at the very time when Pekar wrote those lines, Beneš and Masaryk had already gained British support to proclaim the Czechoslovakian nation state.[12] Both the hurried process of elite formation, the so-called 'combustion of the stages', and the influence exercised by Berlin's model of the nation state, formed the background against which the post-First World War scenario came into place.

Western nineteenth-century experience – according to which the

---

[9] B. Jelavich, *History of the Balkans* (Oxford, 1997).
[10] Cf. F. Fejto, *Requiem pour un empire défunt. Histoire de la destruction de l'Autriche-Hongrie* (Paris, 1992)
[11] Quoted in Fejto, *Requiem pour un empire défunt*, p. 114.
[12] Cf. Fejto, *Requiem pour un empire défunt*.

'nation is the modern socio-political group that corresponds to the individual's ideology'[13] – was uncritically assumed by East-Central European intellectuals. This contributed to the generation of hybrid entities, administrative forms in which the medieval commune cohabited with those specific to the modern world. The dissolution of the 'Dual Empire' did not in itself herald a development towards pluralist democracy and political modernisation. Czechoslovakia on the one hand, and Hungary and Romania on the other, seem to be the most suggestive examples of the way in which the break-up of the empire resulted in the construction of two types of nation states: a federal pluralist one, based on civil society, and another, centralised model, based on a collective ideology of the supremacy of ethnic majorities.

The Czech philosopher T.G. Masaryk thought long and carefully about the new configuration of Europe generally and of East-Central Europe in particular. He was one of the very few thinkers in the region who foresaw the possibility of establishing democracy by overcoming authoritarian forms of government. He spread the idea of the nation state, in particular the right to self-determination of the peoples in the former Austro-Hungarian Empire. In his article 'The New Europe',[14] published in 1916, he offered an interpretation of the First World War and elaborated a programme for a new configuration of post-war Europe. Open diplomacy and disarmament were in his view to become the key issues in European political strategy.[15] In concert with such a programme, Masaryk's political priority was for an independent Czechoslovakia but also for giving consideration and protection to minorities, through granting them rights. Each nation had the right to follow its own destiny. But for all this, the Slovak case was not taken seriously even by partisans of Czech independence. The Bohemian aristocracy, whose attitudes the Czech intellectuals broadly reflected, looked down on the poorer and less modernised regions of Slovakia, whilst the latter's own intelligentsia failed to find the necessary social resources on which to build their own image of cultural independence.

The historical Bohemia was two-thirds Czech and one-third German. The eastern part (Slovakia) was peopled not only by Slavs but also by Magyars. Such diversity seemed initially to be capable of developing

[13] L. Dumont, *Essays on Individualism: Modern Ideology in Anthropological Perspective* (Chicago, 1986).

[14] T.G. Masaryk, *The New Europe*, No. 1, 19 October (London, 1916). See also *Az új Európa. A szláv álláspont* ['The Slavonik Approach'], translated into Hungarian by Domby Bálint (Košice, 1923), pp. 59–112. The original Czech title is *Ceskoslovensky Dennink* (Prague, 1918).

[15] Cf. K.Wilson and J. Dussen (eds.), *The History of the Idea of Europe* (London and New York, 1995).

into a multicultural society. In fact, the ethnic configuration caused contradictions in the political strategies and brought about a series of crises in the relationships between the groups. Czech society was, from the civic and industrial point of view, more emancipated. But even if seemingly better prepared for democracy than other new nations in East-Central Europe, the Czechoslovakian state was not able to withstand the German attack in 1938–9. The absence of a shared political culture between its ethnic groups created great problems on the eve of the Second World War. Echoes of what had happened in the neighbouring Nazi regime played an undeniable role in the public state of mind of the Czechoslovakian people. The influence of National Socialist propaganda on the German groups in Bohemia was a destabilising factor. Finally the differences in political culture, in mentalities, but also in economic standards between the Slovakian and the Czech regions of Czechoslovakia affected the political situation, contributing to the catastrophe of 1938–9.

The cases of Hungary and Czechoslovakia illustrate why the countries in the region were unable to follow the democratic path. Many literary scholars, historians and philosophers became genuine nationalist heroes and were unopposed by other intellectuals. In the realm of ideas, alternatives were often closed off. Ethnic nationalism became dominant, establishing a kind of mono-culture. Even Czechoslovakia – which was economically more developed, and whose population was better prepared for political and cultural pluralism – cannot truly be said to have democratised. The tragedy engulfing the whole of the *Mitteleuropean* societies from the outset of their modernisation to the periods of fascist and communist totalitarian regimes, was therefore as much the product of their own past as of external imposition.[16]

IV

Romania offers an interesting example of the way in which the local political elite confronted, but failed to solve, the problems of the national past. The political debates of the inter-war period were largely dominated by the search for a solution to what they conceived as the problem of 'founding' the state.[17] Their project related to the necessity to organise a new political and administrative Romania. Its components

---

[16] On images of ones own and other nations, and on the use of the internal and the external enemy in the political cultures of East-Central Europe, see the studies published in the volume Laszló Kontler (ed.) *Pride and Prejudice. National Stereotypes in 19th and 20th Century Europe East to West* (Budapest, 1995).

[17] Cf. K. Hitchins, *Romania 1866–1947* (Oxford, 1994).

were Wallachia, Moldavia, Transylvania, Banat, Bukovina, Mara-
muresh, Crishana and Bessarabia, all having a variety of traditions, of
linguistic and religious groups. State unification after the First World
War provided no automatic answer to the problems the country had
confronted since the nineteenth century: poverty, low life expectancy,
high infant death rate, illiteracy, incipient capitalism and ruralism. To all
of this can be added the problem posed by incorporating three and a
half million people of Hungarian, German, Jewish and Ukrainian
extraction in the Romanian state sanctioned by the Versailles Peace
Treaty.[18]

Of the many ways of thinking of the problem of the 'founding' of the
Romanian state, three stand out as being the most influential at the
time. Europeanism advocated rapid and unconditional integration into
Western civilisation. Traditionalism was in favour of a vernacular model
of modernisation. Agrarianism was adopted by those privileging a more
traditional peasant society. The vast majority of politicians and intellectuals of the 1920s subscribed to one or another of these broad views.
Europeanism was represented by two prestigious personalities: the
literary critic Eugen Lovinescu, and the economist and sociologist
Stefan Zeletin. Traditionalism had its most representative advocates in
the writer and journalist Nichifor Crainic and the poet and philosopher
Lucian Blaga. The economist Virgil Madgearu was the main supporter
of agrarianism.[19] The effort of all these theorists was directed to finding
ways out of the country's backwardness. For most Romanian intellectuals it was obvious that nineteenth-century political thought had a
crucial contribution to make in changing the features of state administration and taking the first steps towards integration amongst major
European countries. However, disputes over such general issues as the
costs of industrialisation, of urbanisation, of fast modernisation and of
the wholehearted embracement Western European models resulted in a
kind of stalemate and a waste of important energies. In the absence of
clear theoretical strategies and of an express political wish to renovate
itself, overcoming its inherent étatisme, its excessive centralism and its
backward ruralism, Romania failed to achieve any essential changes
from the pre-war period.

[18] For a comparative presentation of the statistics on the demographic situation of
Romania in the inter-war period (based on Romanian and German documentary
sources) see Hildrun Glass, *Zerbrochene Nachbarschaft. Das deutsch-judische Verheltniss in
Rumänien (1918– 1938)* (Munich, 1996), ch. 2, pp. 25–58.
[19] For a detailed presentation of the trends in Romanian culture and political thinking, see
Hitchins, *Romania 1866–1947*; see also Leon Volovici, *Nationalist Ideology and Anti-
Semitism. The Case of Romanian Intellectuals in the 1930s* (Oxford, 1991), and Z. Ornea,
Anii treizeci. Extrema dreapta româneasca (Bucharest, 1995).

By the next decade, the positions embraced by the rationalists, the modernisers and the champions of Europeanism and individualism lost ground. Their opponents gained the upper hand by propagating nationalist myths. The dictatorships of Charles II and later of General Ion Antonescu were not just the result of an international trend towards right-wing extremism, but also the consequence of a resort to romantic nationalist texts and ideologies. Moreover, nationalists myths and cultural prejudices prevented the diffusion of social-democratic positions, which were rashly rejected because identified with the intelligentsia of linguistic and religious minorities. The Romanian centralist state preferred a closely defined ethnic and cultural society and paid no heed to the contributions of so-called ethnic foreigners.[20] Even where they existed, democratic traditions in Romania and in the neighbouring countries were fragile. The impact of democratic and modern administration was never felt by the populations of Central and Eastern Europe. This made the transference of power from one oligarchy to another easier during regime change.

Part of the intellectual background of the pre-war regime change was the diffusion of philosophical irrationalism. Mystics, existentialists and authors broadly hostile to the 'scientific' spirit characterising West European civilisation were widely read and commented upon, and so were the fathers of the Church and the modern theologians. The crisis of identity experienced in Viennese culture at the end of the nineteenth century echoed loudly in the regions of Central and Eastern Europe in the 1930s and 1940s. Kant's rationalism was neglected, whilst Freud's psychoanalysis became one of the greatest attractions. The liberal tradition of John Stuart Mill and Alexis de Tocqueville was completely overlooked. Kierkegaard, Berdyaev, Nietzsche, Spengler and Heidegger became the main intellectual points of reference for the protagonists of political debate.[21] The dominance of such a literature can be explained with the search for models of thinking that many intellectuals believed would satisfy their neo-romantic understanding of history. Ideas of national or religious uniqueness became, once again, a dominant obsession. The exaggerated impact of speculative texts in the history of political philosophy encouraged a metaphysical vision at the expense of an empirical one. This was not without consequences in political life, encouraging national, mono-cultural and anti-democratic visions.

[20] This point is both documented and argued at a more theoretical level by Leon Volovici. Cf. Volovici, *Nationalist Ideology and Anti-Semitism*.
[21] Cf. Hitchins, *Romania 1866–1947*.

V

From a political perspective, Germany's defeat in 1945 created a power vacuum, resulting in the Soviet Union's post-war dominion of the region.[22] If, up to the war, nationalist texts provided the political orientation of the east, after 1945 they were replaced by Stalinist vulgata. The rallying cry for national advantage was now displaced by a similar cry for the dominance of a sole and omniscient class – sacrifice for the country by sacrifice in the name of the world-wide proletariat. But the political cultures of the post-Second World War regimes did not emerge from indigenous traditions of political thinking. Traces of communism were present in East-Central European countries as far back as the First World War. There were a number of thinkers influenced by Karl Marx's works on political economy and by his theory of historical development, but left-wing radical intellectuals did not enjoy much support. Public opinion was generally hostile and in certain countries communist militants were banned. In the more industrial regions, however, Marxist-oriented social democracy represented a relatively important trend. Besides, Soviet leaders did their best to mask the truth about their regime. The Soviet intelligentsia built an essentially medieval, mystically oriented ideology, and although there was apparent convergence between theirs and West European Marxism, in their version historicist superstitions were prominent. The propaganda machine of Soviet communism was installed in all the states of East-Central Europe. It quickly found advocates, drawing on poorly educated and half-schooled social groups, many of whom had already been manipulated by the previous regime. But for all this, a number of writers who had originally been imbued with communist ideology, publicly demonstrated their abhorrence of it when they grasped the cynicism of the Soviet power.

In the context of the new Soviet regimes, political culture became mere propaganda with the only aim of mass indoctrination through the mystical image of perpetual revolution. The pursuit of the dream of the universal happiness of mankind at any price dominated the period. The Stalinist revolution took full advantage of the lack of pluralism in East-Central Europe. Furthermore, the failure in the

---

[22] History textbook stereotypes were perpetuated from one generation to another, from one political regime to the next. For the situation in the eastern countries, cf. N. Danova, 'L'image de l'autre dans les Balkans', in *Etudes Balkaniques*, 21 (1992), p. 110. On the same topic, see also M. Eliou, 'Utilisations contradictoires de l'appel a l'identité culturelle', in T. Winter-Jensen and P. Lang (eds.), *Challenges to European Education: Cultural Values, National Identities, and Global Responsibilities* (Frankfurt-am-Main, 1996), pp. 157–72.

West fully to appreciate the similitude, remarked upon by Hannah Arendt, between the Nazi and the Stalinist regimes had negative effects on the evolution of the political situation in the East-Central European regimes. François Furet was right to note how late was the emergence of serious reflection on the nature of the extreme left-wing regimes after Second World War, regimes whose ideological character was unprecedented in history. Western European culture regarded Eastern communism as more salient than democracy.[23] Consequently it was only in the 1960s that (older and newer) political thought, as distinct from propaganda, came to have a bearing on intellectual life in East-Central Europe.

The impulse to elaborate theoretical critiques of the totalitarian-communist regimes came from civil society. The memorandum addressed to the communist leader Mátyás Rákosi by the most important Hungarian writers in 1955 requested an annulment of the ban put on the main magazine of the Writers' Union. The document showed that the Hungarian intelligentsia was well aware of the importance of freedom of speech and publication as fundamental rights. The writers' plea for open-thinking was resisted by the aggressive use of bureaucratic interference. At about the same time, the journalist Miklós Gimes stated the programme of the Hungarian democratic intellectuals, whose social-democratic political orientation was to play a defining role in the 1956 Revolution:

What we need is a democracy, a regime where the law defends the citizens or punishes them in absolute fairness. We need a regime where the rights are utterly obeyed: the freedom of expression and of press, the freedom of association, of work and of education; a regime where the people's will can freely manifest itself within the legal system, where the majority respects unconditionally the inalienable rights of the minorities.[24]

It should be said that Marxist thinking itself contributed to the emergence of this new opposition. In the late 1950s, some Marxist writers from Hungary, Yugoslavia, Czechoslovakia and Poland found the courage to support the idea of a pluralist political system against Stalinism and the idea of proletariat dictatorship. The philosopher Georg Lukács – one of the active ideologues of intellectual life in Budapest, the initiator of the Petőfi Circle and animator of Marxist academic debates – developed a comprehensive criticism of the commu-

---

[23] François Furet, *Le passé d'une illusion. Essai sur l'idée communiste au XXe siècle* (Paris, 1995). Cf. the Romanian edition: *Trecutul unei iluzii. Eseu asupra ideii comuniste in secolul XX*, translated by Emanoil Marcu and Vlad Russo (Bucharest, 1996), pp. 383–5. See also Hannah Arendt, *The Origins of Totalitarianism* (New York, 1973).

[24] Cf. V. Tismaneanu, *Arheologia terorii* ['The Archeology of Terror'] (Bucharest, 1992).

nist regime, holding it up to ridicule.[25] During the 1956 Revolution in Budapest, he addressed the following message to the Hungarian youth:

The new government's main task is to develop and realise a democratic, national program. Everybody has to learn from the terrible lessons of the last few days. The most urgent tasks are: a genuine democratic renewal of our national, social, economic and cultural life. This genuine democracy is adequate to sweep away all the remnants of Stalinism. The development of a democratic system of law and popular self-government constitutes the true base for the Hungarian road to socialism, and for then extending Hungary successfully to all aspects of life. It seems to me that the explanation concerning Stalin's 'maniac spirit' and 'criminal feature' have to be searched in spirit and movement: the idea itself of building any society, moreover a society without classes, is in its essence both mendacious and irrational, and a regime based on unlawful actions is by itself a criminal regime.[26]

In 1962, in *Conversations with Stalin*, the Yugoslavian writer, Milovan Djilas, described the Moscow dictator as a monster, with fundamentally utopian ideas, practising violence that extended as far as psychological torture and physical extermination:

The creator of a closed social system, he (Stalin, n.n.) was at the same time its instrument, and in changed circumstances and all too late, he became its victim . . . Unfortunately, even now, after the so-called de-Stalinisation, the same conclusion can be reached as before: those who wish to live and to survive in a world different from the one Stalin created and which still exists and is still as strong as ever, must fight for their lives.[27]

Both Lukács and Djilas, as well as other Marxist intellectuals, not only were alien to the Stalinist terror, but observed that the whole Kremlin ideology was based on non-European traditions of political thought and practice and that it would not end with the dictator's death.

VI

Polish intellectuals in the 1960s also remarked on the deep intolerance characterising the communist regimes. They had a keen understanding of the anomalous character of Stalinist political discourse. They made appeal to past political thought in support of the freedom of the press. Scholars such as Leszek Kolakowski, Oskar Lange, Edward Lipinky, Maria Hirszowitz, Wlodzimierz Brus, Krzysttof Pomian, Bronislaw Baczko and Vitold Kula were prominent in revealing the mystical form of revolutionary communism. Their 'revisionist' works were instrumental in revitalising political activity amongst the Polish intelligentsia.

[25] Cf. A. Kadarkay, *Georg Lukács. Life, Thought and Politics* (Oxford, 1991).
[26] G. Lukács, 'Message to Hungarian Youth', *Szabad Nép* (28 October 1956).
[27] M. Djilas, *Conversations With Stalin* (London, 1962).

Adam Michnik claims that the same 'revisionist' spirit underlies the literary works of K. Brandys, A. Wazyk, W. Woroszylski and J. Bochensky. Regardless of the intrinsic scholarly and artistic merits of their works, these writers succeeded in re-introducing a humanist tradition of ideas, which had been entirely excluded from public debate by totalitarian communism. The publication of their books amounted to political acts in the context of the years from 1956 to 1968. They demonstrated the importance that critical participation in social and political life had in strengthening civil society and in creating an opposition to the official line. So, throughout the 1950s and the early 1960s effective intellectual opposition came more from the Marxist intellectual milieu than from intransigent anti-communist positions.[28]

But the limits of Polish revisionism were all too evident by 1968. The relationship that until then linked the revisionist intelligentsia with the communist party was broken. After that, they could no longer hope for the democratisation of the party. Wladislaw Bienkowski remained one of the very few who still believed in the party's reform, continuing to address himself to the communist leadership rather than to society at large, and drawing their attention to their faults whilst formulating an opposition programme. Admittedly, the Prague Spring had suggested a different scenario, changing, though briefly, the political orientation of the Warsaw opposition. The Polish students hoped for a Dubček of their own. The Czechoslovakian lesson – in which the Polish anti-communists did not believe – became for Adam Michnik a chance for change, since it demonstrated the fragility of the totalitarian *status quo* and Moscow's desperately brutal reaction.[29]

It was at this point that the Polish intelligentsia went back to its own historical past, rediscovering the early twentieth-century traditions re-presented by Brzozowski, Wyspianski, Zeromski and Nalkowski. This was the beginning of the second phase of the intellectual opposition, which Michnik has called the neo-positivist one. The political aspirations of the Polish youth materialised a few years later in the setting up of Solidarity, which became the point of contact between intellectuals and workers, showing the importance of the former's role in the formation of an independent public opinion. The importance of Solidarity was evident to people like Michnik from the very beginning. In 1982, while in prison, he realised Solidarity would not be defeated since it was not the expression of an extremist group; rather its form of social resistance was the result of a general need. He was convinced that the

[28] A. Michnik, *Penser la Pologne. Morale et politique de la résistance*, edited by Z. Erard (Paris, 1983).
[29] Cf. Michnik, *Penser la Pologne*.

Poles were experiencing their last days of the servility first imposed upon them by the Nazis and later perpetuated by the communists. The revolt of 1980 and the action of Solidarity had put an end to this mentality. 'For 15 months people could taste liberty, could be fully aware of their solidarity and their power, feeling themselves again members of a national and civic community.'[30] Michnik's own role as one of the main counsellors of Solidarity explains the contribution of the Polish intelligentsia in structuring an anti-communist and anti-totalitarian political movement. As Vaćlav Havel stated, 'Solidarity was the surest and the most efficacious way of contesting communist power.'[31]

VII

The intellectual traditions from which Czech opposition was born were no less significant than the Polish ones. Charter 77 offered the opportunity for a remarkable civic and socio-political experience, to which many intellectuals contributed throughout the 1980s and the 1990s. The Czech intelligentsia acted in full accordance with their words and ideas. Václav Havel makes frequent reference to the philosopher Jan Patočka, the first 'spokesman' of Charter 77, from whose semi-clandestine school Havel himself claims to have learnt the important lessons of the pluralism of options, of a dissident community, of communication across frontiers, and of a critical approach to past and present. Unlike the Romanian philosopher Constantin Noica, who was more concerned with the collective idea of nation, Patočka put first and foremost his preoccupation with the thinking individual. Havel learnt from Patočka the meaning of a supra-national fraternity of enlightened people. This ideal helped him to resist the oppressive force of the communists. He was thus able to formulate what he called the 'positive madness' that could both mobilise and unify Europe, cutting through the artificial barriers that stood between states ruled by hostile ideologies and administrations. In his speech in Rotterdam, on 13 November 1986, on the occasion of being awarded the Erasmus Prize, Havel pleaded for the role of culture in defeating communism and unifying the two parts of Europe.[32]

Patočka's lesson about the importance of self-awareness had a huge role in structuring Czech dissident thought. They found, in his way of

---

[30] A. Michnick, *Scrisori din închisoare* ['Prison Letters'], Romanian edn (Iasi, 1997), p. 48.

[31] V. Havel, *L'angoisse de la liberté. Choix de discours (1965–1992)*, translated from the Czech by Jan Rubeš and Zlata Chatel (Paris, 1992), p. xx.

[32] V. Havel, *Essais politiques*, texts collected by R. Errera and J. Vladislav (Paris, 1989), p. 234.

stating the relation between *Lebenswelt* (the right to life) and human rights, a philosophy which considered total and free human commitment to be possible through the autonomy of the community and of the civil domain. Such a way of thinking about the individual and his/her public life imposed necessary limits on the action of a supposedly omniscient and globalising state. For Patočka it was impossible to dissociate politics from ethics and philosophy from law. In his *Heretical Essays* we find a concern for a thorough understanding of the relationship between philosophy and politics.[33] It seemed to Patočka that the democratic regime was the only one able to address the human need of opening up towards the other and of setting up a just order. The Czech dissidents took advantage both of his philosophical work, which became a constant cultural point of reference, and of his life, which was in itself an outstanding ethical model.

VIII

In Romania there was no real active resistance against the persecution to which critical reason was subjected. The cultural elite seemed resigned. Unlike Czech and Hungarian intellectuals, Romanian writers were content with a few liberal concessions from the Directorate of Cultural Propaganda.[34] Admittedly, numerous Romanian scholars who were in favour of either liberal and peasant parties, or a more extreme right-wing position were imprisoned. However, even Marxist academics, who approached the contradictions of the regime from the inside, were silenced by Gheorghe Gheorgiu-Dej. The Marxist intelligentsia did not fare better under Nicolae Ceauşescu's national-communist dictatorship. Because of the strict control exercised by the *Securitate* (the Romanian political police), they failed to initiate any civic movements such as those in Hungary, Czechoslovakia and Poland. None the less, the more critical attitude of philosophers such as Henri Wald, and historians like D. Prodan, found a certain echo within small academic and literary circles. A democratically oriented intellectual elite, tacitly dissenting from the dictatorial regime, formed around Professor Henri Wald, a popular lecturer at the University of Bucharest. Echoes of the Hungarian Revolution of 1956 were felt in Timişoara. This was the only city in Romania where students succeeded in organising public debates and street manifestations, and elaborating a Marxist-oriented programme of anti-totalitarian demands. The students were joined by workers, civil servants and farmers. The reason for Timişoara's exceptionalism lies in

[33] Cf. L.A. Lavastine, *Jan Patočka. L'esprit de la dissidence* (Paris, 1998).
[34] Cf. Tismaneanu, *Arheologia terorii*.

the fact that in the western part of Romania, knowledge of the Hungarian language facilitated the penetration of some anti-totalitarian ideas circulating in Budapest, as well as the images of a better material life. The student leaders – who came from the faculties of the Polytechnic of Timişoara –were arrested and expelled and the movement's impact was wholly circumscribed within the Banat region.

A characteristic feature of the 1950s was the lack of interest that the intellectual elite showed in the momentous political events taking place in neighbouring countries. Witness to this is the circle around the ideologist Leonte Răutu, who succeeded in imposing the principle of party spirit in literature and art. While in Poland, under the patronage of the weekly *Po Prostu*, the national confederation of clubs was coming to life, in Romania the intelligentsia remained aloof, contenting itself with the few very modest signs of change after Khrushchev's speech at the twentieth Congress of the Communist Party of the USSR. This was perhaps a sign of resignation as much as a consequence of the repression. Although in its way passionate, discussion in journals and periodicals was equally unsuccessful in awakening political awareness. A number of political issues were discussed in literary papers in particular during the 1980s. Some well-known writers reacted against the dictatorship through their fiction, poetry and essay books. Some of them, such as Mircea Dinescu, also published protest articles in the Western press. Their books of fiction and poetry aimed against the Ceauşescus led in some cases, like that of the poet Ana Blandiana, to their writings' interdiction. They critically analysed the problem of freedom of speech during their meetings at the Writers' Union as did the novelist Gheorghe Schwartz. Yet these attitudes had repercussions only for a small number of intellectuals who were familiar with democratic values. Under communism, cultural leaders were foiled by the promises of the party activists, thus missing favourable opportunities to encourage and develop alternative ideas. This detached attitude was counterproductive. It was perpetuated under both dictatorial regimes in Romania, and that amply explains the dramatic and confused way in which political change took place in 1989. In the absence of a political culture fully aware of its past, and of any alternative political knowledge, the only opposition to Nicolae Ceauşescu's dictatorship eventually came from the revolt of civil society. It was no accident that the focus of the revolt was Timişoara, the city in the western part of the country where a residue of democratic principles was preserved by a population with a multicultural and multiconfessional identity, which had inherited something of the mental reflexes of the cosmopolitan city-dwellers of the time of the Austrian Empire.

IX

The aim of this chapter has not been to provide a description of the evolution of political thought and culture in East-Central Europe, *in extenso*, but rather to highlight those aspects of it which are relevant to understanding how cultural and intellectual traditions, and ideological achievements and failures, impinged on a world that entered late into modernity. What is striking for contemporary analysts is that in states such as Hungary, Poland and Czechoslovakia the social groups which had joined the communist movement were also the first to champion the movement against its party dictatorship.[35] Perhaps, the intelligentsia of Budapest, headed by the Marxist philosophy school, had some memory of the political lessons from the past, such as those of the revolution of 1848. Most likely, in contrast to those countries which had been under the influence of, or components of, the Ottoman and Tsarist Empires, in the states of East-Central Europe the experience of movements dominated by left-wing ideas was decisive. The social democratic traditions, rooted in the *Mitteleuropean* cultural milieu, seemed to retain some effect after the two world wars. It is also possible that the experience of the radical revolution of the Hungarian proletariat led by Béla Kun in 1919 contributed to the maturation of the Marxist left-wing intelligentsia. The case of Georg Lukács, which is not an isolated example, is a suggestive illustration of this.

Direct or indirect participation in debates, theoretical controversies, and even in the political system became a tangible reality in Prague, Budapest and Warsaw in the years between the 1960s and 1980s. The survival of significant elements of civil society made possible the Hungarian, Polish and Czech reform movements. This partly explains the fact that the Hungarian Revolution reached the point of challenging the regime's very right to existence. Historians may be justified in drawing attention to the important fact that, beginning with the events of 1953–6, thinking amongst the East-Central European intelligentsia changed. The observation is rendered all the more credible since the moral and political support of the new democracies is to be found in the theoretical texts of those very intellectuals who directly opposed both left-wing and right-wing forms of totalitarianism.

[35] Cf. Furet, *Le passé d'une illusion.*

13 The limits of the national paradigm in the study of political thought: the case of Karl Popper and Central European cosmopolitanism

Malachi Hacohen

Central European cosmopolitanism demonstrates the limits of the study of political thought in its national context. My argument is not that one cannot write a history of a 'national tradition' in political thought. The fascinating narratives produced for this book are proof enough to the contrary. They seem to me most interesting, however, where the national tradition opens to foreign influences. Such openings often have a transformative effect, but national narratives rarely foreground them. I shall use Central European cosmopolitanism to argue for the relativisation of the national viewpoint in the study of political thought and for the complementarity of national and international perspectives. By interrogating the categories of both 'nationalism' and 'cosmopolitanism', I shall show that there is neither a closed national tradition of political thought that can be historically understood apart from international interaction nor a cosmopolitan tradition that can be understood apart from its national origin. Both nationalism and cosmopolitanism remain useful concepts, a point of departure for understanding and writing the history of political thought, but, standing on their own, they produce impoverished histories. Only their interaction can provide a viable historical account. Accounting for the interaction involves exposing the hypocrisy of nationalist claims to an authentic closed tradition, on the one hand, and disclosing the national origin of cosmopolitanism on the other. This chapter on Central European cosmopolitanism endeavours to do both.

Central Europe provides a natural territory for studying nationalism and cosmopolitanism. The late Habsburg Empire and inter-war Central Europe evinced heightened multicultural interaction, rapid formation of antagonistic ethno-national identities and sporadic rise of cosmopolitan ideas. Ethno-nationalism and cosmopolitanism emerged as divergent responses to culture clash. Ethnic minorities struggled to nationalise their cultures and establish hegemony in areas of ethnically mixed population. When they became, after the First World War, ethnic majorities in newly established states, these efforts intensified. Cross-cultural exchange took place against the expressed wishes, and notwith-standing the protests and denials of the different nationalities. They strove for and claimed authentic national cultures. Cosmopolitans responded by promoting international exchange and proclaiming the unity of humankind. Just as nationalists denied the multicultural making of their own culture, so cosmopolitans ignored the ethno-national dilemmas underlying their effort to rid ethnicity and nationality of significance. Both negotiated across ethno-cultural boundaries, inducing symbioses of ethno-national identities. Central European multicultur-alism was less a product of cosmopolitan pursuit of international dialogue, and more a result of cross-cultural exchanges, generating both cosmopolitan and nationalist discourses. Cosmopolitanism and ethno-nationalism must be studied in the context of multiculturalism.

To trace the simultaneous formation of ethno-national and cosmo-politan identities, discourses and traditions, I propose to focus on progressive Viennese cosmopolitanism, the Vienna Circle's Central European intellectual network and philosopher Karl Popper (1902–94). I shall investigate the role of the network in Popper's life and work and explore the intimate relationship between his cosmopolitanism and the Jewish Question.[1] Pondering reality and dreams in Jewish assimilation and Central European cosmopolitanism, I shall trace the formation of Popper's visions of the Open Society and the scientific community which refashioned the legacy of *fin de siècle* Viennese progressivism into mainstream Western liberalism. Precisely the dilemmas of national integration, I shall argue, inspired visions such as the Open Society. Utopian cosmopolitan commonwealths were the only states where Popper and the Jewish intelligentsia could hope to find a home. Cosmo-politanism emerged as a solution to a particular ethno-national problem.

I

Central European expatriates of Jewish origins have long imagined the late Habsburg Empire as a cosmopolitan golden age. Exiles who had

---

[1] A different version of some arguments developed in this chapter appeared in 'Dilemmas of Cosmopolitanism: Karl Popper, Jewish Identity, and "Central European Culture"', *The Journal of Modern History*, 71 (1999), pp. 105–49. I am grateful to the editors and to The University of Chicago Press for permission to incorporate them into my present text.

been brought up in affluent bourgeois families in *fin de siècle* metropolitan centres recalled a thriving cosmopolitan culture. Stefan Zweig recounted their loss in *The World of Yesterday*.[2] Others who had grown up in the eastern provinces were nostalgic about vanished multiculturalism. Joseph Roth's *The Radetzky March* expressed their yearnings.[3] All wrote under the impression of the triumph of ethno-nationalism and the collapse of Central Europe. They set forth two models of Austrian cosmopolitanism. The first emphasised the Enlightenment heritage, universal humanity and internationalism. The second stressed the imperial idea of supra-national unity in multinational diversity. Both recognised that the Habsburg Empire advanced cosmopolitanism by mediating between universal humanity and cultural particularity.

The exiles' longing for the golden age conflicted with equally powerful testimonies to vicious ethno-national strife under the Habsburgs. In his diaries and correspondence, Franz Kafka frequently despaired at the political and cultural struggles among Czechs, Germans and Jews in Prague. They created, he thought, an impossible situation for Jewish writers, caught in between. Czech Jews writing in German gained acceptance neither among Czechs nor among Germans. They often had an ambivalent relationship to the Jewish community.

Most [Jewish writers] who began writing in German wanted to distance themselves from Jewishness . . . but their hind legs were still stuck to their father's Jewishness and their forelegs found no new ground. Despair over [the situation] was their inspiration . . . That in which their despair found an outlet could not be German literature, [although] outwardly it seemed to be. They existed among . . . linguistic impossibilities.[4]

No national literary tradition left room for them. Their ethno-cultural marginality gave rise to their cross-cultural endeavours, but also set the limits of their audience. The secret of late Habsburg cosmopolitanism was precisely its marginality.

Multinational networks of intellectual exchange gave tangible evidence of Central European cosmopolitanism during *fin de siècle* and inter-war years, but such networks remained thin and fragile. Triumphant nationalism and ethno-politics limited their influence everywhere. Pre-First World War ethnic minorities, turned inter-war national majorities, sought to eliminate any transnational influence and construct an authentic indigenous culture. The networks' members were preponderantly of Jewish origin, everywhere suspect to the ethnic majority. German was their lingua franca, and they critically appropriated German cultural

---

[2] Stefan Zweig, *The World of Yesterday* (New York, 1943).
[3] Joseph Roth, *Radetzkymarsch* (Berlin, 1932).
[4] Franz Kafka to Max Brod, June 1921, *Briefe 1902–1924* (Frankfurt, 1966), p. 337.

traditions. This limited their appeal to non-German intelligentsia, while making them anathema to German nationalists. When Moritz Schlick, the Vienna Circle's head, was murdered by a deranged student in 1936, Viennese papers described him as representative of an alien Jewish philosophy.[5] (Schlick was Prussian, not Jewish, and a German patriot at that.) The legacy of the multinational networks was formidable. Many of their members emigrated West in the 1930s, and reshaped entire disciplines in Western academies. But, precisely on account of their supra-nationalism, they remained marginal in Central Europe.

The failure of cosmopolitanism did not put a damper on multiculturalism. Quite the contrary. In 1869 Czech novelist Jan Neruda (1834–91) protested against the allegiance of the Prague Jews to German culture. The Jews, he argued, 'acted with malice and hatred towards the Czechs' and constituted an alien element in the Czech lands. Alas, he himself was not articulating an 'authentic' Czech discourse. He borrowed Richard Wagner's views, in *Das Judentum in der Musik*, on the inimical German and Jewish spirits. Applying Wagner's ideas to Czechs and Jews, he echoed Marx in 'On the Jewish Question': 'the question is not the emancipation of the Jews, but, rather, emancipation from the Jews'.[6] Given his virulent nationalism and anti-Semitism, his German-Czech-Jewish 'synthesis' may seem surprising, but Czechs often appropriated German and Jewish discourses in constructing Czech identity. All ethnic groups covertly transgressed national boundaries and appropriated rival cultures. Assimilating 'others', they claimed that discourses, identities and traditions formed in multicultural interaction were authentically national.

The contribution of cross-cultural exchange to constructing national identity was most transparent amongst the Jews. The reason is simple: the Jews' relationship to national culture(s) was an open problem throughout Europe. Jewish identity was contested within the Jewish community itself. Traditionalist 'Eastern' Jews regarded Jews as a separate people, united by observance of Jewish law (הלכה), religious tradition, language (Yiddish) and common ancestry. They rejected acculturation on ideological grounds, but manifested various degrees of it in practice (e.g. use of other languages). In contrast, modern 'Western' or liberal Jews – a majority in Vienna and the Czech crown-

---

[5] Prof. Dr Austriacus (Johann Sauter), 'Der Fall des Wiener Professors Schlick – eine Mahnung zur Gewissenserforschung', *Schönere Zukunft* (12 July 1936); reprinted in Friedrich Stadler, *Studien zum Wiener Kreis* (Frankfurt, 1997), pp. 924–9.

[6] Jan Neruda, *Pro strach židovský* ['On the Jewish Fear'] (Prague, 1942), p. 9, quoted in Hillel Kieval, *The Making of Czech Jewry* (New York, 1988), p. 21. Marx's statement was: 'The *emancipation of the Jews* . . . is the emancipation of humanity from *Judaism.*' Karl Marx, 'Zur Judenfrage', in his *Werke* (41 vols., Berlin, 1961), I, pp. 373.

lands – openly debated strategies for acculturation and national integration. Their leaders insisted that in so far as Jews constituted a people, they were united by religion alone. Liberals read the *Aufklärung* (German Enlightenment) into Judaism and spoke of the Jews' universal mission: spreading monotheism, the golden rule, egalitarian citizenship and cosmopolitanism. They denied that Jews were a nation and insisted that they belonged to the nations amongst which they lived. In Austria, this meant that Jews were German. Orthodox Jews charged that liberal acculturation meant assimilation; liberals urged the orthodox to relinquish ghettoised Judaism. Negotiation of identity across cultures, elsewhere covert, here became overt.[7]

The ambiguity of Austrian nationality gave Jews an opportunity missing elsewhere for negotiating Jewish and national identity. Jews were the only ethnic group to adopt enthusiastically the official 'imperial idea', or *Staatsgedanke*. Poor Galician traditionalists and refined Viennese assimilationists, orthodox rabbis and liberal scholars, Zionists and socialists, all declared their loyalty to the dynasty and the supra-national empire. 'Jews are the standard-bearers of the Austrian idea of unity,' stated the liberal Viennese rabbi Adolf Jellinek.[8] 'If one could construct a specifically Austrian nationality,' added his orthodox colleague, *Reichsrat* member Joseph Bloch, 'Jews would form its foundation.'[9] They were not just 'the most loyal supporters of the monarchy, [but] the only ones who were unconditionally Austrian'.[10] Indeed, they were the only minority whose 'golden age of security' depended wholly on the multinational empire's survival.[11] Well into the final days of the First World War, when the empire already lay in ruins, Viennese Jewish papers insisted that, federally reorganised, the multinational empire was viable.[12] The Austrian *Staatsgedanke* seemed to offer a patriotism whose underlying rationale was not ethno-national, but multinational, making

---

[7] For a typology of Jewish politics, see Ezra Mendelsohn, *On Modern Jewish Politics* (New York, 1993). For recent assessments of acculturation: Jonathan Frankel and Steven Zipperstein (eds.), *Assimilation and Community: the Jews in Nineteenth-Century Europe* (Cambridge, 1992).

[8] Adolf Jellinek, 'Jüdisch-österreichisch', *Die Neuzeit* (15 June 1883), p. 225: 'Die Juden . . . sind die Träger des österreichischen Einheitsgedankens.'

[9] Joseph Bloch, *Der nationale Zwist und die Juden in Österreich* (Vienna, 1886), p. 41.

[10] Joseph Bloch, 'Nichts gelernt und nichts vergessen', *Oesterreichische Wochenschrift* (22 June 1917), p. 390: 'In der Tat sind die Juden nicht etwa die treusten Anhänger der Monarchie, sie sind die einzigen bedingungslosen Oesterreicher in diesem Staatsverband.'

[11] On the 'golden age of security': Zweig, *The World of Yesterday*. Hannah Arendt presents the Jews as the state-people *par excellence* in *The Origins of Totalitarianism* (New York, 1951).

[12] David Rechter, 'Neither East nor West: Viennese Jewish Politics in World War One', PhD dissertation, Hebrew University of Jerusalem, 1994.

Jewish participation unproblematic. Jews hesitated not a moment to use this short-term opportunity.

Was Jewish imperial patriotism cosmopolitanism by default? Hardly. The one-sided love affair that the masses of orthodox Galician *Kaiser-treuen* (imperial patriots) had with Franz Joseph reflected their recognition of Austro-Hungary as a 'kingdom of grace' (מלכות חסד), contrasted with the pogroms and 'evil decrees' (תזירות) across the Russian border. Ideologically, however, their *Staatsgedanke* amounted to little more than the traditional 'thou shall always be praying for the welfare of the monarchy, for without the fear of the authorities, people would devour each other alive'.[13] Franz Joseph was a beloved emperor because he permitted the 'Chosen People' a respite in the Diaspora, not because he represented a supra-national idea. Orthodox Jews never developed imperial cosmopolitan designs. In contrast, liberal Jews professed a Jewish cosmopolitan mission, but their cosmopolitanism conflicted with their German nationalism. For Adolf Jellinek, Vienna's chief rabbi 1865–91, Jews superseded national existence, and testified to cosmopolitanism's viability, by becoming exemplary citizens in their respective nations. In Austria, this entailed dedication to *Deutschtum* (German-ness). Enlightenment, emancipation, culture and German nationality were all one. The empire had a civilising mission: German culture must overcome 'regressive eastern cultures', both traditional Jewish and Slavic ones. Jewish orthodoxy thrived on multinational diversity, but had no use for universalism. Many liberal Jews who espoused universalism had little use for diversity.

Liberal cosmopolitanism's Achilles' heel was confounding cosmopolitanism and nationality. Opting for integration into the German nationality, and often making, within a generation, a radical transition from *Shtetljuden* to German-speaking intelligentsia, liberal Jews could not understand the discrepancy between their dreams and those of other nationalities. Why would Czechs not be equally content with integration into the German cultural sphere (*Kulturbereich*)? None the less, negotiating between Jewish identity and German culture, liberal Jews created admirable syntheses, the mark of true cross-cultural interaction. Their commitment to cosmopolitanism need not be questioned, either. In his medieval Jewish history, Moritz Güdemann, Jellinek's successor as Vienna's chief rabbi, reconstituted the Middle Ages as a period of intensive Jewish–Christian cultural exchange.[14] Responding to Herzl's

---

[13] Mishnah *Avot*, III: 2. This tractate recites sayings and dicta of Jewish sages.
[14] Moritz Güdemann, *Geschichte des Erziehungswesens und der Cultur der abendländischen Juden, während des Mittelalters und der neueren Zeit* [1880–8] (3 vols., Amsterdam, 1966).

Judenstaat, he re-affirmed the cosmopolitan Jewish mission, rejecting Zionism and nationalism as backward.[15] Admittedly, the firmest validations of Jewish cosmopolitanism were against Zionism, not against German nationalism. Liberal Jews used cosmopolitanism against Zionism to justify their hopes of integration into the German nation. But it is also true that the rise of anti-Semitism led many to rethink past commitments. A February 1897 meeting of the *Österreichische-Israelitische Union* called for a 'return to the programme of reconciliation of peoples, nationalities, denominations, estates and classes in the name of free thought and progress, in the name of justice and the equality of all citizens before the law'.[16]

This was a pious but also hopeless wish. The liberal Jewish–German synthesis came into a crisis with the emergence of pan-German anti-Semitism in the 1880s. As long as German nationality was defined culturally, liberal Jews could regard themselves as its messengers to the *Ostjuden* and Slavs. Once it became racially defined, they faced exclusion from the German nation. Worsening their predicament, a growing vocal minority of Zionists and Diaspora-Nationalists responded to the rise of anti-Semitism by claiming that Jews were a people and a nation like any other. Zionists strove to rebuild the Jewish community in Palestine; the Diaspora-Nationalists wished to guarantee Jewish cultural autonomy in Europe. Both orthodox and liberal Jews fought the nationalists, the former provoked by their secularism, the latter by their nationalism. Liberals feared that the nationalists would vindicate the anti-Semites and put Jewish emancipation and integration in jeopardy. Yet, they could not be Germans in an age of ethno-nationalism and had nowhere to turn politically. German cosmopolitanism represented the aspirations of the prospective losers of ethno-politics.[17]

Popper's response to the predicament of Jewish-German national cosmopolitanism was to reject both German and Jewish nationalism in favour of uncompromising cosmopolitanism. This may have been the only logical answer, but it was an extremely rare one. It required one to

---

[15] Moritz Güdemann, *Nationaljudenthum* (Leipzig, 1897). See also Güdemann, *Jüdische Apologetik* (Glogau, 1906), esp. chs. 3, 7.

[16] Gustav Kohn, addressing a meeting concerning the coming parliamentary elections, 20 February 1897: *Mittheilungen der Oesterreichisch-Israelitischen Union*, 9, 92 (March 1897), p. 3. See also Werner Cahnman, 'Adolf Fischhof and his Jewish Followers', *Leo Baeck Institute Year Book*, 4 (1959).

[17] This is to imply neither that Viennese progressivism represented the only manifestation of German cosmopolitanism nor that Jews were its only proponents. In my 'Dilemmas of Cosmopolitanism', pp. 112–14, I give a broader survey of Austrian cosmopolitanism, including Catholic cosmopolitanism, socialist internationalism and Austroslavism. The label 'losers of ethno-politics' applies to these, too (as it does to court circles cultivating the imperial idea).

give up both Jewish and German identity. Few intellectuals were willing to go this far. Even assimilated Jews who negotiated away their Jewish identity – or thought they did – insisted on maintaining a German one. Popper's radicalism left him a permanent exile, a citizen only in an imaginary Republic of Letters. Central European intellectual networks allowed the Jewish émigrés to catch glimpses of such a cosmopolitan republic, and to explain the émigrés' nostalgia for Central Europe, but a cosmopolitan Central Europe remained a dream, an invention of exiles contemplating what things might have looked like had the Habsburg monarchy survived. The dream was noble, but it failed miserably – everywhere.

II

Karl Raimund Popper was born to Simon and Jenny Popper on 28 July, 1902 in Vienna. He was a first-generation Viennese, his father's mer- curial rise to the upper bourgeoisie charting the legendary course of upward mobility of Jewish immigrants to the capital. In 1900 both parents renounced their membership in the Jewish community and converted to Lutheranism. While Vienna was overwhelmingly Catholic, Simon Popper shared the anti-clericalism of the Viennese progressives and preferred Protestantism, the *Aufklärung*'s religion. Vienna had the highest Jewish conversion rate of any European urban centre, and Lutheranism was the religion of choice for upper-class Jewish converts. Assimilated Jews remained, however, a small minority, and Jewish acculturation to German culture rarely led to assimilation. Neither acculturation nor religious conversion broke the barriers of ethnicity. Intermarriages were less common in Vienna than in other European cities.[18] Assimilated and non-assimilated upper-class Jews belonged to the same social networks. The Jewish intelligentsia constructed bridges to progressive secular Austrians opposed to anti-Semitism, and together they formed the utopian visions of a secular commonwealth that became the hallmark of *fin de siècle* Viennese progressivism. In such a state, free of religious superstition and ethnic prejudice, the assimilated Jewish intelligentsia would finally find their home: no one would probe their ethnic origins, or challenge their claims to be German. But reality defied utopia. Secular progressive Germans were marginal to their ethnic group. Simon Popper had a good number of close non-Jewish friends,

---

[18] They required that one member of the couple convert to the other's religion, or declare himself/herself *konfessionslos* (without religious affiliation; atheist). Marsha Rozenblit, *The Jews of Vienna: Identity and Assimilation, 1867–1914* (Albany, 1983), esp. ch. 4.

but the Poppers ended up spending much of their life in company with other Jews.

The educational patterns of Viennese Jews mitigated against assimilation. Jews constituted about nine per cent of Vienna's population, but a quarter to a third of gymnasia and university students. (This may explain their preponderance in *fin de siècle* culture.)[19] Since Jews concentrated in three districts (the first, second and ninth), Jewish students often constituted a majority in their schools. *Lycée*-educated Jewish girls, such as Karl Popper's sister, Dora, comprised almost half of Viennese *lycée* students, over two-thirds in progressive ones. There was nothing Jewish about Karl's and Dora's education: it was progressive German education in the *Freie Schule* and *lycée*; and classical German, with a scientific bent, in the *Realgymnasium*. But 'a certain separation of Gentiles and Jews into groups', recalled Arthur Schnitzler, 'could be felt always and everywhere, also therefore in school'.[20] Contrary to their aspirations, neither assimilated nor acculturated Viennese Jews became German Austrians. Much like their predecessors in nineteenth-century Germany, they constituted a German-Jewish community of their own, united by ethnic origins, social class, German education, the Enlightenment's ethos, liberal politics and, of course, the anti-Semites' malice.[21]

Throughout his youth, Popper was surrounded by progressive intellectuals. They rebelled against the Austrian liberals' social conservatism and pursued dialogue with the socialists and the workers. They opted for a bourgeois–proletarian alliance, under the auspices of an enlightened bureaucracy, which would promote social legislation, economic management and scientific education. As several attempts to organise a progressive party ran against the twin obstacles of Catholicism and anti-Semitism and found only limited success, the progressives increasingly channelled their efforts into a large network of associations for educational reform, social welfare, and economic planning.[22] One of them

[19] Steven Beller, *Vienna and the Jews: a Cultural History, 1867–1938* (New York, 1989).

[20] Arthur Schnitzler, *My Youth in Vienna* (New York, 1970), p. 63.

[21] Karl Popper, *Unended Quest: an Intellectual Autobiography* (LaSalle, Il., 1984) (henceforth, *Autobiography*), pp. 12, 31–2, and 'Draft', Popper Papers, Hoover Institute Archives (134, 4, 9) (henceforth, Popper Archives). For Jews in Viennese schools: Rozenblit, *The Jews of Vienna*, ch. 5; David Sorkin, *The Transformation of German Jewry, 1770–1840* (New York, 1987).

[22] Ingrid Belke, *Die sozialreformerischen Ideen von Joseph Popper-Lynkeus (1838–1921) in Zusammenhang mit allgemeinen Reformbestrebungen des Wiener Bürgertums um die Jahrhundertwende* (Tübingen, 1978), esp. pp. 5–56; Albert Fuchs, *Geistige Strömungen in Österreich, 1867–1918* (Vienna, 1949), pp. 133–62; John Boyer, 'Freud, Marriage, and Late Viennese Liberalism: a Commentary from 1905', *Journal of Modern History*, 50 (March 1978), pp. 72–102.

was the Monists, founded by Ernst Mach's disciples in 1911. It was dedicated to the 'scientific' reform of philosophy, education and law. Virtually all Viennese reformers belonged.[23] A socialist family friend took the young Popper to the Monists' meetings.[24] Militantly secular, politically radical, and trusting in social reform, popular education and technological progress, this was the young Popper's social and intellectual milieu. It reflected, to use Friedrich Stadler's term, the late-Enlightenment spirit (*Spätaufklärung*).[25]

Ethno-nationalism was *Spätaufklärung*'s greatest enemy, but the progressives underestimated its danger and responded to it ambivalently. Their ranks included pacifists and federalists, but also German nationalists. They fought anti-Semitism, which offended their humanity and excluded their Jewish members from the nation, but they could see no harm in the expansion of the German cultural sphere in Central Europe. They regarded Slavic nationalism as reactionary. Ethno-politics was, they thought, a passing frenzy. Most of them refused to implicate German nationalism with anti-Semitism. They believed that anti-Semitism was rooted in religious prejudice, and secular education was its proper antidote. Clericalism, not nationalism, was their major enemy.[26] They contested anti-Semitic rhetoric with enlightenment rather than multinationalism.

The Popper family's circle represented the cosmopolitan-pacifist pole on the progressive spectrum. Simon Popper was master of the leading freemason lodge *Humanitas*, and relatives and friends were identified with the Austrian Peace Movement.[27] Freemasons and pacifists gave the clearest expression of Austrian cosmopolitanism. To them, humankind was advancing towards cosmopolitanism. Nationality and religion did not matter, only universal humanity. As a multinational empire, Austria represented a higher developmental stage than national states. Cosmopolitans were the Austrian patriots *par excellence*. They contributed to political harmony and internal peace.[28] Unlike the socialists whose party

---

[23] Friedrich Stadler, *Vom Positivismus zur 'Wissenschaftliche Weltauffassung'* (Vienna, 1982).

[24] *Autobiography*, pp. 12–13.

[25] Friedrich Stadler, 'Spätaufklärung und Sozialdemokratie in Wien, 1918–1938', in Franz Kadrnoska (ed.), *Aufbruch und Untergang: österreichische Kultur zwischen 1918 und 1938* (Vienna, 1981), pp. 441–73.

[26] John Boyer, *Culture and Political Crisis in Vienna: Christian Socialism in Power, 1897–1918* (Chicago, 1995), ch. 4.

[27] Autobiography, pp. 11, 13–14; *Offene Gesellschaft – offenes Universum: Franz Kreuzer im Gespräch mit Karl R. Popper* (Vienna, 1982), p. 23.

[28] Rainer Hubert and Ferdinand Zörrer, 'Die östereichischen Grenzlogen', *Quatuor Coronati Jahrbuch* (1983), pp. 143–66; Gustav Kuéss and Bernhard Scheichelbauer, *200 Jahre Freimaurerei in Österreich* (Vienna, 1959), pp. 137–73; Richard Laurence,

structure forced confrontation with the nationality problem, the free-masons drew no plan for imperial reform. They were content to 'think of themselves as guardians of liberal values and as the intellectual elite of a huge state whose composition gave it the appearance of the international order of humankind in miniature'.[29]

Progressives and socialists alike denied that Jews were a nationality. In *Die Nationalitätenfrage und die Sozialdemokratie* ('The Nationalities Problem and Social Democracy'), Bauer rejected the claims of Galician Jewish socialists for Jewish autonomy. Jews should, and will, assimilate in the majority nationality wherever they live.[30] Likewise, when a 1905 electoral reform in Bukovina, the centre of Jewish Diaspora Nationalism, established a Jewish curia, progressive Viennese Jews led the charge against the 'electoral ghetto' (*Wahl-Ghetto*).[31] They felt that their own German identity was at issue. Striving for recognition as German Austrians, they sought to strip religion and ethnicity of significance – their own first and foremost. The progressive intelligentsia represented a group that, to emancipate itself from its own ethnicity, needed to dissolve all ethnicity and recover universal humanity – Marx's universal class.[32]

The progressives' vision of social reform tended towards utopia. They elaborated grand designs for a future society. Their imagined communities were distinctly modern and reliant on social technology, but they seemed contextless. Neither Theodor Hertzka's *Freiland* (free land) nor Anton Menger's *Arbeitsstaat* (workers' state) nor Josef Popper-Lynkeus' *Nährarmee* (nutrition army) was tailored to the Habsburg Monarchy.[33] This reflected their inability to negotiate imperial problems, but also their universalism. They divested their utopias of any national attribute. They did not design cosmopolitan federations as openly as Kant did, or as polemically as Popper would, but they de-nationalised the state. It would make little sense to regard their utopias as German. The

'Bertha von Suttner and the Peace Movement in Austria to World War I', *Austrian History Yearbook*, 23 (1992), pp. 181–201.

[29] Paul Silverman, 'Law and Economics in Interwar Vienna: Kelsen, Mises and the Regeneration of Austrian Liberalism', PhD dissertation, University of Chicago, 1984, p. 26.

[30] Otto Bauer, *Die Nationalitätenfrage und die Sozialdemokratie* [1907] (Vienna, 1924), pp. 366–381.

[31] Gerald Stourzh, 'Galten die Juden als Nationalität Altösterreichs?', in Anna Drabek, Mordechai Eliav and Gerald Stourzh (eds.), *Prag-Czernowitz-Jerusalem* (Eisenstadt, 1984), pp. 73–117.

[32] Karl Marx, 'Zur Kritik der Hegelschen Rechtsphilosophie. Einleitung', *Werke*, I, p. 390.

[33] Theodor Hertzka, *Freiland: Ein soziales Zukunftsbild* (Leipzig, 1890); Anton Menger, *Neue Staatslehre* (Jena, 1904); Joseph Popper-Lynkeus, *Die allgemeine Nährpflicht als Lösung der sozialen Frage*, 2nd edn (Vienna, 1923).

foundation of the earth was one.[34] The requirements of a good social order were a matter of scientific management, not cultural difference. Even to most nationalists among them, nationalism remained secondary to secular, scientific, popular education (*Volksbildung*). Undoubtedly, they confounded *Aufklärung* and *Deutschtum*. But, for many, it seems, *Deutschtum* was an instrument for realising *Aufklärung*, rather than the opposite. They were less nationalists in a cosmopolitan guise than cosmopolitans in a German guise.[35]

The progressives' denial of ethno-nationalism flew in the face of historical reality. Progressive culture remained marginal. It conflicted with the religious beliefs, nationalist values and ethnic identity of most Germans. There was nothing essentially Jewish about it. Progressive Germans recognised it as their own. Almost every progressive circle had both Jewish and non-Jewish members, but there were relatively few progressive German Austrians. Progressivism made few inroads into the court, the civil service and aristocratic circles. Class and education limited it to the intelligentsia. Even in the academy, where Jews were heavily represented, progressivism represented a minority. Virulent German nationalism dominated much of the student body, and con-servative Catholic and nationalist traditions prevailed in the humanities and social sciences. Through their organisational network, the liberal professions and Vienna's salons and coffee houses, the progressives contributed to the legendary cultural intensity of Vienna. But they remained a narrow segment of the German intelligentsia, allied with a sub-group of an ethnic minority who posed for a short time as a social and cultural elite: Vienna's 'non-Jewish Jews'.

Popper would spend much of his life refashioning progressive philo-sophy and politics. He freed progressivism from its ambivalence about nationalism. Regarding the dissolution of the Habsburg Empire as an unmitigated disaster and holding nationalism, especially German nationalism, responsible, Popper rejected German nationality and dis-sociated the Enlightenment from Germany. He made good on enlight-enment cosmopolitanism,[36] but inherited also its dilemmas. He was just as impatient as the progressives had been with multicultural diversity. As an anti-nationalist, he defended it in the strongest terms, but it existed almost by default, a result of humanity's failure to realise cosmo-politanism fully. Diversity's major benefit was that it created a culture

---

[34] *Babylonian Talmud* (21 vols., Vilna, 1880–92), *Kiddushin*, p. 27b, *Baba Kama*, p. 12b: 'סדנא דארעא חד הוא.'
[35] Steven Beller, 'Patriotism and the National Identity of Habsburg Jewry, 1860–1914', *Leo Baeck Institute Year Book*, 41 (1996), pp. 215–238.
[36] Pauline Kleingeld, 'Six Varieties of Cosmopolitanism in Late Eighteenth-Century Germany', *Journal of the History of Ideas*, 60 (1999), pp. 505–524.

clash that opened closed communities. It was good that immigrants to Vienna 'had to learn German', opening themselves to a new cultural tradition.[37] Precisely as Czech immigrants protested, however, German schools meant German hegemony and Czech assimilation. Popper would not budge. Discounting all national, ethnic and religious identity as culturally primitive and politically reactionary, he posited a universalist vision of the Open Society where none of them counted. His relentless hostility towards Zionism, his rejection of any and all religion (Judaism even more than Christianity), his passionate defence of liberalism and the Enlightenment were a metamorphosis of Viennese progressivism. He remained an assimilated progressive Jew to the end of his life. Through his migration and exile, progressive philosophy, a product of marginal Viennese milieux, made cosmopolitan dreams and dilemmas part of mainstream Western culture.

III

'The breakdown of the Austrian Empire and the aftermath of the First World War . . . destroyed the world in which I had grown up,' wrote Popper in his *Autobiography*.[38] In the immediate post-war years, he experienced revolution, mass hunger and cold. The runaway inflation almost reduced his family to poverty. His sheltered life as an upper-middle-class boy had come to an end. But, beyond his personal misery, he felt that the war destroyed 'the commonwealth of learning' he had known as a child. He would spend his life trying to repair it, shaping visions of science and politics in the image of the lost 'commonwealth' of his youth: free cosmopolitan communities, engaged in critical debates, reconfiguring the Enlightenment's Republic of Letters.

In the scientific philosophy of the Vienna Circle Popper found – for all his lifelong confrontation with it – the legacy of the Enlightenment and of *fin de siècle* progressivism. The circle was the fountainhead of the logical positivist movement which developed, during the inter-war period, an organisational network in Central Europe's urban centres: Vienna, Berlin, Prague, Warsaw, Budapest, Lwów, Bratislava. It had disciples throughout Europe and North America. The circle sought to apply recent advances in logic, mathematics and scientific theory to philosophy. Many members were deeply influenced by Wittgenstein's *Tractatus Logico-Philosophicus* (1922) and declared war on traditional

---

[37] Karl Popper, 'On Culture Clash', in his *In Search of a Better World* (London, 1992), p. 124; Popper, 'Der wichtigste Beitrag seit Aristoteles', *Wissenschaft aktuell*, 1 (September 1980).
[38] *Autobiography*, p. 32.

philosophy, especially metaphysics. Among the more famous were Moritz Schlick, Otto Neurath and Rudolf Carnap. Popper's relationship to the circle was problematic. He developed his philosophy of science in critical dialogue with theirs, but within a framework foreign to positivism, that of the marginal Kantian tradition leading from Jakob Fries (1775–1843) to Leonard Nelson (1882–1927). Recognising his originality, the circle provided him with opportunities that eventually made him a renowned philosopher, but the disjunctions between their positivism and his Kantianism remained a source of constant tension.[39] All the same, having completed *Logik der Forschung* in 1934, Popper became an active member of the circle's network, a 'Central European intellectual'.[40]

By 1934, however, Central European culture was living on borrowed time. Nazism had already claimed Germany and was threatening Austria. In Germany the circle's network could no longer operate openly. Most members lost their academic positions and emigrated when they could. In Austria they were under attack in the academy and suspect to the clerical-fascist dictatorship. Semi-fascist regimes were harassing them in other East-Central European countries, too. None of the circle's annual congresses for scientific philosophy, beginning in 1935, could take place in Central Europe. Instead, they were held in Paris, Copenhagen, Cambridge (England) and Cambridge (Massachusetts). They solidified British and American interest in scientific philosophy and facilitated the circle members' migration. Within a few years, most of them left Central Europe for England and the USA.

In 1935–6 Otto Neurath repeatedly spoke of the circle as a republic of scholars (*Gelehrtersrepublik*). It mattered not that he lived in the Netherlands, and not in Vienna; that Hans Reichenbach was in Istanbul and Carl Hempel in Brussels, not in Berlin; and that Rudolf Carnap was leaving Prague for the USA. The 1935 Paris congress showed that their republic was spreading over the globe, becoming American, British, French, Polish, Scandinavian. They were rebuilding the Enlightenment's Republic of Letters. Launching the *International Encyclopedia of Unified Science*, Neurath concluded his address to the congress with 'vive les nouveaux encyclopédistes!'[41] His bravado was a counsel of despair,

---

[39] *Autobiography*, pp. 72–90 and draft, Popper Archives (134, 12); Herbert Feigl, 'The "Wiener Kreis" in America', in Donald Fleming and Bernard Bailyn (eds.), *The Intellectual Migration: Europe and America, 1930–1960* (Cambridge, Mass., 1969); Malachi Hacohen, *Karl Popper – the Formative Years, 1902–1945* (New York, 2000), chs. 5–6; Stadler, *Studien zum Wiener Kreis*.

[40] Karl Popper, *Logik der Forschung: Zur Erkenntnistheorie der modernen Naturwissenschaft* (Vienna, 1935). Translation: *The Logic of Scientific Discovery* (London, 1959).

[41] Otto Neurath, 'Une encyclopédie internationale de la science unitaire', *Actes du Congrès*

and his Viennese cosmopolitanism utopian as ever. Trying to snatch victory from the jaws of defeat, Neurath imagined the Diaspora as a cosmopolitan triumph.

Popper was less sanguine about cosmopolitanism's immediate prospect, but equally committed to its future. Already in 1927, in a seminar lecture on the *Heimat* idea at the Vienna Pedagogic Institute, he expressed radical cosmopolitanism and deep antipathy to nationalism. A convergence of country and home, Heimat originated with the German romantics. To nineteenth-century liberals, it denoted patriotism and civic culture, but, in inter-war years, it became a leitmotiv of the Austrian fascists. They used it to express local patriotism, attachment to provincial customs, family and religion, and hatred of urban industrial society, parliamentary politics and Viennese culture.[42] The socialists hoped to re-appropriate the concept, but Popper offered them no help. Noting *Heimat*'s amorphous character, he purged the concept of mystical nationalist meanings. He founded *Heimat* on the psychological relationship of individuals to their environment and spoke of school as an educational *Heimat*, but he remained suspicious even of this 'native' environment. It connoted a rejection of the new and different as 'foreign'. It was acceptable as a point of departure, but school should open *Heimat* to new experiences and ideas. *Heimat* existed, but it needed to be overcome.

Popper recognised that *Heimat* established a 'naturally-given primitive *Kulturverband* [cultural community]' that supported larger cultural units, but he did not investigate the transformation of multiple local communities into a nation. Instead, he defined the nation as a *Rechtsverband* (legal association). Legal systems, not cultural heritage, set national boundaries. He insisted that a universal ethic must shape national legal codes, making good citizenship compatible with internationalism. Education should cultivate respect for law, a sense of justice and a critical awareness of social iniquities that demand socialist rectification, but it should not foster patriotism, or *Heimatliebe*. Love is an aesthetic feeling, not a virtue, so there is no duty to love. Patriotic actions violating internationalism are unethical.[43] Threatened by the

---

Internationale de Philosophie Scientifique (8 vols., Paris, 1936), II, pp. 54–9; 'L'encyclopédie comme "modèle"', *Revue de Synthèse*, 12 (1936), pp. 187–201. (Both are also available in his *Philosophical Papers* (Boston, 1983).)

[42] For a more positive evaluation of *Heimat*, emphasising its role in bridging local community and national identity, see Celia Applegate's study of the Palatinate: *A Nation of Provincials: the German Idea of Heimat* (Berkeley, 1990), ch. 1.

[43] The issue has recently resurfaced in academic debates in the USA. See Martha Nussbaum, 'Patriotism and Cosmopolitanism', *Boston Review* (October-November 1994), pp. 3–6 and the responses to Nussbaum in the same issue. Nussbaum's position is identical to Popper: nationality is 'a morally irrelevant characteristic'. 'Where one is

fascist *Heimat*, Popper contained its political force and emotional appeal, first by restricting it to individuals and their environment, then by transforming national collectives into legal associations protecting universal rights.

Popper's cosmopolitanism was already full-blown in this uneven early essay. So also were his difficulties in negotiating national identity. He recognised cultural-historical communities, but divorced nationality and citizenship from them: the latter were legal concepts. National differences appeared insignificant. All nations must conform to the legal code of a yet-to-come world federation. 'From good Germans to good *Weltbürger*', he quoted Eduard Burger, *Die Quelle*'s editor and a socialist school reformer. For socialists, the dictum justified a German national focus. For Popper, good Germans virtually ceased being German, becoming *Weltbürger*. He heaped abuse on German epistemology and *Naturphilosophie* that reflected, in his view, something of a German national character. Their *heimatlicher* superstition, making truth relative to national circumstances, could bring philosophy down. But, Popper seemed to suggest, education could change 'national character' by transforming affective relationships and aesthetic feelings into legal relationships and ethical actions. Love of *Heimat* may develop into an appreciation of nature's beauty, anxieties about 'bad' outsiders into ethical judgements, native (*bodenständige*) art and music into high culture. His suggestions reflected not so much cultural elitism, or authoritarian universalism, as an assimilated Jew's mortal fear of German ethno-nationalism. Excluded from *Heimat* on ethnic grounds, Popper responded by subjecting ethnic and national identities to a universal humanity.[44]

These were daring moves for a young student to make. Progressive cosmopolitanism lost much of its force in the inter-war years. The empire was gone. Versailles (or St Germain) discredited the Austrian Peace Movement. Notwithstanding, Popper adopted the most radical cosmopolitan position available among progressives, and pushed it further. He stood almost alone. Eccentric aristocrats, such as the free-mason Coudehove-Kalergi, could still dream of Pan-Europa. Conservative proponents of the Austrian idea from Hofmannstahl to Roth expressed anti-German sentiments and opposition to nationalism, but they were not progressive universalists. As for the socialists, German

born is just . . . an accident.' Students must be taught that 'they are above all citizens of a world of human beings', 'Patriotic pride is both morally dangerous and, ultimately, subversive of . . . national unity in devotion to . . . justice and equality.'

[44] Karl Popper, 'Zur Philosophie des Heimatgedankens', *Die Quelle*, 77 (1927), pp. 899–908. Burger's quotation is on p. 906.

nationalism always tempered their internationalism. During the inter-war period, they supported unification with Germany. The editor of *Die Quelle* may have gained more than he bargained for when he asked Popper to open the *Heimat* seminar. He provided a platform for a progressive who had made a clean break with German nationalism and refused to compromise cosmopolitanism.

To be sure, Popper's cosmopolitanism involved limited conceptual innovation. His central ideas belonged to Kant: the state as a legal and political entity (not a cultural-historical one), the parallel between civil, national and cosmopolitan rights, the universality of the moral impera-tive, and the division between aesthetics and ethics (ruling out deriva-tion of moral imperatives from aesthetic judgement).[45] But political realism and government pressure constrained Kant's cosmopolitanism. His republican government and international federation were a future prospect, a conjecture about historical progress that would lead human-kind to a cosmopolitan age, the descent of the Kingdom of Ends upon earth. In reality he faced an absolutist monarchy, first an enlightened one (under Frederick II), then a reactionary one. There were many escape clauses for an absolutist monarch. The security of the state was a supreme imperative. Under no circumstances was resistance to the monarch permitted. Rebellion was 'the greatest crime'. A country in the midst of Europe (i.e. Prussia), subject to pressures from powerful neighbours, was exempted from a republican constitution.[46] The moral imperative was universal, but its political fulfilment was problematic and required caution.

Young Popper would have none of it. With typical single-mindedness – reflecting philosophical consistency, moral uprightness, obstinacy and more than a touch of political naïveté – he collapsed Kant's future and present, conjecture and reality. He freed Kant's cosmopolitanism from its historical and political limits, daringly proclaiming its universal validity, here and now.

Popper affirmed cosmopolitanism in the face of vicious ethno-politics that left him with no intellectual or political home and diminished his academic prospects. 'The unfavourable circumstances of the time', as the Viennese social theorist Felix Kaufmann delicately put it in a recommendation for Popper, required that Popper teach at a

---

[45] Immanuel Kant, 'Über den Gemeinspruch: Das mag in der Theorie richtig sein, taugt aber nicht für die Praxis' [1793] and 'Zum ewigen Frieden' [1795], *Gesammelte Schriften (Akademieausgabe)* (29 vols, Berlin, 1912), VII; Kant, *Critique of Judgement* (Oxford, 1952), second book, 'Critique of Aesthetic Judgement'.

[46] Kant, 'Theorie [und] Praxis', esp. pp. 297–300; Kant, 'Zum ewigen Frieden', esp. pp. 372–3; Kant, 'Der Streit der Fakultäten' [1798], *Gesammelte Schriften*, VII, pp. 79–94, esp. note p. 86.

Hauptschule, secondary school for gymnasium rejects.[47] By 1935, sensing the impending disaster, Popper was desperately looking for a way out of Central Europe. After much travail, he accepted an offer from Canterbury University College in Christchurch, New Zealand, and, in January 1937, left Austria forever.[48] Ethno-nationalism shattered Central European culture and drove him to exile. He responded, in exile, by imagining Central Europe as the Open Society.

The Open Society and Its Enemies was Popper's war effort. As German troops swarmed over Europe, and the Japanese advanced towards New Zealand, he worked feverishly on the book, thinking at times that he might be writing civilisation's testament. *The Open Society* explained, he thought, the reasons for the rise of Fascism, the surrender of Central European democracies, the major issues at stake in the war, and the principles for social reconstruction afterwards. Completed in February 1943, the work consisted of three controversial critiques of Plato, Hegel and Marx that traced modern totalitarianism to humankind's 'venerated intellectual leaders'. Popper opined that the fascist drive to return to 'tribal' society fed on anxieties arising from the rapid changes in open societies. He found these anxieties expressed in both Plato and Hegel. Plato conspired to halt Athens' economic development and substitute an authoritarian regime for democracy. Hegel twisted progressive philosophy and politics, so they fit the mould of Prussian 'tribal nationalism'. In contrast, Marx and the socialists were essentially progressive democrats, but the scientific pretensions of Marxism resulted in the socialists' belief in historical inevitability. This weakened the ability and resolve of the working class to confront Fascism, leaving Central European democracies defenceless. Their enemies took advantage of their vulnerabilities and destroyed them.

The Open Society joined the familiar sociological narrative of development from tribe to civil society to Kant's and Nelson's narrative of the transition from nationalism to cosmopolitanism. Conservative German historian Eduard Meyer, whose work *Geschichte des Altertums* ('History of the Ancient World') Popper used extensively to familiarise himself with ancient Greece, spoke of the passage from *Stamm* (tribe) to *Staat* (state), *ethnos* to *polis* in early Greek history and alluded to the close relationship between the *polis* and the national state.[49] Nation thus came

---

[47] Kaufmann to the Academic Assistance Council, 28 October 1936, *Felix Kaufmann Nachlaß, Sozialwissenschaftliches Archiv*, Constance. See also Popper to Kaufmann, late November 1936 (011226).

[48] On Popper's emigration, see my 'Karl Popper in Exile: the Viennese Progressive Imagination and the Making of *The Open Society*', *Philosophy of the Social Sciences*, 26 (December 1996), esp. pp. 455–7.

[49] Eduard Meyer, *Geschichte des Altertums*, 2nd edn (5 vols., Stuttgart, 1915).

naturally to follow tribe. Popper added humanity, converting Meyer's reactionary nationalist narrative into a progressive cosmopolitan one. Tribe, nation, humanity became stages in the history of civilisation.

Western history was a continuous struggle between progressive imperialism and reactionary nationalism. Classical Athens was the first open society, the first to break the chains of 'tribalism', overcome myth, magic and custom, and found politics on *logos* and law. Secular, commercial, democratic and cosmopolitan, it embodied the progressive imperial ideal, but, eventually, succumbed to totalitarian Sparta. Later, Alexander the Great and the Roman Empire advanced universalism. 'From Alexander onward, all the civilised states of Europe and Asia were empires, embracing populations of infinitely mixed origin. European civilisation [has] remained international or, more precisely, inter-tribal ever since.'[50] In the nineteenth century tribal nationalism reared its ugly head once again. Hegel and German intellectuals supported Prussian nationalism and, within a century, Central Europe succumbed to German barbarism. Nazi racism was the highest stage of nationalism, its inevitable conclusion. Nationalism must be reined in if post-war Europe is to be an open society. An international legal order would best accomplish such a task.[51]

Central European conceptions of nationality and imperialism shaped Popper's account. Imperial Austria made *Volksstamm* (tribe; race; ethnicity) the basis of claims for *Nationalität* and cultural autonomy. Popper spoke therefore of 'tribal nationalism' (in current parlance, 'ethnonationalism').[52] But there were no good and bad nationalisms: he would not second a cultural *Deutschtum* any more than an ethnic one. The only nation he recognised was a political one, founded on the French Revolution's concept of citizenship. His charitable view of the British Empire reinforced the Habsburg legacy. Like other Central European émigrés to England, he thought the British Commonwealth the largest free community on earth. It extended hospitality to him in England and provided a war refuge in New Zealand. German totalitarianism and British 'democracy' were at war. If the democratic cosmopolitan empire could be saved, nationalism might subside and enlightenment spread. The Open Society represented the last metamorphosis of the multi-national Habsburg ideal, projected on to the British Empire.

Alone among liberals of his generation Popper challenged the princi-

---

50 Karl Popper, *The Open Society and Its Enemies* (2 vols., London, 1945), II, p. 48. All references are to the first edition, unless otherwise indicated.
51 Ibid., I, ch. 10; II, ch. 12.
52 Auriel Kolnai's use of 'tribal egotism' in *The War Against the West* (London, 1938) may have suggested the term 'tribal nationalism' to Popper, but it seemed so fitting because it both connoted primitivism and conformed to official terminology.

ples of national self-determination and the national state. Nationalities did not really exist. German thinkers from Herder to Fichte to Hegel invented them to serve the interests of reactionary states.

> The idea that there exist natural units like nations or linguistic or racial groups is entirely fictitious . . . The principle of the national state . . . owes its popularity solely to the fact that it appeals to tribal instincts[53] . . . None of the theories which maintain that a nation is united by common origin, or a common language, or a common history, is acceptable, or applicable in practice. The principle of the national state . . . is a myth. It is an irrational, a romantic and Utopian dream.[54]

Wilson's and Masaryk's 'well meant' effort to apply national self-determination consistently throughout Central Europe – 'one of the most mixed of all the thoroughly mixed regions of Europe' – was an incredible folly that brought about Versailles' failure. 'An international federation in the Danube basin might have prevented much.'[55] National Socialism represented the culmination of the national state. So did the tragedy of Bosnia, he said in his 1994 Prague speech. If the principle of national self-determination did not lose its authority, post-communist Central Europe could also fall prey to ethnic terrorism. The only remedy was abandoning self-determination, recognising state boundaries as conventional, sanctioning the *status quo*, and establishing an armed international organisation to guarantee peace. National identities were false, reactionary and utopian. Individual, imperial and cosmopolitan identities were true, progressive and possible.[56]

Popper ingeniously deconstructed nationality, pointing out its complex historical formation and diffused character, but he never extended this mode of questioning to imperialism. The nation state was historicised and delegitimised; empires went unexamined and were vindicated. His recollection of historical episodes of imperialism was selective. He recalled Alexander's cosmopolitanism, the Napoleonic Code and Habsburg multinationalism, not Spanish colonialism, the Middle Passage and Nazi *Lebensraum*. Imperialism represented cosmopolitanism's possibility; this was enough. The historicity of imperial

---

[53] Popper, *The Open Society*, I, ch. 9, n. 7(1).

[54] Ibid., II, p. 49.

[55] Ibid., II, ch. 12, n. 53.

[56] Ibid., I, ch. 5, n. 13(2); ch. 6, n. 44 (in later editions Popper expanded this note to rebut Hans Morgenthau's dismissal of an international legal order); ch. 9, n. 7; II, p. 238; ch. 12, ns. 19, 53; ch. 13, n. 2(1); Karl Popper, 'Kant's Critique and Cosmology', in *Conjectures and Refutations* (New York, 1963), esp. p. 182; Popper, 'Epistemology and Industrialisation', in *The Myth of the Framework* (London, 1994), pp. 185–7; Popper, 'On Culture Clash', pp. 118–21; Popper, 'Prague Lecture', www.lf3.cuni.cz/aff/p2_e.html (access through The Karl Popper Web: www.eeng.dcu.ie/~tkpw/).

identities – past or future – never became an issue. They were divested of historical specificity. They did not emerge from historical identities, but overcame them.

Popper was convinced that if we deconstruct false collectives and get to the individual, we will have reached the truly universal. Yet, cosmopolitan identity seemed abstract and unreal. Popper himself conceded that 'concrete groups' – families, churches, voluntary associations, possibly even ethnic communities – would remain even in the Open Society. They would continue to fulfil some of the functions that kinship groups had in the 'closed society'. Indeed, they were essential: people, Popper said unsympathetically, will 'try to satisfy their emotional social needs as well as they can'.[57] But 'emotional social needs' remained foreign to him, implicated with Fascism. He never negotiated between the closed and the Open Society, ethnicity and cosmopolitanism, or showed their possible convergence in his future cosmopolitan federation.

There was no room for negotiation with Fascism. Popper's uncompromising universalism, his categorical rejection of the claims of closed communities against the cosmopolitan Open Society, ought to be understood in the context of Central European ethno-nationalism. Kantian universalism made his polemical rejection of particularity possible, but it did not require it. Central Europe did. Popper acknowledged 'diversity' and – with the exception of Jewish religion and nationality which, he insisted, must be given up – assailed any effort to suppress difference. In one of his last public appearances, he acerbically suggested that Germany's and France's 'homogenous populations' were due to 'political and educational means suppressing minorities or dialects'.[58] To be sure, he thought that ethnic and religious differences were insignificant. Diversity existed, but, unlike universal humanity, it was no cause for celebration. His refusal to celebrate diversity reflected determination not to eliminate difference, but to ensure it does not infringe on universal humanity. The first response to the racist argument that those who are different are inferior and cannot be members of the nation is *not* that we ought to respect difference; it is that we are all equally human and entitled to equal rights as citizens.

The Open Society defended this universalist vision eloquently. Central Europe ensured that it remained utopian, making it impossible for Popper to close the gap between national communities and cosmopolitanism. Ethno-nationalism first gave rise to cosmopolitan dreams, then made them impossible. But Popper would not give up. He searched

[57] Popper, *The Open Society*, 2nd edn (London, 1952), I, p. 175; p. 171 of the American edition (Princeton, 1950).
[58] Popper, 'Prague Lecture'.

throughout Western history for cosmopolitan moments to provide instruction and encouragement for those fighting Fascism. He found Socrates, Pericles and classical Athens. They became the origin of the Open Society.

IV

The vision of a democratic cosmopolitan empire dominated *The Open Society* from beginning to end, but the failure of classical Athens captured Popper's imagination like no other. For a generation no longer educated in the ancient Greeks, it is difficult to imagine earlier periods' intense engagement with them. German historians rewrote Athenian history each time Germany went through a major political change, taking sides in Athenian domestic and foreign conflicts.[59] Conservative nationalists, such as Meyer, pleaded for Sparta. Liberals, in Germany and England alike, sided with Athens. Prussian reformer Wilhelm von Humboldt, Victorian progressive George Grote, and historian F.M. Cornford idealised classical democracy.[60] The noted Viennese liberal classicist, Theodor Gomperz, had made Athens the site of the Greek enlightenment. Popper used Gomperz, Grote and Meyer extensively, radicalised the progressives' view of Athens and rebutted Meyer's defence of Sparta. To Popper, Plato's attack on Athens was treason to the Open Society. Imagining ancient wars and philosophical disputes in the frame of Second World War, Popper divided Greek *poleis*, politicians and intellectuals into two camps, democratic and totalitarian. He fought one's war against the other. Totalitarian Sparta and the Athenian aristocracy sought to dismantle Athen's empire. Athenian imperialism had to be vindicated.

Popper moulded Athenian imperialism in the image of Viennese progressivism. Drawing an idealised picture of Athens, he interpreted extant literary sources in a manner many classicists found questionable, rejected evidence conflicting with his view and, on occasion, speculated where none existed. Reading Pericles' Funeral Oration as a realistic rather than rhetorical depiction of Athenian life, he expounded on Athenian liberty, equality, cosmopolitanism, magnanimous imperialism, cultural achievement and, above all, individualism.[61] Likewise, he inter-

---

[59] Beat Näf, *Von Perikles zu Hitler?* (Berne, 1985).

[60] Wilhelm von Humboldt, *The Limits of State Action* (Cambridge, 1969); George Grote, *Plato and Other Companions of Socrates* (London, 1865); Francis Cornford, *Before and After Socrates* (Cambridge, 1932); Theodor Gomperz, *Griechische Denker* (3 vols., Leipzig, 1896), I, part iii; Eduard Meyer, *Geschichte des Altertums*, IV–V.

[61] Popper assumed both that Thucydides accurately reported Pericles' speech and that it faithfully described Athenian life. He ignored parts of the speech contradicting his

preted Socrates and the sophists as propounding modern egalitarian views of justice, democracy and individualism. The Great Generation of Athenian philosophers and politicians before and during the Peloponnesian War (431–404 BC) was cosmopolitan.[62]

Contrary to Popper, it is unlikely that Pericles, or any classical Greek, articulated an 'individualist' view of the *polis*, liberal concepts of liberty and justice, or a cosmopolitan vision of international politics.[63] To be sure, Thucydides' Pericles contrasted favourably the Athenians' leisurely private business with the Spartans' regimented life, but to him, democracy's magic was the voluntary and spontaneous service individuals rendered to the city, their ability to move swiftly between private and military life. Thucydides' Pericles never questioned the subordination of individual to *polis*. Indeed, Athenian political grandeur was the central theme of 'Pericles'. Thus, in the Funeral Oration: 'Mighty indeed are the marks and monuments of our empire . . . Future ages will wonder at us, as the present age wonders at us now . . . for everywhere we have left behind us everlasting memorials of good done to our friends or suffering inflicted on our enemies.'[64]

Progressives have used the abolition of slavery as the litmus test of historical progress. It was impossible for Popper to deny Athenian slavery, but he invented an Athenian abolitionist movement. He elicited anti-slavery sentiments from sophists Lycophron, Alcidamas and Antisthenes.[65] All three were reputed to have been influenced by Gorgias. Popper established, therefore, the 'School of Gorgias'. The school embodied the Great Generation's ideals and led the Athenian abolitionism.[66] Other intellectuals joined. Sophists Hippias and Protagoras were members. They delivered speeches in the *Protagoras* about humanity's common origins and individuals' equal share in justice and political knowledge. (Neither Hippias nor Protagoras made any explicit reference to slaves or barbarians.)[67] Socrates was a member, too: did he

---

interpretation, and Pericles' other orations in the *History* that reflected power politics. Thucydides, *History of the Peloponnesian War*, trans. by R. Warner (New York, 1972), II, 40–4; II, 35–46, 60–4.

[62] *The Open Society*, I, chs. 5, 10.

[63] To use Isaiah Berlin's terminology, the Greeks did not possess a concept of 'negative liberty', the idea that the individual should be protected against state and society. Isaiah Berlin, 'Two Concepts of Liberty', in *Four Essays on Freedom* (New York, 1969). For the opposite view: M. H. Hansen, *The Athenian Democracy at the Age of Demosthenes* (Oxford, 1991).

[64] Thucydides, *History*, II, 41. Athenian 'individualism' was, indeed, one of Thucydides' themes, but he understood it differently from Popper: 'each man cultivates his own intelligence with a view to doing something notable for his city' (I, 70).

[65] For a detailed discussion of Popper and Lycophron see my *Karl Popper*, ch. 9.

[66] *The Open Society*, I, pp. 58–9, 100–103, 133–4, 161–2, 236–7 (n. 48).

[67] Plato, *Protagoras*, trans. by W.K.C. Guthrie, in *The Collected Dialogues of Plato*

not recognise the rationality of a slave in the *Meno* by using him to prove an axiom in geometry?[68] The attacks by the Old Oligarch, Plato, and Aristotle on slaves' unruliness in Athens proved the strength of Athenian abolitionism. The enemies of democracy combined criticism of Athenian pluralism with reproaches for Athenian indulgence towards slaves and foreigners.[69] They knew well that cosmopolitanism gave rise to abolitionism and were determined to squelch the Open Society before it abolished slavery forever.[70]

Popper underestimated the social limits of Athenian criticism. Athenian philosophers and dramatists may have recognised the conventional nature of slavery, perhaps even its injustice, but we have no record of opposition to slavery in Athens, political or intellectual. Aristotle contested the conventionalist (i.e. anti-naturalist) view of slavery in the *Politics*, so it was likely a competing discourse.[71] Plato questioned gender roles in the *Republic* and proposed abolishing the family. Such recognition of the social construction of fundamental distinctions could conceivably extend to slavery.[72] Euripides showed in his tragedies women, children and slaves as noble heroes, and gods and men as brutes. In the *Bacchae*, he reversed all distinctions of gender, age and race considered essential to the *polis*.[73] If he could turn upside-down social hierarchy and reverse social roles in his plays, it is not inconceivable that he, and others, entertained doubts about slavery. Yet, the debate on the injustice of slavery that was possible in principle did not take place historically; we are left with hints of heretical thoughts that intellectuals may have entertained. Slavery was essential to the *polis*, especially to the economically developed democratic *poleis*.[74] A city without slaves was utopian. Abolition would be tantamount to discarding private property and would probably necessitate the wide introduction of serfdom, along the Spartan model. Theoretical reflections about the justice of slavery were possible; practical abolitionist

(Princeton, 1963), 320d–323a (Protagoras' myth of common origins), 337d–338a (Hippias on 'kinship by nature').

[68] Meno 82b, trans. G.M.A. Grube, *Five Dialogues* (Indianapolis, 1981).

[69] Pseudo-Xenophon (Old Oligarch), *The Constitution of the Athenians*, in *Aristotle and Xenophon on Democracy and Oligarchy*, trans. by J.M. Moore (Berkeley, 1975), I 10–12; II 7–8; Plato, *Republic*, trans. by G.M.A. Grube and C.D.C. Reeve (Indianapolis, 1992), 557b–e, 562e–563b; Aristotle, *Politics*, trans. by Ernest Barker (New York, 1946), 1313b11.

[70] *The Open Society*, I, pp. 35–6, 58–9, 161–7, ch. 5, n. 13, ch. 8, n. 48.

[71] Aristotle, *Politics*, 1225a–b.

[72] Plato, *Republic*, 453a–461e.

[73] Euripides, *Alcestis, Bacchae, Trojan Women, Iphigineia in Aulis*, in *The Complete Greek Tragedies*, ed. by David Grene and Richmond Lattimore (4 vols., Chicago, 1959–60).

[74] Moses Finley, 'Was Greek Civilisation Based on Slavery?', in his *Economy and Society in Ancient Greece* (New York, 1982).

proposals were not. An Athenian abolitionist movement was highly improbable.[75]

Popper may have also exaggerated Athen's cultural openness. Athens proved more receptive to foreign influences than other Greek cities: commercial traffic through the Piraeus brought foreigners, with different dialects and dress, to the city. Conservative critics drew the same connections Popper did among commercialism, cosmopolitanism, cultural diversity and democracy, but Popper took their sarcastic portrayals of Athens literally. Athenian liberties were also more precarious than Popper conceded. Athens permitted unprecedented freedom of speech, but it did not protect it legally. The audience decided the limits of tolerance. Philosophers and dramatists wrote, spoke and performed at their own risk. They could, and were, sued for impiety. Popper regarded Socrates' execution as a single fateful aberration. It was not. Protagoras and Euripides both ended up in exile, possibly after judicial proceedings. Athenian intolerance was not just a myth created by democracy's enemies.[76]

Popper's idealisation of Athenian imperialism flew in the face of evidence of brutality. Athenian rule was not mild, but as harsh as Athens deemed necessary to accomplish its objectives: political hegemony and financial exploitation.[77] Thucydides remains our major literary source on Athenian imperialism. He recorded and analysed its growing harshness during the Peloponnesian War, describing two memorable episodes, Mytilene (427 BC) and Melos (416 BC). In the first, the Athenians almost put to death, or reduced to slavery, the population of a rebellious ally. In the second, they actually did so to a small island that refused to join their empire. Thucydides dramatised the episodes and may have omitted information explaining Athenian actions, but his testimony of the brutality remains incontrovertible. Popper doubted it and decided to overlook it. Even if 'wanton attacks' occurred, they should not obscure the glory of cosmopolitan imperialism.[78]

---

[75] '[Philosopher Michael] Foster (who worked out all your references) and [Roman historian Ronald] Syme . . . both maintained that your picture of a humanitarian liberal equalitarian movement in Athens had no foundation . . . [B]oth thought you had read back nineteenth-century liberalism into an era where there was not the faintest gleam of it as a political force or a "movement".' J.D. Mabbott to Popper, 8 July 1947 (Popper Archives (28, 10)).

[76] A.H.M. Jones, 'The Athenian Democracy and Its Critics', *The Historical Journal*, 11 (1953), pp. 1–26 thinks otherwise. His sympathetic account of Athenian freedoms is close to that of Popper.

[77] Moses Finley, 'The Athenian Empire: a Balance Sheet', in *Economy and Society*.

[78] Thucydides, *History*, III 2–50, v 84–116. Both Jones, 'The Athenian Democracy', and Moses Finley, 'The Melian Dialogue', in Thucydides, *History*, appendix 3, believe that Athens behaved in accordance with Greek norms. They challenge Thucydides' anti-Athenian bias and question his narrative of growing harshness. They do not dispute,

Seeking to vindicate progressive dreams against Fascism, Popper read his political hopes for Central Europe into classical Athens. The disintegration of the Habsburg monarchy doomed the progressives' hopes for a democratic empire. No agent for cosmopolitanism existed any longer. Classical Athens was both a democracy and an empire. So was Britain: a maritime liberal commonwealth, fighting a continental totalitarian enemy.[79] Sparta – a military caste ruling over serfs, closing the borders to foreign influences, maintaining an autarkic rural economy – was the epitome of the closed society. To Popper, it resembled Nazi Germany. The Peloponnesian War became Second World War. In ancient Greece, Popper finally discovered his ideal empire: classical Athens. It mattered little that it happened two millennia ago, far from Central Europe. Kant's cosmopolitan federation transcended place and time. Where the Habsburg Empire failed, Athens succeeded. Progressive imperialism triumphed over nationalism and ethno-politics. Against Athens' conservative critics, Popper defended his vision of a democratic cosmopolitan empire advancing human emancipation. Where he found success once, the exile could hope, amidst global ruins, for another.

V

In a scholarly world where Grote and Cornford drew the boundaries of acceptable criticism of Plato, the post-war debate on totalitarianism and ancient philosophy would not have taken place. Popper made it possible. He showed that philosophy was entangled with totalitarianism from its origin, and utopianism, intellectual conceit and political ambition were intertwined among philosophers from Plato to Hegel to Toynbee. He exposed not only masters, but also a tradition. Not the radical right alone was implicated, but classical liberal education, too. Still, Popper retained a belief in the 'West' and the Greeks' crucial role in its formation. He distinguished between the historical and the 'ideal' West, identifying the latter with the Open Society, rationality (i.e. critical discussion) and Athenian democracy.[80] Against the ideal West, he posited the closed society. Societies that had not developed critical

---

however, his reports of Athenian brutality. Popper was unsure: *The Open Society*, I, p. 158.

[79] Steven Beller suggested to me the British-Athenian parallel and emphasised that it must have informed *The Open Society*.

[80] He quoted approvingly (*The Open Society*, I, ch. 7, n. 12) Richard Crossman (*Plato Today* (New York, 1939), p. 93): 'Socrates showed that philosophy is nothing else than conscientious objection to prejudice and unreason . . . All that is good in our Western culture has sprung from this spirit . . . [This] is the only force which can break the dictatorship of force and greed.'

discourse were closed. Advanced polities had closed and open dimensions, but they had moved furthest away from the closed society. People entered relationships, formed groups and exited communities based on choice and preference, not blood relations. Change in the Open Society was rapid, and conflict permanent, but there was no way back: 'we must go on into the unknown'.[81]

How did one open a closed community? Popper suggested that cross-cultural interaction in a multinational empire could do so: 'tribalist exclusiveness and self-sufficiency could be superseded only by some form of imperialism'.[82] Empires permitted enlightenment to penetrate ghettoes and lowered barriers among ethnic groups. He was willing to see an imperial metropolis temporarily gain at the expense of the peripheries for the sake of an eventual dissolution of the boundaries between centre and margins. The possibilities for abuse – by nationalism, no less – were colossal, but Popper somehow hoped that empire would promote *Aufklärung* rather than racial *Deutschtum*. Like other Austrophiles, he regarded Prussia and Austria, German nationalism and Habsburg imperialism, as conflicting and enlightenment and empire as concordant. Still, Central Europe demonstrated that empire did not tame nationalism; nationalism undermined empire.

Assuming success, how multinational, or culturally diverse, would the cosmopolitan empire be? Would the triumph of enlightenment over the ghetto not imply a universal (progressive) German identity? Most Germans, Czechs and Jews concurred that the *Aufklärung* was German. Was it not pseudo-universal? Popper denied this – and with good reason. Ideas emerging from national contexts may well have universal potential. Moreover, cosmopolitanism and *Spätaufklärung* were projects of the Central European Jewish intelligentsia as much as – nay, more than – of German intellectuals. All the same, the dilemmas of universalism were real, and, like most liberals, Popper was not able to negotiate effectively between nationalism and cosmopolitanism, communal diversity and universal humanity, the closed and Open Society.

The gap between cosmopolitan dream and ethno-national realities came back to haunt Popper with a vengeance. He presented his views on the Jewish Question as flowing from his cosmopolitanism. He thought that anti-Semitism disclosed the natural hostility of an indigenous community towards strangers. Assimilation was a moral imperative, and Jewish nationality and religion were impediments to cosmopolitanism. He got the relationship between assimilation and cosmopolitanism wrong. Assimilation under threat violated cosmopolitanism. Precisely

[81] Popper, *The Open Society*, I, p. 177.
[82] Ibid., I, p. 158.

assimilation's failure gave rise to cosmopolitanism. Assimilated Central European Jews rejected Jewish identity, but failed to gain acceptance into their nations. Imagined cosmopolitan communities were the only societies they hoped would accept Jews. Cosmopolitanism was a precondition for assimilation, not vice versa.

Popper thought that there was little worth saving in Judaism. He regarded the Hebrew Bible as the fountainhead of tribal nationalism. Hearing as a young boy the biblical story of the Golden Calf, said Popper, he had recognised the roots of religious intolerance in Jewish monotheism. Oppressed and persecuted, Jews in the Babylonian exile created the doctrine of the Chosen People, presaging modern visions of chosen class and race.[83] Both Roman imperialism and early Christian humanitarianism threatened the Jews' tribal exclusivity. Jewish orthodoxy reacted by reinforcing tribal bonds, shutting Jews off from the world for two millennia. The ghetto was the ultimate closed society, a 'petrified form of Jewish tribalism'.[84] Its inhabitants lived in misery, ignorance and superstition, their separate existence evoking the suspicion and hatred of non-Jews and fuelling anti-Semitism. Enlightened Jews should help their unfortunate co-religionists make the transition to the modern world. Integration into non-Jewish society was the only solution to the Jewish problem. Any stumbling block must be removed. Even a merely religious community carried the stigma of Jewish ethnic, or national, separateness. Better go the extra step and dissolve the community altogether.

Zionism was a colossal mistake, and Israel a tragic error. They retarded a solution to the Jewish Question, and incited a national conflict between Jews and Arabs. 'The *status quo* is the only possible policy in that maze of nations which peoples Europe and the Near East,' and Zionism disrupted the *status quo* in Palestine.[85] Once Israel was established, Popper recognised the need to prevent annihilation of the Jewish community there, and 'strongly opposed all those who sympathise with the Arab attempts to expel them'.[86] But Israel's treatment of Arabs elicited his harsh condemnation:

Of all the countries benefiting from European civilisation, only South Africa and Israel have racial laws that distinguish between rights of different groups of citizens. The Jews were against Hitler's racism, but theirs goes one step further. They determine Jewishness by mother alone. I opposed Zionism initially because I was against any form of nationalism, but I never expected the Zionists

[83] Karl Popper, 'Toleration and Intellectual Responsibility', in his *In Search of a Better World*, pp. 188–90; Popper, *The Open Society*, I, pp. 6–8, 179 (n. 3); II, pp. 21–2.
[84] Popper, *The Open Society*, II, ch. 11, n. 56.
[85] Draft of *Autobiography*, Popper Archives (135, 1), section 20.
[86] Ibid.

to become racists. It makes me feel ashamed in my origin: I feel responsible for the deeds of Israeli nationalists.[87]

Popper treated Jewish religion, nationality and ethnicity as if they were interchangeable and reducible to race. In fact, they were intricately related both historically and theologically. Divergent Jewish communities viewed the relationship differently. Liberal Jews discovered enlightenment cosmopolitanism in Judaism. Zionist socialists rejected traditional religion, but negotiated between Jewish nationality and socialist internationalism. Even traditional Jews defined themselves more as a religious community bound by belief and practice than in ethnic terms. Besides, Jewish ethnicity was no more incompatible with the Open Society than other ethnicities whose continued existence Popper tolerated. He was prescient in observing the emergence of Jewish racism under the conditions of ethno-national conflict in Israel. 'The connection between religion and nationalism is most dangerous,' he said, especially when the Hebrew Bible sanctioned genocide.[88] Still, obnoxious, discriminatory and oppressive as Israeli laws and policies may have been, physical genocide has been neither their goal nor end-result, so they could not be 'one step further' than Hitler's racism.

Many assimilated Viennese Jews shared Popper's anti-Jewish convictions. Liberal Jews' critique of Zionism and of Jewish orthodoxy was almost equally fierce. Such discourses have prompted scholars to hypothesise about Jewish self-hatred and its origin in the assimilationists' acceptance of enlightenment pseudo-universalism. Admittedly, Popper expressed ambivalence about his Jewish background. He claimed to have cut his cords to Jews, yet felt 'ashamed' in his origin and 'responsible' for the Zionists. None the less, an explanation in terms of the 'pathology' of assimilation is inadequate. Popper's rhetoric expressed not hatred of the self, but concern for it. He did not internalise antisemitic norms, trying to transform a despised Jewish self into a respectable one. He was anxious lest Jewishness and Zionism provoke ugly and contemptible anti-Semitism. Not cosmopolitanism, but anti-Semitism made it impossible for him to negotiate between Jewish identity and cosmopolitan principles. Jews, he knew, would not be accepted as such. They had to disappear as Jews. They could only become cosmopolitan citizens in a Kantian Kingdom of Ends. Central European reality intruded into cosmopolitan dreams.

Popper's analysis of anti-Semitism explains his fervent assimilationism:

---

[87] My interview with Popper, 26 January 1984.
[88] My interview and Popper, 'Toleration', pp. 188–90.

My father had decided that living in an overwhelmingly Christian society imposed the obligation to give as little offence as possible – to become assimilated. This needed some courage, for it meant to arouse the hatred, and the attacks, of organised Judaism . . . [But] anti-Semitism was to be feared, and it was the task of all people of Jewish origin to do their best not to provoke it. It was most understandable that people who were despised for their racial origin should insist that they were proud of it. But the logic of this racial pride was, obviously, mutual contempt, and ultimately racial war . . .

In Austria, anti-Semitism was very largely the resistance of an autochthonous population against infiltration from outside . . . The Jews *were* 'guests' in Austria . . . I believe that [they] were treated as well, or better, than one could expect. There was almost every career open to Jews. [But t]he situation changed radically for the worse with the dissolution of the Austrian Empire . . . The Jews achieved full equality, at least before the law and, understandably but not wisely, invaded politics and journalism . . . The influx of the Jews into the parties of the left contributed to the downfall of these parties.[89]

In these staggering statements, Popper draws us back from cosmopolitan dreams to ethno-political realities. Anti-Semitism was to be feared at all times and places. Jews were not to expect fulfilment of cosmopolitanism's promise, but to accommodate themselves to anti-Semitism. They were wrong to take advantage of openings in society and stupid to draw attention to their wealth and success. Popper reversed the roles of persecutor and victim. Jews infiltrated Austria, invaded politics and journalism, attacked assimilationists, provoked anti-Semitism. By assuming leadership positions among the socialists, they contributed to the triumph of Fascism. Retaining Jewish identity, they triggered a racial war that brought their own destruction. Popper's discourse descended from cosmopolitanism dangerously close to anti-Semitism.

Mortal fear of anti-Semitism accounts for Popper's willingness to tamper with cosmopolitanism. Liberal and assimilationist Jews imagined a cosmopolitan community accepting them, but anti-Semitism constantly reminded them of the hopelessness of cosmopolitanism. Reality conflicted with dream. Anti-Semitism was a given, an immutable, if regrettable, fact, the response of a native population to strangers. Jewish identity, in contrast, seemed a variable, subject to change. Popper, like many progressives, thought the price of integration right. Confusing assimilation with cosmopolitanism and pretending that humanity would remain intact if threats forced Jews to disappear, he gave up a tribal religion to join humanity. The refusal of most Jews to join seemed reactionary and treacherous, putting assimilation at risk by fuelling anti-

---

[89] Draft of *Autobiography*, section 20 (later 21), Popper Archives (135, 1). I used the corrected typescript (pp. 140–1), but retained phrases that appeared in the earlier holograph (21 pages long). See also p. 142 of the slightly later version (137, 3).

Semitism. Recalcitrant Jews, rather than anti-Semites, became the Jewish problem.

The triumph of ethno-nationalism throughout Central Europe made reconciling German and Jewish identities impossible. The result was an indeterminate identity for assimilated Jews. If assimilation were possible, Popper would become a German Austrian. But neither would anyone but progressives accept him as German any time after 1880, nor would he, sworn enemy of nationalism, wish to become one. Enlightenment cosmopolitanism appealed to Popper and liberal Jews precisely because of their life in-between cultures and their indeterminate identity. The German *Aufklärung* may have been their cosmopolitanism's source, but few Austrians secure in their German identity promoted cosmopolitanism. Jewish intellectuals appropriated enlightenment traditions because they promised a home, an alternative to the ethno-national *Heimat*.

'There . . . always will be [a] "Republic of Scholars",' avowed art historian Ernst Gombrich, a Viennese émigré and a close Popper friend.[90] Claiming membership in such an imagined cosmopolitan community, Popper rejected Jewish identity. 'I do not consider myself "an assimilated German Jew",' he told a critic of his *Autobiography:* 'this is how "the *Führer*" would have considered me.'[91] Could he be included in the Jewish Year Book, inquired an editor in 1969. No, answered Popper, 'I am of Jewish descent, but . . . I abhor any form of racialism or nationalism; and I never belonged to the Jewish faith. Thus I do not see on what grounds I could possibly consider myself a Jew.'[92] What was he, then? 'I do not feel myself an Englishman [but] a Central European who works in England,' said Gombrich.[93] 'We scientists or scholars, *res publica litterarum*, stick together and our home is our work.' So Popper, Gombrich and other émigrés thought of themselves both as 'Central Europeans' *and* as citizens of a timeless and contextless Republic of Letters.

The émigrés' professions of identity must always be consulted, but they cannot always be accepted. Identities are not merely personal self-identifications; they also have collective historical dimensions. 'Once labels [such as "Jew"] are applied to people, ideas about people who fit

[90] Ernst Gombrich, 'Austria Later Awarded Me All Sorts of Orders . . .', in Friedrich Stadler and Peter Weibl (eds.), *Vertreibung der Vernunft: The Cultural Exodus from Austria*, 2nd edn (New York, 1995), p. 333.
[91] Popper to M. Smith, 7 August 1982, Popper Archives (407, 17).
[92] Popper to Michael Wallach, 6 January 1969, Popper Archives (313, 10). He softened his stance in later years, agreeing to be included in Herlinde Koelbl's *Jüdische Portraits: Photographien und Interviews* (Frankfurt, 1989), pp. 189–90.
[93] Gombrich, 'Austria', p. 333.

the label come to have social and psychological effects. In particular, these ideas shape the ways people conceive of themselves and their projects [and] provide what we might call scripts: narratives that people can use in . . . telling their life stories.'[94] 'Assimilated Jew' is an ascribed identity, not a self-identification, but it captures well 'the social and psychological effects' that shaped the émigrés' life chances and imagination. Their self-identification as cosmopolites and Central Europeans represented an effort to overcome the collective identity ascribed to them, but they were not successful. 'Collective identities . . . are products of histories; and our engagement with them invokes capacities that are not under our control.'[95] Their force in shaping experience and imagination may be such that they become social reality. In contrast, 'Central Europe', the Republic of Scholars and the Open Society remained projects, imagined communities, not historical ones. Using 'assimilated Jew' to describe and analyse Popper and the intelligentsia, I neither follow in 'the *Führer*'s' steps nor deny cosmopolitanism. I simply recognise that collective identities both invoked and set limits to cosmopolitanism. I hope, with Popper, for a world where such limits will no longer exist.

Marginal and utopian, Central European cosmopolitanism tottered for decades on the brink of disaster, then succumbed to ethno-nationalism. It represents the Central Europe we would like to remember, the vanished dreams that migrated West with refugee intellectuals, or went up Auschwitz's chimneys in smoke. Popper immortalised them in the Open Society. His cosmopolitanism was not free of problems, but neither his assimilationism nor his anti-Zionism was a logical conclusion of his cosmopolitanism. Rather, they reflected the impossible situation of Central European Jewry. In different contexts – in the contemporary USA, for example – Jewish identity has proved perfectly compatible with integration. In a new Middle East, Zionism may prove compatible with cosmopolitanism. As the recent revival of the debate on cosmopolitanism shows, the prospects for Popper's vision seem better today than at any time in the twentieth century. It would be a mistake to give up on its emancipatory potential.

Central European cosmopolitanism has so far attracted scant attention because the national paradigm remains hegemonic. This paradigm does not allow one to trace an international community, rooted in the experience of an ethnic minority across different Central European

---

[94] K. Anthony Appiah, 'Liberalism in Difficulty', a paper submitted to the Intellectual History Seminar 'Liberalism and Its Critics' at the National Humanities Center, September 1999.

[95] Ibid.

countries, and ending up as a global Diaspora. To serve as a useful analytical category, the nation must open to the international, but also be deconstructed into local sites for the formation of knowledge, with ethnic and class fault lines often drawing the boundaries of such sites. Such analytical use of the nation does not conflict with Popper's critique. Imagined national communities 'flourish despite . . . their roots in myths and lies' and often constitute the logic of the historical situation. But, if 'there is . . . no large place for reason in the construction of identities', there is room for their rational management.[96] Following the imperative of rational management, Popper demystified national identity; following the imperatives of humanity and citizenship, he invented cosmopolitan identity. Historians collide with Popper only if they accept nations as holistic entities, principles in no need of explanation.

Still, antipathy to the nation creates major difficulties for cosmopolitanism. The greatest, and the one least addressed, is the lack of cosmopolitan solidarity. Cosmopolites are commonly people who have themselves crossed political and cultural boundaries, who thrive on cultural hybridisation, see in closed communities a threat and wish to make the whole world a home. They may recognise the needs of rooted people, but they have little sympathy for them and no alternative source of solidarity to the national, ethnic or religious community. Central European cosmopolites were blind to their own homelessness and to the bonds tying their Republic of Letters. Theirs was a solidarity formed, under external nationalist threat, among members of an ethnic minority, acculturated in the national culture, wishing but unable to assimilate, searching for a cosmopolitan homeland.[97] Could they really hope to extend these bonds, formed in particular historical experiences, over the globe? How could they hope to appeal to people who were perfectly at home in their relatively closed communities? 'In democratic ages', said Tocqueville, 'the bond of human affections widens but loosens.'[98] The broader the bonds of obligation and loyalty stretch, the looser they are. The challenge of the next generation of cosmopolites is to find resources for cosmopolitan patriotism and cultivate them. Only then will reality begin striving towards a cosmopolitan utopia.

[96] Kwame Anthony Appiah, *In My Father's House: Africa in the Philosophy of Culture* (New York, 1992), p. 178. Appiah speaks here of identities in general.
[97] I explore the themes of homelessness and the pursuit of homeland in 'Karl Popper in Exile'.
[98] Alexis de Tocqueville, *De la démocratie en Amérique*, ed. by J.P. Mayer, 2 vols., in *Oeuvres Complètes* (Paris, 1961), II. p. 106. A conversation with historian David Hollinger has evoked these reflections on solidarity as a problem for cosmopolitanism.

Disciplines, canons, and publics: the
history of 'the history of political thought'
in comparative perspective

Stefan Collini

> It is always desirable that a part of the education of those persons who
> are either born into, or qualified by their abilities to enter, the superior
> political grades of society, should be instruction in history, and that a
> part of the study of history should be the history of political theory.
>
> (T.S. Eliot, *Notes Towards the Definition of Culture* (London, 1948), p. 88)

I

As a social critic, T.S. Eliot could scarcely be accused of an excess of
relativism. Here, his assertion of what is 'always desirable' is, of course,
part of his coolly mandarin tone, and that tone is the natural vehicle for
the assumption that there is a class, largely selected by birth, destined to
control the political affairs of a country, an assumption clearly intended
as a calculated provocation in the Britain of the 1945 Labour government. The passage is, in these respects, characteristic of the later Eliot's
persistent attempt, in the face of disagreeable social change, to appear to
be taking the assumptions of the day before yesterday for granted. But as
the sequence 'education', 'instruction' and 'study' suggests, one assumption which Eliot could indeed take for granted was that, in
referring to 'the history of political theory', he was referring to something that was by this date an acknowledged part of an established
academic practice. It was, as we shall see, part of his conservatism to
presume that the larger academic practice in question was 'the study of
history', yet even in this detail the passage offers a usefully concise, if
somewhat oblique, indication of the themes of this 'Postscript'.

The declared purpose of *The History of Political Thought in National
Context* is to address the relationship between the enterprise conventionally labelled 'the history of political thought' and the political cultures of
the different countries within which it has been practised. As the editors'
Introduction puts it, the volume aims at 'the twofold objective of putting

national traditions within the context of their own political culture and discussing the more general relationship between the history of political thought and political discourse at large'. This is clearly a valuable approach to the topic, and nothing I say in what follows should be taken as suggesting that the two-way relationship between the systematic study of past political thinking and the characteristics of particular political cultures, with their distinctive discourses, preoccupations and varying histories, can be neglected.

However, in this 'Postscript' I should like to shift the focus in several ways. After all, it may be characteristic of practitioners of the history of political thought who are lodged in departments of politics that, in seeking to account for the variety of forms the enterprise has taken, their inclination is to look to the varieties of national *political* culture. By contrast, I want in the first part of this chapter to suggest that we gain at least as much understanding of this variety by attending to the different *intellectual* and *academic* cultures as to the different national 'political discourses'. In particular, we need to attend to the different ways in which 'the map of the disciplines' has been drawn in different academic cultures, and this is something with deep roots in their respective intellectual traditions often stretching far back into the nineteenth century or even beyond. In the second section, I want briefly to consider some of the different relations in which a canon of 'classic' texts may stand to the contemporary practice of an academic discipline. This may help us to isolate certain structural features of the enterprise of 'the history of political thought', at least as it has been most influentially practised in the English-speaking world, which in turn may enable us to account for some of the recurrent, and even repetitive, controversies that have marked its own history. In this section, therefore, comparison between countries is replaced by comparison between disciplines. In the third section, I touch briefly on the limitations of 'discipline history': in particular, I call the conventional opposition between 'narrow professionalism' and 'a public role' into question, and I suggest that we need instead to consider a variety of relations to overlapping 'publics'. This leads to a polemical conclusion about who may be best equipped to write the history of the enterprise of 'the history of political thought'. If what I have said in the earlier sections is persuasive, it will become clear that the answer may not be 'historians of political thought'.

Let me first enter one caveat about the problems involved in doing comparative intellectual history (which, implicitly, is what these chapters collectively offer to do). There is no single enterprise or entity corresponding to what in English-speaking countries has most often been called 'the history of political thought', and this immediately raises the question of how far these chapters are about the same, or even about a meaningfully comparable, thing. There is a fundamental difficulty to be faced in all attempts to undertake comparative studies in cultural history: since the units or objects of comparison are culturally defined, the exercise of comparison always implicitly posits a kind of overarching or transcendent category of which each of the national examples is a kind of variant or sub-set; but in practice, this larger category is always likely to bear the marks of the national version with which the historian is most familiar. The ostensible 'comparison' then all too easily ends up neglecting the specificity of other cultural patterns in order to fasten on to the presence, or more polemically the absence, of an entity or activity described in terms derived from the historian's own culture. As Michel Trebitsch expressed it recently, summarising an extensive literature, there is no escaping 'le fait que les comparaisons s'opèrent toujours d'un point de vue national, ce qui les empêche d'élaborer de véritables outils comparatifs et les enferme dans des catégories purement abstraites. Le *tertium comparationis*, la grill commune d'analyse qu'implique toute comparaison, loin de dégager des signifiés commensurables, n'est le plus souvent que la projection sur l'autre d'un point de vue strictement national.'[1]

This is certainly true where the activity or entity in question is supposed to be 'the history of political thought'. This term itself already slices up reality in slightly different ways from various near-analogues in English, and the lack of exact correspondence only becomes more pronounced as we move across 'l'histoire des idées politiques', 'Geschichte der Staatslehre', 'la storia delle dottrine politiche' and so on. And each of these terms in turn has encompassed a variety of referents depending upon the more exact chronological, cultural and institutional location of their use. In making comparisons here, therefore, we need to recognise the heuristic function which the (anglophone) notion of 'the history of political thought' plays in organising the enquiry (and in providing the rationale for this volume). My relatively sparse remarks about the situations in other countries are intended to do no more than to provide an occasional reminder of the historical specificities built into this organising notion.

---

[1] Michel Trebitsch, 'L'histoire comparée des intellectuels en Europe: quelques points de méthode et propositions de recherche', in Michel Trebitsch and Marie-Christine Granjon (eds.), *Pour une histoire comparée des intellectuels* (Paris, 1998), p. 40. Trebitsch is at this point particularly citing the work of Michel Espagne, especially his 'Sur les limites du comparatisme en histoire culturelle', *Genèses*, 17 (1994), pp. 112–21.

II

While the broad areas of human interest denoted by such generic terms as history, literature or philosophy clearly both antedate, and continue to exceed the boundaries of, any particular pedagogic activity, the enterprise known as 'the history of political thought' initially came into being and derived its identity from an educational practice. Of course, an interest in aspects of the past of any human activity may be pursued under all kinds of disciplinary labels and under none. But there is none the less a significant difference between, on the one hand, the terms we may retrospectively use to designate the intellectual interests of a particular individual or group and, on the other, the title of a 'subject', an academic practice carried on in certain established institutional contexts. No doubt there were scholars undertaking enquiries in the late nineteenth and early twentieth centuries into what we may wish to call 'the history of aesthetic thought' or 'the history of epistemological thought' and so on, but these were not at the time (or perhaps since) recognised as the labels of separate 'subjects'. However, if one is interested in the historical development of 'the history of political thought', one is interested in an aspect or episode of the intellectual and institutional history of academic disciplines within this period. In other words, although there had been, needless to say, a long tradition of systematic reflection upon politics, it was not the case that some previously existing activity called 'the history of political thought' was, in this period, taken into the universities; rather, that notion, in the forms in which we are familiar with it, is the *creation* of these disciplinary practices.

The social and institutional roots of these practices lie in two developments in particular: first, a very significant expansion, most dramatic in the United States, of systems of higher education, which involved an increase in the numbers of students and teachers, the introduction of new subjects into the established curricula and the elaboration of a professionalised academic identity; and second, an expansion of the traditional governing classes, including a marked growth in the numbers of civil servants of all kinds, including, for the leading European nations, colonial administrators.[2]

It was against this background that the aspiration to develop a 'science of politics' took on a new and more pedagogic form, particularly where it could be seen to offer an appropriate training for a future political and administrative elite, as was the case, for example, with

[2] This and the following paragraph draw upon my *Public Moralists: Political Thought and Intellectual Life in Britain 1850–1930* (Oxford, 1991), pp. 248–9.

Emile Boutmy and his courses in 'les sciences politiques' at the Ecole Libre des Sciences Politiques in Paris, with J.W. Burgess and his teaching of 'government' at Columbia, or with J.R. Seeley and his lectures on 'political science' in Cambridge. A central place in these enterprises was occupied by what was usually referred to as 'the theory of the state', a subject on which Aristotle and Hobbes were understood to be no less relevant authorities than, say, Bluntschli or Sidgwick. At the same time, the immense impact of German historical scholarship was still being felt across a range of intellectual activities outside Germany, especially those activities which wished to lay claim to an academic title as 'science'. One of the more obvious ways in which this impinged on the nascent study of politics was in the so-called comparative method, with its tracing of the lines of descent, notably from Aryan roots, of modern political forms.[3] This was frequently married without noticeable friction to an emphasis which it would be too narrow to describe simply as Hegelian, but which was an integral part of that idealism which pervaded German historical thinking and thus left its mark elsewhere, namely the belief that the skeleton of world history in its centrally political dimension could be traced in the most reflective forms of the political consciousness of each epoch. We also need to remember the immense hold of classical humanism over the German educated class and the possibilities for cultural criticism suggested by that ethos, especially for mounting a case against liberalism or even modernity as such (a tradition diffused, notably in the United States, by later generations of German émigrés). These strands coalesced in a fresh interest in charting the phases of the history of political ideas, an interest one can see developing in that series of works which begins with Gierke and Bluntschli in Germany from the 1860s onwards, with Janet in France from the 1870s, with Pollock and later Figgis and the Carlyles in England from the 1880s and 1890s, and with Dunning and others in the United States from the 1890s and 1900s.

Each of these examples has its own complex history, of course, but for the purposes of a comparative survey, one way to disentangle the different strands of the story is to see the various incarnations of 'the history of political thought' as a coming together in specific institutional contexts in the late nineteenth and early twentieth centuries of four different impulses.

The first impulse came from the tradition of moral philosophy which elaborated itself in early modern Europe, and which in the course of the

[3] See Stefan Collini, Donald Winch and John Burrow, 'The Clue to the Maze: the Appeal of the Comparative Method', in S. Collini, D. Winch and J. Burrow, *That Noble Science of Politics: a Study in Nineteenth-Century Intellectual History* (Cambridge, 1983), pp. 207–46.

eighteenth and nineteenth centuries became more self-conscious about a certain continuity or canon of major figures. Academically, this tradition had its strongest roots in the study of the classics, but it also came to be a central feature in the teaching of philosophy as that subject began to be institutionalised in universities in Europe and the United States in the course of the nineteenth century. As such an academic or pedagogic practice, of course, the point was not principally to study the *history* of moral philosophy, but to study *moral philosophy*, but it was also true that in continental European countries, in particular, commentary upon the classics of philosophy remained at the heart of an education in philosophy.

The second impulse, which only acquired self-conscious form in the course of the nineteenth century, was what (as I indicated earlier) was usually referred to as 'the theory of the state'. In all countries this had strong roots in the law; the focus was upon the formal-legal analysis of the structure and functions of government, embedded within a larger jurisprudential discourse which touched the boundaries of moral philosophy at one extreme (the nature of rights, obligations and so on), especially in those societies where the natural law tradition was strong, and which engaged with current decisions in constitutional and public law on the other. This last point of contact was obviously strongest in those countries which combined a written constitution with an inheritance of Roman law, a category to which Britain conspicuously did not belong.

The third impulse derived from the dominant nineteenth-century style of political or constitutional history, which encouraged an interest in the history of the political ideas and attitudes that had been operative in earlier periods. A major part of the rationale for attending to this kind of history was that it was often thought an essential element of understanding or explaining those past political practices or events that had shaped the modern polity, in the form, for example, of the ideas supposedly informing the evolution of civil liberties in seventeenth- and eighteenth-century England or the theories alleged to have inspired the French Revolution and so on. The topical and ephemeral writings which provided many of the sources for such inquiries were, it is worth remarking, worlds away from the abstract treatises with which the moral philosophers concerned themselves.

The fourth and final impulse was clearly subsequent to the others chronologically and was in a sense secondary to them, for it involved the expression of a kind of academic self-consciousness, namely an interest in the history of earlier attempts to study politics and to develop some general theories and methods for doing so. It may now be difficult to imagine prescribing Montesquieu's *De l'esprit des lois* or Austin's *Lectures on Jurisprudence* as how-to-do-it books for the aspiring student of politics, but these and similar works came to figure on late nineteenth-century syllabuses for this more narrowly methodological reason as well as for reasons of piety and cultural legitimation. More or less all academic disciplines eventually generate some such parade of ancestors and precursors, and wherever the notion of the disciplinary identity of political science began to appear at all strongly, as in the United States above all, then a sequence of works of past political theorists came to be attended to as providing the requisite genealogy.

The results of the interplay or blending of these different impulses varied depending on the intellectual traditions and institutional settings within which they took place, but there were certain broad similarities, including the way in which these developments deposited a strikingly heterogeneous collection of past writings in syllabuses by the end of the nineteenth century. It is certainly not easy to see how otherwise to account for the juxtaposition of, say, Kant's *Grundlegen zur Metaphysik der Sitten*, Blackstone's *Commentaries on the Laws of England*, the Abbé Sièyes's *Qu'est ce que c'est le tiers état?* and Burgess's *Political Science and Comparative Constitutional Law*. Although national traditions in these matters were more significant at the end of the nineteenth century than at the end of the twentieth, there was even then a certain amount of international contact and mutual influence, especially stemming from the authority of German models: Bluntschli's *Allgemeine Staatslehre*, first published in 1851 and translated into English in 1885, served as a set text in Oxford and Johns Hopkins as well as in Heidelberg. Indeed, the English translation, entitled *The Theory of the Modern State*, was undertaken by a team of Oxford scholars led by D.G. Ritchie precisely in order to meet the needs of the first cohort of students to take the 'political science' option in the Oxford Modern History Schools. It was revealingly described by Ritchie as 'an attempt to do for the European State what Aristotle had accomplished for the Hellenic'.[4] As this suggests, these texts were not at this point regarded as landmarks in the history of thinking about politics, but as substantive guides to the nature of politics itself. The shift from the latter status to the former was particularly notable at Cambridge, where Seeley's initial vision of an inductive science of political institutions was eventually diluted into papers in the history of political thought without some of the familiar

---

[4] For Bluntschli's place in the Oxford syllabus, see Julia Stapleton, *Englishness and the Study of Politics: the Social and Political Thought of Ernest Barker* (Cambridge, 1994), pp. 57–8; for Johns Hopkins, see John G. Gunnell, *The Descent of Political Theory: the Genealogy of an American Vocation* (Chicago, 1993), pp. 32–3.

sequence of texts from Aristotle to Burke ever losing their place in successive syllabuses.[5]

Considering this history in more structural terms, one might say that the enterprises which, from their beginnings in the late nineteenth century, came to be labelled as 'the history of political thought' were carried on at the points of intersection or overlap among four related academic disciplines – philosophy, law, history and politics – and the particular shape taken by the enterprise in any given time and place was largely determined by which of these subjects has exerted the greatest gravitational pull or dominance. The demonstration of this point would require a more detailed account of syllabuses and committees and so on than is appropriate here, but the career of Ernest Barker may be allowed to provide a neatly symbolic representation of these shifts in disciplinary affiliation.

Educated in 'Greats' at Oxford in the 1890s, Barker absorbed the dominant idealist ethos, and later claimed he had gained his 'general conception of political science' from T.H. Green's *Lectures on the Principles of Political Obligation*. Increasingly, however, Barker came to treat 'law as the institutional essence of the state', and he was actively involved in the (ultimately unsuccessful) attempt in 1915 to establish a 'Master of Civil Science' degree at Oxford, the programme of which 'took law rather than philosophy as its mainstay'. Following his election to the newly founded Cambridge chair of political science in 1927, Barker found himself in a history faculty still partly loyal to its Seeleyan inheritance, though this did not prevent him from turning what had once been papers in 'political science' and 'comparative politics' into papers in 'the history of political thought'. But the disciplinary wheel still had one further revolution to make, and in 1950 the aged Barker figured as one of the founders of the Political Studies Association, the first professional body in Britain devoted to the study of politics.[6] The point, of course, is not that Barker's work underwent unusually drastic changes – he was hardly noted for his intellectual volatility, and he carried on explicating the work of Aristotle and company through all these shifts in professional identity – but rather that the institutional fate of 'the history of political thought' depended upon movements among the larger disciplinary ice floes.

At this point, it may be worth reminding ourselves again of how these curricular developments were implicated in larger cultural and institutional histories. One brief comparison must stand in here for a more

---

[5] See Collini et al., and *That Noble Science*, pp. 349–51.
[6] I take these details of Barker's career from Stapleton, *Englishness and the Study of Politics*, pp. 29, 64, 60–1, 130, 198–9.

systematic survey of these variations. In the United States in the late nineteenth and early twentieth centuries, the rapidly multiplying and expanding institutions of higher education sought, in a somewhat hostile social environment, to establish and defend their legitimacy in terms of 'scientific objectivity', ostensibly distanced from mere partisanship though still directed at practical ends, such as 'social reform'. Attempting to provide such an education for a wide range of citizens and not just for a small governing class, universities and even colleges founded a series of departments of 'social science', including very notably 'political science', which has even been spoken of as a distinctively American invention.[7] As John Gunnell and others have argued, the notion of 'political theory' grew up as part of the academic practice of 'political science'; as a result, in the United States, 'the subfield of political theory has characteristically been the locus of self-reflection about the state of political science, its past and its future prospects'. Indeed, Gunnell suggests that 'many of the images of political theory that have populated the field and held its practitioners captive . . . have been generated within, and have little sense and reference outside, this academic practice'.[8] It was this notion of 'political theory' which attempted to legitimate itself by 'providing itself with an authoritative past and a philosophically compelling self-image', that is to say by appropriating a supposed 'tradition' of great political theorists of the past from Plato to Mill (or whoever was held to be the most recent exemplar). Many other forces were to help shape and complicate this story, to be sure, not least the enormous impact of émigré European scholars from the 1930s onwards, yet even that episode can be seen as partly testifying to the power of the disciplinary matrix. After all, the likes of Strauss, Arendt, Vogelin and others tended, in their native settings, to be at least as readily characterised as philosophers or cultural critics, engaging in cultural conversations which had several academic and non-academic settings. It was partly their academic location once in the United States, and partly the genealogy which 'political theory' had given itself in its constant conflict with the dominant empirical and behavioural trends within political science, which resulted in the con-

---

[7] See the classic polemic by Bernard Crick, *The American Science of Politics* (London, 1959). For contrasting historical accounts, see John G. Gunnell, 'The Historiography of American Political Science', and David Easton, 'Political Science in the United States: Past and Present', both in David Easton, John G. Gunnell and Luigi Graziano, *The Development of Political Science: a Comparative Survey* (London, 1991); see also the more tendentious story of decline from public involvement to professionalised scientism told in David M. Ricci, *The Tragedy of Political Science: Politics, Scholarship, and Democracy* (New Haven, 1984).

[8] Gunnell, *Descent of Political Theory*, p. 2; see also John G. Gunnell, *Political Theory: Tradition and Interpretation* (Cambridge, Mass., 1979), ch. 1.

Disciplines, canons and publics 289

tributions of these figures being largely identified as those of 'political theorists'. The dynamics of this conflict with the institutionally dominant empirical approaches, and the resulting intra-disciplinary focus, surely continue to inform recurrent features of work in 'the history of political thought' in the United States to this day.

In France, by contrast, the field of 'la science politique' has historically been much weaker.[9] The Faculté de Droit was the presiding institutional framework within which the study of constitutional and public law long retained its 'formal-legal' character. Conversely, in the Faculté des Lettres moral philosophy and the history of philosophy were strong, and those venerable enterprises provided between them a much more purely philosophical framework within which to consider those classic texts which elsewhere were becoming the subject matter of 'the history of political thought'.[10] The most spectacularly successful interloper here was Durkheimian sociology (which grew out of moral philosophy initially), but the intellectual thrust of this enterprise was precisely to dissolve superficial political phenomena into the more fundamentally explanatory 'social facts'. Insofar as any education in 'politics' developed before the early twentieth century, it reflected the intimate links between the elite institutions, especially the *grandes écoles*, and the upper reaches of the already highly bureaucratic French state. The early development of L'école libre des sciences politiques, popularly known as 'Sciences Po', is revealing here: the independent institution which Boutmy intended as a haven for the sceptical, anti-doctrinaire study of recent history in the English manner became progressively more and more a training-ground for future members of the administrative class. No very distinct notion of 'la science politique' developed: instead this term became the label given to 'une science carrefour', the meeting-ground of a series of more specific or practice-oriented enquiries which were and have remained, in Pierre Favre's terms, 'des sciences d'État plus que des sciences politiques'.[11] Both within the Facultés de Droit and within Sciences Po (and still more within the Ecole Nationale

---

9 See Jean Leca, 'La science politique dans le champ intellectuel français', *Revue française de science politique*, 32 (1981), pp. 653–78; an extended and updated version of this article appeared as 'French Political Science and its Subfields', in Easton et al., *Development of Political Science*, pp. 147–86. See also the work of Pierre Favre, 'Les sciences d'état entre déterminisme et libéralisme: Émile Boutmy et la création de L'école libre de sciences politques', *Revue française de science politique*, 32 (1981), pp. 429–65; and, notably, Favre, *Naissances de la science politique en France 1871–1914* (Paris, 1989).

10 See Jean-Louis Fabiani, *Les philosophes de la République* (Paris, 1987), ch. 2, on the encompassing role of 'philosophy' within the structure of French higher education in the late nineteenth and early twentieth centuries.

11 See Favre, 'Les sciences d'état', p. 461.

d'Administration founded after 1945) there was comparatively little call for work in 'the history of political thought' conceived on an Anglo-American model, though at Sciences Po there did develop a strong tradition of studying the role of political ideas within French politics.[12]

These are, of course, the merest thumbnail sketches, intended simply to indicate the *kinds* of contrasts that could be explored in a fuller treatment.[13] It is also true that I have here focused on the two academic cultures which were perhaps the most widely divergent in the late nineteenth and early twentieth centuries; other pairings (e.g. France and Italy) would more clearly bring out resemblances and mutual influence. And it is evident that since at least the 1960s and 1970s, academic cultures have become progressively internationalised so that one could track a growing convergence in fields where the contrasts between national intellectual traditions had previously been more to the fore.

In thinking about the development of academic disciplines in the late nineteenth and early twentieth centuries, we always need to bear in mind the intellectual prestige and structuring power during that period of a broadly historicist framework. This was most evident in Germany and in the German-influenced parts of Europe (which in this period meant pretty much the whole of Europe), but it was in many ways no less true in the United States despite the later emphases on the ahistorical, or even anti-historical, character of so much American social thinking. As Carl Schorske put it recently, speaking of American academia in the early decades of the century:

We are inclined to forget today how recently history as a mode of understanding suffused the world of learning. Within the curriculum, the disciplines presented themselves in a historical frame: the *history* of economic or political thought, the *history* of literature, the *history* of philosophy. This temporal organisation governed both introductory and prestigious advanced courses within each discipline. It also implied a progress in understanding based on the ingestion of past achievements and their transcendence in each field of learning.[14]

---

[12] See, for example, the standard manual edited by Jean Touchard, *Histoire des idées politiques* (2 vols., Paris, 1959); and more recently the work of René Rémond, such as his *Pour une histoire politique* (Paris, 1988).

[13] I have attempted to explore the British case in a little more detail elsewhere: 'A Place in the Syllabus: Political Science at Cambridge', and Epilogue, 'A Nebulous Province: the Science of Politics in the Early Twentieth Century', in Collini et al., *That Noble Science*; Collini, *Public Moralists*, ch. 6, 'Their Title to be Heard: Professionalisation and its Discontents', and ch. 7, 'An Exclusively Professional Subject: the Jurist as Public Moralist'. See also Julia Stapleton, 'Academic Political Thought and the Development of Political Studies in Britain 1900–1950', unpublished DPhil. dissertation, University of Sussex, 1985.

[14] Carl Schorske, 'The New Rigorism in the Human Sciences, 1940–1960', *Daedalus*, 126 (1997), pp. 292–3. The title of this issue of *Daedalus* is 'American Academic

This model certainly prevailed in the teaching of politics. David Easton later complained about the education in political science which he received at Harvard in the dying days of this dispensation (in the 1940s): he had hoped that 'political theory' might have provided a principled account of the methods and coherence of the discipline, 'but theory turned out to be devoted largely to the study of the history of political thought'. This, though interesting in itself, 'did not fulfil what might have been one of the functions of theory in, say, economics, chemistry, or physics, namely, the conceptualisation of the discipline in part or as a whole'.[15] The 'behaviourist revolution' of the 1950s and 1960s (in which Easton played a prominent part) accentuated the gulf which already separated the pens-in-the-top-pocket political scientists from their colleagues who had inherited the task of teaching 'theory': the troubled marriage declined into mere co-existence, with each party increasingly leading a separate life in terms of conferences, professional journals and so on.[16]

In the United States above all, and, increasingly in the course of the twentieth century, in Britain as well, 'the history of political thought' thus came to be an activity pursued very largely in departments of politics which were heavily invested in quite other intellectual concerns and procedures, and this helps to explain some of the recurring features of the disputes surrounding the activity in the past half century or more. In the early days of the establishment of these departments, the appearance on syllabuses of a sequence of culturally accredited classic figures lent a patina of respectability to the enterprise, associating it with the prestige of the classics and of philosophy. The study of such figures then became progressively more and more marginal to the main business of such departments, although of course it was precisely this cultural capital which Straussians in the United States or Oakeshottians in Britain tried to marshal against the overwhelmingly empirical and behavioural inclinations of the preponderant elements of the discipline. Such conflicts have been one expression of the fact that these departments have more and more tended to be divided between 'theorists' and the rest (that is, all those engaged in the empirical, quantitative and comparative study of political institutions and behaviour). As a result, the history of political thought tended, and perhaps still tends, to be

Culture in Transformation: Fifty Years, Four Disciplines'; it contains several other useful essays on the history of American academic culture.

[15] Easton, 'Political Science in the United States', pp. 277–8.

[16] Tom Bender's general observation about American academia may be relevant here: 'Very few new departments have been created anywhere since Second World War, and even fewer have been abolished.' Thomas Bender, 'Politics, Intellect, and the American University', *Daedalus*, 126 (1997), pp. 30–1.

taught by those who also teach courses in contemporary political philosophy: the relevant professional framework within which Hobbes or Locke (or whoever) might be studied thus tended to be provided by contemporary theoretical analyses of 'authority', 'rights' and so on.

The roots of much subsequent methodological dispute are discernible in this institutional arrangement. 'Political theory' could absorb its inheritance from moral philosophy without producing overly disruptive conflicts of professional allegiance or turf wars, but the more the *historicity* of the 'history of political thought' came to be insisted on, the more the inheritance from history threatened to dissolve altogether the sense of sharing any sort of common enterprise with other colleagues in politics departments. Becoming deeply learned in the religious and cultural history of the Holy Roman Empire in the fourteenth century would be a somewhat eccentric choice for anyone aspiring to become president of a Political Science Association, but it might be a natural intellectual development for someone attempting a deeper under-standing of the work of Marsilius of Padua. Such a specific and remote focus would not, of course, seem at all out of place in a history department – indeed, it would conform to the professional norm – and it is hardly surprising that much of the methodological debate about historicity and anachronism that stirred the sub-field of 'the history of political thought' in Britain and America in the 1960s and 1970s was provoked by scholars associated with those few places where the enter-prise was (as Eliot assumed it should be) the institutional property of a history department rather than of a politics department.

III

At first glance, it is easy to assume that 'the history of political thought' will share a common structure with a range of enterprises labelled 'the history of x', where 'x' is the name of a branch of human activity or of an academic subject. This may seem to be particularly true of those cases where the conventional form of such histories is given by a canon of 'classic' texts. But on closer inspection, these other enterprises them-selves turn out to vary in interesting ways, not least in the different relations between the history and the contemporary practice of the 'same' discipline, and it may help to isolate some of the distinctive characteristics of 'the history of political thought' if one briefly tries to place it on a grid of such variations.

One model is provided by the history of science. Although this once upon a time took the form of a canon of great scientific works, from Thales to Einstein (or whoever), largely studied by distinguished or retired scientists no longer engaged in creative research, it has for at least a couple of generations now been a relatively autonomous branch of history. Not only are budding physicists or chemists not introduced to their discipline via a parade of great founders or precursors, but departments of the history of science often do not have even vestigial links with the science departments whose history they are ostensibly studying. In terms of journals, conferences, learned associations and the other paraphernalia of professionalism, the history of science is not part of the practice of 'science'.

A second model is provided by the history of economics. Here, there has long been a recognised canon of great economists from the past, such as Smith, Ricardo, Walras and company, and a closer relation between their ideas and current professional practice is assumed than in the case of the history of the natural sciences. None the less, the subject itself is not defined by a canon of such names: budding economists are not inducted into the discipline by studying the works of these figures, and there is on the whole a clear distinction in the subject between practising economists and historians of economic thought, even though some of the former still occasionally devote themselves to the study of some particularly congenial past master. Until recently, a historian of economic thought was a creature most departments kept for purely ceremonial and celebratory purposes, but in the past few decades 'the history of economics' has started to become a flourishing sub-field of its own, with dedicated journals such as *The History of Political Economy.*

A somewhat similar but interestingly distinct model is provided by the history of geography. The relatively underdeveloped disciplinary identity of the subject at the highest academic level and its lack until recently of structuring theoretical paradigms has meant that no canon of classic texts with recognisable affinities to current practice has been established. But 'geographical thought', in the broadest sense, is obviously a human activity with a long history, and so enthusiasts can choose to study the work of a very diverse list of predecessors who are united only by having given systematic attention to the spatial distribution of those physical and social properties of the world which have since been identified as the subject matter of geography – Strabo, Hakluyt, Montesquieu, Mackinder and so on. The relation of such studies to the current discipline of geography is weak both institutionally and intellectually.

In all three of these examples there is a pretty clear distinction between the current practice of any one of the disciplines and the independent or at best subsidiary practice of the enterprise of 'the history of . . .' that discipline. A striking contrast is provided by those disciplines where this distinction is much less clear cut, or at least where a canon of classic texts has some claim to *be* the discipline.

The academic study of English literature provides one example, where the subject matter of the discipline was until very recently, and in many places still is, defined in terms of the canon of 'great authors', often parodied as the long march from Beowulf to Virginia Woolf. But this list was of course quite distinct from any assembly of purportedly 'great critics' who might have been thought to instantiate the methods and achievements of the discipline, especially as in modern times the critics become more and more professional and not themselves writers or even general men- or women-of-letters. And in this case the two lists are obviously not on a par: the budding student could be taught to use the approach of, say, Empson to study Milton, but not (at least in any but a weird sense) the approach of Milton to study Empson. The result has been the formation of two very unequal canons, where English literature, prescriptively defined, is constituted by those major past writings thought to possess 'literary interest', while the history of literary criticism offers a set of influential or exemplary approaches (largely to the criticism of the figures in the first canon). This latter canon has rarely achieved a more than subsidiary or marginal status in the teaching of the subject, and its study has not really developed into a professional sub-discipline of its own.

In this respect, a somewhat different model is provided by another canon-based discipline, that of philosophy. Here, while it is true that the student has long been inducted into the mysteries of the craft by reading the classic texts from Plato to Kant (or Wittgenstein or Quine or wherever the succession is thought to have temporarily and locally halted), it has not been quite as clear as in English that the texts *are* the subject matter of the discipline. There has always remained a difference between philosophy and the history of philosophy, albeit a difference which is unclear and constantly contested: problems in epistemology or metaphysics and so on constitute the subject matter in a way which is at least partly independent of the discussion of such problems in the work of previous philosophers. And of course there is not in philosophy quite the same distinction that I have just remarked in English between the list of authors who are its subject matter and a secondary list of authors who are its most famous practitioners – there could be Wittgensteinian critiques of Plato but there could also be Platonist readings of Wittgenstein. Genuinely to engage with the arguments of a philosopher is to *do* philosophy; to criticise the work of a poet is not to *write* poetry. It is true that there has come to be something of a separate sub-field of 'the history of philosophy', but it is exclusively cultivated by those trained as philosophers (rather than as historians), and for some, at least, of its practitioners this is actually a rival way of 'doing philosophy' – indeed, it is in their view the only intellectually defensible way.[17]

I want to suggest that 'the history of political thought' has been an ineliminably hybrid activity which has, at different times and places since the late nineteenth century, exhibited features of all of these models without wholly corresponding to any one of them. Perhaps the closest resemblance has been to the history of moral philosophy. But in fact the canon of great political theorists as it was built up in the late nineteenth and early twentieth centuries was influenced by very different concerns, most notably by the political historians' judgements about which writers had been influential in affecting the course of actual political developments. Figures such as Machiavelli or Rousseau or eventually Marx, who were not part of the more venerable moral philosophy canon, owed their prominence to this kind of judgement (which was often mistaken, of course, or at least very disputable), and the more the study of political history was expected to yield an inductive science of politics, the greater the say the political historians had in deciding who was a significant political theorist. Such concerns also shaped the broader contours of the story: George H. Sabine's much-used (and subsequently much-pilloried) *A History of Political Theory*, first published in 1937, was written on the assumption that 'theories of politics are themselves a part of politics', and he accordingly organised his survey in terms of the three major political forms which he identified in conventional (post-Hegelian) terms as 'the city-state', 'the universal community' and 'the national state'.[18] And the same was true for more local studies. In the introduction to his *Political Thought in England from Locke to Bentham*, first published in 1920, Harold Laski noted that with the decline of the notion of Divine Right towards the later seventeenth century, disputes over the fundamentals of politics also diminished, producing 'a relative barrenness of abstract ideas'. The reader is still on the first page and the suspicion is forming itself that Laski may rather have regretted that he was not assigned a philosophically more exciting century. But reassurance is swift in coming, and comes in a form which English readers of the first part of this century could be expected to find persuasive: 'The eighteenth century had an importance in English politics which the comparative absence of systematic speculation can not conceal', an importance he spells out in terms of the development of the constitution, the beginnings of the party system and so on. And in its

---

[17] See, for example, the essays in Part I of Richard Rorty, J.B. Schneewind and Quentin Skinner (eds.), *Philosophy in History* (Cambridge, 1984).

[18] George H. Sabine, *A History of Political Theory* (1937; London, 1951), pp. 7, 11–15.

detail the book constantly combines these heterogeneous perspectives – for example, 'Nothing . . . is more important in the history of English political philosophy than to realise that from Stuart times the Nonconformists were deeply bitten with distrust of government' and so on.[19]

Moreover, although it is true that in every discipline membership of the canon, at least at the margins, is responsive to shifts of fashion within the already-established discipline, it is clear that during the formative period of 'the history of political thought' developments both in the wider intellectual world and in contemporary politics itself were always likely to exercise a powerful influence on the prescribed lists of texts. The earliest syllabuses in Britain, for example, usually jumped from the Ancient World directly to the Renaissance or even to the mid-seventeenth century, but turn-of-the-century concerns about the legal status of corporations and the relations of Church and state were among the causes directing attention to the political theory of the Middle Ages.[20] Similarly, contemporary disputes about sovereignty and conscience in the early twentieth century invested the political thought of the late sixteenth and early seventeenth centuries with a new significance, and prompted figures such as Laski to set about editing early texts on religious toleration and the rights of resistance.[21] Once one recognises the role of such local and temporary forces in shaping the formation of what has become the canon of political theory, and especially once one recognises the extent to which in its common twentieth-century form it represents something of a compromise between the preoccupations of the moral philosophers and the late nineteenth-century's ambition for a science of political development, it becomes clear that the resulting collection of texts written at very different levels of abstraction from or immersion in that political history can hardly be regarded as constituting a 'tradition', still less, as it has sometimes been grandly celebrated, 'the tradition'.

In some ways, it is curious that in Britain and America the history of political thought came to be regarded as a semi-autonomous discipline at all. After all, it might be thought that as politics came to be recognised as one social science among others, alongside economics, sociology and so on, as increasingly it did in the early twentieth century, especially in the United States, so the place occupied in both teaching and research by the history of political theory would correspond to the Founding

---

[19] Harold J. Laski, *Political Thought in England from Locke to Bentham* (London, 1920), pp. 2, 217.

[20] The inspiring presence here was, of course, Maitland, but the fruits of this impulse were evident in the historical work of J.N. Figgis, A.J. Carlyle, Cecil Woolf and others.

[21] For example, his 1924 edition of the *Vindiciae contra Tyrannos*.

Parents model suggested by economics. And in fact, some of the more crudely triumphalist histories of the social sciences produced in the 1920s and 1930s, again above all in the United States, *did* try to make the pasts of all these disciplines conform to that model, in which Chapter One disposed of pretty much everybody from Aristotle to Herbert Spencer, after which the pace slowed down a bit. But this model never wholly displaced the by now well-entrenched canon of works in 'political thought', even though that disparate collection of polemical and philosophical writings was never going to function very well as the theoretical component of a largely empirical discipline, as the 'methodology' of 'political science' (and there has remained something odd about the idea of introducing students in Poli Sci 101 to the methods of their discipline by reading Hooker or Bodin, though it is an open question whether that oddity arises more out of the curious institutional development of the history of political theory than from something amiss in the ambitions of an empirical political science itself).

This very hybridity also meant that a demanding sense of the historicity of the texts studied was always more likely to make itself felt than in 'purer' fields, and this has in turn raised troubling questions about the principles of selection and the methods of study. The history of philosophy legitimately deals with what, in any time and place, is thought to have been *philosophically interesting* past philosophy (the rest is sometimes rather loftily assigned to 'intellectual history'). But it is not so obvious that the rationale for the canon of texts in the history of political thought is that it focuses on what is now regarded as *politically interesting* past political thought, except in the vacuously diluted sense that *any* past political thought can be interesting. There may be several reasons at the beginning of the twenty-first century for studying the work of Bartolus of Sassoferato, but the *political* benefits of learning how to deploy the authorities of Roman law against the Holy Roman Emperor's claim to *imperium* cannot be one of them. It may make somewhat more sense to say that the enterprise singles out those past texts which are thought to be the *theoretically interesting* bits of past political thinking, though as soon as one descends below a certain level of abstraction this can only be true if one believes one is excavating the 'foundations' of later conceptual elaborations. But none of these rationales can permanently fend off the demands of history, and reflection on the range of models mentioned earlier suggests the general conclusion, which is particularly pertinent to 'the history of political thought', that the less tight the connection with the contemporary practice of a particular discipline, the readier its historians have been to recognise that they are inescapably involved with a wider intellectual history.

Canons, it has to be recognised, generate unhistorical interpretations. The professional and pedagogical investment in that particular selection of texts results in a disproportionate importance being assigned to alleged connections and contrasts between works in the canon, even when these have no actual historical foundation. It also tends to smooth out differences in genre and level of abstraction between works within the canon. And of course it produces practitioners who tend to be systematically ignorant of the work of 'lesser' figures and of the broader milieux within which all these works were written. One consequence of this pattern is that work on canonical figures tends to attract the greatest professional rewards. One of the noticeable features of disputes over 'the canon' of classic texts in several disciplines in recent decades, including English and the history of political thought, is that even many of those who make, in general terms, the strongest revisionist case for attending to a much wider range of hitherto neglected types of writing still tend to obey the professional imperatives which dictate that influential careers are most readily furthered by concentrating on those writers to whom the highest proportion of their fellow-professionals will already have some reason, pedagogic or practical, to pay attention.

IV

Disciplines are unstable compounds. What is called a 'discipline' is in fact a complex series of practices, whose unity, such as it is, is given as much by historical accident and institutional convenience as by a coherent intellectual rationale. These practices almost invariably incorporate layers or residues from some previous form of the constituent activities, elements which do not necessarily have an intrinsic connection with those concerns which many current practitioners might regard as being at the core of the discipline (symptomatically, disciplines always provoke a lot of talk about 'cores'). From time to time efforts are made to purify this heterogeneous bundle: new definitions, methodological prescriptions, curricular re-organisations, the founding of breakaway professional societies and so on.

No sketch of the bundle of activities that have been carried on under the heading 'the history of political thought' can claim any adequacy unless it brings out the shifting and hybrid nature of the enterprise. Simply within the English-speaking world, the variety of labels under which these activities have been carried on and which have each deposited something in subsequent conceptions of the enterprise is baffling in its diversity: 'The theory of law and politics', 'The principles of political obligation', 'Comparative politics', 'Theories of the state',

'Moral and political philosophy', 'Introduction to political science', 'The study of politics', 'The classical tradition', 'Theory', 'The history of political ideas', 'Political theory', 'The history of political thought' and so on. Each of these labels bespoke a somewhat different intellectual and pedagogic ambition, but none started from scratch. The processes by which 'The theory of law and politics from Aristotle to Sir Henry Maine' became 'The history of political thought from Plato to Nato' are complex, but they are not principally part of the subject matter of the history of political thought itself. They belong to that category of phenomena now largely studied by intellectual historians and historians of higher education.

It therefore seems to me a mistake to encourage the writing of the history of 'the history of political thought' in purely internalist terms as a form of that old-fashioned discipline-history which, in other areas, has in recent years begun to be displaced by approaches which attempt to place academic developments within a much broader social and intellectual context, including the context of the relevant 'political cultures'.[22] American academic culture has been particularly well served in this respect, and it seems to me that attempts to explore national variations in the history of 'the history of political thought' might benefit from considering the kind of work done on that particular culture by such scholars as Thomas Bender, Gerald Graff, Thomas Haskell, David Hollinger, Dorothy Ross and others.[23] As one, perhaps surprising, example of the kind of illumination this might yield, I would cite the interesting parallels between the history of political thought and the story of the discipline of English literature in the United States as told by Graff. Three features of this story may be briefly mentioned here. First, there are the repetitive disputes about the subject matter and approach of the discipline, which usually involve pitching some version of 'the great tradition' against whatever form was currently being taken by 'the new rigorism' (philology, historical scholarship, the New Criticism and so on). Second, there is what Graff terms, critically, 'the passive pluralism of the department', that is, the way in which new sub-fields and approaches are permitted to establish themselves *alongside* the existing fields, co-existing in 'patterned isolation' within the same

---

[22] I attempted to spell out some of the drawbacks of this kind of 'discipline history' in '"Discipline History" and "Intellectual History": the History of the Social Sciences in France and England', *Revue de synthèse*, 109, 3–4 (1988), pp. 387–99.

[23] See, for examples, Thomas Bender, *Intellect and Public Life* (Baltimore, 1993); Gerald Graff, *Professing English: an Institutional History* (Chicago, 1987); Thomas Haskell (ed.), *The Authority of Experts* (Bloomington, 1984); David Hollinger, *Science, Jews, and Secular Culture: Studies in Mid-Twentieth Century American Intellectual History* (Princeton, 1996); Dorothy Ross, *The Origins of American Social Science* (Cambridge, 1991).

institutional framework without either genuinely engaging each other or becoming entirely autonomous. And third, there is the constant dialectic between justifications in terms of a principled withdrawal from society and claims for some form of social utility, a dialectic which was as much at work in the late nineteenth century as, in altered form, in the late twentieth. There is no need to labour the similarities with recurring features of the story of the history of political thought as an academic subject. There is also an interesting chronological correspondence in the phases of the two disciplines, with the 'generalist counter-attack' on the scientific pretensions of philological scholarship in English enjoying some success in the period 1895–1915, followed by a reassertion of 'scientific' method against mere criticism in the 1920s and so on; or, in terms of political thought, the displacement of Dunning by Merriam. Each of these possible points of correspondence would need to be explored in detail, and perhaps challenged; they are here offered simply by way of illustration of what is to be gained from looking at a broader history than that provided by 'the history of political thought' itself. And of course, as the enquiry is pushed further in the direction of transnational comparisons, a whole literature on the comparative study of higher education also comes into view.[24]

Emancipating ourselves from the narrow perspective of discipline-history may also help us to account for a further characteristic of recent writing about the study of the history of political thought, namely the jeremiad about 'withdrawal' and 'loss of function'. We all know how the tune goes. There was once a golden age in which there were no hard and fast distinctions between intellectuals, scholars and academics, who all engaged in public debate on the great issues of the day while also cultivating their scholarly inquiries. But then a narrow professionalism supervened, and now academics in their ivory towers are concerned only with the development of their particular discipline and have lost all contact with public discussion in the world outside the walls.

The fact is, of course, that, far from being unique to the history of political thought, some such lament is a recurring feature of a certain sort of tendentious discipline-history, as indeed it is of writing about the topic of intellectuals more generally.[25] This lament obviously meets various polemical and nostalgic needs, but as history it is largely false or, at best, a gross over-simplification. We need to think, instead, of a series

---

[24] For one, highly relevant, example from this large literature, see Fritz Ringer, *Fields of Knowledge: French Academic Culture in Comparative Perspective, 1890–1920* (Cambridge, 1992).

[25] For a striking example of the genre which focuses on political science, see Ricci, *Tragedy of Political Science*; one of the best-known polemics which generalises the case is Russell Jacoby, *The Last Intellectuals* (New York, 1987).

of overlapping publics, in the plural, and a historically variable range of strategies for engaging with them. This is not the place to argue that case at length, but it may be appropriate to draw out one implication of it here, namely, that any attempt to chart the shifting engagement over time of a particular category of intellectual figures with their various publics will have to be a story about social roles and expectations more generally.[26] There cannot be, in other words, an explanation from within the history of 'the history of political thought' itself for the different strategies of public participation and comment which its practitioners may have adopted.

In writing about a series of mid and late Victorian intellectual figures in Britain I found the notion of the 'public moralist' helpful, but I would say here that even that should not, in my view, be regarded as a timeless role, always equally available. It depended upon a particular conjunction of circumstances – a certain forum or arena for public debate, certain shared moral values, certain relations to a governing elite and so on. Similarly, we should surely not speak as though there were a universal or perennial professorial role: what is allowed or expected at a particular time has to be understood as part of a larger history of the standing of universities in a culture, of the means for reaching certain publics, of the requirements of professionalisation and so on.

By the same token, we should not speak of 'professionalisation' as though it involved the complete elimination of a non-specialist audience. In his discussion of a range of academic literary and cultural critics in his *Secular Vocations*, Bruce Robbins highlights the inadequacy of thinking of a simple dichotomy between 'the professional' and 'the public' figured in terms of a contrast between 'inside' and 'outside'.[27] Other defects of this dichotomy apart, it obscures the extent to which a form of public legitimation needs to be represented 'within' the values of professionalism themselves. One telling indication of this is the way in which exercises in self-justification or other responses to the views of an imagined 'outside' public recurrently feature in all forms of professional discourse. All specialists are driven to describe their activities in ways which build some kind of social utility into the description, however indirect or long-term the connections between the specialist activity and the larger utility are said to be.[28] The insistence by some contemporary historians of political thought that their work is not 'mere antiquar-

---

[26] I very briefly sketch this argument in Stefan Collini, 'My Public is Bigger Than Yours: Professors, Critics, and Other Intellectuals', *Journal of the History of the Behavioral Sciences*, 30 (1994), pp. 380–7.

[27] Bruce Robbins, *Secular Vocations: Intellectuals, Professionalism, Culture* (London, 1993).

[28] This point is amply confirmed in Preston King (ed.), *The Study of Politics: a Collection of Inaugural Lectures* (London, 1977).

ianism' because it reveals the foundations of 'our' current concepts (or uncovers alternatives to them) is yet another instance of this pattern.

For all these reasons, we should, I think, be wary of stories of simple 'decline' or even 'retreat'. There has never been one single 'general public' nor, conversely, should we think of all writing by contemporary academics as only reaching a specialist readership.[29] Identifying the actual publics which any particular piece of past writing may have reached is a notoriously perilous enterprise, and as Francis Mulhern has reminded us in another context: 'The ideal match of inscribed addressee and contingent reader cannot happen in the absence of favouring extra-textual conditions.'[30] The intellectual history of the 'history of political thought' needs to be as much about these 'extra-textual conditions' as about the ideas of individual teachers of the subject.

This is, in the end, only to re-state a familiar case, of course, but it may none the less, given the theme of this volume, be a pertinent one. For the truth, unwelcome as it has proved to be to political theorists, is that much of what has in the past been done in the name of 'the history of political thought' has been, whatever other merits it may have possessed, very poor *history* indeed. It would be a pity if work in the much more minor sub-field of the history of 'the history of political thought' should prove to be open to the same charge.

[29] I have tried to argue this at greater length in 'Before Another Tribunal: the Idea of the "Non-Specialist Public"', in Stefan Collini, *English Pasts: Essays in History and Culture* (Oxford, 1999), ch. 16.

[30] Francis Mulhern, 'English Reading', in Homi K. Bhabha (ed.), *Nation and Narration* (London, 1990), p. 261.

Index

Adams, W.G.S., 139, 141
Adler, Mortimer J., 157
Adorno, Theodor W., 48–9, 102, 110 n.
Agulhon, Maurice, 215–17
Alatri, Paolo, 103
Albert, Hans, 45
Albertoni, Ettore, 104
Alcidamas (the sophist), 269
Alexander (the Great), 265–6
Al-Farabi, Abu Nasr, 115
Alfieri, Vittorio, 86
Allen, R.E., 23 n.
Angermann, Erich, 42
Annan, Noel, 151, 152 n.
Ansell-Pearson, Keith, 187 n.
anti-Semitism (and rejection of), 116,
    219, 232, 250, 253, 254–6, 273, 274,
    275–7
Antisthenes (the sophist), 269
Antonescu, Ion, 238
Appiah, K. Anthony, 278 n., 279 n.
Appleby, Joyce, 113
Applegate, Celia, 261 n.
Aquinas, Thomas, 11, 15
Arendt, Hannah, amongst US immigrants,
    113; definition of politics, 191; influence
    at Berkeley, 117; in German accounts of
    totalitarianism, 43; on Jewish attitudes to
    the state, 251 n.; philosophical use of
    past, 116–17, 196, 288
Aristotle, 27, 31, 37–8; canonical status, 1,
    108, 284; definition of the political,
    190–1; feminist critiques of, 122–5; in
    Oxbridge and other curricula, 140–1,
    284; medieval and Renaissance
    interpretations of, 15; Popper's
    treatment of, 270, 284, 286, 287, 297,
    299; pre-Socratics, 22–3; rejected in
    behavioural revolution, 108–9;
    unrepresentative character of, 17–18
Aron, Raymond, 208
Ashcraft, Richard, 35 n., 129
Asquith, Herbert, 138

Astell, Mary, 124
Augustine, 11, 15
Aulard, A., 197
Austin, John L., 160, 164, 202 n., 286
Austriacus, J.S., 250 n.
Azouvi, François, 212

Baczko, Bronislaw, 241
Baer, M.A., 109 n.
Bagehot, Walter, 140, 150
Bahro, Rudolf, 55
Bailyn, Bernard, 112, 260 n.
Baker, Keith Michael, 2 n., 164 n., 222,
    223, 227
Baldini, E.A., 98–9 n.
Ball, Terence, 4, 130 n., 160 n.
Balmand, Pascal, 215 n.
Bambach, Charles R., 60 n.
Barash, Jeffrey Andrew, 60 n.
Barcia, F., 59, 99 n.,
Barker, Ernest, 138–9, 140, 141–3, 144,
    147, 149, 150, 152, 153, 157, 158, 287
Baron, Hans, 173
Barry, Brian, 135 n., 151, 156, 158
Barry, J., 163 n.
Bartolus (of Sassoferato), 297
Battaglia, Felice, 89, 90, 91, 97, 105
Bauer, Otto, 257
Bayle, Jean-Louis Loubet del, 217
Beard, Charles, 111
Becker, C., 112 n.
Becker, J.J., 216
Bédarida, François, 207
behaviourism (behavioural revolution), 54,
    64, 107–9, 118–20, 129, 291
Belke, Ingrid, 255 n.
Bell, Daniel, 45, 52, 118 n.
Beller, Steven, 255 n., 258 n., 272 n.
Bender, Thomas, 291 n., 299
Benn, Tony, 171
Bentham, Jeremy, 122, 123, 140
Beonio Brocchieri, Vittorio, 88, 89, 96
Berdyaev, Nicholas, 238

303

IDEAS IN CONTEXT

Edited by QUENTIN SKINNER (*General Editor*),
LORRAINE DASTON, DOROTHY ROSS and JAMES TULLY

Recent titles in the series include:

Titles marked with an asterisk are also available in paperback